WOODROW WILSON AND WORLD POLITICS

WOODROW WILSON AND WORLD POLITICS

*America's Response to
War and Revolution*

N. Gordon Levin, Jr.

OXFORD UNIVERSITY PRESS
LONDON   OXFORD   NEW YORK

OXFORD UNIVERSITY PRESS
Oxford   London   Glasgow
New York   Toronto   Melbourne   Wellington
Nairobi   Dar es Salaam   Cape Town
Kuala Lumpur   Singapore   Jakarta   Hong Kong   Tokyo
Delhi   Bombay   Calcutta   Madras   Karachi

printing, last digit: 20 19 18 17
Printed in the United States of America

FOR
MY MOTHER AND FATHER
EVELYN AND NORMAN LEVIN
AND FOR
MY WIFE ELAYNE

PREFACE

my thesis

The purpose of this book is to present an integrated analysis of the theory and practice of Wilsonian foreign policy in the 1917–1919 period. My aim, therefore, has not been to achieve anything approaching a complete narrative coverage of American foreign relations during World War I. I have sought instead to discuss those events and ideological tendencies which seemed to me most central to an understanding of the essence of the Wilson Administration's approach to world politics. Moreover, while I have tried not to ignore the very real differences over specific policy issues which existed within the Wilson Administration, my main emphasis has been in the direction of establishing, and illustrating in concrete circumstances, the over-all international goal which the President and his leading advisers all came to share. This ultimate Wilsonian goal may be defined as the attainment of a peaceful liberal capitalist world order under international law, safe both from traditional imperialism and revolutionary socialism, within whose stable liberal confines a missionary America could find moral and economic pre-eminence. In our own time this basic Wilsonian vision, at once progressive and conservative, continues to motivate America's foreign policy decision-makers.

It will become quickly apparent to readers of this book that I am intellectually indebted to the works of Louis Hartz, Arno Mayer, and William Appleman Williams. In the case of my thesis adviser Louis Hartz, however, the debt happily has not been merely an intellectual one. His personal advice and encouragement were of great assistance to me in the preparation of this study. Other friends, Theodore P. Greene, Stephan Thernstrom, and John William Ward, were kind enough to read this manuscript and give me the benefit of their suggestions. The careful editorial work of Caroline Taylor and Sheldon Meyer at the Oxford Press also improved the manuscript. I am happy, in addition, to be able to acknowledge a profound personal debt to Gabriel Kolko and to Norman Pollack. Without their unselfish aid, the example of their own passionate scholarship, and the constant support of their warm friendship I am not sure that this book could have been finished. Finally, my greatest debt is to my wife Elayne. Not only was her help invaluable during our months of work together in manuscript collections, but her loving presence throughout the years of writing helped me to continue to the end.

N. G. L., Jr.

Amherst, Mass.
August, 1967.

ACKNOWLEDGMENTS

For giving me permission to quote from copyrighted and manuscript material I should like to thank the following: Bobbs-Merrill Company, Inc., for *The War Memoirs of Robert Lansing;* Harper & Row, Publishers, Inc., for *The Public Papers of Woodrow Wilson,* edited by Ray Stannard Baker and William E. Dodd; Harvard College Library, for the Papers of Joseph C. Grew; Houghton Mifflin Company, for *The Intimate Papers of Colonel House,* edited by Charles Seymour; Rachel Baker Napier in behalf of the heirs of Ray Stannard Baker, for *Woodrow Wilson, Life and Letters* and *Woodrow Wilson and World Settlement,* by Ray Stannard Baker; Princeton University Library, for the Woodrow Wilson Manuscripts Collected by Charles Lee Swem; G. P. Putnam's Sons, for *The Drafting of the Covenant,* by David Hunter Miller; Charles Scribner's Sons, for *Russia from the American Embassy,* by David R. Francis, and *What Really Happened at Paris,* by Edward M. House and Charles Seymour; and Yale University Library, for the Papers of Gordon Auchincloss, William H. Buckler, William C. Bullitt, Edward M. House, Frank L. Polk, and Sir William Wiseman.

CONTENTS

INTRODUCTION

WAR, REVOLUTION, AND WILSONIAN LIBERALISM

The main outlines of recent American foreign policies were shaped decisively by the ideology and the international program developed by the Wilson Administration in response to world politics in the 1917–19 period. It was these years which saw both America's entrance into World War I and the Bolshevik Revolution in Russia, the two seminal events with whose endless consequences the foreign relations of the United States have since been largely concerned. In the midst of these events, Wilsonians laid the foundations of a modern American foreign policy whose main thrust, from 1917 on, may be characterized as an effort to construct a stable world order of liberal-capitalist internationalism, at the Center of the global ideological spectrum, safe from both the threat of imperialism on the Right and the danger of revolution on the Left.

It was the Wilson Administration, in its response to the challenges of war and revolution, which forcefully articulated this conception of liberal-internationalism, a conception which had been both manifest and latent in the policies of earlier American statesmen. For Wilson, as for many of his successors in the ranks of American decision-makers, the national interest became merged with liberal ideology in such a way that he could act simultaneously as the champion of American nationalism and as the spokesman for internationalism and anti-imperialism. The policy of building a rational international-capitalist order served for the Wilson Administration, at one and the same time, the varied but related tasks of countering Germany's atavistic imperialism,* of answering Lenin's demands for world revolution, and, finally, of maximizing the moral and economic expansion of the liberal American nation-state. The crucial importance of Wilsonianism, then, in the context of twentieth-century American foreign relations, lies in the fact that the Wilson Administration first defined the American national interest in liberal-internationalist terms in response to war and social revolution, the two dominant political factors of our time. While many in his own generation resisted Wilson's vision of the United States as the prime mover in the creation of collective international defenses of world political and commercial order against threats from the Right and the Left, later generations of American decision-makers would seek fully to realize Wilson's design during World War II and, especially, during the Cold War that followed.

1. THE WILSONIAN VISION OF AMERICAN LIBERAL-EXCEPTIONALISM

Basic to any understanding of Wilson's foreign policy is an awareness of his complete faith in America's liberal-exceptionalism. For the President, the United States represented a new departure among the nations in both a moral and a political sense. With the evils of militarism and pre-liberal reaction left behind in Europe, America had an historic mission to disseminate the progressive values of liberal-internationalism and to create a new world order. In Wilson's completely liberal ideology, imperialism and militarism were seen as essentially European phenomena associated with a past which America had escaped. In Wilsonian terms, American exceptionalism consisted in the complete tri-

* The use of the word "atavistic" in this study is based on Joseph Schumpeter's concept of imperialism as a "social atavism," i.e. old-fashioned and irrational and vestigial in a period of supposed possible liberal-capitalist rationality and harmony.

umph of liberal-capitalist * values in the United States, a triumph which ensured that American foreign policy could not be guided by the atavistic values of traditional European imperialism. America, was for Wilson the incarnation of the progressive future of European politics and diplomacy, after Europe had cast off the burdens of its militant and pre-bourgeois past in favor of more rational liberal-capitalist development. The President never doubted that American liberal values were the wave of the future in world politics. Soon the whole world would follow the lead of the United States to the establishment of an international system of peaceful commercial and political order.

For Wilson, then, American national values were identical with universal progressive liberal values, and an exceptionalist America had a mission to lead mankind toward the orderly international society of the future. Europe, however, was, in Wilsonian terms, seen to be still imprisoned in a combative "Hobbesian" state of

* At this point I should indicate the manner in which I use such concepts as liberal-capitalism, liberal-exceptionalism, liberal-capitalist internationalism, etc. Liberalism and liberal-capitalism both refer to a system of socio-political values and institutions characterized by political liberty, social mobility, constitutional government, and the capitalist mode of production and distribution. The concept of American liberal-exceptionalism was developed by Louis Hartz in *The Liberal Tradition in America.* He argued that the United States was an almost purely liberal society from the outset. The United States was exceptional: unlike other nations, it did not have to advance from feudalism toward liberal values and institutions. Thus, while being a liberal in Europe has meant the advocacy of values and institutions which are not necessarily universally accepted in one's own country and which are often opposed by both the Left and the Right, in the United States "liberalism" has come to stand loosely for those political elements most anxious to use state power for moderately reformist ends in a society all of whose political culture is dominated by the classic form of liberalism defined above.

Finally, the phrases liberal-capitalist internationalism and liberal-internationalism are used interchangeably in this study to refer to the Wilsonian vision of a global situation beyond power politics to be characterized by open world trade and by great power co-operation within a framework of world law and international-capitalist commercial relationships. In Wilson's view, moreover, the projected triumph of such a liberal-capitalist world order over traditional imperialism would represent the realization of America's liberal mission to lead mankind to a victory over the unenlightened past. Ironically, when Wilsonian liberal values became involved in world politics they were confronted by the very enemies of liberalism who were absent from the domestic American political universe.

nature, in which the balance of power and armed strength were the only things upon which nations could rely for their self-preservation. In Wilson's view, it was America's historic mission to bring Europe into a peaceful international order based on world law. The Wilsonian goal was to create an international civil society, or social contract, making orderly and responsible world citizens out of the hitherto aggressive European nations. Wilson sought to "Lockeanize," or to Americanize, the global political system by creating a world society under law, to be preserved through the moral and material strength of the international social contract embodied in the League of Nations.

Implicitly, these Wilsonian values were in large part congruent with those of European liberal-internationalists and democratic-socialists,* whose basic orientation was to make more rational and orderly the existing world system of competing nation-states, while avoiding the extreme solution of socialist revolution advocated by Lenin. In their own way, such European liberals and socialists as Joseph Schumpeter and Karl Kautsky joined Wilson in believing that, Lenin's proscriptions to the contrary, the international-capitalist system could still put behind it the militant imperialism of the past and could increasingly stabilize itself through peaceful trade and through economic development of the backward areas of the world. If the world system of competing imperialist nation-states could be liberated from atavistic and militaristic forms of traditional imperialism, and could also be restructured in a more rational Wilsonian fashion, then Lenin's predictions of inevitable conflict among capitalist nations might be refuted, and a new world system of international-capitalist

---

* In this study, a basic distinction is drawn throughout between democratic-socialism and revolutionary-socialism. Democratic-socialism refers to groups or parties seeking to achieve socialist goals by constitutional means within the context of traditional state authority. In this sense, except for its most radical proponents, the term democratic-socialism may be used inerchangeably with social-democracy. The term revolutionary-socialism will be used to indicate groups or parties seeking to achieve socialist goals by the use of violent or extralegal means outside the confines of existing state authority.

order might, in the future, avoid the related threats of war and revolution.

Unlike the European liberals and democratic-socialists, who operated in societies in which pre-liberal military and traditional values were still powerful, however, Wilson was the leader of a nation-state in which pre-liberal values and classes did not exist. For this reason, Wilson's ideology permitted him to conceive of himself as acting, at one and the same time, with perfect internal consistency, as the defender of American national interests and as the champion of liberal-internationalism. For Wilson, there was no conflict between the needs of a burgeoning American political-economy to expand commercially and morally throughout the world and the European liberal-internationalist and moderate democratic-socialist program of a progressive, rationalized, and peaceful international-capitalist system. In other words, a Wilsonian America was to be the historical agent of the world's transformation from chaos and imperialism to orderly liberal rationality.

In Wilsonian terms, America both participated in and yet, at the same time, transcended the existing system of international politics. America thus interacted as a nation-state with others in the "Hobbesian" realm of world politics and shifting alliances, while America was simultaneously the carrier of values seeking to rationalize and to pacify that very political universe. While the European moderate Leftist was often forced to think in class terms when he sought to oppose national imperialism, the Wilsonian was faced by no such dilemma since America itself embodied the very ideology of liberal-internationalism which, in Europe, was the property only of certain classes but not of whole nations.

2. THE WILSONIAN ANTI-IMPERIALISM OF LIBERAL ORDER

In general terms, there were essentially two separate but related strategies which Wilson could follow in his anti-imperialistic

mission to liberalize or to Americanize international politics. On
the one hand, the President could use America's moral influence
in an effort to absorb all the conflicting elements in world politics
into a new liberal-international system under a League of Nations. Such an absorptive anti-imperialist approach was evident
both in the Wilsonian attempts to offer American mediation
in the interests of facilitating a constructive liberal settlement of
the European War prior to 1917, and in the Administration's
postwar efforts at Paris to construct a new liberal European order
through the League of Nations. On the other hand, however, the
President could use American power to compel the most atavistic
and militant practitioners of the Old World's imperialist politics
to enter into a new international society of law and stability. Such
a more forceful American anti-imperialist approach was, of course,
evident in the Wilsonian response to Imperial Germany after the
submarine crisis of early 1917. Yet, in a larger sense, it could be
argued that both of these Wilsonian anti-imperialist approaches
were combined in the war against German autocratic imperialism,
since, in the President's mind, despite his lingering distrust of Allied war aims, the anti-German Entente alliance increasingly became the possible nucleus for a progressive and inclusive postwar
system of American-inspired liberal world order.

All forms of Wilsonian anti-imperialism were, however, clearly
anathema to the values of Leninist revolutionary-socialism. In the
first place, Wilson's reformist desire to use America's moral leadership to construct a liberal world community emphatically challenged Lenin's belief in the inability of the international-capitalist
system peacefully to resolve its own internal contradictions through
gradual rational reform. Thus, while Wilson had developed his liberal anti-imperialist vision of a League of Nations prior to the emer-
gence of Leninism, after 1917 the League would also become, in
Wilsonian statements, implicitly and explicitly an anti-Leninist
effort to resolve the contradictions of world imperialism by means
of reform and without revolution. In the second place, Wilson's
efforts to transform the Entente's struggle against the Central

Powers into a crusade for international-liberalism was in direct opposition to Lenin's desire to transform the war into a world revolution. Naturally, Lenin and other revolutionary-socialists saw the threat to their hopes in a Wilsonian ideology which provided a way for socialists in the Allied countries to legitimize possible support for the Entente's war effort. Lenin sought to make a clear distinction between war and revolution, while Wilson and Kerensky created ideologies which appeared to give a quasi-radical legitimization to the war against German autocratic imperialism by making the war of the moment the precondition of progress in the future. For all these reasons, then, Wilsonianism and Leninism came into conflict after 1917, as two opposed methods of moving the world from an imperialistic past to a progressive future.

On one level, this conflict between Wilsonian and Leninist values was acted out in the arena of revolutionary Russian politics. In wartime Russia, Wilsonians sought initially to buttress the pro-Allied liberal-nationalist regime of the March Revolution, in order to save the moral and material strength of a liberalized Russia for the anti-German coalition. Then too, even after failing to prevent the triumph of Russian Bolshevism, the Wilson Administration continued its limited efforts, by means of intervention and diplomacy, to end the single-party rule of the Bolsheviks and hopefully to bring Russia back to the lost liberalism of the March Revolution. Beyond Russia, however, Wilsonianism and Leninism clashed implicitly in relation to Wilson's attempts to reform traditional imperialism, without socialist revolution, through the politics of gradual liberalism. The impact on world politics of Wilsonian reformist liberalism was anti-Leninist as well as anti-imperialist.

Broadly speaking, Wilson's non-revolutionary anti-imperialism sought to use America's moral and material power to create a new international order, safe from the related threats of war and revolution, in which America could serve mankind from a position of political and economic pre-eminence. Yet the attainment of such a stable American-inspired world order was dependent, ultimately, on the Administration's ability to contain the world's anti-imperialist forces within the confines either of orderly liberal reform or of legitimized liberal war. Indeed, Wilsonians feared that unless America could remain in control of all progressive international movements, Leninist revolutionary-socialism might capture Europe's masses and destroy not only atavistic imperialism, but all liberal values and institutions as well. Somehow then, Wilson had to use either liberal reform or liberal war to destroy traditional imperialism, while at the same time maintaining the inviolability both of the nation-state system and of world capitalist order in the face of the challenge posed by the more radical anti-imperialism of Leninist revolutionary-socialism.

In the final analysis, Wilsonian ideology sought essentially to end traditional imperialism and the balance of power, without socialist revolution, by reforming world politics from within. The Wilsonian problem was how to be *in* but yet not completely *of* the existing international political system. Thus, while the United States, under Wilson, would aid the Allied coalition to defeat Germany and to liberate the Slavic peoples of Eastern Europe, it would do so only with the hope of eventually reintegrating a liberalized but non-revolutionary Germany into a new co-operative world structure of law and liberal order under the League of Nations. The American nation-state could, therefore, participate in a world war alongside a major European military alliance and, at the same time, hope to remake the alliance into an agency of liberal-international reform.

The heart of the matter is that Wilson's conception of America's exceptional mission made it possible for him to reconcile the rapid growth of the economic and military power of the United States with what he conceived to be America's unselfish service to humanity. Yet, this Wilsonian reconciliation between national power and liberal internationalism was ultimately more successful in the realm of theory than in the universe of political and diplomatic action. At the Paris Peace Conference, for example, Wilsonian efforts to use American economic and political power on behalf of a more moderate peace led, in part, to the involvement of American power in a postwar extension of the Entente alliance. Indeed, the absorption of Wilson's America into the alliance politics of postwar Europe was a constant possibility so long as the Administration ultimately saw American and Allied power as a safer agent to transform and to control Germany than some form of social revolution. Ultimately then, in their search for a new rational international capitalist order, safe from war and revolution and open to the commercial and moral expansion of American liberalism, Wilsonians would find it easier to enter than to transcend the traditional diplomatic system.

For the President, however, the hope of this liberal transcendence was kept alive by his vision of the League of Nations. In Wilsonian terms the League not only secured the peace with Germany, it also created an ongoing structure capable of handling all future international contradictions and imperialist threats to world order. In broader terms still, the President saw the League of Nations as the fulfillment of his long effort to use America's moral and material power to move the world from a warlike state of nature to an orderly global society governed by liberal norms. Indeed, even if all nations could not be transformed immediately into liberal polities on the American model domestically, they all could hopefully be brought, through participation in the League of Nations, at least to play the role of orderly citizens in a new Lockean world system of liberal-capitalist harmony. Finally, then, Wilson envisioned the League as an American-inspired international social contract, guaranteeing a world liberal order made safe from traditional imperialism* and revolutionary-socialism,

* In this study, the concept of traditional imperialism refers to the entire existing structure of world politics in the late nineteenth and early twentieth centuries, a structure characterized by alliance systems, military preparedness, and especially by great power rivalry for colonies and spheres of influence in the underdeveloped world. The concept of the "old diplomacy," developed by Arno Mayer in his *Political Origins of the New Diplomacy*, largely corresponds to my usage of the term traditional imperialism in this study. This usage also relates to the inclusive sense in which both Wilsonians and Lenin-

within which the leadership of the liberal-exceptionalist United States would be welcomed by mankind.

ists used the concept of imperialism, while each offered, of course, quite different analyses of the roots of imperialism and quite different anti-imperialist programs. Moreover, even if, on another plane of analysis, the ideological basis for a new American imperium can be seen to have been latent in Wilson's vision of a new liberal world order led by the United States, it nonetheless remains true that the Wilsonian position was opposed to traditional imperialism as defined above.

WAR AND REVOLUTION 1

Wilson messianic ?

I

War and Revolution, I: Wilsonianism and Leninism, The Ideological Setting of Conflict

The world views of both Woodrow Wilson and Vladimir I. Lenin, like those of most messianic political thinkers, were centered on a dominant faith or myth. At the core of Wilson's political creed was a conception of American exceptionalism and of the nation's chosen mission to enlighten mankind with the principles of its unique liberal heritage. In Lenin's case, the central myth concerned the imminent liberation of mankind from liberalism, capitalism, and imperialism through the means of a proletarian revolution led by a knowledgeable socialist vanguard. From this basis, Leninist ideology would challenge not only Wilson's ultimate goal of a capitalist-international system of free trade and liberal order, but also the President's final decision to achieve this aim by fighting a liberal war against Germany in the interests of universalizing self-determination and democracy throughout Europe. In 1917, these two mutually exclusive visions of world history came directly into conflict when Lenin and Wilson both became, almost simultaneously, major historical actors.

1. LIBERAL AND REVOLUTIONARY SOCIALIST CRITIQUES OF IMPERIALISM

Woodrow Wilson's vision of a liberal world order of free trade and international harmony did not oppose but rather complemented his conception of the national interests of American capitalism. By the turn of the century it was clear to Wilson that the growth of the American economy, especially in heavy industry, meant that America would soon be competing for the markets of the world with the other major industrialized powers. The future President also correctly saw that the Spanish-American War and the subsequent annexation of the Philippines marked the realization by the nation that the next frontier to be conquered consisted of the fertile export market of Asia. Indeed, this new frontier had to be conquered lest the United States burst with the goods its new industrial system was capable of creating. On the eve of his first presidential campaign, Wilson told the Virginia General Assembly that "we are making more manufactured goods than we can consume ourselves . . . and now, if we are not going to stifle economically, we have got to find our way out into the great international exchanges of the world." [1]

A constant *leitmotif* in Wilson's speeches both before and during his campaign for the presidency in 1912 was the concern that recession and stagnation might overtake the American economy if exports were not drastically increased. Wilson also insisted that, in order to achieve the commercial expansion necessary for American prosperity, it would be necessary to remove certain structural defects in the American economy. In this connection, he emphasized the inadequate credit facilities provided by American banking institutions for export expansion [2] and also stressed his opinion that the merchant marine was inferior to those of America's competitors in international trade.[3] Wilson also attacked the high protective tariff because, among other reasons, its rates brought retaliation against American goods by other countries. The essence of trade was reciprocity, and one could not sell unless one was also willing to buy.[4] Wilson had no doubt that technological efficiency guaranteed American success in international commercial competition, and that, given a chance, "the skill of American workmen would dominate the markets of all the globe." [5]

Wilson's Secretary of the Treasury, William G. McAdoo, was no less convinced than the President that American economic sta-

[handwritten margin note: Wilson for free trade]

[handwritten note at bottom: Sounds like what we hear today.]

bility was dependent on the movement of surplus products into the mainstream of foreign commerce.[6] He championed, therefore, all Wilson's efforts to remedy the defects in American capitalism which were inhibiting our export expansion. In the same vein, McAdoo worked tirelessly throughout most of Wilson's first term for the passage of an act to create a government-supported merchant marine to prevent foreign competitors from shutting the United States out of world markets by discriminatory freight rates.[7] McAdoo also understood that reciprocity was basic to any effort to avoid depression by a policy of export expansion and that for this reason, among others, Wilsonian efforts to lower the tariff were wise.[8] Finally, McAdoo was fully aware of the relationship of banking reform to the growth of America's commercial role in the world. Writing in the summer of 1915, McAdoo said of the Federal Reserve Act that "this great piece of financial legislation has put this country in position to become the dominant financial power of the world." [9]

In this general area of commercial expansion, it is also significant that, under Wilson, Chairman Joseph E. Davies and Vice Chairman Edward N. Hurley of the Federal Trade Commission conceived of the role of the FTC, in part, as one of coordinating joint government-business efforts to make American capitalism rational, co-operative, and efficient. Davies and Hurley hoped thereby both to enhance the stability of the American economy and to increase its competitive potential in world trade.[10] In late 1915, Davies proudly announced at an exporters' convention that it was the purpose of the Federal Trade Commission to aid "in the development of the power and greatness of this nation as an industrial, commercial and financial nation in the world." [11] In a similar vein, Secretary of State William Jennings Bryan told the first National Foreign Trade Convention, meeting in Washington in the spring of 1914, that the Wilson Administration was "earnestly desirous of increasing American foreign commerce and of widening the field of American enterprise." [12] Bryan also emphasized that the State Department would work to "obtain for Americans equality of opportunity in the develop-ment of the resources of foreign countries and in the markets of the world." [13]

It is little wonder that Wilson's speeches and letters in 1916 radiated pride in what his first Administration had done to promote American trade abroad. Time and again Wilson stressed the aid given by the Federal Reserve Act, the Federal Trade Commission, and the Commerce Department to American exporters, and called on the nation's business leaders to rise to their global opportunities.[14] It should be noted, however, that the Wilsonian program of commercial expansion did not go uncriticized domestically. On the Right, some Republican and Progressive nationalist spokesmen, such as Theodore Roosevelt, Albert Beveridge, George Perkins, and Henry Cabot Lodge, were not willing to see tariffs lowered as a means of increasing exports, and they were not averse to having exports expanded by the alternate method of international economic rivalry backed by naval preparedness. On the Left, socialists questioned the very concept of trade expansion itself, arguing that there was no real surplus to export, but only those goods which the lower classes were not able to consume at existing price and income levels. Beyond the question of underconsumption, socialists and some radical liberals also saw a danger of navalism, imperialism, and war in any vigorous program of export expansion. In the Center, however, the Wilsonian position implicitly held, against both conservative and radical critics, that it was possible to have economic expansion and yet to avoid such traditional imperialistic practices as protection, economic warfare, and navalism. Yet, in order fully to understand how Wilson could ideologically fuse commercial expansionism with a form of anti-imperialism, it is now important to grasp that, for the President, export was the necessary material aspect of a national mission to spread the values of American liberalism abroad in the interests of world peace and international liberal-capitalist order.

In essence, Wilson approached the question of America's export trade from the perspective of the Puritan sense of "a call-

like we do today w/ China.

ing." Like the Puritans, who placed earthly vocations, or callings, in a larger context of service to God and man, Wilson saw the enlargement of foreign commerce in terms of a duty in the service of humanity. During the early years of the war, and American neutrality, the President coupled his exhortations to American businessmen of commercial expansion with a messianic conception of the service which America was able to provide to a suffering world whose productive facilities had been upset by the struggle. "The war," he claimed, "has made it necessary that the United States should mobilize its resources in the most effective way possible and make her credit and her usefulness good for the service of the whole world." [15] In this sense, the competitive advantage in world trade which America possessed due to her technological and productive efficiency was, for Wilson, not a threat to other nations, but rather a godsend. The peaceful triumph of America in the markets of the world was, therefore, to be both a service and a lesson for a suffering humanity. In Wilson's terms:

America has stood in the years past for that sort of political understanding among men which would let every man feel that his rights were the same as those of another and as good as those of another, and the mission of America in the field of the world's commerce is to be the same: that when an American comes into that competition he comes without any arms that would enable him to conquer by force, but only with those peaceful influences of intelligence, a desire to serve, a knowledge of what he is about, before which everything softens and yields, and renders itself subject. That is the mission of America, and my interest, so far as my small part in American affairs is concerned, is to lend every bit of intelligence I have to this interesting, this vital, this all-important matter of releasing the intelligence of America for the service of mankind.[16]

The fusion which Wilson made here of America's economic and political missions reveals the roots of the President's combined vision of moral and material expansion. The commercial health of America was, for Wilson, the visible evidence of underlying political and moral strength. Having ideologically unified liberalism, capitalism, and missionary-nationalism, Wilson never doubted that "all the multitude of men who have developed the peaceful industries of America were planted under this free polity in order that they might look out upon the service of mankind and perform it." [17] For the President, the extension of American trade around the world was inseparable from the export of American liberalism. In his eyes the national purpose was one of seeking "to enrich the commerce of our own states and of the world with the products of our mines, our farms, and our factories, with the creations of our thought and the fruits of our character." [18] Toward the end of his first term, Wilson addressed a Salesmanship Congress in Detroit in words that speak volumes as to the unity of his world view of liberal-capitalist expansionism:

> This, then, my friends, is the simple message that I bring you. Lift your eyes to the horizons of business; do not look too close at the little processes with which you are concerned, but let your thoughts and your imaginations run abroad throughout the whole world, and with the inspiration of the thought that you are Americans and are meant to carry liberty and justice and the principles of humanity wherever you go, go out and sell goods that will make the world more comfortable and more happy, and convert them to the principles of America.[19]

New Freedom foreign policy in regard to China and Latin America, during Wilson's first term, exemplified the relation of the President's ideology of moral and material export to his liberal anti-imperialism. In the Far East, Wilsonian concern for the territorial integrity, stability, and political independence of China was not an abstract anti-imperialist position arrived at in an economic and social vacuum. Actually, Wilson's opposition to the traditional policies of spheres of influence and territorial annexation in China was inextricably bound up with his concept of the type of liberal world order of commercial freedom within which the genius of American capitalism could best win its rightful place in the markets of the world. Since Wilson never questioned his basic assumption that American commercial and moral expansion into China contributed to the welfare of the Chinese people, there was a unity in his mind of both his allegiance to the export of American surplus products and his opposition to traditional imperialism in China.[20] In this connection, the Wilson Administration refused to continue the Taft policy of encouraging an American banking group to participate in a projected financial consortium of six major powers for China. The President took the position that the terms of the planned Six-Power Consortium threatened the political and economic independence of China, and that large segments of the American banking community had been refused admittance to the program.[21] In opposing United States participation in the Consortium, Wilson was not however, opposing the principle of the expansion of American capitalism into underdeveloped areas. On the contrary, the Administration felt that, once free of the restraints of the Consortium, the American banking and business community as a whole could do a better job of serving the Chinese with the aid of the Departments of State and Commerce.[22]

In Latin America, Wilsonian policy sought to relate American economic expansion to the creation of an hemispheric system of free trade and liberal-capitalist order to be led by the United States. Wilson, McAdoo, and Commerce Secretary William C. Redfield were all anxious to promote the extension of American financial and commercial activity in South America, and they emphasized government support to this end.[23] Adding his voice, Secretary of the Navy Josephus Daniels argued that since America had to sell her surplus products abroad in order to maintain domestic prosperity, American businessmen had best learn how to conquer the markets to the South.[24]

Yet, if Wilsonians envisioned a commercial hemispheric harmony transcending power politics, it is also true that in the sensitive Caribbean area the Wilsonian urge to export liberalism and protect America's commercial and strategic interests from any European encroachments led to armed interventions to maintain stability.[25] In late 1915 House recorded:

He [Lansing] laid some memoranda before me concerning the Caribbean countries which he thought needed attention. He believes that we should give more intimate direction to their affairs than we would feel warranted in doing to other South American states. He puts them in the same category with Santo Domingo and Haiti and believes we should take the same measures to bring about order, both financial and civil, as we are taking in those countries. I approved this policy and promised to express this opinion to the President.[26]

As regards Mexico, however, Wilson successfully resisted pressure to apply the traditional interventionist and conservative solutions of Republican nationalism to the problems created by the Mexican Revolution. Instead, he slowly developed a policy of aid to the Mexican Constitutionalists to the end that Mexican feudalism would be destroyed and broad-based land ownership established.[27] Wilson hoped that these changes, coupled with education, would create the prerequisites for liberalism, capitalism, and stability in Mexico.[28]

In the light of coming events in Russia and the future confrontation of Wilson and Lenin, it is important to understand at this juncture that the revolution which Wilson came to support in Mexico was conceived by him to be basically liberal-capitalist rather than socialist in intent. There is no evidence that the President ever changed his mind about a statement that he made in 1913 to the British diplomat Sir William Tyrrell: "the United States Government intends not merely to force Huerta from power, but also to exert every influence it can to secure Mexico a better government under which all contracts and business concessions will be safer than they have ever been." [29] In short, Wilson held that the avoidance of crude economic exploitation and of traditional imperialist practices in Mexico and Latin America would lead both to increased legitimate American investment to the South and to a just liberal-capitalist hemispheric order.[30] In this fashion both the material and moral missions of American liberal-expansionism could be fulfilled.

Wilson and House hoped to cap their vision of an American-inspired and American-led liberal order in the Western Hemisphere with a Pan-American Pact providing for mutual guarantees as to arbitration, disarmament, and territorial integrity.[31] Even though the pact was not actualized, Colonel House recorded some thoughts concerning it which serve to illustrate the universal scope of the Wilsonian non-socialist critique of existing world politics. "It was my idea," wrote House, "to formulate a plan, to be agreed upon by the republics of the two continents, which in itself would serve as a model for the European nations when peace is at last brought about." [32] Indeed, the hope that somehow America could supply the answer to the problems of war-torn Europe became a major element in Wilsonian foreign policy from 1914 to 1917. In the President's eyes, it should be remembered, the vast wartime expansion of America's export trade was a means of American aid to mankind. In defense of his policy of neutrality, Wilson argued that "we can help better by keeping out of the war, by giving our financial resources to the use of the injured world, by giving our cotton and our woolen stuffs to clothe the world." [33] This missionary ideology of foreign aid through export also extended to a vision of the role which America might play as the reconstructor of devastated Europe in the postwar period. In a statement capturing his conception of the redemptive power of business and international trade, Wilson affirmed early in 1916 that:

Somebody must keep the great stable foundations of the life of nations untouched and undisturbed. Somebody must keep the great economic processes of the world of business alive. Somebody must see to it that we stand ready to repair the enormous damage and the incalculable losses which will ensue from this war.[34]

This Wilsonian vision of a role for the United States in European reconstruction was intimately related to the President's awareness that the export trade of 1914–16 had made America the major financial power in the world. This development had necessarily greatly enlarged the potential influence of American capitalism on

the international commercial and political scene. "We have become not the debtors but the creditors of the world," Wilson told
an audience at Shadow Lawn on the day before the 1916 election,
adding, "We can determine to a large extent who is to be financed
and who is not to be financed . . . we are in the great drift of
humanity which is to determine the politics of every country in the
world." [35] The President's realization that the United States was
"becoming by the force of circumstances the mediating nation of
the world in respect of its finances" was clearly a major element in
his confident assertion that "we shall someday have to assist in re-
constructing the processes of peace." [36] The fact that the aggregate
resources of the national banks of the United States exceeded by
three billion dollars the aggregate resources of the Bank of
England, the Bank of France, the Bank of Russia, the Reichsbank
of Berlin, the Bank of Netherlands, the Bank of Switzerland, and
the Bank of Japan, helped to give Wilson confidence that America
was better prepared than ever before to "lead the way along the
paths of light." [37] The ultimate Wilsonian hope was to use
America's expanding commercial and political influence to establish
on a worldwide scale the type of liberal-capitalist order of commercial freedom which had been the goal of his concern for
American moral and material expansion in China and Latin
America. To this end, the President, in close co-operation with
Colonel House, opted for the role of mediator in the World War.
Indeed, House's missions to Europe as Wilson's emissary during the
1914–16 period may be seen as efforts to convince the European
powers that their best interests would be served by a negotiated
peace to be made lasting by their mutual co-operation with the
United States in the creation of a new political and economic
world system in which the seas would be free, territorial integrity
mutually guaranteed, and financial expansion into underdeveloped areas handled in a co-operative atmosphere. In such a world,
traditional imperialism would be obsolete and American liberal-
expansionism could prosper in an atmosphere of peaceful international-capitalism.

In 1912 Colonel House wrote a utopian novel entitled *Philip Dru: Administrator*, whose protagonist, upon becoming dictator of America, succeeds in bringing Germany into an Anglo-American inspired world order "of peace and commercial freedom," within which "disarmaments were to be made to an appreciable degree, customs barriers were to be torn down, zones of influence clearly defined, and an era of friendly commercial rivalry established." [38] During his actual trips to Europe, between 1914 and 1916, House used all his diplomatic skills in an effort to reintegrate Germany into a harmonious international-capitalist concert of Western powers led by England and the United States. In the spring and early summer of 1914, on the eve of war, House sought unsuccessfully to bring about an Anglo-German *rapprochement* around the principles of concert of power, naval disarmament, and peaceful commercial rivalry.[39] In his Diary, House recorded his conception of the best way to approach the Kaiser in the interests of a rational world system of economic and political order:

My purpose is to try to show the Emperor that if he will consent to take the initiative in the matter I have in mind, it will rebound greatly to Germany's commercial and material welfare. It is not in my mind to suggest to him to lessen at all his military organization or to disturb his Continental relations. It is only to try to show him that an understanding with Great Britain and the United States will place him in a position to curtail his naval program and open up a wider field for German commerce, besides insuring the peace of the world.[40]

The Colonel's desire to reintegrate Germany into a stable Western international structure was intensified by the outbreak of war in August 1914. Writing to James W. Gerard, the American Ambassador in Germany, House expressed the hope that the Kaiser would consider a peace based on mutual disarmament and territorial guarantees. "With Europe disarmed and with treaties guaranteeing one another's territorial integrity," the Colonal reasoned, "she [Germany] might go forward with every assurance of industrial expansion and permanent peace." [41] On his second peace mission to Europe, in early 1915, House sought to fuse America's export-oriented concern for freedom of trade and neutral rights with an appeal to Germany's leaders to exchange their traditional reliance on national power for an Anglo-German *détente* based on freedom of the seas and peaceful commercial expansion.[42] In the fall of 1915, House sought to present his position to Count Bernstorff, the German Ambassador to America:

During the conversation we spoke of peace overtures, and of when and how they might begin. I impressed upon him my belief that no peace parleys could be started until Germany was willing to consent to abolish militarism and Great Britain to abolish navalism. I enlarged upon Germany's splendid opportunity for industrial advancement with the freedom of the seas assured, and I made it clear that the one thought uppermost in the mind of the Western Allies was a peace free from the menace of another such war.[43]

At the core of House's vision of Western unity was a program through which the bitterly competitive process of financial and commercial expansion by the advanced nations into the undeveloped world could be restructured in a rational and co-operative manner. In the Colonel's conception, the American desire to maintain the Open Door in colonial areas for the export of American surplus products was joined to the liberal impulse to end a major cause of imperialist conflict by reforming world politics from within. As House explained it to British leaders in early summer 1914:

My plan is that if England, the United States, Germany and France will come to an understanding concerning investments by their citizens in undeveloped countries, much good and profit will come to their citizens as well as to the countries needing development. Stability would be brought about, investments would become safe, and low rates of interest might be established.[44]

Co-operative management of the world's backward areas also provided, in House's mind, further means of bringing Germany into a peaceful international-capitalist world system. In his *Philip Dru: Administrator*, House had already sketched out a program in which Germany would be allowed commercial expansion in Latin America, the Balkans, and the Near East.[45] On his actual peace missions, the Colonel often urged upon Allied and German leaders the possibility of sublimating Germany's expansive energies into less aggressive channels by giving her financial opportunities in the undeveloped areas.[46]

In the light of House's efforts to place the "backward" peoples into the context of a harmonious liberal world order, a dimension was added to Wilson's own desire to use American mediation and financial power to reconstruct and reunify the Western world. Wilson tended to view American neutrality and peace-making as a duty due to the system of world leadership by the great "white" nations of the West, a position which would be reinforced by the imminent challenge of Bolshevism to that system from the Left. Secretary of State Robert Lansing records a significant comment of Wilson's made just after the German declaration of unlimited submarine warfare in February 1917, in which the President made explicit his vision of world liberal peace based on unified Western commercial and political leadership:

The President, though deeply incensed at Germany's insolent notice, said that he was not yet sure what course we must pursue and must think it over; that he had been more and more impressed that "white civilization" and its domination over the world rested largely on our ability to keep this country intact as we would have to build up the nations ravaged by the war.[47]

On close analysis, then, Wilsonian liberal anti-imperialism emerges as a limited form of international reformism. That is to say, Wilson opposed traditional exploitive imperialism involving territorial annexations, armed force, protectionism, and war. The President did not, however, question either the structural inequitability of the commercial and financial relationships between the agrarian and the industrialized areas of the world or the correlative economic and political world predominance of the West. Wilson's basic concern, inspired both by the expansive needs of American capitalism and by his own liberal-internationalist ideology, was to make more rational and humane the existing world economic and social relationships. The mandate system, which he was to advocate at Paris, was a classic example of his paternalistic orientation. In essence, Wilson and House were reformers with a faith that there was a potential for peace and justice latent in the international-capitalist system which would develop once it was liberated from imperialist irrationality. This Wilsonian position was, of course, to the Left of the views of many Republican and Progressive nationalists vis à vis America's role in the world, but it did not go far enough in its anti-imperialism for many socialists, who insisted that capitalism per se was the root cause of imperialism and war. In this connection, Wilson's world view was not unlike that of such English non-socialist anti-imperialists as Norman Angell, E. D. Morel, and J. A. Hobson, who also offered a rational and democratic critique of protectionism, navalism, secret diplomacy, and colonialism. Along with Wilson and House, these liberals argued that Britain and Europe would prosper best under a commercial and political concert of power which would guarantee free trade, international-capitalist stability, and peace.[48]

Undoubtedly the most complete expression of the Wilsonian anti-imperialism of liberal order may be found in the conceptions of formal international co-operation which Wilson and House developed in the 1915–16 period. By 1916 Wilson hoped to associate America in a postwar union with other leading powers, including Germany, to achieve disarmament, freedom of the seas, mutual territorial guarantees, and international arbitrations.[49] Writing to House on the eve of the Colonel's departure for his third peace mission to Europe, Wilson succinctly expressed his vision of a co-operative international order of commercial freedom:

I agree with you that we have nothing to do with local settlements, —territorial questions, indemnities, and the like—but are concerned only in the future peace of the world and the guarantees to be given for that. The only possible guarantees, that is, the only possible guarantees that any rational man could accept, are (a) military and naval disarmament and (b) a league of nations to secure each nation against aggression and maintain the absolute freedom of the seas.[50]

The emphasis here on the freedom of the seas recalls again the intimate connection in Wilsonian ideology between the needs of an expanding American capitalism and the goals of international liberalism and anti-imperialism. In accepting his renomination for the presidency in September 1916, Wilson made this connection clear by affirming:

We have already formulated and agreed upon a policy of law which will explicitly remove the ban now supposed to rest upon co-operation amongst our exporters in seeking and securing their proper place in the markets of the world. The field will be free, the instrumentalities at hand. It will only remain for the masters of enterprise amongst us to act in energetic concert, and for the Government of the United States to insist upon the maintenance throughout the world of those conditions of fairness and of even-handed justice in the commercial dealings of the nations with one another upon which, after all, in the last analysis, the peace and ordered life of the world must ultimately depend.[51]

An exchange of memoranda between Lansing and Wilson in early 1917 also shows that concern for commercial freedom and an international Open Door were basic elements in the President's hopes for a liberal postwar order.[52] By the latter half of 1916, Wilson's speeches, which were full of the mission of American capitalism to reconstruct a war-torn world, also affirmed the closely related duty of America to join a future concert of powers in the maintenance of international peace and justice.[53] Beyond war there hopefully lay a liberal-internationalist community of civilized powers, inspired by the moral and material expansion of America, which would guarantee world peace, international law, and freedom for commercial expansion. As the President told an audience in Indianapolis during the campaign of 1916:

I have said, and shall say again, that when the great present war is over it will be the duty of America to join with the other nations of the world in some kind of league for the maintenance of peace. Now, America was not a party to this war, and the only terms upon which we will be admitted to a league, almost all the other powerful members of which were engaged in the war and made infinite sacrifices when we apparently made none, are the only terms which we desire, namely, that America shall not stand for national aggression, but shall stand for the just conceptions and bases of peace, for the competition of merit alone, and for the generous rivalry of liberty.[54]

At the very time, however, that Wilson was formulating his vision of a liberal future, a Russian political exile in Switzerland was developing an ideological assault not only on traditional imperialism but on liberal-capitalist anti-imperialism as well.

The efforts of Wilson and House to reform world politics within a context of international-capitalism fitted the world view of the German socialist theorist Karl Kautsky, but not that of Lenin. It is for this reason that the Lenin-Kautsky controversy concerning socialism's reaction to imperialism, a controversy raised above mere sectarianism by the Russian Revolution, is vital to an understanding of the Wilson-Lenin confrontation itself.

In a series of articles written during the early years of World War I, Kautsky developed his theory that military and territorial imperialism were not inevitable phenomena in the behavior of capitalist nation-states. Kautsky felt that imperialism, in the classic sense of the term, was a *policy* pursued by capitalist powers, rather than being an inevitable *phase* or stage of capitalist development.[55] This distinction, which may at first glance seem to be merely an effort to split hairs, is crucial, for it allowed Kautsky to suggest that there were other methods or policies through which the advanced industrial capitalist states of the West might expand into the undeveloped agrarian areas of the world besides navalism, militarism, territorial colonialism, and protectionism.[56] Kautsky believed that he saw tendencies in international-capitalist behavior which suggested that sophisticated bourgeois statesmen would soon realize that war and militarism were irrational and upsetting to the orderly processes of world finance and trade.[57] Indeed, Kautsky saw the possibility of enlightened and cartel-oriented capitalists opting for a worldwide policy of peace, free trade, disarmament, and co-operative development of backward areas. The term given by Kautsky to this possible bourgeois policy of world peace was ultra-imperialism.[58] Clearly, Colonel House, whose peace missions to Europe we have seen to have been in large part efforts to reconstruct a unified and liberalized international-capitalist community led by the Western powers, provides a classic example of what Kautsky meant by the ultra-imperialist statesman.

Yet if Kautsky, like all social democrats, was both encouraged and discouraged by progressive tendencies he perceived in bourgeois circles, Lenin was not. Kautsky's formulation of the possibility of a peaceful change from a system of militarism and war to one of rational ultra-imperialism was a direct threat to Lenin's revolutionary socialist position. For, whatever his intentions, Kautsky had buttressed the axiom of reformist liberalism that the progressive tendencies inherent in capitalism and liberalism were not yet exhausted. Lenin's writings in the 1915-17 period are full of efforts to counter both Kautskyism and liberal anti-imperialism by claiming that imperialism and war were not mere policies which an enlightened liberal-capitalism might discard. Instead, Lenin insisted that imperialism was an essential part of the final stage of capitalist development, and could be ended only by socialist revolution.

Lenin's theory of imperialism emphasized that the mutual need of all monopoly-capitalist nations to find outlets for their surplus capital, created by domestic underconsumption, led to an inevitable economic and political division of the undeveloped world among the powers.[59] Yet no such division of the colonial areas of the world could be permanent and stable, according to Lenin, since the balance of power among the competing capitalist states would shift with the passage of time, necessitating a redivision of

spheres of influence by force of arms.[60] It was therefore the
"contradictions" inherent in the process of capitalist expansion
which militated against Kautskyite and liberal hopes for the
peaceful evolution of international capitalism. Lenin asked socialists, in addition, to compare "the extreme disparity in the rate of
development of the various countries and the violent struggles of
the imperialist states, with Kautsky's silly little fable about ultra-
imperialisms." [61] So far as Lenin was concerned, the concept of
the unity of international-capitalism was conceivable of realization
in only one of two forms: either as a temporary union of many
capitalist states in military and commercial alliance against one or
two others, or as a union of major capitalist powers for the purpose of destroying a revolutionary-socialist state.[62] Clearly, then,
the Bolshevik view of the League of Nations was previewed in
Lenin's writings well before 1917.

For Lenin, Kautsky's major sin lay in his (Kautsky's) tendency
to blunt the revolutionary spirit of the masses by drawing off their
discontent into what the Bolsheviks conceived to be, verbal and
harmless assaults on imperialism from the tame perspective of
bourgeois pacifism.[63] Lenin scorned all liberal anti-imperialist no-
tions of disarmament, arbitration, and free trade, arguing that
such Kautskyite solutions were mere utopian palliatives in the era
of monopoly-capitalist imperialism from which only socialist revolution could rescue mankind.[64] Lenin was quick to condemn
Wilson's peace initiatives in the winter of 1916–17, seeing them
as part of a moderate socialist and liberal movement to create a
non-revolutionary peace of compromise among the imperialist
powers, which peace would then be covered with the rhetoric of
bourgeois pacifism.[65] In this connection, Lenin was often at pains
to claim that no democratic or anti-imperialist peace was possible
under capitalism, and, therefore, to speak, as did Kautsky, of the
possibility of the attainment of a more just international order
without revolution was to accept the utopian abstractions of
bourgeois pacifism.[66] Obviously, Lenin's form of anti-imperialism
was far removed from the Wilsonian liberal-internationalist con-

cern for a peace of accommodation among the powers. It should
be noted, as well, that Lenin also opposed the efforts of moderate
socialist elements to hold a conference at Stockholm during the
war in the interests of agitation for a speedy compromise peace.
The German Sparticists and the Russian Bolsheviks attacked the
Stockholm Conference as an exercise in imperialist peace-making
covered by a gloss of reformist rhetoric.[67]

Lenin's opposition to what he conceived to be any form of a
peace through a capitalist accommodation is perhaps best exemplified by his attitude on the self-determination question. The
Leninist position on self-determination was more universal in its
scope than that of Wilson, in that it insisted on socialists' working for the independence of all subject peoples, whether in Russia, the Dual Monarchy, Asia, or Africa, and not simply those
controlled by the Central Powers.[68] Lenin's assumption was that
socialist support for the breakup of all empires might encourage
bourgeois nationalism in the short run, but that in the end the
triumph of socialism in the newly freed states would lead to the
voluntary amalgamation of free revolutionary states into large and
economically viable socialist units.[69] From this revolutionary perspective on the national question, Lenin opposed all liberal- and
moderate-socialist peace proposals which sought to return international politics to a modified *status quo ante bellum.* For Lenin,
the Stockholm slogan of peace without annexations or indemnities was too moderate in that it did not call for a revolutionary
effort to free peoples subjugated or annexed by the major powers
prior to 1914.[70] While other socialist theorists on the far Left,
such as Rosa Luxemburg, were scornful of nationalism in Asia,
Africa, and Eastern Europe because they feared bourgeois domination, Lenin was willing to risk co-operation with bourgeois
nationalism in wars of national liberation in order to strike a revolutionary blow at what he conceived to be the system of world
domination by the capitalist West.[71] Indeed, Lenin's stress upon
the revolutionary-socialist implications of self-determination in
Asia proved to be a major cause of early British opposition to Bol-

shevism.[72] In the final analysis, Lenin's implacable hostility to the influence of the West in the undeveloped areas of the world, coupled with his insistence on a revolutionary-socialist peace, helped to form the ideological gulf separating the Leninist world view from that of Wilsonian liberal anti-imperialism.

2. DEMOCRACY, AUTOCRACY, AND BOLSHEVISM

Wilson's conception of the origin of the world war was a basic component of his American exceptionalist ideology, and his conception was closely related as well to his desire to use the moral and economic strength of America to establish a liberal world order. In Cincinnati, late in the 1916 campaign, Wilson addressed himself to the causes of the European holocaust:

Nothing in particular started it, but everything in general. There had been growing up in Europe a mutual suspicion, an interchange of conjecture about what this Government and that Government was going to do, an interlacing of alliances and understandings, a complex web of intrigue and spying, that presently was sure to entangle the whole of the family of mankind on that side of the water in its meshes.[73]

Several things should be noted in relation to this statement. First of all, by placing the locus of responsibility for the war on "European" phenomena, such as secret diplomacy and entangling alliances, Wilson remained consistently within the ideological pattern formed by his fusion of liberal anti-imperialism and American exceptionalism. While Lenin saw the war as the inevitable result of competition among imperialist nations in an era of monopoly capitalism, Wilson blamed atavistic and irrational patterns of European national behavior and retained a faith in the peaceful and orderly potential of international-capitalism in general and of American moral-commercial expansionism in particular. Nonetheless, despite the great differences between the liberal-capitalist and the revolutionary-socialist critiques of the war,

the two ideologies had one thing in common. From the particular
levels of abstraction which each afforded, it was possible to transcend views of the war held by the partisans of the nations involved and to see the conflict critically and objectively as a historical experience emerging from a particular set of political and
economic institutions. This was true even if the definition of
those institutions offered by Wilsonians and Leninists differed
greatly. Indeed, many American radicals and socialists retained
positions of critical objectivity *vis à vis* the war during the 1914–
18 period, which positions could be placed on an ideological con-
tinuum at varying points between the poles of liberal and socialist
anti-imperialism. The problem becomes further complicated,
however, by the fact that by April 1917 the President had moved
from his position of liberal objectivity toward the war to a position advocating liberal war against Germany in association with
the Entente. The point was that the very missionary liberal
nationalism which gave Wilson his neutral and critical objectivity
toward the war was also paradoxically capable of supplying an ideological basis for American participation in a war against German
autocratic imperialism. To understand fully the Wilsonian transi-
tion from liberal mediation to liberal war, it is necessary to consider both the problem of German submarine warfare and the
presence within the Wilsonian anti-imperialist mind of certain
latent ideological tendencies which would help to motivate an
American liberal war against Germany.

The submarine warfare used by Germany during the war could
not help but be threatening to Wilson, whose vision, both of
America's expansionist mission and of a liberal world order, was
so deeply related to a concern for freedom of the seas and the
maintenance of international law. The President sought to make
his position on the necessity to defend American rights on the
seas clear to an audience in Topeka, Kansas, early in 1916:

There are perfectly clearly marked rights guaranteed by international
law which every American is entitled to enjoy, and America is not

going to abide the habitual or continued neglect of those rights. Perhaps not being as near the ports as some other Americans, you do not travel as much and you do not realize the infinite number of legitimate errands upon which Americans travel—errands of commerce, errands of relief, errands of business for the Government, errands of every sort which make America useful to the world. Americans do not travel to disturb the world; they travel to quicken the processes of the interchange of life and of goods in the world, and their travel ought not to be impeded by a reckless disregard of international obligation.[74]

This conviction, that Americans were justified in traveling to serve the world commercially, was often affirmed by the President during his speaking tour of the Mid-West on behalf of his military preparedness program in the early weeks of 1916.[75] In this connection, it should be kept in mind that by the end of 1915 American exports to the Allies had grown to such proportions that the recession which plagued the country early in Wilson's first term had been overcome by the effects of the immense war trade.[76] Related to the material issue, however, was the fact that, for Wilson, the very process of defending the nation's rights on the seas became an important aspect of America's unique liberal service to mankind. If it was the exceptional destiny of the United States to feed, clothe, and morally instruct the world, it was also its duty to maintain the rule of law on the high seas for the benefit of all neutral trading nations. As the chief representative and trustee of neutral rights, Wilson was convinced that the mission of the United States was "to assert the principles of law in a world in which the principles of law have broken down." [77] In defending America's neutral rights, then, the President was as certain as always that there was complete unity between the national interest of the United States and the values of liberal-internationalism. This was the uniqueness of America, a nation which since its inception had "undertaken to be the champions of humanity and the rights of men. Without that ideal there would be nothing that would distinguish America from her predecessors in the history of nations." [78]

It must be emphasized that Wilson and his leading advisers made a clear moral distinction between British naval encroachments on commerce alone and the German submarine threat to both trade and lives.[79] After the torpedoing of the *Lusitania*, it was clear that Wilson was prepared, if pressed, to go to war with Germany on an issue which he saw as involving basic principles of neutral rights and international law.[80] Convinced that unrestricted submarine warfare posed a total challenge to the liberal world order which it was America's duty to foster, the President told his audiences on the preparedness tour that the armed forces of the United States were ready to defend those American rights which were identical with universal human rights, and that the defense of basic principles by force was preferable to ignoble compromise.[81] Speaking in Washington in late February 1916, Wilson expressed succinctly his willingness to take America to war, if that were necessary to defend her most cherished ideals:

America ought to keep out of this war. She ought to keep out of this war at the sacrifice of everything except this single thing upon which her character and history are founded, her sense of humanity and justice. If she sacrifices that, she has ceased to be America; she has ceased to entertain and to love the traditions which have made us proud to be Americans, and when we go about seeking safety at the expense of humanity, then I for one will believe that I have always been mistaken in what I have conceived to be the spirit of American history. . . . I would be just as much ashamed to be rash as I would to be a coward. Valor is self-respecting. Valor is circumspect. Valor strikes only when it is right to strike. Valor withholds itself from all small implications and entanglements and waits for the great opportunity when the sword will flash as if it carried the light of heaven upon its blade.[82]

The President also felt that the armed defense of American and neutral rights would not be at odds with but would rather complement his conception of America's responsibility to join a postwar community of powers in the maintenance of international peace and justice.[83] In short, Wilson's response to German submarine warfare proved that a propensity for war in defense of the particular and universal values of American liberal-nationalism was latent in his thought well before the actual entry into the war.

Nevertheless, the President hoped to be able both to defend his principles and to keep the United States at peace. The Wilson-House vision of a reunified Western world functioning with liberal-capitalist harmony has already been discussed at length. Indeed, the President's conception of America's duty to pacify Europe and reconstruct a liberal world order seemed often to assert itself most strongly in his thought at those times when the submarine issue seemed about to force a final break between the United States and Germany.[84] The climactic Wilsonian peace effort of the winter of 1916–17 reflected both Wilson's desire to co-opt Germany into a liberal concert of powers and a fear on the President's part that an imminent resumption of unrestricted submarine warfare by Germany might force the United States to enter the war.[85] The evidence also suggests that, until February 1917, Colonel House never fully gave up the hope that a German-American conflict could be avoided through the voluntary acceptance of the Wilsonian vision of Western commercial and political unity by Germany's leaders.[86]

Wilson and House were both concerned with the consequences of a total Allied victory over the Central Powers. Should German power be crushed, it was possible that Tsarist imperialism would menace the West.[87] Then too, both the President and House were disturbed lest high-handed actions by the British navy and Allied plans for postwar economic competition indicate that British-naval- and protectionist-oriented Toryism might overcome British liberalism and constitute a serious postwar threat to freedom of the seas and the international commercial Open Door.[88] Such apprehensions as to the possibilities latent in total Entente victory served to counterbalance the Wilsonian urge toward war with Germany over the use of submarines, and to reinforce the Wilson-House conviction that only a compromise peace without victory could provide the foundation necessary for international liberal stability.[89]

Because Wilson has such a strong urge to re-establish Western liberal-capitalist unity under American guidance, another ideological element was needed to justify fully war with Germany to the President. This element was supplied to the Administration by House and Lansing in the form of the theory that the World War was a conflict between aggressive German autocracy and defensive Allied democracy. This theory was capable of neutralizing Wilson's counter tendencies to view the war, from the perspective of liberal American exceptionalism, as having emerged from a welter of universal "European" institutions such as alliances, secret diplomacy, and militarism. The autocracy vs. democracy concept also gave an ethical finality to the schism in Western unity which Wilson was hesitant to accept irrevocably until March 1917, when the resumption of German unrestricted submarine warfare led the President finally to believe that Imperial Germany could not be peacefully reintegrated into a liberal-capitalist international community. Wilson's eventual full acceptance of the autocracy vs. democracy concept also, as we shall see, widened the gulf between him and Lenin.

In Colonel House's wish-fulfillment fantasy, *Philip Dru: Administrator*, the American dictator Dru appeals to the British people over the head of their anti-American conservative government, thereby achieving its replacement by a liberal regime with whom Dru co-operates in creating an Anglo-American-sponsored program designed to uphold "the peace and commercial freedom of the world." [90] House himself, despite his desire to include Germany in a postwar commercial and political community of the powers, did place his greatest hopes for the future on what he conceived to be the enlightened liberalism of such British leaders as Sir Edward Grey, a man, according to the Colonel, of "unselfish outlook, broad vision and high character." [91] By the end of 1915, House had come to believe that Grey shared with Wilson the vision of the maintenance of postwar stability and interna-

tional freedom of trade through a league of major Western powers.[92] This faith in the possibility of a future Anglo-American
partnership in the maintenance of liberal world order was the
basis of the moderately pro-Allied character of House's mediation
efforts during 1915 and 1916. Given the commanding position of
Germany on the war map in the early stages of the war, his concern for a liberal compromise peace would alone have been
enough to bring the Colonel's sympathy to the beleaguered Allied
cause in the interests of maintaining a balance of power as the
basis for negotiation. When one adds the submarine issue and
pronounced liberal Anglophilia to the formula, however, it is even
easier to see why the Colonel's mediation efforts operated on the
assumption that all peace proposals had to have prior Allied approval and should in no way interfere with necessary Entente military activity.[93] House felt that, even if the Entente ought not to
achieve total victory, it must not lose.

In a larger sense, moreover, the evidence suggests that, although House's over-all aim as a mediator was to bring about the
peaceful reintegration of Germany into a liberal-capitalist world
order, by early 1915 the Colonel had in reality grave doubts about
the willingness of autocratic Germany to enter a Wilsonian international community. These doubts were much stronger than similar fears House had as to the future intentions of reactionary elements in the Entente. Indeed, there ran through the Colonel's
correspondence and diary a stream of concern, broken by momentary periods of optimism as to German developments, to the
effect that an aggressive Germany, dominated by the military,
constituted a future threat to America, and that Germany would
try to place a diplomatic wedge between the United States and
the Allies in order to win an imperialist peace based on the
German-dominated war map.[94] As he came to see the German
autocracy as the principal threat to his and Wilson's vision of a
liberal world order, House felt increasing solidarity with the Allies
as the defenders of democratic values.[95] The Colonel wrote to
Wilson early in 1916 that were Germany to win a victory "the

war lords will reign supreme and democratic governments will be imperilled throughout the world." [96] Earlier, House had theorized that English power was not objectionably exercised due to the existence of British democracy,[97] and that only a democratic Germany could be a "satisfactory member of the society of nations." [98] By early 1916, through negotiating the House-Grey Memorandum, the Colonel succeeded in making explicit his conception that the United States should co-operate with the Allies, peacefully if possible but with force if necessary, in ending the war and creating a new international order on Wilsonian terms.[99] House's goal remained the same as it had been on his first trip to Europe in early summer 1914, namely, to foster a new and rational concert of liberal-capitalist powers. By 1916, however, the Colonel had well advanced the ideological process through which, with the impetus of German submarine warfare, this goal would no longer be sought by the diplomacy of mediation and would become a Wilsonian war aim.

Secretary of State Lansing was far more committed than the somewhat ambivalent House to the theory that Imperial Germany could not be an acceptable partner in a liberal world community. By the summer of 1915, Lansing was convinced both that German submarine warfare was symptomatic of a total threat to democracy posed by German absolutism throughout the world, and that the United States should be prepared to take part in the war, if necessary, to prevent the Central Powers from either winning or breaking even.[100] During 1916 and early 1917, Lansing was worried by Wilson's and House's efforts in the area of mediation, and was also concerned by the President's periodic efforts to prod the British on the question of neutral rights. The Secretary felt that such policies might result at best in a compromise peace with German imperialism, and at worst in an irrevocable split between the United States and the Allies, leading to a German victory.[101] Convinced that only democracies were fit partners for a peace league, Lansing opposed any plan to include the Central Powers in a projected postwar concert of nations.[102]

With the German declaration of resumption of unrestricted submarine warfare in February 1917, Lansing pressed unrelentingly for war. Angered by Wilson's hesitation to make the final decision to enter the conflict that as President he had tried so long to end, Lansing repeatedly emphasized the necessity for a liberal crusade to defeat German absolutism and thereby lay the foundation for permanent peace in universal democracy.[103] Writing to a close friend in late February 1917, Lansing affirmed his view "that modern civilization is threatened by military Absolutism and that the only hope of a permanent peace lies in the triumph of the principle of Democracy." [104] We shall see that Lansing's militant commitment to liberalism proved important not only as a basis for an Administration opposition to German autocracy but because it later became a basis for the hostile Wilsonian response to the Bolshevik challenge to the values of liberal-capitalism.

It is not surprising, then, that neither House nor Lansing opposed the subtle but steady process through which Sir Edward Grey, while appearing to encourage Wilsonian mediation efforts, was in reality working to enlist American influence and power behind the achievement of Allied war aims. Of course, this British policy was in no sense predetermined to succeed. Had Germany's leaders been willing to give up their hopes for a total victory, to abandon submarine warfare and accept their defeat on the seas, and to use their military superiority on the land to sue openly for an honest compromise peace in late 1916, there is no doubt that they could have seriously undermined the Wilson Administration's ties with the Allies. This was true because whatever political, ideological, and economic ties were growing between the Wilson Administration and the embattled Allies in the 1914–16 period, there always remained, especially in the President's mind, an element of suspicion of Allied imperialism and a continued irritation with Britain's wartime naval and blockade policies. Moreover, until the Germans made their final decision to try for total victory through unlimited submarine warfare, Wilson remained more committed than House, and especially more committed than

Lansing, to the vision of an American-inspired liberal world order to be built on the foundations of a true compromise peace without victory for either side.

Wilson himself proved far less prepared to accept completely the autocracy vs. democracy theory of the war than either of his two principal foreign policy advisers. It is true, of course, that at times Wilson seemed to reveal a latent moral commitment to the Allied cause; one evening in the fall of 1915 he confided to House that "he had never been sure that we ought not to take part in the conflict and if it seemed evident that Germany and her militaristic ideas were to win, the obligation upon us was greater than ever." [105] Nonetheless, despite his latent tendency to make an identification between the cause of the Entente and the values of American missionary liberalism, the main thrust of Wilson's thought and action in the 1914–17 period was in the direction of critical and objective neutrality toward the war coupled with an effort to end the conflict by mediation and the re-establishment of international commercial and political stability. In this connection, Wilson looked upon the House-Grey negotiations of early 1916, which implied extremely close Anglo-American co-operation, as part of the mediation process and in no sense a commitment to go to war in alliance with the Entente.[106] In fact, Wilson's anger both with Allied reluctance to ask him to move for peace and with British infringements on American neutral rights was instrumental in his decision to act publicly for peace in December 1916 despite Allied objections.[107] In the end, it took not only the resumption of unrestricted German submarine warfare in February 1917 but also the liberal March Revolution in Russia to bring the President to accept the war on the terms of a conflict between autocracy and democracy.

The presence of the Tsarist regime among the Allies, in addition to British recalcitrance on neutral rights, had been of concern to Colonel House as he tended more and more to see in the Entente the nucleus for a liberal postwar world. The Colonel was convinced of the possibility that a separate peace could be arranged between Russian and German reactionaries, for, as he told

Wilson, "there is no doubt that the Russian bureaucracy and the German militarists have some understanding and will work together so far as the Russian and German people will permit." [108] This fear of a relationship between German and Russian reaction was, of course, evidence that House saw the war as a potential liberal crusade even prior to American entry. The news of the March Revolution thrilled House, who had "been fearful lest bureaucratic Russia and autocratic Germany would link fortunes and make trouble for the democracies of the world"; [109] and he urged Wilson, as the great liberal of modern times, to recognize the new Russian Government as soon as England and France did so. [110]

The significance of the March Revolution was also grasped by Lansing, who sought to convince Wilson that "the Russian Government founded on its hatred of absolutism and therefore of the German Government would be materially benefitted by feeling that this republic was arrayed against the same enemy of liberalism." [111] Actually, the reactions of House and Lansing were typical of those of many liberals in the United States and the Allied countries, who responded to the March Revolution by claiming that it had purified the Entente cause of the stigma of Tsarist reaction, and thereby removed the last barrier to seeing the war ideologically in terms of a contest between autocracy and democracy. [112] Wilson himself, in the Cabinet meeting of March 20, 1917, "spoke of the glorious act of the Russians, which in a way had changed conditions," but added the doubt that he could "give that as reason for war." [113] By April 2, when he asked Congress for a declaration of war, however, Wilson had clearly resolved the question of Russia in his mind and had adopted the House-Lansing view of the significance of the March Revolution both to the Allied cause and to America's war aims:

Does not every American feel that assurance has been added to our hope for the future peace of the world by the wonderful and heartening things that have been happening within the last few weeks in Russia? Russia was known by those who knew it best to have been always in fact democratic at heart, in all the vital habits of her thought. . . . The autocracy that crowned the summit of her political structure, long as it had stood and terrible as was the reality of its power, was not in fact Russian in origin, character, or purpose; and now it has been shaken off and the great, generous Russian people have been added in all their naïve majesty and might to the forces that are fighting for freedom in the world, for justice, and for peace. Here is a fit partner for a League of Honor.[114]

For the next three years Wilson would seek to defend this vision of a liberal Russia against the threats posed both by German imperialism on the Right and by Bolshevism on the Left.

The ideological implications of the President's final conversion to the autocracy vs. democracy theory of the war also extended beyond the Russian question, however. We have seen that Wilson and House sought to end the split in the Western community of nations through mediation, and that the President took his mission as world reconstructor and peace-maker with great conviction. If, however, the Entente alliance could be transformed by the Russian Revolution and Wilsonian participation into the nucleus of a postwar liberal world system, then America could enter the war without doing violence to Wilson's overriding desire to create a liberal-capitalist community of Western powers. The unchanged goal of reintegrating Germany into a reunified West could eventually be accomplished in a postwar climate of universal democracy, despite the momentary unwillingness of Germany's existing rulers to accept a peaceful role in a liberal world order. Assuming that a Germany liberalized by war would be generously treated by a democratic Entente at the eventual peace conference, the President saw no necessary contradiction between his desire on the one hand for a liberal war against German imperialism and his hope on the other for a compromise peace to form the basis of a new commercial and political world harmony. Indeed, Wilson told Congress in his war message that "only free peoples can hold their purpose and their honour steady to a common end and prefer the interests of mankind to any narrower interest of their own." [115] Then too, once it was accepted that the

war was caused by German militarism, rather than by general
"European" imperialistic practices, as Wilson had originally held,
it was possible for Wilsonians to handle their American exceptionalist distrust of possible Entente imperialism by emphasizing
a belief in the peaceful proclivities of liberal states. What was
basically needed, according to Wilson, was the remaking of a
peaceful liberal-capitalist Germany which could act with international restraint and responsibility. Until then, German imperialism had to be fought militarily.

In a larger sense, it could be said that the decision to bring the
United States into the war solved the problem of finding a
method of actualizing the President's world view by firmly wed-
ding American military strength to Wilson's missionary liberal-
internationalism. Actually, Colonel House had been urging this
seemingly contradictory fusion of national power and international-liberalism on the President since 1914. On the one hand,
the Colonel insisted that Wilson's voice could carry prestige
abroad only if American dignity were maintained in Mexico and
if the United States embarked on an impressive program of military and naval preparedness.[116] House was also convinced that
American firmness in regard to German submarine warfare was
essential to the retention of the respect of the Allies and their
willingness to co-operate with the United States in building a
postwar world.[117] On the other hand, the Colonel often declared
that it was his and Wilson's purpose to eliminate militarism and
navalism,[118] and that the President, in working for peace and a
new world order, should seek to "rally the liberals of the world"[119]
even possibly in opposition to conservative elements in the
Entente.[120] It should be stressed, however, that House did not
feel that he was inconsistent in trying to join nationalism with
liberal anti-imperialism. As if to reassure Wilson on this point,
the Colonel wrote in the spring of 1916 that "your desire to stop
the war and your willingness to help maintain the peace of the
world afterwards would not be inconsistent with a demand for a
navy commensurate with these purposes."[121]

In reality, Wilson seemed as able as House to combine the exercise of national power with an appeal to international-liberalism. The President's willingness to use American military force against Germany in defense of his conception of the freedom of the seas has already been discussed. In late 1916 Wilson responded to House's theory that friction with Great Britain was caused by commercial rivalry by suggesting, "let us build a navy bigger than hers, and do what we please." [122] At the same time, however there is no doubt that Wilson conceived of himself as "speaking for liberals and friends of humanity in every nation" in a struggle for a new international system of peace, disarmament, and commercial freedom against entrenched reaction.[123]

Only a supreme faith in the universal righteousness of their conception of America's national interests could have enabled House and Wilson to conceive of themselves as operating simultaneously as the wielders of traditional forms of national power and as the leaders of world liberalism. The point was, as has been shown, that Wilson's vision of a liberal world order of free trade and international harmony was not opposed to but rather served to complement his conception of the national interests of American liberal-capitalism.[124] Wilsonian foreign policy in an era of war and revolution, then, can best be understood as a combination of liberal opposition to imperialism and of missionary nationalism, and this is the basic explanation of why, once the President accepted it, the concept of a war to make the world safe for democracy served to hold both the national and international elements of the Wilsonian world view in balance. Yet, if Wilson was able to maintain a balance between national considerations and liberal internationalism, his conservative and radical domestic critics were not.

The Republican opposition was unprepared to accept the image of America as the leader of liberal anti-imperialism, while the President's socialist and radical critics never fully accepted the use of American national power. On the international scene as well, the President faced challenges from the Left and the Right, which threatened to upset the precarious Wilsonian balance established between national considerations and liberal-internationalism. On the one hand, the use of American military power against the Central Powers tended to encourage militant imperialist elements in the Entente who were willing to collaborate with American power in the interests of victory, but who did not at all share Wilson's concern for the eventual reintegration of a liberalized Germany into a stable postwar community of powers. Ironically, the very weakness of German liberalism intensified Wilson's crusade against German imperialism, thereby unavoidably aiding Entente extremism at the same time. On the other hand, to the extent that he maintained even a limited and controlled revolutionary liberal posture, the President tended to encourage socialist forces on his Left, whose desire to use class politics to attain a new international system threatened both the President's goal of liberal-capitalist world order and his ultimate reliance on traditional diplomatic and military methods during war and peace negotiations. Even Wilson's calls during the war for democracy in Germany as a pre-condition of peace would help to cause the German Revolution of 1918, from which emerged a socialist threat to both capitalism and liberalism in Germany. In this connection, while ambivalent relations between Wilsonianism and democratic-socialism would be possible, Bolshevism would prove a more lasting challenge to the President's dream of liberal world order than would autocratic Germany.

Lenin's opposition to all efforts in the direction of a compromise peace of liberal reformism has already been discussed, but Lenin was no less opposed to any form of liberal or socialist rationale for participation on either side in the war. Since, after April 1917, it would be Wilson's role to give liberal legitimization to the Entente cause, some consideration of Lenin's approach to the issues of liberal war in general and the March Revolution in particular is essential to full comprehension of the ideological roots of the Wilson-Lenin conflict.

In Lenin's view, the world war was simply a conflict among

capitalist-imperialist powers for the division of the underdeveloped areas of the world, and as such merited the unqualified opposition of all international-socialists.[125] Since all wars on the part of the major powers after 1870 were essentially imperialist struggles for annexations and not defenses of homelands, and since both sides in the world conflict were equally predatory, it naturally followed for Lenin that it was wrong for socialists to support the war efforts of their respective countries either on the ground of national defense or by way of opposing the imperialism or social system of the enemy.[126] For Lenin, the only socialist policy to follow in the face of imperialist war was that of a revolutionary attack on one's own government. Only such a policy of civil war could rescue socialism from what Lenin felt were the opportunistic and social patriotic attitudes of the majority socialist parties in the warring countries. As Lenin saw it, the strong support given by these parties to their respective governments in the war resulted both from the fact that their working class leaders had become too dependent on parliamentary methods for political action and from the fact that a small group of privileged workers—the labor aristocracy—were benefitting from the profits of imperialism.[127] In a larger sense, however, Lenin's contempt for democratic-socialism was rooted in his fundamental position that republican government did not mean the end of bourgeois rule over the workers and that, therefore, only opportunists and petty bourgeois democrats placed any faith in democratic procedures.[128] We shall see that it was this Leninist dismissal of all the values of liberal democracy, which, as much as anything else, motivated Wilsonian hostility to Bolshevism. Also important in the context of the Wilson-Lenin conflict, however, was the fact that Lenin's rejection of traditional liberal values was coupled with an assault on all forms of war under capitalism in such a way as to form a position completely at odds with Wilson's projected war for a new liberal world order in league with Russian and Entente liberalism.

In his writings, Lenin totally rejected the notion that the war was a conflict between autocracy and democracy rather than a struggle for the division of the world among two capitalist coalitions, and he insisted as well that the liberal-capitalism of the Entente was not less imperialistic than the autocratic-capitalism of the Central Powers.[129] In this connection, Lenin had already speculated prior to March 1917 as to whether or not, as many Russian social-democrats held, a republican revolution in Russia would legitimize socialist support for the Russian war effort. Lenin concluded, before the event, that under a republican form of government Russia would still be capitalist and therefore would still be waging an imperialist war.[130] With the victory of the liberal revolutionaries over Tsarism in March 1917, it comes as no surprise to find Lenin opposing all liberal- and moderate-socialist efforts to arouse war enthusiasm in Russia and claiming that no change in war aims could alter the imperialist nature of the war.[131] Lenin also indicted the Provisional Government as the servant of Entente imperialism to which, he held, Russia's liberal leadership was tied by the strings of financial indebtedness and secret treaties.[132] Writing in *Izvestia* in June 1917, Trotsky supported Lenin by arguing that with the state apparatus of Russia still in the hands of the bourgeoisie, the revolution had not changed the character of the war in the slightest.[133] Bolshevism demanded neither a liberal peace nor a liberal war, but called instead for socialist revolution throughout Europe. In so doing, it posed a total challenge to the Wilsonian world view.

In the chapters which follow, we shall be concerned with analyzing, in some detail, the ideological and diplomatic interaction which developed between Wilsonianism and Leninism during the 1917–19 period. In the broadest terms, it could be said that the challenge which Lenin posed for Wilson was related to the general question as to whether or not liberalism had a progressive role left to play in world history. For example, in countries such as Germany and Russia, where liberal-capitalism had not yet completed its historical task of defeating traditional reaction, Wilson would seek to revitalize the progressive potential of liberalism, whereas Lenin would seek to destroy both reaction and liberal-capitalism in one final socialist revolution. In a real sense, then, Wilsonianism represented liberalism's opportunity to regain its progressive dynamism and to end atavistic imperialism while, at the same time, containing revolutionary-socialism.

II

War and Revolution, II:
Wilsonianism and the Rise of Bolshevism

Russian politics provided perhaps the supreme test for a Wilsonian wartime program which sought to relate the immediate necessities of a conventional power political confrontation with German imperialism to the more long-range Administration goal of building a worldwide order based on liberal anti-imperialism. Events in Russia tended to bring home dramatically, to Wilsonians, the difficulty involved in placing the struggle against German autocratic imperialism in an ideological and political context which would move international relations away from the atavistic practices of traditional imperialism, while, at the same time, preventing the total restructuring of world politics by the revolutionary Left. In short, the Wilsonian problem was to set a wartime course on the basis of moderate and rational anti-German liberalism, thereby avoiding both the latent threat of pro-war Entente imperialism and the danger of anti-war revolutionary socialism.

Specifically, however, it is possible to say that two broad approaches to the issues posed by war and revolution in Russia emerged within the Wilson Administration in the immediate aftermath of the Bolshevik Revolution. On one side, Colonel House hoped to bring Russia back to liberal-nationalism through a policy of liberalizing Allied war aims. Presumably, in House's view, this change was to make possible the absorption of Bolshevism into a liberal war consensus. On the other, more conservative

Administration elements surrounding Secretary of State Lansing were suspicious of the Allied Left and were also oriented more in the direction of an overtly anti-Bolshevik position in Russia. It was not long before the interaction of these two tendencies gave a somewhat erratic quality to Wilsonian efforts to contain Russian Bolshevik influence and power during 1917 and early 1918. By the time of the signing of the Brest-Litovsk Treaty, however, the balance had tipped in the direction of growing support in Washington for those anti-Bolshevik *and* anti-German Russian elements who wanted to bring Russia back into the war.

On July 27, 1917, Colonel House discussed the international situation with A. Lawrence Lowell. In the course of the conversation, House argued, in effect, that:

The idea ought to be made current among the socialists and the too advanced liberals that they must go slow or they will bring about a revulsion of feeling that will result in reactionary policies gaining the ascendency. He [House] says that Russian radicals are today doing more than any other influence on earth to secure the victory of autocracy and Toryism, and to impede the growth of democracy.[1]

Similarly, in late February 1918, House and Wilson "discussed the trend of liberal opinion in the world and came to the conclusion that the wise thing to do was to lead the movement intelligently and sympathetically and not allow the ignoble element to run away with the situation as they had done in Russia." [2]

Both the examples just cited above speak volumes regarding the nature of Wilsonian anti-imperialism. Neither House nor Wilson ever really doubted that Wilsonian liberalism, and not socialism, was entitled to exercise an "intelligent and sympathetic" leadership of the anti-imperialist cause in world politics. We have seen, in the preceding chapter, that the essence of Wilsonian foreign policy was the effort to bring about a rational and moderate reform of the international political-economic system, along limited anti-imperialist lines, without, in the process, threatening to undermine liberal-capitalism, the nation-state system, or the com-

mercial-political world leadership of the advanced Western powers.

The President's ultimate vision was the creation of a peaceful
international world order, within which American commerce and
liberal ideals would be pre-eminent. House and Wilson sought, in
other words, to combine liberal reform with a non-revolutionary
conception of international-capitalist stability, and to fuse internationalism with nationalism in a program universalizing the
commercial freedom needed by an expanding American economic
system. Since the President sought essentially to reform and to
humanize the traditional factors of international politics rather
than to demand structural changes in the world's economic and
social patterns, Wilsonian liberalism remained a strictly limited
reformist ideology capable both of legitimizing and of accom-
modating itself to traditional forms of national power. Indeed,
Wilson and House saw no fundamental inconsistency between
their role as wielders of the armed forces of a great power and
their desire to lead the movement of liberal opinion in the world.
In a related fashion, Wilson and House were able to switch from
a position of American liberal-exceptionalism totally critical of
European imperialism in general, to an association with the Entente powers in a war against German imperialism in particular.

Wilson's and House's vision was challenged, however, by socialist elements who persisted in viewing imperialism as an inevitable
stage of capitalist development rather than as a political anach-
ronism existing only in autocratic Germany. Somehow, the
American and European Left had to be convinced, through the
orderly and sympathetic guidance of Wilsonian ideology, that the
defeat of German arms and the democratization of German politics were the essential prerequisites to the attainment of a peaceful liberal international system. House and Wilson hoped that a
liberalization of Allied war aims would accomplish the under-
mining of German imperialism from within, while, at the same
time, channeling the anti-imperialist passion of the Allied-American Left away from radical goals and into the more moderate pro-
war path of the Wilsonian anti-imperialism of liberal order.

In the years before America entered World War I, Colonel House had sought to integrate Imperial Germany into an Anglo-American-led world system of peaceful commercial order. The events of early 1917, however, finally confirmed House's growing feeling that a Germany dominated by its traditional military-imperialist power structure could never play a rational role in international politics. Indeed, after April 1917 House was as convinced as Wilson or Lansing that there could be no question of compromise or negotiation with a Germany dominated by autocratic and military elites.[3] In contrast to Lansing's skepticism regarding the anti-imperialist potential of German liberalism, however, the Colonel remained confident during 1917–18 that it was possible to extend an effective propaganda appeal to the German moderates in the midst of conducting a war against German militarism. Thus, while House opposed any compromise peace based on the prewar *status quo* in regard to territory so long as the German political system remained autocratic, he did repeatedly urge a moderation of Allied peace terms, as well as frequent reaffirmations of the President's projected postwar vision of international commercial and political stability, in the hope of providing incentives to the German liberals to take power from the military and bring Germany voluntarily into a Wilsonian world order.[4] The President largely accepted this approach, and a dominant concern of Wilson's wartime addresses was the effort to assure German moderates both that the war was being conducted against the German military autocracy rather than against the German people, and that there was a place for the commerce of a democratic Germany in a future liberal-international order.[5] The President perhaps best fused these themes in a section of his reply to the Papal peace proposal of August 1917:

Responsible statesmen must now everywhere see, if they never saw before, that no peace can rest securely upon political or economic restrictions meant to benefit some nations and cripple or embarrass others, upon vindictive action of any sort, or any kind of revenge or deliberate injury. The American people have suffered intolerable wrongs at the hands of the Imperial German Government, but they desire no reprisal upon the German people, who have themselves suffered all things in this war, which they did not choose. They believe that peace should rest upon the rights of peoples, not the rights of Governments—the rights of peoples, great or small, weak or powerful—their equal right to freedom and security and self-government and to a participation upon fair terms in the economic opportunities of the world, the German people, of course, included if they will accept equality and not seek domination.[6]

The House-Wilson appeal to German moderates was, however, not the only example of the Administration's desire to combine participation in a global power struggle with the guidance of the world liberal movement. As mentioned earlier, House was deeply concerned with the problem of establishing effective control over those elements of the Allied Left whose anti-imperialist zeal threatened to upset Entente class unity before the achievement of victory over German arms. Late in 1917 the Colonel was especially anxious over the "danger of the people taking matters into their own hands as the Russians had," and he warned Balfour, the British Foreign Secretary, to use skill in handling the British political situation and not to blunder along as most of the Entente leaders had been doing.[7] In mid-February 1918, House and Wilson sent the liberal journalist Ray Stannard Baker to investigate the "disruptive influences" at work among war-weary labor and radical elements in Europe who were attracted by the Bolshevik Revolution.[8]

The delicate problem was that for the Wilsonian conception of the politics of war and revolution to be actualized the Allied Left would have to remain loyal to a liberalized Entente while, at the same time, the German liberals and moderate-socialists were deserting the German state. War aims revision was needed, therefore, to purify the Wilsonian-Entente cause so that democratic-socialists and liberal anti-imperialists in the Allied countries could see their way clear to move toward a world free of traditional imperialism while remaining loyal to the liberalized anti-German war effort. House was certain that if Entente war aims could be modified and publicized in a Wilsonian framework there would be much less difficulty in controlling the American and Allied Left.[9] The President also saw the necessity of co-opting as much of the Entente Left as possible into the pro-war liberal consensus.[10] Wilson's description to House of his basic intent in the reply to the Pope reveals both the President's desire to carry on a dialogue with the Allied Left and his awareness that in so doing he ran the risk of antagonizing the Entente Right:

I have tried to indicate the attitude of this country on other points most discussed in the socialistic and other camps. I have not thought it wise to say more or to be more specific because it might provoke dissenting voices from France or Italy if I should,—If I should say, for example, that their territorial claims did not interest us.[11]

In a larger sense this letter points up anew that the ambiguous essence of the Wilsonian position was the effort to maintain a delicate balance between the claims of liberal-internationalist ideology and the demands of the more traditional aspects of international power politics.

There is no doubt that during the war the power of Wilsonian liberal rhetoric helped to legitimize support for the war effort among most moderate elements of the Allied Left.[12] If, in domestic affairs, Wilson's policies of progressivism proved a powerful antidote to radicalism, so too, in international affairs, the President's projected world order of legality and trade, bound by a fraternity of the leading powers, was appealing to liberals and moderate socialists who sought a non-revolutionary transformation of world politics. In effect, Wilson's Fourteen Points legitimized an Allied war against the imperialism of the Central Powers by emphasizing both the need of greater self-determination for the nationalities subject to the Central Empires and the vision of a new liberal world order of disarmament and free trade to be guaranteed by a League of Nations. Thus, Allied radicals could orient toward their governments in a crusade against the imperialism of the Central Powers while reassuring themselves that

Wilson's vision of postwar liberal-internationalism would effectively checkmate the hopes of Allied imperialists to capitalize on victory in a more traditional annexationist fashion. Moreover, under the impact of Wilson's ideology combined with the wartime evidence of German imperialism in Eastern Europe, many on the Allied Left would find it increasingly difficult to sustain a totally critical stance in relation to their Entente governments unless, of course, they could share Trotsky's expectation that a political victory for the Left was imminent in *all* European capitals, including those of the Central Powers. Naturally, the Bolsheviks reserved particular scorn for Allied socialists who broke faith with the vision of imminent and universal revolution and oriented instead toward Wilson's liberal legitimization of the Allied cause.

Writing in early summer 1918, William G. Sharp, the American Ambassador to France, accurately described the "safety-valve" effect which Wilsonian ideology had on the French Left in wartime. In an added flash of insight Sharp also predicted the President's coming role at the Paris Peace Conference in the sublimation of radical passions:

Paradoxical and strange as it may seem, the counsel of President Wilson, and his constructive measures, exert a vastly greater influence upon shaping the thought of the socialistic mind in France—sometimes of an iconoclastic tendency—than do any other leaders of the Allied Powers. The reason, perhaps, is not far to seek; it has confidence in his motives. In my judgement, that influence has been a valuable asset, and far more powerful in restraining the radical actions of this particular group than is generally understood. They have time and again reiterated their own principles as being in full accord with those enunciated by President Wilson, and I would not be at all surprised that coming events would so shape themselves as to give such an unusual situation great weight in harmonizing the discordant elements which will have to be dealt with in making the terms of peace.[13]

Indeed, it was only in Russia, where the rise of Bolshevism created a historical situation hostile to the politics of pro-war liberal anti-imperialism, that the Wilsonian program for control of the Left by co-optation was tried and found wanting.

During the summer and early fall of 1917 the liberal-nationalist leaders of Russia's Provisional Government * sought to stabilize their own power, popularize the war against Germany, and pacify the Russian Left. The Provisional Government sought to achieve these ends with a Wilsonian-oriented program which combined efforts to arouse liberal-nationalist fervor against German autocratic imperialism with discreet efforts to have Allied war aims purified of their imperialistic aspects.[14] Both House and Boris Bakhmeteff, the Russian Provisional Government's Ambassador to Washington, were united in advocating a program of anti-imperialist Allied war aims as the best means both of avoiding a radical-inspired separate Russo-German peace and of maintaining Russian political unity under liberals loyal to the Entente alliance.[15] In essence, House hoped to apply the normal politics of liberal sublimation to Russian radical passions. Ultimately, this hope would help to pave the way for his and Wilson's unsuccessful efforts to reintegrate even a triumphant Bolshevism into the liberal crusade against German autocracy. As we shall see, however, some Administration figures who gathered around Lansing —occasionally including Wilson as well—opposed in general most efforts to meet the Allied and Russian Left halfway, even for purposes of control. The Lansing group favored, in particular, a firm anti-communist stance in Russia from the outset of Bolshevik rule.

Colonel House's faith in the ability of Wilsonian ideology ultimately to moderate radical extremism and to foster a progressive and pro-war context of class unity is well exemplified by his apparent confidence both that Russian Bolshevism represented only a temporary manifestation of extremism within the anti-imperialist camp, and that this aberration would soon be transformed by Russian moderates and reabsorbed into a revitalized liberal-nationalist consensus. In the weeks immediately following the

* In this study, the concept of Russian liberal-nationalism will be used, sometimes interchangeably with Russian democratic-nationalism, to refer to the program of those Russian political elements, supported by the Wilson Administration, who sought to unify revolutionary Russia around pro-Allied, anti-Bolshevik, and liberal values and institutions.

November Revolution, House seemed to accept the view of some Provisional Government representatives that popular support for Bolshevism would dissolve if the Allied powers went ahead with war aims revision as a constructive answer to the Bolshevik ideological challenge, while avoiding an overt clash with Lenin which might gain support for Bolshevism in Russia.[16] As opposed to Lansing, who, we shall see, saw Bolshevism as completely irreconcilable with liberalism, capitalism, and nationalism, House tended to conceive of Leninism more as an ephemeral expression of thoughtless radicalism soon to be reintegrated into a healthy democratic Russia committed to a crusade against German autocracy within the limits of the anti-imperialism of liberal order.

In the late fall and early winter of 1917–18 the President appeared to join House in the latter's confidence that Bolshevism would not for long divert Russia from the path of democratic-nationalist stability. Shortly after the November Revolution, Wilson wrote to Congressman Frank Clark to say that he had by no means lost faith in the Russian situation, adding that "Russia, like France in the past century, will no doubt have to go through deep waters but . . . her great people . . . will in my opinion take their proper place in the world." [17] Wilson's faith in the Russian outcome was no doubt reinforced by the fact that, despite the counsels of Lansing, the President, like House, tended at first to characterize Bolshevism as an extreme form of democratic anti-imperialist idealism whose radical energies might be guided by rational argument back into the fold of responsible Wilsonian pro-war liberalism. Speaking to the A.F. of L. Convention on November 12, 1917, Wilson voiced an almost condescending puzzlement in regards to the alleged naïveté of Bolshevik reforming idealism:

May I not say that it is amazing to me that any group of persons should be so ill-informed as to suppose, as some groups in Russia apparently suppose, that any reforms planned in the interest of the people can live in the presence of a Germany powerful enough to undermine or overthrow them by intrigue or force? Any body of free men that compounds with the present German Government is compounding for its own destruction.[18]

As yet seemingly unable to grasp the fact that Bolshevik ideology sought the total revolutionary transformation of international politics, including those of the Central Powers, Wilson saw the communists as fuzzy idealists in danger of trusting German militarism. In this vein the President told his Cabinet in late November that the actions "of Lenine and Trotsky sounded like *opéra bouffe*, talking of armistice when a child would know Germany would control and dominate and destroy any chance for the democracy they desired." [19] Along with House, Wilson hoped that a presentation of Allied war aims in an anti-imperialist framework would cause Bolshevik extremism to lose its force and become reabsorbed into the conventional guidelines of the pro-war liberalism of the March Revolution. Speaking to a Joint Session of Congress on December 4, 1917, Wilson affirmed that the Allied cause was one with the cause of anti-imperialism. He added that:

The congress that concludes this war will feel the full strength of the tides that run now in the hearts and consciences of free men everywhere. Its conclusions will run with those tides. All these things have been true from the very beginning of this stupendous war; and I cannot help thinking that if they had been made plain at the very outset the sympathy and enthusiasm of the Russian people might have been once for all enlisted on the side of the allies, suspicion and distrust swept away, and a real and lasting union of purpose effected. Had they believed these things at the very moment of their revolution and had they been confirmed in that belief since, the sad reverses which have recently marked the progress of their affairs toward an ordered and stable government of free men might have been avoided.[20]

Like many of Wilson's and House's statements in this period, this one made no clear-cut distinction between the Bolsheviks and the Russian people and left unclear whether stable liberalism was to result from a new democratic moderation on Lenin's part after his conversion to Wilsonian anti-imperialism or whether stability was to be the result of the Russian masses opting for Wilsonianism against Bolshevism. In a sense Wilson seemed to be calling for a coalition between the Bolsheviks and other political elements in Russia to form a pro-war and ordered democracy allied with a purified Entente.

In any event, pressures on Wilson increased in early 1918 moving the President to legitimize continuation of the war in the minds of the Russian Left. In addition to Colonel House, David R. Francis, the American Ambassador to Russia, argued that the Russian people would only fight "for a democratic peace, for the fruits of the revolution, if appealed to by a country whose unselfish motives they recognize as they do ours." [21] In late December 1917 the Inquiry, an organization set up by Wilson and House to provide expert planning for American policy orientations at an eventual peace conference, recommended in a memorandum a Russian policy consisting largely of war aims liberalization to prove to the Russians "that the diplomatic offensive is in progress and that the Allies are not relying totally upon force." [22] The Inquiry memorandum also expressed a conviction close to that of Colonel House, that the generalized anti-capitalist radicalism of revolutionary Russia could be successfully channeled into the path of the more responsible and safe anti-autocratic crusade against German imperialism:

It is often overlooked that the Russian revolution, inspired as it is by deep hatred of autocracy, contains within it at least three other great motives of serious danger to German domination: 1) anti-capitalist feeling, which would be fully as intense, or more intense, against German capitalism . . . 3) a powerful nationalist feeling among the Moderates, who will either return to power or at least exercise a strong influence in Russia. The revolution, therefore, must be regarded not only as inherently difficult for the Germans to manage and to master, but as being in itself a great dissolving force through its sheer example. [23]

This conviction, shared both by the Inquiry and by House, that somehow the moderates would either return to power or would at

Lansing anti-Bolshevik
more
House tried to steer
Russia towards
liberalism

WAR AND REVOLUTION II   61

least exercise a strong influence on Russian politics, goes a long
way toward explaining why the "House wing" of the Administration was wary of making any clear verbal distinctions between
Russia and Bolshevik Russia in early winter 1918. In some manner the power of Wilsonian liberal ideology would have to help
the Russian moderates lead the Bolsheviks back into the March
Revolution framework of pro-war democratic-nationalism.

Of all Wilson's advisers, Colonel House, armed with the Inquiry memorandum, played perhaps the central role in the conception and composing of the Fourteen Points Address, delivered
on January 8, 1918,[24] at a time when the Brest-Litovsk talks had
been recessed following the revelation of the extent of Germany's
imperialistic demands on Russia. The attitude expressed toward
Bolshevism in this address clearly exemplified the House approach
of making little in the way of clear distinctions between liberal
Russia and Bolshevik Russia. A week before the speech House
decided that the best American policy would be one of offering
sympathy "for Russia's efforts to weld herself into a virile democracy, and to proffer our financial, industrial and moral support in
every way possible." [25] In the planning sessions for the January 8
address House advised Wilson against an assault on the Bolshevik
Government, urging instead the approach of promising sympathy
and aid for "Russia" against Germany, which was ultimately the
basis for Point Six of the Fourteen.[26] Moreover, the opening
paragraphs of the address were in part seemingly complimentary
to the Bolshevik negotiators for their refusal to accede to Germany's demands. Indeed, rather than emphasizing a firm distinction between the Bolsheviks and the Russian people, the tone of
the address was one of hope that the "present leaders" of the
Russian people were about to recognize the folly of negotiating
with German imperialism and to move in their foreign and domestic policies toward the values of liberal-nationalism:

The negotiations have been broken off. The Russian representatives
were sincere and in earnest. They cannot entertain such proposals of
conquest and domination. . . . The Russian representatives have

insisted, very justly, very wisely, and in the true spirit of modern democracy, that the conferences they have been holding with the Teu-
tonic and Turkish statesmen should be held within open, not closed,
doors, and all the world has been audience, as was desired. . . .
There is, moreover, a voice calling for these definitions of principle
and of purpose which is, it seems to me, more thrilling and more
compelling than any of the many moving voices with which the
troubled air of the world is filled. It is the voice of the Russian people. They are prostrate and all but helpless, it would seem, before the
grim power of Germany, which has hitherto known no relenting and
no pity. Their power, apparently, is shattered. And yet their soul is
not subservient. They will not yield either in principle or in action.
Their conception of what is right, of what it is humane and honorable for them to accept, has been stated with a frankness, a largeness
of view, a generosity of spirit, and a universal human sympathy which
must challenge the admiration of every friend of mankind; and they
have refused to compound their ideals or desert others that they
themselves may be safe. They call to us to say what it is that we desire, in what, if in anything, our purpose and our spirit differ from
theirs; and I believe that the people of the United States would wish
me to respond, with utter simplicity and frankness. Whether their
present leaders believe it or not, it is our heartfelt desire and hope
that some way may be opened whereby we may be privileged to assist
the people of Russia to attain their utmost hope of liberty and ordered peace.[27]

Latent in these words, of course, was the possibility of a clear
Wilsonian distinction between the "Russian people" and "their
present leaders," that is, the Bolsheviks. Indeed, we shall see that
under the impact both of Lansing's articulate anti-Bolshevism and
of the growing evidence that Lenin fully repudiated the values
and institutions of liberalism, Wilson, by late February 1918,
would come to reject any plans for aiding a strictly Bolshevik
regime in Russia against Germany. Nevertheless, at the time of
the Fourteen Points Address the influence of House was strong
and the Bolsheviks had not as yet irrevocably burned their bridges
to liberal-nationalism by disbanding the Constituent Assembly.
For these reasons, it was still possible for Wilson on January 8 to
blur the distinction between Bolshevik values and the values of

Russian liberal-nationalism, and for the President even to seek to assure the Bolsheviks of his own anti-imperialist credentials. Naturally, such efforts were assumed by the President and House to result in an absorption of Leninism into a pro-war Russian consensus of democratic-nationalism, and not, in any sense, to result in a conversion of Wilsonianism to the values of revolutionary-socialism. As will be shown, only socialists, and some liberals to the Left of House, would seek to unite Wilson and Lenin against German imperialism partly on Lenin's terms.

As if inspired by the Fourteen Points Address, Newton D. Baker, the Secretary of War, issued a memorandum, apparently in mid-January 1918, arguing that any overt American support for anti-Bolshevik elements in Russia would aid Germany. Baker hoped that, under the impact of German imperialism and Wilsonian ideology, Russian radicalism would be converted to a democratic and pro-Allied position:

Our only chance in Russia is to reestablish, as quickly as possible, confidence in our absolute honesty and disinterestedness, in the hope that we may thereby help the Russians to establish a government in sympathy with democratic ideals, and in the further hope that the sincerity of the Germans may become patent, thus forcing Russia to the conclusion that, after all, her true interests must lie in a vigorous continuation of the war.[28]

So vague was the House-inspired rhetoric of the Fourteen Points Address in regard to an undifferentiated "Russia" that many Left-liberals in the United States wishfully and mistakenly assumed that the Administration was about to recognize the Bolshevik regime. Lansing even had to reassure Boris Bakhmeteff, the worried Provisional Government's Ambassador to Washington, that no American recognition of Lenin was intended.[29] Probably House would have been surprised at Bakhmeteff's anxiety, since the Colonel's Diary indicates that there was close communication between both House and the Ambassador on the portions of the address concerning Russia.[30] The problem arose, however, from the fact that in early January 1918 House and Wilson appeared to feel that the liberalization of Allied war aims might bring the Bolsheviks themselves back to liberalism, while Bakhmeteff apparently wanted war aims liberalization only to win the Russian people completely away from Bolshevism. The distinction is subtle but important. In its largest sense, the issue was between those led by House, who felt that the ideological power of Wilsonian liberalism could bring even Lenin back into the Kerensky posture of support for a war by a united liberal-nationalist Russia against German autocracy for a new world order, and those led by Lansing, who saw no hope of domesticating Lenin within the confines of pro-war liberalism. Before turning to a consideration of Lansing's militant anti-Bolshevism, however, it should be re-emphasized that House never intended his projected Wilson-Lenin fusion to be other than on Wilson's terms, whereby revolutionary-socialist passion would be moderated by the progressive controls of a pro-Allied version of anti-imperialism. In other words, the Fourteen Points Address makes sense only if we assume that Wilson and House felt that Lenin was going to act exactly as Kerensky would have done, or that Kerensky would actually replace Lenin. Of course the January 8 address had sought not only to co-opt the Allied Left into the war effort, but also to avoid offending the Allied Right. The problems raised by such an attempt to join both Right and Left in a moderate Wilsonian consensus would, however, only become fully apparent at the Paris Peace Conference to come.

If, for a time following the November Revolution, House, and to a large extent Wilson as well, retained hopes of keeping the Russian revolutionary experience unified and liberal, Secretary Lansing and his colleagues in the Department of State did not hesitate to make early and clear distinctions between the adherents of the March and November Revolutions. This tension within the Administration, dividing those like House, who wished to enlist a liberalized Bolshevism against Germany, from those like Lansing, who preferred a crusade against both German imperialism and Bolshevism, expressed attitudes which also existed, in more extreme form, to the Left and the Right of the Wilson Administration as a whole. By spring 1918, however, even Colonel House, as we shall see, would come to define "Russia" predominantly in terms of an anti-Bolshevik and liberal-nationalist Russia.

Unlike Colonel House, Secretary Lansing had no real vision of uniting the Allied and Russian Left behind the war, under the guidance of Wilsonian anti-imperialist values. Indeed, Lansing apparently trusted only those aggressively loyal and anti-radical elements which comprised what might be termed an "Administration-Left." These groups, including the A.F. of L. and the Social Democratic League (pro-war socialists), needed no coaxing to serve the war effort. Along with such men as Samuel Gompers and William English Walling (the latter an influential pro-war socialist), Lansing was prone to characterize the position of any political group to the Left of the A.F. of L., indulging in radical criticism of the Administration or the Allies, as constituting a disloyal threat to legal authority in the conduct of foreign relations, and, also, as providing objective aid to German imperialism. In this general connection, both Lansing and the Administration-Left looked upon all plans for an international conference in Stockholm of socialist groups from all the belligerent countries as symptomatic of the entire challenge posed by what they considered to be irresponsible or pro-German radicalism to the Entente war effort and to the March Revolution in Russia.[31] Moreover, as opposed to House, who was anxious to incorporate much of the radical anti-imperialist critique within a liberalized Wilsonian war aims consensus, Lansing appeared more concerned lest public concessions to anti-imperialist ideology aid Germany by robbing the supposedly nationalistic masses in Italy and Russia of their will to fight on for national aggrandizement.[32]

The President, who was torn between the differing approaches of House and Lansing toward wartime radicalism, did largely share the Secretary's conviction that much wartime radical activ-

ity, such as the agitation for a Stockholm Conference, was inspired, directly or indirectly, by Berlin.[33] Indeed, we shall see
later that a growing conviction in Washington, to the effect that
the actions of the extreme Allied Left were objectively, even if
unconsciously, serving the aims of German imperialism, would act
as one of the dominant determinants of Soviet-American relations
as the Wilson Administration moved toward its decision to intervene in Siberia. In a message to the Russian Provisional Government on May 26, 1917, the President sought to counteract the
peace program of the Russian Left in part by emphasizing the
German interest in an early peace:

The war has begun to go against Germany, and in their desperate desire to escape the inevitable ultimate defeat, those who are in authority in Germany are using every possible instrumentality, are making
use even of the influence of groups and parties among their own sub-
jects to whom they have never been just or fair or even tolerant, to
promote a propaganda on both sides of the sea which will preserve for
them their influence at home and their power abroad, to the undoing
of the very men they are using.[34]

The point is that the President was only willing to adopt the
House approach, of co-opting the Left by means of persuasion
into the ordered pro-war framework of liberal anti-imperialism, up
to a point. The heart of the matter was that Wilson was less prepared to compromise with the Left than either House or the New
Republic-oriented liberals who went much further even than the
Colonel in seeking to accommodate the American war effort to
the values of radical anti-imperialism. Actually, on many occasions
the President joined Lansing and the Administration-Left in chal-
lenging the responsibility and loyalty of Left-liberals and socialists
who were unwilling to be convinced or controlled by Wilsonian
rhetoric.[35] It should also be noted that the wartime record of the
Wilson Administration on civil liberties illustrates that when
pressed by the radicals the President was willing to use legalized
force as well as persuasion to maintain national war unity.[36]

The House-Lansing differences as to the best method for the
Administration to use in controlling radicalism extended naturally
into the area of Russian policy as well. While House, as we have
seen, hoped initially to bring the new Bolshevik regime into a
more liberal framework through war aims purification, Lansing
had no hopes for moderating Lenin into a Kerensky. The Secretary decided immediately after the November Revolution that an
understanding between Wilson and Lenin was politically and
morally inconceivable. In early August 1917, Lansing had already
developed a neo-Burkean analogy between the French and Russian Revolutions which held that Russia was fated to pass
through a period of despotic "Jacobin" terror before ordered liberty could be re-established by arbitrary military power.[37] With
the coming of the Bolshevik Revolution itself Lansing recorded
his conviction that the Russian terror would "far surpass in bru-
tality and destruction of life and property the Terror of the
French Revolution."[38] By early December 1917, according to
Lansing, he and Wilson had agreed in principle that recognition
of a Bolshevik regime per se in Russia was out of the question.
This was not only because Bolshevism was seen as having aided
German imperialism by upsetting the pro-war and liberal-nationalist Provisional Government, but also because the Secretary saw
Bolshevik authority as merely that of a minority faction which
had arbitrarily imposed class despotism on parts of Russia by
force.[39] For Lansing it was inconceivable that an American Government dedicated to "the supremacy of the popular will operating through liberal institutions" could accept any despotism,
whether of autocratic or proletarian makeup.[40] In the light of
these views, it is not surprising that in early December 1917 the
Secretary convinced Wilson as to both the wisdom of extending
secret financial aid to the pro-Allied and anti-Bolshevik armies of
General Kaledin in the hope of re-establishing stability and an
eastern front in Russia, and the desirability of not recognizing
Bolshevik claims of control over traditional Russian railway interests in Manchuria.[41]

In the Secretary's view, Bolshevism represented a threat not only to liberal-nationalism in Russia but to Western civilization itself. Lansing characterized the Bolsheviks as ignorant armed idealists who lacked all respect for nationalism as a concept and were determined "to overthrow all existing governments and establish on the ruins a despotism of the proletariat in every country." [42] Since recognition of Bolshevism in Russia might encourage its spread, the Secretary felt that "the correct policy for a government which believes in political institutions as they now exist and based on nationality and private property," was to leave such "dangerous idealists alone." [43] While House hoped to reintegrate Bolshevism into the orderly and anti-autocratic consensus of Wilsonian war liberalism, Lansing's abhorrence of communism was such that in the midst of a liberal crusade against the German Right the Secretary could be moved to observe that the ordered and intelligent despotism of the German military and political elites was for him ultimately preferable to a "despotism of ignorance . . . productive of disorder and anarchy." [44] Fortunately for Lansing, however, the continued existence of pro-Allied and anti-Bolshevik Russian elements during the war allowed him to avoid the necessity of choosing between Lenin and the Kaiser and to continue opposing both Bolshevism and German imperialism in the interests of a liberal-nationalist Russia.

Finally, in terms of the early Lansing-House dichotomy on the problem of Bolshevism, it is important to note their differing reactions to Trotsky's December 29, 1917, appeal for the peoples and governments of the Allied countries to enter into negotiations for a peace which would guarantee universal self-determination. Lansing reacted with contempt, both because Trotsky had appealed to the propertyless masses rather than to society as a whole and because the universal and revolutionary quality of the Bolshevik position on national self-determination fundamentally challenged the existing international structure.[45] By contrast, the following selection from the diary of House's son-in-law, Gordon Auchincloss, illustrates the confident House approach of seeking to incorporate revolutionary ideology into the diplomatic and political service of the Wilsonian anti-imperialist war for liberal international stability:

> On Thursday, January 3rd, 1918, a great deal of my time was spent communicating to Mr. House the exact situation in Russia in connection with the Brest-Litovsk peace negotiations, and particularly the statement made by Trotsky to the Allied Governments. It is a remarkably able paper and presents an extraordinary opportunity for a strong diplomatic drive which would be bound to cause a great deal of trouble in Germany between the Socialists and the Pan-Germans.[46]

Apparently House was confident enough in Wilson's ability to control the Allied Left to believe that really only the German elites needed to fear revolutionary ideology. Lansing was far less sanguine about the relationship of radical thought to the war effort.

In addition to Lansing, other individuals close to the Administration advocated various ways of making the distinction between Bolshevism and Russian liberal-nationalism after the November Revolution. Such observers as Maddin Summers, the Consul General at Moscow, and Arthur Bullard, the director of the Committee on Public Information (CPI) in Russia, were quick to inform Washington of their conviction that Bolshevism represented the rule of an undemocratic minority which was contemptuous of liberal institutions and was willing to retain power by terror.[47] In a similar vein, George Creel, the chairman of the CPI, wrote to Wilson in late December 1917 in regard to American propaganda in Russia, suggesting that aid could be productively given only in co-operation with an anti-Bolshevik government based on liberal institutions.[48] Then too, in connection with American propaganda abroad, the chairman of the Inquiry, Sidney Mezes, wrote to House suggesting that only those propagandists be sent by the United States to Russia who were in sympathy "with the Russian Revolution but not with the Bolsheviki." [49]

Early in 1918, Samuel Gompers also called for a clear-cut anti-Lenin stand on the part of the Administration, claiming that:

The real, democratic, practical revolutionaries of Russia, men who have made the revolution, are standing firmly for the democratization of Russia, and for the proper orderly government of that country. I am informed on good authority that the six radical daily papers of Petrograd are opposed to the bolsheviki and for democratic institutions.[50]

During January 1918 the dissolution of the Russian Constituent Assembly by the Bolsheviks went a long way toward ending whatever hopes for the liberalization of the Bolshevik regime were still alive among the Administration personnel in Russia and Washington.[51] Finally, within the State Department, Russian expert Basil Miles developed a position, in a series of policy memoranda, which combined a modified version of House's desire to control Bolshevism by reintegrating it into a liberal Russian consensus with a more Lansing-oriented tendency to make explicitly clear that a purely Bolshevik regime in Russia was morally and politically unacceptable to America.[52]

So far as the President himself was concerned, we have seen, especially in the case of the Fourteen Points Address, that Wilson in large part shared House's desire to reintegrate Bolshevism into the liberal war effort. Indeed, as late as January 21, 1918, Wilson showed some interest in a plan suggested by Senator Robert L. Owen under which the United States would extend informal recognition and aid to the Bolsheviks as a means of maintaining Allied influence in Russia.[53] Yet we have also seen that, during the same period, the ambivalent Wilson was also impressed by the more militantly anti-Bolshevik orientation and advice of Lansing. Almost on the eve of the Fourteen Points Address, for example, we find that Wilson's concern over the revolutionary implications of Trotsky's note of December 29, 1917, had a good deal in common with Lansing's reactions to the same note.[54] Moreover, Wilson's letters in late January 1918 often reflected dismay and anger over the Bolshevik dissolution of the Constituent Assembly in Russia.[55] In any event, after early 1918 the main drift of Wilson's thought in relation to Leninism would have more to do with finding a liberal-nationalist alternative to Bolshevism than with trying to co-opt the Bolsheviks into a democratic Russian order.

On February 9, 1918, Samuel Gompers sent Wilson a memorandum on European socialism written by the committed war-socialist W. E. Walling. Walling, as suggested earlier, was bitterly opposed to any policy of concessions to the Left in the Allied countries or Russia which sought either to enlist radicals in the war effort or to subvert Germany from within. He was in total opposition to House's orientation of controlling radicalism by sympathetic absorption. The President read Walling's statement and quickly sent it on to Lansing, assuring the Secretary that Walling's work contained "an unusual amount of truth." [56] In this particular memorandum Walling had argued that any encouragement of Bolshevism redounded to the benefit of German imperialism since Walling saw Germany's socialists as more subservient and less prone to revolutionary agitation than those of the Allied democracies. Thus, in Walling's view, if Bolshevism were encouraged the Allied countries might suffer revolutionary-socialist upheaval, but German imperialism would remain untouched and aggressive since German socialism would fail to rise against military dominance in Germany. This argument gave a paradoxically pro-war and pro-Allied twist to the classic Left-socialist critique of the moderate character of German social democracy. In addition, Walling's memorandum also opposed any recognition of the Bolsheviks which might aid their worldwide class war against all governments, including those of the Entente.[57]

Lansing himself had come to the conclusion weeks earlier that the Bolsheviks were as hostile to democracy as to autocracy and that to recognize Lenin's government "would encourage them and their followers in other lands." [58] Naturally then, the Secretary joined Wilson in enthusiastic appreciation of Walling's views, which, according to Lansing, represented "a keen apprecia- tion of the forces which are menacing the present social order in nearly every European country." [59] It is not surprising that, on February 19, 1918, Lansing and Wilson ruled as "out of the ques- tion" a French suggestion that the United States join France in giving the Bolshevik Government material and financial support in the event that it should decide to defend Russia against Ger- man aggression.[60] Moreover, on February 23, Lansing explicitly told Assistant Secretary of State Breckinridge Long that the United States would refuse on principle to offer material and mil- itary aid to the Bolsheviks, even in the event they should resist the Germans. The Secretary emphasized in his discussion with Long that the Bolsheviks were ultimately more dangerous to American security than was Germany, since Bolshevism denied both nationality and property rights and had threatened America with revolution. Finally, Lansing confided to Long that he, Lan- sing, and Wilson had discussed the Bolshevik problem on the previous day and had decided that the United States would not recognize or deal with Lenin's regime even on a basis of wartime expediency.[61] Thus, even though one of the basic sources of Soviet-American antagonism was Bolshevism's disruption of Rus- sia's war effort against Germany, Wilsonian abhorrence of revolu- tionary-socialism was such that had Lenin desired to conduct a revolutionary war against Germany while maintaining strict Bol- shevik control in Russia the Wilson Administration was not pre- pared to recognize or assist a purely Bolshevik regime. It is of course, true, as recent historical scholarship has emphasized, that Lenin had no desire to continue the war or to rejoin what he saw as an imperialistic Entente alliance.[62] However, and this is the heart of the matter, in late February 1918, when Lansing and Wilson decided not to aid a purely Bolshevik regime against Ger- many, they obviously did not know that Lenin was not contem- plating a revolutionary war against Germany for the defense and/or the extension of Bolshevism. This problem will be considered in more detail in the next chapter, but it should be emphasized here that just as the Bolsheviks were not prepared to sacrifice their revolutionary principles to get Allied assistance against Germany, so too the Wilson Administration was not willing to embrace the Bolsheviks against the Germans unless Lenin was prepared to turn his regime into one of constitutional democracy.

While certain differences have been stressed in this chapter for purposes of analysis, it should be said that the gap between the Wilson of the Fourteen Points Address and the Wilson of late February 1918 was not really too wide. At the time of the partly House-inspired January 8 address Wilson had in no sense, despite the vagueness of his language, been prepared to accept Bolshevism in its pure form. Rather it seems probable that he had mistakenly assumed that Lenin was about to adopt the policies of Kerensky. Indeed, it was only in such a circumstance that the Wilson Administration would consider fully supporting Lenin against the Germans. In other words, Lansing did not have to turn Wilson against the theory and practice of revolutionary-socialism. The President and House both had always opposed class warfare and violent revolution and had hoped that Bolshevism would disappear in a rebirth of pro-Allied Russian liberalism. Lansing, however, did help Wilson to see that he could not alter Bolshevism itself with just the rhetoric of liberal anti-imperialism. It is true, as will become evident soon, that the House approach toward Russia was not totally abandoned. Moreover, Wilson's moderate anti-imperialism would also become an effective safety valve for the non-Bolshevik radicalism of Europe during the Paris Peace Conference. Nevertheless, during the rest of the war the central problem for Wilsonian Russian policy would largely be one of developing a clear-cut alternative to both Bolshevism and German imperialism in Russia. Somehow a democratic-nationalist Russia would have to be fashioned, if not for the purposes of the wartime alliance, at least to help solidify the liberal international order to come with victory.

III

War and Revolution, III: The Wilson Administration and Russian Politics, from the Bolshevik Revolution to the Siberian Intervention

The rise of Bolshevism to power in wartime Russia in no way changed the commitment of the Wilson Administration to the support of a liberal-nationalist Russia against German imperialism. On the one hand, Wilsonians rejected the advice of Left-liberals and socialists who sought to unite Wilson and Lenin in a revolutionary war against both Imperial Germany and anti-Soviet Russians. On the other, the Administration opposed any tendency toward an anti-Bolshevik compromise peace with Germany at the expense of Russian and/or Eastern European national interests. In essence, then, the Wilsonian position remained, throughout the war, rooted in a commitment to Russian liberal-nationalism.

In this general context, moreover, America's eventual participation with Japan in the Siberian Intervention of August 1918 is best seen as the climax of a months-long Wilsonian search for some viable and moral means to oppose both German imperialism and Bolshevism, and to defend Russian liberal-nationalism. Furthermore, we shall also see that this effort at American-Japanese collaboration, in bringing political and social stability to Siberia, formed an important stage in the Administration's wartime attempt to sublimate Japan's latent imperialistic energies by co-opting Japan into an orderly and rational system of international capitalist co-operation among the great powers interested in commercial expansion in Asia. At the Paris Peace Conference, the President would continue his wartime efforts to integrate both

Japan and a non-Bolshevik Russia into a commercial and political world order of peace, trade, and law.

1. REVOLUTIONARY WAR, GERMAN IMPERIALISM, AND WILSONIAN LIBERALISM

While the Administration moved, during the spring of 1918, steadily away from further efforts to absorb Bolshevism into a Wilsonian consensus of orderly liberal war, there were political elements to the Left of House who continued, even after the ratification of the Treaty of Brest-Litovsk, to try to bring about a Wilson-Lenin united front against German imperialism. Raymond Robins, director of the American Red Cross Commission to Russia, was the major spokesman for a program of direct military and economic aid to the Soviet Government, a program calculated to provide a new barrier to German expansion in the East.[1] Robins felt that a policy of co-operation with Lenin would "lead inevitably to the modification, adjustment, and softening of the hard and impossible formulas of radical socialism," while also directing "the forces supporting the Soviet Power against Germany."[2] Robins's expressed hopes in regard to the softening of radical-socialist intransigence indicate that, despite their willingness to campaign longer than House for an American-Bolshevik *rapprochement*, most liberals of the Robins-*New Republic* persuasion hoped to unite Wilson and Lenin largely on Wilson's terms. Indeed, it was only a few American socialists, coming to desire the defeat of German imperialism in 1918, who sought to fuse Wilsonianism and Leninism into a pattern of revolutionary war which was more Bolshevik than liberal in orientation. In any event, all wartime efforts to join Wilson and Lenin against Germany failed. This was not only due to the committed anti-Bolshevism of the Administration, but also to the unwillingness of the Bolsheviks to allow their revolutionary ideology to evolve into democratic-nationalism and be absorbed into the pro-war anti-imperialism of liberal order.

Despite the hopes of some Robins-oriented American Left-liberals, the Bolshevik Government showed no real readiness during its first months in power either to modify its revolutionary-socialist aims or to seek an understanding with a Wilsonian liberalism which Bolsheviks saw as essentially another form of capitalist-imperialism.[3] As we saw in an earlier chapter, Lenin's opposition to any non-revolutionary peace of international-capitalist understanding, his refusal to make distinctions between the two warring coalitions, and his contempt for any efforts on the part of patriotic liberals and socialists in any belligerent country to unify all classes behind the war through purification of war aims, all served to separate the Bolshevik leader ideologically from Wilson. After November 1917, Lenin's approach to the issues of war and peace was equally anti-Wilsonian.

Since Lenin was convinced that Russia's peasant masses demanded peace as well as land, that it would take months to build a new and reliable Red Army out of the remnants of the shattered Tsarist Army, and that the immediate revolutionary potential of the German proletariat was uncertain, he determined, in winter 1918, to make an expedient peace with victorious Germany rather than to risk the total destruction of Bolshevism by German arms.[4] Moreover, Lenin had no desire either to aid, or to be used by, "Anglo-French imperialism." For this reason, and also because he feared reviving, through any *rapprochement* with the Entente, those pro-Allied but anti-Bolshevik political and military elements which had been defeated in November, Lenin was certainly not prepared to respond positively to Wilson's appeals, in the Fourteen Points Address and elsewhere, for a return to anti-German liberal-nationalism in Russia.[5]

It is true that a strong Left-communist faction opposed Lenin's peace policy in the Brest-Litovsk period. This faction advocated armed resistance to the demands of German imperialism as revealed at the conference table. However, and this is the heart of the matter, those Bolsheviks such as Bukharin and Radek who called for war against Germany wanted to conduct such a conflict in the context of a purely revolutionary war for the defense and expansion of Bolshevism. They did not advocate a revival of the Wilsonian-oriented Provisional Government's position of patriotic war for the Russian nation-state and for a liberalized Entente.

This Left-communist or Bukharinite position is best understood against the background of the international revolutionary euphoria which pervaded the ranks of Bolshevism after the November Revolution and fostered in Petrograd hopes of imminent and universal socialist revolution throughout Europe.[6] The proponents of revolutionary war held that the European socialist revolution could be precipitated first in Germany if the German workers were given the example of armed Bolshevik resistance to German imperialism.[7] They further maintained that any compromise peace between the Bolshevik regime and the Central Powers would represent both a sellout of the German proletariat and, in terms of the ultimate survival of Bolshevik *élan* and power, an unwise policy, in that it would place the interests of Soviet nationalism ahead of Bolshevik duty to the world revolution.[8] At the same time, however, it must be re-emphasized that the radical purism which led the revolutionary war faction to oppose a compromise with German imperialism also made any plan for co-operation between the Bolsheviks and the Entente against German aggression completely anathema to these Left-communists.[9] In Bukharin's terms, the goal of a revolutionary war against Germany was not a *rapprochement* between Bolshevism and the imperialist alliance opposed to the Central Powers. It was rather the precipitation of a socialist revolution which would sweep over both Germany and the Entente.[10] Clearly, there were no potential allies for the Wilsonian anti-imperialism of liberal order among the Left-communist opponents of Lenin's plans for an expediential peace with German imperialism.

Actually, no Bolsheviks were prepared either to define a possible war against Germany in non-revolutionary terms that would be acceptable to the Wilson Administration or to move toward liberal democracy within Russia as a means of unifying all potentially anti-German political and military elements. This was true also of Trotsky who, of all the Bolsheviks, had the most contact with representatives of the Entente. Trotsky was indeed ready, in the absence of revolution in Europe, to ask for Allied economic and military aid both in order to resist German aggression and to forestall the threat of Entente-sponsored intervention by Japan in Siberia.[11] Trotsky made it clear however, that if, unlike the Left-communist purists, he was willing to co-operate with the Entente on a limited basis against Germany, he would do so entirely in terms of mutual expediency and only provided that the Allies recognized Bolshevik authority throughout Russia and ceased all support of anti-Bolshevik elements.[12] This was not the sort of a partnership with a liberal-nationalist Russia which the Administration had enjoyed briefly after the March Revolution. It was also not the sort of partnership in liberalism and war which Wilson had envisioned for the United States and Russia in the Fourteen Points Address.

While Lenin never ceased to favor a policy of peace on the best possible terms with Germany, even he was willing, in the event the Germans clearly intended to crush Bolshevism, to defend the revolution in part by taking "potatoes and ammunition from the Anglo-French imperialist robbers." [13] As his tone suggests, Lenin, if forced against his better judgment to resist Germany with Allied aid, did not intend any political *rapprochement* with the Entente or Wilson in the process, however. Indeed, if the Germans forced his hand Lenin would have fought as a revolutionary. Having favored revolutionary war in theory prior to assuming power, Lenin opposed the position of the Left-communist revolutionary war faction on tactical rather than on ideological grounds, and he, like Trotsky, would have used Allied aid to conduct as revolutionary a war as possible both within Russia and abroad.[14] The following selection from a decree written by Lenin and published by the Council of People's Commissars in *Pravda* and *Izvestia* on February 22, 1918, at a time when the Bolshevik leaders mistakenly assumed that the Germans did not intend to halt

their advance in Russia, shows that whatever resistance Lenin intended to mount against the Germans was to be conducted in a
revolutionary-socialist and not a liberal-nationalist framework:

5) The workers and peasants of Petrograd, Kiev, and of all towns,
townships, hamlets and villages along the line of the new front are to
mobilize battalions to dig trenches, under the direction of military experts 6) *These battalions are to include all able-bodied members of
the bourgeois class, men and women, under the supervision of Red
Guards; those who resist are to be shot.* 7) All publications which oppose the cause of revolutionary defense and side with the German
bourgeoisie, or which endeavor to take advantage of the incursion of
the imperialist hordes in order to overthrow Soviet rule, are to be sup-
pressed, able-bodied editors and members of the staffs of such publications are to be mobilized for the digging of trenches or for other
defence work. 8) *Enemy agents, profiteers, marauders, hooligans,
counter-revolutionary agitators and German spies are to be shot on
the spot. The Socialist Fatherland is in danger! Long live the Socialist
Fatherland. Long live the international socialist revolution.*[15]

Also important in this connection is the fact that a conditional
feeler, sent to Washington by Lenin and Trotsky on March 5,
1918, via Raymond Robins, to discover whether American aid
would be forthcoming in the event the Germans forced the Soviets to fight, stipulated that any arrangements with the United
States were to be based on the assumption "that the internal and
foreign policies of the Soviet government will continue to be directed in accord with the principles of international socialism."[16]
Thus, while Wilson hoped for the rebirth of a unified liberal
Russia to rejoin the struggle against German autocracy, the Bolsheviks, if they fought at all, were prepared to conceive of resistance to Germany only in terms of a revolutionary-socialist
struggle against both German imperialism and the Russian bourgeoisie.

For its part, the Wilson Administration was definitely not prepared to support a revolutionary war against Germany and the
Russian middle classes conducted by and for the Bolshevik re-

gime. As shown in the preceding chapter, Colonel House hoped to convince the Bolsheviks to allow themselves to be integrated into a liberal-nationalist Russian framework, and in late February 1918, Lansing and Wilson categorically opposed any military or economic aid to an unmodified Leninist government. Lansing's "hard line" on Bolshevism was buttressed by the reports to the State Department from Maddin Summers, the American Consul General at Moscow, who shared the Secretary's contempt for the values and practices of the November Revolution.[17] Summers's cables emphasized that the Bolsheviks were incapable of uniting responsible middle class forces in resistance to the Germans, and Summers argued that, unless a truly national—that is, non-Bolshevik—army were formed to fight against Germany, many of the Russian bourgeois elements might rally to the Germans as restorers of order against Lenin.[18] It is obvious then, in the light of the world view of men such as Lansing and Summers, that any suggestion of supporting Bolshevism, against not only Germany but the Russian bourgeoisie as well, would have been anathema to both men. The evidence also suggests that the State Department's fear that Trotsky's projected Red Army might be used to promote social revolution was an element in Washington's decision to reject Robins's pleas for military aid to the Bolsheviks in the late winter and early spring of 1918.[19] Moreover, one of the prime motives for America's eventual military intervention in Siberia would be the desire to provide Russia's liberals with an Allied alternative to Germany as a restorer of social stability against the Bolsheviks.

In the light of the extent of the hostility toward the Bolshevik regime on the part of the Wilson Administration, it is worth questioning as to whether or not there was any inclination on the part of Washington to favor a policy of accommodation with Germany against the threat of Bolshevism in the East. In point of fact, some abortive efforts along these lines were made during the war by certain political elements in both England and the Central Powers. In this connection, Lenin and Trotsky always considered

it possible that the warring imperialist coalitions would decide
that they had best end the civil strife within international-capitalism and join to make a compromise imperialist peace at the expense of Bolshevik Russia.[20] If such an Allied-German *rapprochement* had in fact been achieved on the basis of opposition to
Bolshevism, it would have been a highly ironic historical development. In that case, the Bolshevik movement, whose revolutionary thrust and survival potential depended in large part on
the continued existence of war-producing contradictions within
world capitalism, would have been itself the cause of a unification
of the international imperialist structure; the very triumph of
Lenin would have hastened the development of the tendencies
which Kautsky had described as ultra-imperialism.

Some sophisticated conservative elements in England, gathered
around Lords Milner, Haldane, and Lansdowne, advocated a
compromise peace with Germany. These men abhorred the brutal
slaughter which was rending Europe and threatening to bring socialist revolution in its wake, and they assumed that Germany
would become a responsible member of an orderly international
community of conservative powers if she were guaranteed commercial freedom, the maintenance of her autocratic political
structure, and a largely free hand in Eastern Europe in the context of a compromise peace arrangement.[21] It is fitting that, in a
recent study, George Frost Kennan, who expresses admiration for
Lord Lansdowne's vision of a compromise peace with Germany,
should also feel called upon to present a mild apology for the
terms of the German-imposed treaty of Brest-Litovsk.[22]

In Germany there were some moderate-imperialist groups ready
to answer the Lansdowne call. During the war the mildly annexationist and centrist parties in Germany carried on a prewar tradition of moderate imperialism by continuing to compromise with
the dominant conservative and annexationist military-political
forces.[23] Indeed, by the time the Brest-Litovsk Treaty was rati-
fied with the support of the German middle class parties, the dis-
pute between the moderates and the Ludendorff elements in re-

gard to Germany's foreign policy was not really a fundamental one over the general aim of German economic and political dominance in Eastern Europe. The question was really a more pragmatic one as to whether such German control was to be gained and maintained by the indirect methods of diplomacy and political influence or by the more direct methods of military conquest or annexation.[24] From this moderate-imperialist background emerged the Lansdowne-oriented efforts of such statesmen as Czernin, Erzberger, Max of Baden, and Kuhlmann, to effect a compromise peace with the Entente, partly on a basis of mutual anti-Bolshevism, whereby Germany would give concessions in France and Belgium to gain a largely free hand for the Central Powers in organizing the political-economy of Eastern Europe.[25] An excellent contemporary analysis of the aims of this compromise peace tendency among German moderate-imperialists was included in one of the earliest memoranda to originate from the Inquiry:

There appear to be two schools of German imperialism at the present time, represented perhaps by the Fatherland Party and by the Kuhlmann-Helfferich groups. They differ considerably in tone, in domestic politics, perhaps even in spiritual values. But there is a tacit agreement on two points: (1) that Germany's immediate future is the domination of the eastern part of the continent; (2) that this domination depends upon access to the supplies of the outer world. It is upon the method of attaining the second point that they really disagree. Kuhlmann and his group wish to attain it by "accommodation," by a reconciliation with the western nations which at the present time is equivalent to a surrender of the Near East to the Germans.[26]

It should be re-emphasized that the rise of Bolshevism was seen by many German moderate-imperialists as facilitating this "reconciliation with the western nations."

For its part the Wilsonian Administration remained, during the war, as opposed to an anti-Bolshevik understanding with German imperialism as it was to an alliance with Bolshevism against both Germany and the Russian middle classes. In other words, Washington refused to move toward early versions of either the appeasement or the popular front orientations of the 1930's. Far from being attracted to a compromise or Lansdowne peace, built in part on the appeasement of German expansionism in the East, Wilson instead was terribly anxious throughout the war lest a premature peace would permit Germany to establish a vast sphere of imperial control in Eastern Europe and in Asia Minor.[27] Speaking in Washington on June 14, 1917, the President voiced his fears of German imperialism in the Balkans and the Near East and argued that "the eagerness for peace that has been manifested from Berlin" was explicable in terms of Germany's successes in the East.[28] Nor did the rise of Bolshevism in any way weaken Wilson's determination not to come to terms with German imperialism. The President's speeches in the winter and spring of 1918 were full of denunciations of any plan to arrive at an understanding with Germany at the expense of Eastern Europe.[29] Late in the war Wilson spelled out his position on Germany and the East to State Department Counselor Frank Polk. The President wanted Polk to discontinue the Department's secret efforts to discuss peace terms in Switzerland with di Fiori, a centrist and moderate-imperialist anxious to arrange a compromise peace for Germany:

I hope with you that Herron will not go any further with these conversations with di Fiori. In the first place, though the basis of discussion proposed by di Fiori is in some respects a very fair and promising one, you will notice that the usual thing has happened. There is absolutely no mention of the situation in the East. These suggested terms ignore the existence of Russia, and it is plain to me that Bavaria would have no difficulty in inducing the Prussian government to propose negotiations on this basis, because I am convinced that it is not only ready to agree to concede practically anything that it is necessary to concede in the West and in the Balkans, if only it is left with a free hand in the East and Southeast.[30]

And, while Lansdowne and Milner were willing to negotiate peace with the German Government as traditionally constituted,

the Wilson Administration was agreed that peace could be discussed only with a liberalized Germany.[31]

In both Germany and Russia, Wilsonian wartime policy sought
to align with the liberal Center against alternatives open on the
Left and the Right. While Wilson did not want a socialist revolution in Germany, he was not willing to join Lansdowne in accepting a compromise peace with German imperialism and autocracy. The President sought to find the middle ground between
Lenin and Lansdowne by pushing for just enough democratic
change in Germany to qualify her for reintegration into a peaceful American-inspired system of international-capitalist order. It is
important to note that Wilson was convinced that German imperialism in Eastern Europe and the Near East constituted a direct threat to his export-oriented vision of an Open Door world to
be characterized by a peaceful and uninhibited commercial expansion of all the major powers into the underdeveloped areas.[32]

In relation to Imperial Germany, then, the President sought a
program which could appeal to German moderates and, at the
same time, not constitute an appeasement of German imperialism, past or present. Such a balance was not easy to strike, and
Wilson's war addresses in effect demanded more domestic radicalism and national effacement from Germany's moderates, whether
liberals or socialists, than they were prepared to give.[33] This was
not surprising, since the Fourteen Points were not oriented toward a peace without victory based on the *status quo ante*. Instead, the Fourteen Points combined proposals for a new liberal
world order with demands which even moderates in the Central
Powers could not rationally have been expected to accept before a
decisive military defeat. Thus, because of his unwillingness to ap-
pease even moderate-imperialists in the Central Powers, Wilson
succeeded in prolonging the war, in paving the way for the German Revolution, and in uniting disparate elements of the Allied
Left and Right behind the liberal war effort. Yet, at the same
time, of course, the President also endangered his vision of a
postwar liberal world order. On the Right, many Allied and

American political elements, who were anxious to prolong the war against German imperialism for traditional reasons, had no desire eventually to reintegrate a liberalized Germany into a new cooperative world community. On the Left, some Allied and American socialists would give various forms of *de facto* support for the anti-German war effort in its late stages, in the hope of preserving Bolshevik Russia from the German threat and of seeing the destruction of German and Austrian imperialism lead directly to socialist developments throughout Europe.

At the Paris Peace Conference, the Wilson Administration, in the face of such pressures, would turn partly to a Lansdowne-like program of an anti-Bolshevik understanding with moderate German forces of order in an effort both to limit Allied extremism and to contain the German Revolution within the bounds of liberal order and a reconstructed international-capitalist system. In other words, if Wilson in his zeal to reform Germany by means of liberal war ignored the appeal of anti-Bolshevik Lansdownism during the war, the main thrust of the President's policy at the Paris Peace Conference would be in the direction of healing the war-engendered splits in an international-capitalist system threatened by socialist revolution and the possibility of renewed conflict. In this sense, Wilsonian policy at the Paris Peace Conference would represent in part a return to the prewar House-Wilson mediation efforts aimed at integrating Germany into a commercial and political system of peace and stability. It could even be argued that, by constituting the threat that he did to world order, Lenin paradoxically helped Wilsonian efforts to reform traditional imperialism into a Kautskian ultra-imperialism of international-capitalist co-operation among the major powers. Yet, as a contradiction, the Wilsonian punitive orientation toward German imperialism also lived on at Paris to complicate the Administration's postwar effort.

In terms of the more limited issue of wartime American-Soviet relations, however, the President's often stated purpose to stand by Russia against German imperialism led to mistaken hopes on the Left and mistaken fears on the Right, that some sort of American-Bolshevik tie might be in the offing. As we have seen, however, the Wilson Administration was as unwilling to desert the Russian liberals by allying with a totally Bolshevik Russia against Germany as it was to abandon even a Leninist Russia to German control. The Wilsonian solution was to seek the rebirth of a liberal-nationalist and pro-Allied Russia with which to ally against Germany. By March 1918 Wilsonians were speaking of support for "Russia" and the "Russian people," but not directly equating these terms with the existing Bolshevik regime.[34] In a note given to the Japanese Government on March 12, 1918, the State Department conveyed the sense of this distinction.

In the view of the Government of the United States recent events have in no way altered the relations and obligations of this Government towards Russia. It does not feel justified in regarding Russia either as a neutral or as an enemy, but continues to regard it as an ally. There is, in fact, no Russian government to deal with. The so-called Soviet government upon which Germany has just forced, or tried to force, peace was never recognized by the Government of the United States as even a government de facto. None of its acts, therefore, need be officially recognized by this government; and the Government of the United States feels that it is of the utmost importance, as affecting the whole public opinion of the world and giving proof of the utter good faith of all the governments associated against Germany, that we should continue to treat the Russians as in all respects our friends and allies against the common enemy.[35]

To a message from Wilson which had pledged American support for "the people of Russia in the attempt to free themselves forever from autocratic government," the Bolsheviks replied, for their part, on March 15, 1918, with the revolutionary hope that "the happy time is not far distant when the laboring masses of all countries will throw off the yoke of capitalism and will establish a socialistic state of society, which alone is capable of securing just and lasting peace." [36] Despite the early hopes of House and Wilson, the ideological gap, between Bolshevism's revolutionary socialist approach to war and peace and the Administration's orderly liberal anti-imperialism, was not bridged.

In Washington, whatever else it did, the Bolshevik ratification of the Brest-Litovsk Treaty largely removed the embarrassing possibility of the Bolsheviks launching a revolutionary war, against both Germany and the Russian middle class liberals, which the Wilson Administration would have been morally unable to support. After Brest-Litovsk, it would be easier for Wilson to move toward a policy which combined opposition to both Leninism and Kaiserism in revolutionary Russia, and sought to "check anarchy, help lay the foundation for an orderly future and hinder the enslavement of Russia by Germany." [37] Ultimately, the Wilsonian opposition to both Bolshevism and German imperialism would fuse into one struggle for the resurrection, at least in one part of Russia, of the liberal and pro-Allied order of the March Revolution. Between March and July of 1918, the potential nucleus for such an anti-Bolshevik and anti-German Russia would appear in Siberia.

2. TOWARD WILSONIAN LIBERAL INTERVENTION IN SIBERIA

In the spring and early summer of 1918, many factors helped to move the Wilson Administration toward a policy of military, political, and economic intervention in Siberia. Underlying all these factors, however was the desire of the President and his advisers to support these Russian elements, favorable to a pro-Allied order of liberal nationalism, whom Wilsonians felt were menaced, in differing and yet paradoxically interrelated ways, by both German imperialism and Bolshevism.

In one sense, this continuing Wilsonian desire to revive the values and institutions of the March Revolution was testimony to the successful efforts of the representatives of the deposed Provisional Government to persuade official Washington that the struggle against German imperialism in Russia was inextricably bound to the ongoing struggle of Russian liberal-nationalism

against Bolshevism. The successful propaganda course to be followed by representatives of the March Revolution was set as early
as December 1917, when, a few weeks after the Bolshevik Revolution, a confidential memorandum, emanating unofficially from
the Russian Provisional Government's Embassy in Washington,
was circulated among the leading members of the Wilson Administration.[38] This memorandum held that the United States
should not lose faith in Russia, despite the temporary triumph of
Bolshevism, because all actions of the Bolshevik regime, even the
possible signing of a separate peace with Germany, could in no
sense be "recognized as binding and representative of Russia's
aims." [39] Seeking "objectively" to link Bolshevism with the aims
of German imperialism, the memorandum argued that, whatever
Lenin's revolutionary hopes might be, the success of Bolshevism
in disrupting the social and national order of Russian liberalism
could only mean that Russia was now open to German penetration.[40] The solution, according to the Russian Embassy's analysis,
was the development of an Allied program designed to aid the
forces of Russian democratic-nationalism against both Bolshevism
and German imperialism:

This imminent danger of a success of German autocracy can be para-
lyzed only in case the process of further political disintegration and
economic chaos in Russia is stopped and followed by an active and
constructive movement for political unity, democratic stability, economic progress and welfare . . . This understanding is accompanied
by an emphatical distinction between the Russian people and its pass-
ing rulers of violence,—those who are leading the country to disaster
and, by deliberate action or through blindness of fanaticism, are con-
tributing in fact to the strengthening of autocracy in Germany. . . .
Support has to be given to the sound and constructive forces which
arise throughout the present chaos in Russia, so as to enable them to
vanquish the destructive and demoralizing activities of extremism
backed by fraudulent German plans.[41]

The memorandum concluded by outlining a projected economic
and political program whose aim would be the amalgamation of

various anti-Bolshevik and anti-German regional groupings into a unified liberal Russia.[42] During the period from March to July 1918 repeated appeals on the order of this original Embassy memorandum reached Washington from various centers of Russian anti-Bolshevik activity inside and outside of Russia. These were essentially appeals for American and Allied support of anti-Bolshevik and anti-German Russian elements who were anxious to repudiate the Brest-Litovsk Treaty, to re-establish the social and political order of the March Revolution, and to resume the war as an ally of the Entente. These same messages also often urged the Allies to begin a program of joint military and economic intervention in Siberia, in which Japanese influence would be balanced by that of the United States.[43] The significance of these appeals from the viewpoint of an analysis of Wilsonian policy formation becomes clear when it is noted that early in 1918 the Administration had vetoed an Allied plan for unilateral Japanese action in Siberia on the assumption that such an action would appear imperialistic and might possibly unify all Russians under the Bolsheviks in an alliance with Germany against Japan.[44] However, the diplomatic dispatches between March and July 1918 clearly suggested that so long as an intervention were a joint one, in which America had as much influence as Japan, it would have the support of the overwhelming majority of anti-Bolshevik Russians.

Indeed, so great was the desire for some outside help against Bolshevism on the part of liberal and conservative Russian elements that some of these began even to consider the idea of turning to Germany as an ally against Lenin. In the late spring and early summer of 1918 a steady stream of information reached the State Department to the effect that influential middle and upper class political groups in Russia were looking increasingly to Germany for the restoration of social order.[45] During the same period, members of the Wilson Administration at home and abroad often coupled advocacy of intervention in Siberia with warnings that many anti-Bolshevik Russians who had hitherto been anti-

German would soon turn to Germany for aid against the Bolsheviks unless an American-Allied intervention could somehow provide them with a way effectively to oppose both Bolshevism and
German imperialism.[46] In June 1918 Colonel House, who by
then favored a policy of American economic intervention in Siberia, urged Henri Bergson to tell Wilson "that Russia could not
compose herself without aid from either the Central Powers or
the Entente, and if the Entente did not attempt it, Russia would
turn to Germany." [47]

Also aware of this last trend was William C. Bullitt, the one
representative of Left-liberalism in the State Department. He
wrote in late June to a supposedly sympathetic House, asking the
Colonel:

What do you think of the argument which is being advanced by gen-
tleman investors of all races at present, to wit, that the Russian aristocracy and the bourgeoisie is about to join hands with Germany
against the Soviets, and that, therefore, we must join hands with the
aristocracy and the bourgeoisie against the Soviets in order to get one
jump ahead of the Germans? To me this is the supreme diplomatic
non sequitur.[48]

For Bullitt this argument was a non sequitur primarily because,
like so many other Left-liberals and socialists in America and the
Allied countries, he was willing to consider some sort of alliance
with Russian Bolshevism in a revolutionary war against both Germany and the anti-Bolshevik Russians. Administration decision-
makers, however, to say nothing of their domestic critics on the
Right, could be expected neither to permit Germany to restore
social order in Russia nor to resist these German plans in the
manner desired by Bullitt and Robins. In the first place, we have
seen that Wilsonians, despite their opposition to Bolshevism, rejected any concept of an anti-Bolshevik understanding with Germany during the war. To have permitted Germany to use her military and economic power as the rallying point for Russian liberals
and conservatives would have meant a long step toward both the

recognition of a German sphere of influence in Russia and the eventual signing of a Lansdowne-like compromise peace giving Germany a largely free hand in the East. Indeed, once Germany became the recognized defender of all Russian anti-Bolshevik elements the only way to have resisted German power in Russia would have been through an alliance with Lenin. While this solution of an anti-German Wilson-Lenin union appealed to some on the Left in the spring and summer of 1918, Wilsonian policy-makers were never prepared to ally with an unmodified Bolshevik regime against both Germany and the Russian anti-Bolsheviks. This was especially true so long as the alternative of backing Russian liberal-nationalism against both German imperialism and Bolshevism appeared in Washington to remain open, and diplomatic dispatches in the winter and spring of 1918 did continue to indicate that even if some Russian defenders of the values of the March Revolution might be willing to turn in desperation to Germany as a last resort against Lenin, most anti-Bolsheviks ultimately preferred Entente aid in restoring political order and annulling the Treaty of Brest-Litovsk.

In mid-June 1918, a State Department memorandum, originating from Lansing's office, considered the probable results of an inter-Allied intervention in Siberia and also analyzed many of the complexities stemming from the juxtaposition of Bolshevism, anti-Bolshevism, and German imperialism in revolutionary Russia:

The more natural position for Germany to occupy, and at present the most dangerous possibility, is for her to assume the role of protector of all anti-Bolshevik elements in Russia who are now disgusted with the wreck and ruin wrought by the Bolshevik government and hold out to them the prospect of some stable form of government which will insure the protection of their property and the establishment of conditions under which they can resume their ordinary avocations with food to keep them from starvation. If Allied assistance is much longer delayed the anti-Bolshevik element in Russia will certainly turn to Germany for this protection. The fact is that while Germany in a way has been using the Bolshevik element either directly through bribes of some of its leaders or as a result of the principles of govern-

ment they espouse and practice, Germany is appealing to the conservative elements of Russia as their only hope against the Bolshevik.
Germany's policy in Russia since the overthrow of the Czar has been
based upon a well-settled plan of action, namely to deprive Russia of
her power of resistance by supporting the disastrous propaganda of
the extreme radicals which resulted in complete demoralization and
disorganization of her army, the overthrow of the provisional government, the coming into power of the Bolshevik and the Brest Litovsk
peace treaty and thus created such intolerable conditions throughout
Russia as to make the greater part of the Russian people prefer even
Germany's domination to Bolshevik rule. Examples of Germany's
success in the execution of this plan are to be seen in Finland and
Ukraine where all of the more conservative elements which stand for
the protection of property rights and public order after having abandoned all hope of Allied assistance were driven by desperation to request German protection from the Bolshevik terror. It would, therefore, seem most important to prevent the further consummation of
Germany's plan throughout the balance of Russia by timely intervention, which, in any view of the matter, could not make the situation
worse. On the contrary the greater part of the Russian population,
which is at present opposing the Bolshevik would be able to speak
and act freely and concentrate their efforts behind the allies with the
ultimate view of establishing a government free from German influence.[49]

The most obvious point in this analysis is that the Department
saw a "timely intervention" directed against both unmodified
Bolshevism and German imperialism as the best means of preventing wavering liberal and conservative Russian elements from
deserting the Allied cause and accepting the expansion of German
influence in Russia as the price of Berlin's assistance against Lenin. Equally of interest, however, is this sophisticated analysis
of the German-Bolshevik relationship. We have previously seen
ample evidence of the Department's realization that the Bolsheviks
were sincere revolutionary-socialists opposed to both liberal and
autocratic-capitalism. As this memorandum illustrates, however,
the Department also reasoned that since, for quite different reasons, both Lenin and the German Government wished to destroy
the pro-Allied order of Russian liberal nationalism, it was possible

Collusion between Soviets & Germany?

that they had co-operated to this end. In this connection it is significant that American diplomatic correspondence from Russia in late 1917 had been full of charges of collusion between Berlin and the Bolshevik movement, and that three weeks after the November Revolution Lansing himself expressed his anguish that democratic Russia had not been able to "resist the intrigues of German agents and prosecute with courage and vigor the war which the free peoples of the world are waging against Prussian militarism." [50] At the same time Lansing speculated that Lenin and Trotsky might "be acting entirely in Germany's interest, but I cannot make that belief harmonize with some things which they have done. In fact they may be honest in purpose and utterly dishonest in methods." [51] The June 1918 memorandum quoted above left open the question of whether Germany had been using the Bolshevik Government "directly through bribes of some of its leaders or as a result of the principles of government they espouse and practice." In his published memoirs Ambassador Francis also grappled with the problem of the German-Bolshevik relationship, and he made it clear that it was possible for Wilsonians to see the Bolsheviks as both German accomplices and sincere social revolutionaries:

While I have no doubt that Lenin was a German agent from the beginning and disbursed German money, I believe, and so wired the Department, that his real purpose was promotion of world-wide social revolution. He would have taken British money, American money, and French money and used it to promote his purpose. . . . Germany's desire to demoralize Russia and break up the Provisional Government gave Lenin his opportunity, of which he made good use.[52]

Ultimately the crucial point for Wilsonians was not whether the Bolsheviks were in reality linked to Berlin; it was that, even discounting any overt German-Bolshevik connection, the Bolshevik overthrow of the pro-war Provisional Government was seen in Washington as being objectively of benefit to the interests of German imperialism in Russia. It will be remembered that the

December 1917 memorandum emanating from the Russian Provisional Government's Embassy in Washington had argued that, whatever Lenin's intentions, the objective results of his actions could not help but aid German imperialism. In a similar vein Francis cabled Lansing in the midst of the Brest-Litovsk crisis arguing that Lenin and Trotsky "may possibly not have been Germany's agents continuously but if had been could not have played more successfully into Germany's hands." [53] It is obvious that this sense of Bolshevism as the unconscious agent of German imperialism played a major role in Wilsonian assessments of Germany's grand design in Russia. As we have just seen, the heart of the Departmental analysis in the memorandum of June 1918 is centered on the conception of Germany's dual strategy of first aiding Bolshevism to disrupt the pro-Allied Provisional Government and then switching roles in Finland, the Baltic states, and the Ukraine to reappear as the counterrevolutionary defender of social stability in an effort to consolidate the predominant position of German economic and political power in the formerly Russian areas "liberated" by the Treaty of Brest-Litovsk. Even the fraudulent Sisson Papers, which sought to portray the Bolsheviks as mere German agents and traitors to socialism, could not ignore the fact that in the winter of 1918 the Germans were definitely turning on the Bolsheviks and supporting conservative elements in Finland, the Baltic states, and the Ukraine.[54]

Such assumptions made it easier for official Washington to conceive of actions taken against Bolshevism on behalf of liberal Russian elements as also constituting blows against growing German influence in Russia. Powerful political and ideological forces were making anti-Bolshevism a corollary to the Wilsonian war effort against Germany. On one level it was necessary to oppose the Bolshevik movement because it sought to undercut the remaining power of pro-Allied Russian national-liberalism and thereby, consciously or unconsciously, to help realize the first phase of Germany's grand design for Russia. Then too, if Germany were in the process of deserting the Bolsheviks, all the more reason for Wilsonians to oppose Lenin so that the anti-Bolshevik Russians might not be won to Germany. This was especially true since the Administration was opposed on moral grounds to the Left-advocated alternative of joining a totally Bolshevik Russia in a revolutionary war against both German imperialism and the Russian anti-Bolsheviks. Largely in response to such concerns, the cables reaching the State Department from American diplomatic personnel in Russia during the months immediately following the Brest-Litovsk settlement almost uniformly expressed opposition to Bolshevism and urged a policy of support for anti-Bolshevik and anti-German elements in Siberia.[55]

It is true that the Wilson Administration, between March and June of 1918, continued to resist British and French pressure for military action in Siberia. This was both because Wilsonians doubted the military wisdom of certain grandiose Entente hopes for reviving an eastern front, and because there was a lingering fear in Washington that the entrance of Japanese troops into Siberia might alienate otherwise pro-Allied Russians.[56] Nevertheless, it is equally true that the appeals of American diplomats, Allies, and anti-Bolshevik Russians for some sort of intervention in Siberia were not totally lost on Wilson and Lansing. After March 1918, the evidence suggests an increasing desire on both their parts to find a moral way to satisfy Entente urgings and come to the aid of non-Bolshevik and pro-Allied Russian liberals in the creation of a Siberia free of radical socialist revolution and of German penetration.

In April 1918, Wilson informed Lansing of his interest in the several nuclei of self-governing authority which were springing up in Siberia, and the President added that it would give him "a great deal of satisfaction to get behind the most nearly representative of them if it can indeed draw leadership and control to itself." [57] In May, Wilson continued to express an interest in non-Bolshevik Siberian developments; he asked Lansing to follow attentively what the Cossack leader Semenov was accomplishing to see if there were "any legitimate way in which we can assist." [58]

On May 30, William Wiseman, a British intelligence officer, reported to London on a conversation with the President in which Wilson had said:

If we could have put a large British-American force into Vladivostok, and advanced along the Siberian Railroad, we might he [Wilson] thought, have rallied the Russian people to assist in defense of their country. But if we relied mainly on Japanese military assistance we should rally the Russians against us, excepting for a small reactionary body who would join anybody to destroy the Bolsheviki. I [Wiseman] remarked that in any case it was not possible to make the situation worse than it was now. He said that that was where he entirely disagreed. We would make it much worse by putting the Germans in a position where they could organize Russia in a national movement against Japan. If that was done he would not be surprised to see Russian soldiers fighting with the Germans on the Western Front. 'Then,' I said, 'are we to do nothing at all?' 'No,' he said, 'we must watch the situation carefully and sympathetically, and be ready to move whenever the right time arrived.' His [Wilson's] own idea was to send a Civil commission of British, French, and Americans to Russia to help organize railroads and food supplies, and, since currency is worthless, organize a system of barter. He would send such missions to Vladivostok and Murmansk. Of course, it would take a long time before any results could be expected from such a movement. If in the meantime we were invited to intervene by any responsible and representative body, we ought to do so. An oral or secret agreement with Trotsky would be no good since he would repudiate it.[59]

It is evident that Wilson desired to intervene in Russia on behalf of a broadly based and representative group of anti-German Russian elements. The President opposed unilateral Japanese action lest it alienate Russians from the Entente and make Germany's task of organizing Russia easier by giving the Germans access to all segments of the Russian population save perhaps "a small reactionary body who would join anybody to destroy the Bolsheviki." Though Wilson might have reflected that Bolshevism would hardly have been an issue very long in a Russia totally organized by Imperial Germany. In any event, the crucial point to note is that Wilson himself wished, if possible, to rally such broad-based Russian national support for the Allies against the Germans, and that he would have liked to have been invited "to intervene by any responsible and representative body." Moreover, the President's concluding remarks regarding Trotsky suggested that Wilson was extremely dubious as to Bolshevik capabilities of supplying that "responsible and representative" type of invitation. On June 14, 1918, Wiseman reported that Wilson, while despairing of receiving any invitation to intervene from the Bolsheviks, was prepared to act if invited either by the *de facto* Russian Government (that is, the Bolsheviks) or by some body really representing Russian opinion. Very soon, however, Wilson would ignore the Bolsheviks entirely and move toward an intervention in Siberia in support of anti-Bolshevik and anti-German Siberian elements.

Upon reflection, it becomes clear that the entire question of a possible Bolshevik invitation to the Allies to intervene in Siberia involved problems of an insolvable nature. The Bolsheviks claimed, but had not yet really consolidated, revolutionary-socialist control of Siberia. Moreover, the Bolsheviks were naturally opposed to any foreign interference with their authority, whether by the Entente or by the Central Powers, and Lenin and Trotsky sought, therefore, to survive by balancing one imperialist camp against the other. Thus, even if a renewed German threat had forced the Bolsheviks to seek Allied aid, Entente troops and civilian personnel could have been admitted only if the Allies had been willing to accept total Bolshevik control in the areas of intervention. But could the Wilson Administration have been expected, even against Germany, to have agreed to buttress the shaky control of a purely Bolshevik regime in Siberia contrary to the wishes of those liberal-nationalist Russian elements who remained loyal to the Provisional Government of the March Revolution and who still possessed considerable moral and official influence in Washington? In any event, the President waited in vain for any Bolshevik invitation to intervene in Siberia, and, as we shall see, both events and Wilsonian ideological inclinations

soon combined to move the Administration toward increased in-
difference to Bolshevik claims of revolutionary-socialist authority
in Siberia and toward policies involving implicit support for the
efforts of pro-Allied and non-Bolshevik Russian elements to win
control of Siberia.

In this direction, Lansing cabled Thomas Nelson Page, the
American Ambassador to Italy, on June 4, 1918, expressing his essential agreement with the program of the League for Regeneration of Russia.[60] This particular League's program had been sent
by Page to the Department earlier, and it called for Allied support of a democratic Russian regime which would oppose both
the Bolsheviks and the Germans.[61] Then too, in late spring 1918
there was considerable support among Wilsonian decision-makers
for a non-military program of economic assistance designed to
penetrate Siberia with American goods and liberal values in an
effort to aid responsible Russian elements in curbing both German economic influence and the prevailing social-economic upheaval.[62] Wilson expressed special enthusiasm to Lansing on
June 19 regarding the views of a clearly anti-Bolshevik member of
the All-Russian Union of Co-operative Societies who had pleaded
for Allied economic aid to the Societies in their effort to bring
social order to Russia's East and to make possible Siberian resistance to the Germans. The President felt that such co-operatives
might "be of very great service as instruments for what we are
now planning to do in Siberia." [63] Some further evidence of Wilson's sympathies may be gleaned from his reaction to Madame
Botchkarova, Colonel in the Russian women's Battalion of
Death, who visited the White House on July 10. Botchkarova
told of Russia's sufferings and, clasping Wilson around the knees,
pleaded for economic and military assistance against the Bolsheviks. Wilson, according to one account, "sat with tears stream-
ing and assured her of his sympathy." [64]

In June 1918 a division of Czech troops on its way to the Allied lines in France via the Trans-Siberian railway found itself in
conflict with the recently established Bolshevik authorities in Si-

Displays that Wilson, while true, while the motion was an idealist that Wilson, he also walked a tightrope + had a pragmatic rather...

beria. In the course of the conflict, anti-Bolshevik elements rallied to the side of the Czechs throughout Siberia and, by the end of June, they and the Czechs had succeeded in bringing most of Russia east of the Urals back under the control of non-Bolshevik and pro-Allied Russians.[65] The Wilson Administration quite naturally showed immediate interest in the Czechs and their anti-Bolshevik Siberian allies as the potential nucleus for a pro-Entente and orderly Siberia free from German influence. On June 13, 1918, Paul S. Reinsch, the American Minister in China, enthusiastically cabled to the Department his view of the possibilities opened up by the presence of the Czech troops in Siberia:

It is the general opinion of the Allied representatives here in which I concur that it would be a serious mistake to remove the Czecho Slovak troops from Siberia. With only slight countenance and support they could control all of Siberia against the Germans. They are sympathetic to the Russian population, eager to be accessories to the Allied cause, the most serious menace to extension of German influence in Russia. Their removal would greatly benefit Germany and further discourage Russia. If they were not in Siberia it would be worth while to bring them from a distance.[66]

Wilson, obviously interested in Reinsch's dispatch, told Lansing that "there seems to me to emerge from this suggestion the shadow of a plan that might be worked, with Japanese and other assistance. These people are the cousins of the Russians." [67]

The concern expressed by Reinsch as to countering German influence in Siberia had particular reference to the threat seemingly posed by hundreds of liberated German-Austrian prisoners of war who were fighting with the Siberian Bolsheviks against the Czechs and their anti-Bolshevik Russian allies. Indeed, ever since the signing of the Brest-Litovsk Treaty the Administration and its representatives abroad had been fearful that large numbers of liberated and Bolshevik-armed German war prisoners would aid in the suppression of a pro-Allied and liberal Siberia and would also serve as the opening wedge for eventual German penetration of the Russian East.[68] In connection with these Administration anxieties as to the roles of Germany, the armed prisoners, and the Bolsheviks in wartime Siberia, it is important to keep in mind that the State Department saw German policy in Russia as calculated to move from an early stage of co-operation with Bolshevism against pro-Allied liberal-nationalism to a second stage of increased German influence in alliance with anti-Bolshevik groups. In this sense the German prisoners in Siberia appeared to Washington to be active in the first stage and to embody the potential threat of the second stage. Many of these issues were well expressed by Reinsch, who cabled Lansing his views on the Bolshevik-prisoner threat in Siberia two weeks before his enthusiastic cable of endorsement for aid to the Czechs:

Reports received here from all sources indicate extreme need for Allied action in Siberia. German influence extending eastward while armed prisoners, though strategically unimportant, facilitate pro-German organization. West Siberia, source of supplies, is at stake. Positive action is required in order to prevent Russian moderate elements in despair accepting German influence. Bolsheviks waiting for social revolution in western Europe cannot resist nor effectually organize.[69]

Against this background, it is not surprising that American representatives in Russia saw in the Czechs a possible way to save Siberia from Germany and Bolshevism. In the late spring and early summer of 1918, the diplomatic dispatches from Russia were almost uniformly enthusiastic in their portrayal of a Siberia in which Czech troops in league with pro-Allied and anti-Bolshevik Russian elements were successfully defeating a coalition of Siberian Bolsheviks and pro-Bolshevik armed war-prisoners.[70] The military and political events taking place in the city of Samara as detailed to the Department in a report from Dewitt Clinton Poole, the American Consul at Moscow, may stand as a microcosm of the larger developments being reported to Washington from throughout the Russian East:

Siberian Cooperatives' league interviewed . . . have all expressed
earnest hope that Czechs will be left in predominating present positions while new Siberian government is consolidating. Williams reports citizens of Samara, fearful of departure of Czechs, are hastening
organization of forces intended (1) to prevent the return of the Bolsheviks and (2) obstruct German advance across Volga. Provisional
city government consists of delegates to constitutional Assembly and
members of previous municipal administration. Czechs have given
over part of the city to local guards. All quiet.[71]

Almost miraculously, it seemed, events had conspired to present
the Wilson Administration with the opportunity in Siberia to
support liberal Russian elements who were both anti-Bolshevik
and anti-German.

In order more fully to understand the Administration's readiness to support the Czechs, however, it is helpful to turn again to
the memorandum concerning intervention in Siberia which had
originated from Lansing's office. This memorandum exhibited a
surprisingly keen awareness of the great hostility to German imperialism which existed among the world's socialists in general and
the Bolsheviks in particular in the aftermath of Brest-Litovsk.
Taking this hostility into account, the memorandum reasoned that:

It is of the greatest importance that whatever statement may be made
by the Allies as to the purpose of military intervention be addressed
to the Russian people as a whole ignoring the factional differences
among them and treating them as a disorganized mass. This would
leave the door open for cooperation with the Allies by the Bolsheviks
themselves if they desire to avail themselves of the opportunity. But,
assuming that the Bolsheviks will object to such intervention it becomes necessary to ascertain what elements in Russia would be es-
tranged by the movement.[72]

Apparently the possibility of having Allied troops in Russia gave
the memorandum's author enough confidence in the ultimate triumph of justice for him tentatively to adopt a variation of the
House approach to Bolshevism. However, in analyzing this statement it must be stressed that what the memorandum proposed was

neither that the Bolshevik regime be recognized nor that it be assisted in a revolutionary war against the Germans and the Russian bourgeoisie, but rather the hope that the door be left open for possible Bolshevik absorption into a widely based anti-German program of Allied intervention in Siberia. In addition, it is clear from the last sentence of this statement that its author did not really expect the Bolsheviks willingly to give up power and become one Russian faction among many in an Allied sponsored social-political program. Indeed, the original Bolshevik Revolution had been directed against just such a pro-Allied and broadly based liberal-nationalist regime. The State Department author remarked earlier in the memorandum that the Bolsheviks were "very jealous of any interference with the success of their particular theories of government," and he must have been essentially convinced that the Bolsheviks would accept no foreign assistance against Germany which did not include a recognition of the complete domestic authority of Bolshevism.[73]

The Wilson Administration, however, was never prepared to accept complete Bolshevik rule in Russia in order to enlist Lenin against Germany. It is true that there was some vague sentiment within the Administration in favor of getting a Bolshevik invitation for Allied intervention in Russia, and it is also true that some ambivalent efforts were made by the Department in May to stimulate Bolshevik anti-Germanism by curbing the efforts of American diplomatic personnel in Siberia to give overt aid to anti-Bolshevik elements.[74] Nevertheless, whatever halting attempts to arrange an unofficial anti-German *modus vivendi* with Lenin that did originate in Washington in the winter and spring of 1918 were more than counterbalanced both by the moral unwillingness of Wilsonians to recognize the domestic authority of the Bolshevik regime and by the Administration's concern lest even a minor American *rapprochement* with Lenin alienate anti-Bolshevik and pro-Allied Russians and perhaps even push such groups toward an alliance with the Germans against the Bolsheviks.[75] In any event, a full reading of the June 17, 1918, memorandum reveals that its au-

thor's analysis moved rapidly past the doubtful possibility of
Bolshevik absorption into an Allied intervention to what obviously seemed to him the far more likely possibility of a German-Bolshevik alliance against Allied action in Siberia. Such a situation would have its advantages, the memorandum reasoned, both
because it would permit a clear-cut union of the Allies and the
Russian anti-Bolsheviks against Germany and also because it
would prevent Germany from "playing a double game with both
the Bolshevik and the elements opposed to the Bolshevik in Russia." [76] With the Germans and Bolsheviks linked and discredited
in the eyes of Russians, the author of the memorandum felt that
the Allies rather than the Germans would loom as the legitimate
saviors of anti-Bolshevik Russia from revolutionary-socialism:

With Germany so closely linked with the Bolshevik in the minds of
the Russian people who oppose that organization, the further extension of German influence would be curtailed. In this connection it
should be borne in mind that only the more conservative elements in
Russia have been so far for war with Germany. These are naturally
hostile to the German influences with every natural inclination to co-
operate with the Allies if given the opportunity. . . . In conclusion I
will say that, in my opinion, if a stable form of government, such as
would appeal primarily to the Russian people who are opposed to the
German influence in Russia, could be established through military intervention, in Asiatic Russia, or even over that half of Asiatic Russia
lying east of Irkutsk, the moral effect upon the balance of Russia
would be incalculable. It would give hope to all as well as furnish a ref-
uge to those who could avail themselves of the opportunity of going
there and greatly strengthen the position of the Allies in the conduct
of the present war.[77]

Considering the State Department's desire to establish a pro-Allied
and non-Bolshevik Siberia, it is not surprising that the June 17
memorandum also spoke of the possibility of using the Czech
troops in the Russian East. In general terms the political and military situation in Siberia in June 1918 appeared to fulfill the Wilsonian vision of liberal Russians opposing both Bolshevism and
German imperialism.

Recently historians have partly obscured the complex nature of American intervention in Siberia by attempting to portray it as motivated almost exclusively by *either* an anti-German *or* an anti-Bolshevik intent on the part of the Wilson Administration.[78] The confusion arises from a tendency to view these two motives as mutually exclusive, when, in reality, they were fused in a Wilsonian desire to oppose both Bolshevism and German imperialism on behalf of a pro-Allied and liberal-nationalist Russia. It also could be argued that anti-Bolshevism was the natural corollary to any Wilsonian war effort in Russia so long as revolutionary-socialism was ruled out on moral grounds either as a weapon against German imperialism or as an acceptable social system for Russia. Of course Lenin's unwillingness to see the Entente as either morally or politically superior to the Central Powers also helped make him objectively pro-German in the eyes of official Washington. In short, Lenin was just as opposed to the idea of aiding the Entente or the pro-Allied forces in Russia as the Wilsonians were opposed to the idea of solidifying Bolshevik control in Russia in the process of opposing German imperialism.

The Czech troops did offer an excellent opportunity for the Administration to ally with Siberian elements favorable to the internal and international values of the March Revolution against what seemed to Washington to be a concrete manifestation of German-Bolshevik co-operation. In a confidential memorandum written early in July Lansing argued that America had a clear duty to aid the Czechs against both the Germans and the Bolsheviks in Siberia:

This responsibility is increased and made almost imperative because they are being attacked by released Germans and Austrians. I do not think that we should consider the attitude of the Bolshevik Siberians who have furnished arms to the German and Austrian prisoners for the purpose of attacking the Czecho-Slovaks. . . . As soon as the danger from German and Austrian aggression is over the military forces will be withdrawn unless Russia desires further cooperation on their part in resisting the Central Powers and their allies.[79]

It must be emphasized that when Lansing recommended American military aid to the Czechs in Siberia he was fully aware that the Czechs and their anti-Bolshevik Russian allies were combating the Siberian Bolsheviks as well as the German prisoners.[80] In this connection the Secretary wrote to Wilson on June 23:

The situation of the Czecho-Slovak forces in western Siberia seems to me to create a new situation which should receive careful consideration . . . it appears that their efforts to reach Vladivostok being opposed by the Bolsheviks they are fighting the Red Guards along the Siberian line with more or less success. As these troops are most loyal to our cause and have been most unjustly treated by the various Soviets ought we not to consider whether something cannot be done to support them? . . . Is it not possible that in this body of capable and loyal troops may be found a nucleus for military occupation of the Siberian railway? [81]

If this letter explicitly fused anti-Bolshevism and anti-Germanism, these motives were implicitly combined on July 8 when Lansing and the Japanese Ambassador Ishii "considered the possibility of a friendly attitude by the Russians toward the Czecho-Slovaks thus aided and also the possible consequence of their forming a nucleus about which the Russians might rally even to the extent of becoming again a military factor in the war." [82] Such a program operationally meant hostility to the Bolsheviks, who were fighting both the Czechs and the Siberian anti-Bolsheviks and who were opposed to any plan of bringing Russia back into the war within the context of the Entente alliance. Indeed, the late spring and early summer of 1918 was a period in which the Bolsheviks, desperately seeking to survive between the two power blocs until a socialist revolution could sweep Europe, moved in the direction of a temporary and expediential *rapprochement* with German power in the face of mounting Entente pressures in the northern ports and Siberia.[83] Thus, although he was wrong in assuming that Wilson intended to send the Czechs west to fight the Germans in European Russia, General Tasker Bliss, America's representative on the Supreme War Council, was in the largest sense correct when he held that "if the Japanese and the other Allies strengthen the Czecho-Slovaks, I cannot see that it can have any other object than to overturn the present so-called Government in Russia." [84]

On July 17, 1918, the State Department sent to all Allied Ambassadors a detailed *Aide-Memoire* which told of America's decision to intervene in Siberia with Japan, and outlined the aims of such a military-economic program. America's purpose was to support the Czechs and loyal Russians in building a liberal Siberia free of German control, and not to use Russia as a new battleground for Entente armies:

Military action is admissible in Russia, as the Government of the United States sees the circumstances only to help the Czecho-Slovaks consolidate their forces and get into successful cooperation with their Slavic kinsmen and to steady any efforts at self-government or self-defense in which the Russians themselves may be willing to accept assistance. Whether from Vladivostok or from Murmansk and Archangel, the only legitimate object for which American or Allied troops can be employed, it submits, is to guard military stores which may subsequently be needed by Russian forces and to render such aid as may be acceptable to the Russians in the organization of their own self-defense.[85]

When it is remembered that these words were written by men who knew that the Czechs had been joined by anti-Bolshevik and pro-Allied Russian elements (that is, "their Slavic kinsmen") in combat against Siberian Bolsheviks and the liberated German war-prisoners, the fact that America's action was directed both against German influence and against Bolshevism in Siberia becomes even more manifest. In June 1919 Wilson sent a message to the Senate concerning the motivation for America's intervention in Siberia. At this time the President's choice of words revealed more specifically what the *Aide-Memoire* of July 1918 had meant by "efforts at self-government":

This measure was taken in conjunction with Japan and in concert of purpose with the other Allied Powers, first of all to save the Czecho-Slovak armies which were threatened with destruction by hostile armies apparently organized by, and often largely composed of, enemy prisoners of war. The second purpose in view was to steady any efforts of the Russians at self-defense, or the establishment of law and order in which they might be willing to accept assistance.[86]

While it is possible to debate exactly what Wilson did mean by the "establishment of law and order" in Siberia, there can be no doubt that he did not mean a Bolshevik Siberia.

The original *Aide-Memoire* of July 17, 1918, concluded by outlining a program of economic and social relief in Siberia to be conducted by "a commission of merchants, agricultural experts, labor advisers, Red Cross representatives, and agents of the Young Men's Christian Association." [87] This first real venture in American foreign aid had several motives, among which both humanitarianism and the fear of German political-economic penetration of Siberia were definitely prominent. Nevertheless, it is also important to stress that foreign aid for Siberia had definite anti-Bolshevik implications as well. American merchants, labor experts, and Y.M.C.A. men were not going to Siberia to buttress Bolshevism. They would seek rather to export the goods and values of American liberalism in the hope of establishing a system of democratic-nationalist stability in the Russian East. Lansing concisely combined all these motives in his projection of the purpose of civilian relief in Siberia:

A peaceful commission of representatives of various phases of society, to-wit, moral, industrial, commercial, financial, and agricultural, with a political High Commissioner at its head; should proceed at once to Vladivostok with the announced purpose of assisting, insofar as they are able, the Russian people by restoring normal conditions of trade, industry and social order. Through those means the territory would be made safe for all people and the Germans and Austrians would be prevented from acquiring domination by force over the regions and from enforcing their will upon the Russian people. This commission should proceed westward from Vladivostok following as closely as possible, with due regard to safety, the Czecho-Slovaks. The final destination should depend in large measure upon their reception by the Russians and the resistance made to the military forces.[88]

Finally, it is worth noting that Wilson was highly impressed by the conception of the role of American civilian relief in Siberia which was advanced by the extremely anti-Bolshevik Russian expert George Kennan.[89]

On August 3, 1918, Lansing wrote an angry letter to Frank Polk in regard to the desire of the English and French to join Japan and the United States in intervening in Siberia:

The participation of these two Governments will give the enterprise the character of interference with the domestic affairs of Russia and create the impression that the underlying purpose is to set up a new pro-Ally Government in Siberia, if not in Russia. It is unfortunate that London and Paris do not see this and let the United States and Japan handle the situation without seeking to interfere.[90]

Considering all the evidence, it seems to me that this statement should be read not as a disavowal of anti-Bolshevik intent in Siberia on Lansing's part, but simply as an expression of the Administration's unwillingness to join in overt Allied dictation of Russian politics. There can be no doubt either of Lansing's desire to assist pro-Allied and anti-Bolshevik elements in Siberia or of his awareness that the Czechs were allied with such Siberian groups in opposition to the Siberian Bolsheviks as well as the German prisoners. Yet it is also true that in the summer of 1918 Lansing and Wilson were prepared neither to avow openly the anti-Bolshevik implications of their assistance to the Czechs nor to move toward a system of overt Allied political control in Siberia.[91] This inhibition was due in part to the persistent Wilsonian fear that the Allies intended to establish both a new eastern front and an anti-Bolshevik military dictatorship in opposition to Washington's more limited goals of aiding the Czechs and helping to stabilize Siberian liberal-nationalism. On July 12, 1918,

Wiseman wrote to Arthur Murray to emphasize that Wilson would immediately withdraw support from any intervention plan which had reactionary, monarchist, or anti-republican tendencies.[92] The inhibition was also due in a larger sense to the fact that the Administration sought to find a middle ground between its critics on the Left, who opposed intervention in Siberia as anti-Bolshevik, and its critics on the Right, who had long been insisting on firm anti-German and anti-Bolshevik action in Siberia. The Administration's solution was to refer to a desire to aid "Russia," which is best read as Wilsonian shorthand for a liberal and pro-Allied Russia.

The heart of the matter is that since the Administration recognized the March Revolution as the only valid expression of the Russian revolutionary impulse, it was possible for Washington implicitly to oppose Bolshevism while explicitly denying any intent either to interfere in Russia's internal affairs or to further counterrevolution in Russia. The Wilsonian definition of counterrevolution in Russia was a desire to reinstate Tsarism and not a desire to overthrow Lenin in favor of democratic-nationalism. Wilsonians appeared to feel that they were not intervening in Russia's internal affairs so long as they were simply steadying the efforts of "Russians" (that is, liberal Russians) to re-establish non-Bolshevik and anti-German democratic institutions in Siberia. That is to say, as long as in Wilsonian ideology the *real* Russia was implicitly defined as the Russia of the March Revolution, with the "objectively" pro-German Bolsheviks beyond the pale until they were willing to become patriotic social-democrats, the fiction that American policy in Siberia did not constitute an interference in Russian internal politics could be maintained by Washington. In the Wilsonian mind the United States was just acting as the impartial and disinterested friend of the "Russians" who were utilizing the opportunity given them by the Czechs to reconstruct Siberian political life along the lines of pro-Allied liberal order. In this general vein Lansing enthusiastically told Wilson on September 9, 1918, that:

Wilson did not make
decisions in a vacuum —
what were the pressures
exerted by the Right in U.S.?

110   WOODROW WILSON AND WORLD POLITICS

Our confidence in the Czech forces has been justified and the fact
that now a Russian military force of equal strength has joined them
combined with the gratifying reception given the Czechs by the civilian population of the localities occupied is strong evidence to prove
that the Russians are entirely satisfied to cooperate with the Czechs
in Russia and that assistance to the Czechs amounts to assistance to
the Russians.[93]

Considering all the evidence there can be no question that for
Lansing the only "Russians" really worthy of the name were non-
Bolshevik and pro-Allied.

Operationally, then, Wilsonian non-interference in the internal
politics of Siberia really amounted to a tendency to see all non-
Bolshevik and pro-Allied elements as an undifferentiated mass
known as "Russia" and a refusal to interfere in the disputes among
the rival claimants of anti-Bolshevik and anti-German authority.
On August 2, 1918, Acting Secretary of State Frank Polk cabled to
Caldwell, the American Consul at Vladivostok, to say that "this
Government sympathizes with the desire of patriotic groups in Siberia to secure the restoration of order and the welfare of the
population but is not prepared to assist any one movement or
group as distinct from others." [94] This statement, with its emphasis on the "restoration of order," is a superb example of the
Wilsonian tendency in practice to exclude the Bolsheviks from
the field of Russian politics within which American neutrality was
to be operative. In other words, America was neutral when it
came to choosing among conservative, centrist, and moderate-
socialist Siberian elements. The Administration was not neutral,
however, as between the liberal order desired by all these groups
as a whole and the alternative of total Bolshevik rule. Indeed, in
fall 1918 there were many efforts on the part of the State Department to make it clear that American reluctance to choose among
the rival patriotic and anti-Bolshevik Siberian groups was in no
sense to be interpreted as a lessening of America's desire to see
Bolshevism kept out of Siberia.[95] Lansing wrote to Boris Bakhmeteff, the Provisional Government's Ambassador to Washington,

outlining both the Administration's fundamental anti-Bolshevism and its neutrality only in relation to the various Russian claimants of non-Bolshevik authority:

As you are aware, this Government is not, at the present time, prepared to recognize any new government in Russia, though we watch with interest and hope for the future the various efforts which are being made to restore law and order under a stable government. I note that the conference at Ufa includes the names of many distinguished Russians and shall be very glad to be kept advised as to the progress of this movement. As you are aware, the purpose of the United States to assist Russia by any practical means which may be devised remains unchanged. The fact that this Government does not see its way clear at the present time to recognize political movements at Ufa and elsewhere must not be construed as a lack of sympathy with the efforts of the Russian people to erect a government which is able to protect individual rights and to perform its international obligations.[96]

Documents concerning the Administration's plans for currency reform in Siberia also reveal that Washington hoped a stable pro-Allied Siberia would eventually join a reconstituted liberal-nationalist regime throughout Russia.[97]

The anti-Bolshevik implications of America's Siberian intervention were of course strongly reinforced by Washington's reaction to the political repression instituted by the Bolsheviks in the wake of the attempt on Lenin's life. The month of September 1918 saw strenuous efforts on the part of the Wilson Administration to bring world opinion to bear against the Red Terror in Bolshevik Russia.[98] In late September Lansing was even more convinced than he had been in July of the need to use the Czechs as a shield for the anti-Bolshevik Russians:

The Russian communities of the Volga region, which have been friendly to the Czecho-Slovaks, being unarmed, will be at the mercy of the Red Guards, who have committed such monstrous crimes within the past six weeks in Moscow and other cities, if the Czecho-Slovaks withdraw to the east of the Urals. I must confess that I sympathize with the spirit of the Czecho-Slovaks when they say that they cannot abandon their helpless friends to certain massacre and pillage. I believe that the world would be disposed to condemn such a course, and that the Czecho-Slovaks with their high sense of honor would rather die on the Volga than bear the charge of such ingratitude. It seems to me that we must assume that the Czecho-Slovak force west of the Urals will remain there and do the best they can to protect the friendly Russian communities from Bolshevik excesses.[99]

The collapse of Germany in fall 1918 in no sense lessened the desire of Wilsonians to aid anti-Bolshevik Siberians. Indeed, as will be seen in a later chapter, the removal of the fear of a German penetration of Siberia only permitted the motive of anti-Bolshevism, which had been implicit in the intervention from the outset, to come into its own as the explicit reason for continued American involvement in the Russian East.

Finally, however, a complete understanding of the place of the Siberian intervention in the grand design of Wilsonian world policy is not possible without some consideration of the problem of Japan. Certain historians have put Japanese-American relations in the forefront of their discussions of the Siberian intervention, and have argued in effect that the real motivation for Wilson's decision to intervene was a desire to check potential Japanese imperialism in the Russian East.[100] Recently, however, other historians have emphasized, more correctly I believe, the more inclusive interpretation: that the Siberian intervention is best viewed in the context of growing wartime efforts in Washington to achieve co-operation between America and Japan against the threats of German imperialism and Bolshevism in Asia.[101] From the Administration's standpoint, the Siberian intervention was in essence an uneasy experiment in American-Japanese collaboration aimed at containing German imperialism, checking Bolshevism, and co-opting a hopefully moderate Japan into an orderly Wilsonian system of rational international-capitalist co-operation among the major powers interested in commercial expansion in the Far East. Thus, while it is true, on one level of analysis, that Washington hoped American participation with Japan in Siberian affairs would check potential Japanese imperialism in the area, it is more important to note that larger Wilsonian policy aims involved a projected co-operation between America and Japan in the creation of a new anti-German and non-revolutionary liberal order for Asia.

An earlier chapter analyzed Colonel House's efforts, in the 1914–17 period, to convince the leading powers that a major step in the direction of world stability would be the adoption of a co-operative orientation to the problem of investment in underdeveloped countries. It is important now to emphasize that the Colonel was prepared to apply this approach to the Far Eastern problems posed both by militant Japanese expansionism and by the traditional competition of the powers for commercial-financial opportunities in underdeveloped China. Early in the war House showed that he hoped to avoid a direct clash over the Open Door with Japan, a nation with whose "aspirations for colonization in Manchuria" he had sympathy.[102] By fall 1917, House had come to favor a plan under which China would agree to be governed by a trusteeship of three, whose members would represent Japan, China, and all the other major powers, respectively. The proposed trusteeship was to last "long enough to put China in order, develop a civilization and purchasing power, and take her out of the backward nations and make her a blessing rather than a menace to the world."[103] The Colonel hoped that Japan would come to see that her rational interests could best be served by the creation of a stable and prosperous China, able to serve as a market for Japanese manufactures and as a source of food and raw materials for Japan.[104] In classic liberal-internationalist style, House hoped to rationalize, to reform, but not to restructure fundamentally the existing economic and political relationships between the advanced and backward areas of the world. In a letter to Wilson in September 1917, House made even more explicit his program for maintaining the Open Door in China by containing the legitimate expansion of Japanese national-capitalism within the orderly limits of a system of international-capitalist cooperation in China:

We cannot meet Japan in her desires as to land and immigration, and unless we make some concessions in regard to her sphere of influence in the East, trouble is sure sooner or later to come. Japan is barred from all the undeveloped places of the earth, and if her influence in the East is not recognized as in some degree superior to that of the Western powers, there will be a reckoning. A policy can be formulated that will leave the open door, rehabilitate China, and satisfy Japan.[105]

In other words, Japan would have to be brought to see that the rewards of expansion were more obtainable in an orderly structure of international commercial rationality than through a program of traditional imperialism.

The search for a Japanese-American *rapprochement* was also carried on by the State Department in the 1915–18 period. At the time of Japan's twenty-one demands on China in 1915, Lansing had unsuccessfully advocated a compromise whereby the Open Door for American commerce in China would have been preserved in return for what amounted to American acquiescence in Japanese expansion in Manchuria and Shantung.[106] It is true that during 1915 and 1916 Wilson and his Administration sought, largely in opposition to Japan, to promote the Open Door, to extend American economic expansion in China, and to defend Chinese territorial integrity. It is also true, however, that in these years Lansing never lost his desire to come to a final agreement with Japan in Asia.[107] This desire was naturally reinforced in 1917 when the United States and Japan found themselves in effect allies against Germany. In this context, the Lansing-Ishii agreement of November 1917 emerged as an effort, prompted in part by the war, finally to gain Japanese acceptance of the Open Door and the principle of Chinese territorial integrity in return for a vague American recognition of the "special interests" of Japan in Manchuria and northern China.[108]

By way of corollary to the Lansing-Ishii understanding, the Administration also moved in 1917 and 1918 toward participation in the Second Consortium, a program of financial co-operation among the major powers in the area of Chinese affairs. It was hoped in Washington that the consortium approach would wean Japan away from a commitment to an imperialistic policy of spheres of influence and bring about Japan's absorption into a stable international-capitalist system of commercial freedom and great-power harmony in China.[109] Thus, the Administration sought to support moderate elements in Japan who were willing to seek expansion within a framework of the Open Door and political-financial co-operation with the United States.[110] In a letter to Secretary of Commerce Redfield, Lansing succinctly outlined the aims of America's consortium policy which sought to control Japan by co-optation:

As to the suggestions in your letter and in that of Mr. Oudin that we have lost interest in the future of China or have handed her over to exploitation by Japan, permit me to say that such is far from the case. On the contrary, we maintain a very great interest, if possible, an increased interest in China, but, the circumstances in which the world now finds itself are such that it is not desirable for us to compete with Japan, other nations being eliminated from competition, and we are now, as far as possible, joining with Japan. This is done for the very practical reason that it is better to do so than to leave the field undisturbed for Japan.[111]

The wartime policy of *rapprochement* with Japan was further reinforced by Administration fears lest pro-German military elements in Japan gain the ascendancy and bring Japan into an imperialistic alliance with Germany.[112] Events in the years to follow would prove that such anxieties, if premature, were in no sense unrealistic.

The point of this discussion is not to argue either that the course of Japanese-American relations was free of suspicion and friction during the war, or that the road to attempted Japanese American co-operation in Siberia was a totally smooth one. We

have already seen that the Administration refused to support unilateral Japanese action in Siberia during the winter of 1918. There
was also a good deal of friction between Japan and the United
States in the late spring and early summer of 1918 over the question of the type of contribution the Japanese were to make to the
military phase of the joint Siberian intervention.[113] It should also
be noted both that Lenin counted on rivalry between America
and Japan in Asia to protect the Bolsheviks and that there was
considerable anxiety among some Administration advocates of a
policy of intervention in support of anti-Bolshevik and anti-German Siberians lest German or Bolshevik propaganda drive an irreparable wedge between America and Japan.[114] Nevertheless,
these Bolshevik hopes and interventionist fears in regard to Japanese-American friction proved largely groundless in the short run,
since the politics of war and revolution in Russia which moved
the Administration toward intervention in Siberia also reinforced
Washington's wartime propensity for co-operation with Japan on
America's own terms.

On March 5, 1918, the State Department sent a note to the
Japanese Government arguing that, at that point, the United
States felt unilateral Japanese intervention in Siberia to be ill
advised. It read in part:

The Government of the United States has been giving the most careful and anxious consideration to the conditions now prevailing in Siberia and their possible remedy. It realizes the extreme danger of anarchy to which the Siberian provinces are exposed and the imminent
risks also of German invasion and domination. It shares with the
governments of the Entente the view that, if the intervention is
deemed wise the Government of Japan is in the best situation to un-
dertake it and could accomplish it most efficiently. It has moreover
the utmost confidence in the Japanese Government and would be
entirely willing . . . to entrust the enterprise to it. But it is bound in
frankness to say that the wisdom of intervention seems to it most
questionable.[115]

While this note rejected immediate and unilateral Japanese action, its tone was nonetheless friendly and it joined the Japanese

in recognizing that anarchic social conditions and German imperialism were legitimate causes of concern in regard to Siberia. A
few weeks later Lansing reasoned in a private memorandum that
it would be a mistake to alienate Japan since any eventual military action in Siberia would in part depend for its success on enthusiastic Japanese participation.[116] It will be remembered also
that by late spring 1918 diplomatic dispatches had made it clear
to the Wilson Administration that anti-Bolshevik and anti-
German Russian elements would not object to Japanese intervention in Siberia so long as the United States participated as
well. It was only natural, therefore, that Wilsonian plans to assist
the Czechs and their Russian allies against social anarchy and
German imperialism should have provided for a co-operative role
for Japan. In short, just as Washington sought to contain Japanese imperialism in China by absorbing Japan's expansive energies
into an international financial consortium, so too Washington
hoped to co-opt Japanese power into a Wilsonian-oriented program for the aiding of pro-Allied liberalism in Siberia. Lansing
was especially anxious to harness moderate Japanese power to
American aims in Siberia, and in this connection he wrote to
Frank Polk:

I have received your letters in regard to the progress—or rather lack
of progress—in the negotiation with Japan in regard to the Siberian
situation and I am very much obliged to you for keeping me so closely
advised. I draw the conclusion that politics in Japan have been the
real difficulty in completion of an agreement. It seems to me that a
formula might be found which would satisfy the chauvinists in Japan
and at the same time the general spirit of our proposal. I have always
believed that in the end Japan would have to have a superiority in
numbers but that at the outset an equal number of Americans and
Japanese should be landed in order not to excite Russian opposition.[117]

For his part, Colonel House, while annoyed at last-minute Japanese demands in regard to the procedures of intervention, was
nonetheless both enthusiastic over the consortium approach to

China and hopeful that Japan might be brought to eschew the traditional imperialistic path of Germany in favor of a rational program of commercial-financial expansion in partnership with the United States and the Entente.[118] Early in July, House outlined for Wilson a plan to encourage Japanese moderation by allowing Japan reasonable room for expansion. A more liberal Japan would presumably follow America's guidance in Siberia and conduct her expansion within the context of an international-capitalist harmony in the Far East:

Viscount Ishii motored out from Boston this afternoon to see me. We had a very friendly and frank talk. Among other things I told him that many thought Japan stood at the parting of the ways and had not determined whether she would follow the German or the American civilization. I pointed out the advantage to his country of following the international ideals set forth by you. If Japan would do this I thought she would find America ready to help her extend her sphere of influence. He was very receptive, and said that the foundation of your policy was justice to all nations, and that he hoped Japan was to be included. He stated that within recent years there had been a growing tendency on the part of Russia to exclude the Japanese from Siberia, although they continued to let Koreans and other Asiatics go in. He thought that the position of Japan would become intolerable if her citizens were to be deprived of such an outlet. I expressed my sympathy with this view and believed he would find the United States cooperating with the Japanese to bring about a more liberal policy. If this could be done, he was sure that Japan would be willing to follow our lead in any policy that might be determined upon regarding Siberia. It has been my opinion for a long time that unless Japan was treated with more consideration regarding the right of her citizens to expand in nearby Asiatic, undeveloped countries, she would have to be reckoned with—and rightly so.[119]

In a similar vein, William Sharp, the American Ambassador to France, wrote enthusiastically to Wilson on August 8, 1918, to support Siberian intervention as a means both of defending Siberians against anarchy and of providing the United States with firm commercial connections for postwar exports to Russia. Sharp was particularly pleased, however, by the implications for American-Japanese harmony which he saw in the proposed joint intervention:

As a concluding observation on this question, I am not at all sure but that, growing out of the aftermath of the war, it will be found that the binding in closer ties of mutual confidences between America and Japan, through their common intervention in Russian affairs, will evolve a stabilization of conditions, working mightily for world peace. America can never again enjoy her isolation and immunity, as in the century past, from the danger of being embroiled in international controversies. As a co-ordinating and dependable member of the League of Nations, Japan is very essential to its perpetuity. Indeed, I consider the new Entente established between the United States and Japan as a triumph for our diplomacy and of far reaching effect.[120]

In late 1918 and throughout 1919 the Wilson Administration would continue its attempts to bring Japan into an anti-Bolshevik world order of liberal-capitalist harmony. Yet, in a larger sense, these efforts to arrange for Asian stability ultimately formed but one phase of the climactic Wilsonian effort at the Paris Peace Conference to build a world free both of traditional imperialism and of revolutionary socialism. Had President Wilson been able to achieve these aims, and erect a rational and peaceful liberal-capitalist world order under a League of Nations, he would not only have succeeded in his implicit goal of refuting Lenin's vision of inevitable intra-capitalist conflict and revolutionary necessity; he would also have achieved his central aim, at once both progressive and conservative, of establishing, on the grave of German imperialism, an American-inspired world system, beyond both atavistic imperialism and socialist revolution, a centrist liberal world order in which, for Wilson, America's moral and material pre-eminence would have been assured.

PEACE AND REVOLUTION 2

IV

Peace and Revolution, I: The Wilson Administration
and the Problem of German Reintegration at
the Paris Peace Conference

Two contradictory Wilsonian approaches to the problem of Germany dialectically interacted at the Paris Peace Conference, ultimately to create an ambiguous American policy toward the future role of the leader of the Central Powers. One of these approaches, the reintegrationist tendency, was oriented toward the inclusion of a democratized Germany in a new non-revolutionary community of liberal nation-states. This reintegrationist orientation, supported ideologically by the President's reformist anti-imperialism of liberal order, was marked by efforts to moderate Allied, and especially French, economic and territorial demands on Germany in the interests of securing world peace and preventing the further spread of Bolshevism. At the heart of the reintegrationist position on Germany was the Wilsonian vision of a universal international commercial and political system, led by American missionary liberalism, and free from both traditional imperialism and revolutionary socialism.

Wilsonian policy at Paris was also marked, however, by an almost equally strong and necessarily conflicting punitive approach toward Germany. If the Administration's reintegrationist tendency was supported in part by the concern that the German Revolution might go too far to the Left and destroy liberal-capitalism along with autocratic-militarism, the punitive tendency was supported paradoxically by the reverse fear that the moderate German Revolution that Wilsonians defended against Bolshevism had not really destroyed the reactionary roots of German militarism. Unwilling to opt for real solidarity with Germany's more revolutionary socialist elements, the Wilsonian decision-makers were often forced, for reasons of policy and diplomatic necessity, to accept various forms of military controls on a probationary Germany which they still distrusted. Moreover, the President's loyalty to France and to the national aspirations of the new Slavic states of Eastern Europe led him to approve territorial demands on Germany which, despite their moderation by comparison with the more extreme French demands, were far in excess of what Germany's moderate-socialist and liberal-nationalist leaders were prepared to accept willingly. These new German leaders had hoped to use Allied fear of Bolshevism and Germany's mild democratization to win a compromise peace and entrance for Germany into a postwar anti-Leninist community of democratic states. Yet, in counting on the reintegrationist tendency of Wilsonian policy to aid them, the German leaders forgot Wilson's commitment to Slavic nationalism. They also underestimated the possibility that Wilsonians would be somewhat influenced by the French desire to place the prime responsibility for containing Bolshevism on the new anti-German states of Eastern Europe that were to be guaranteed by the League of Nations.

Ultimately, the dialectical interplay between these reintegrationist and punitive tendencies in Wilsonian policy at Paris led to a situation in which American power was co-opted into the maintenance of the moderately anti-German settlement which American statesmen had ambivalently helped to create. Convinced that America's liberal-exceptionalism assured no contradiction between his position as leader of a powerful nation-state and his role as spokesman for world liberalism, the President chose to moderate Allied demands by the judicious use of America's economic and political power. If, however, American power could often moderate the peace program of the Allies, it could also, in the absence of any desire on the Administration's part either to challenge the givens of international politics in a revolutionary fashion or to aid

Germany excessively, create simultaneously the possibility of its own absorption into the defense of the resulting compromise settlement. Indeed, this absorption of American power into the maintenance of a moderately punitive European settlement had been a dominant goal of British policy at Paris, and the hope of some of the more far-sighted French leaders as well. It is not surprising then, that the League of Nations, a product of the interplay of reintegrationist and punitive tendencies at Paris, ended by combining the qualities both of a new community of democratic states under international law and of an extension of the Entente alliance against Germany into the postwar period. For Wilson, however, in the last analysis the League legitimized the absorption of American strength into European politics by seeming to contain the promise of the triumph of American-inspired world liberal order over both traditional imperialism and revolutionary-socialism.

1. TOWARD WILSONIAN REINTEGRATION OF POSTWAR GERMANY

The Administration's reintegrationist orientation toward Germany at Paris stemmed from two mutually reinforcing Wilsonian desires: the urge to restructure world politics in a liberal direction under American leadership, and the desire, by so doing, to check revolutionary-socialism with the force of ordered international reform. In other words, to be fully understood, the American efforts at Paris to moderate the anti-German demands of the Allies at the Peace Conference must be seen as expressions both of Wilson's American exceptionalist anti-imperialism and of Wilsonian anti-Bolshevism. Let us now briefly consider, in turn, the contributions of Wilsonian liberal anti-imperialism and of Wilsonian anti-communism to the American reintegrationist position toward Germany at Paris.

On September 27, 1918, President Wilson opened the fourth Liberty Loan campaign in New York with what was to prove to be his last major war address. At a climactic moment in this speech, the President managed to state succinctly his anti-imperialist vision of an American-inspired liberal order for the postwar world:

There can be no leagues or alliances or special covenants and understandings within the general and common family of the League of Nations . . . and more specifically, there can be no special, selfish economic combinations within the League and no employment of any form of economic boycott or exclusion except as the power of economic penalty by exclusion from the markets of the world may be vested in the League of Nations itself as a means of discipline and control. . . . all international agreements and treaties of every kind must be made known in their entirety to the rest of the world. Special alliances and economic rivalries and hostilities have been the prolific source in the modern world of the plans and passions that produce war. It would be an insincere as well as insecure peace that did not exclude them in definite and binding terms.[1]

At the core of this Wilsonian program was the desire to achieve both economic and political harmony in the international arena. In political terms, the President envisaged a world-wide order of liberal states, free of traditional military alliance systems, in which an unstable balance of power system was to be superseded by a stable and inclusive community of power embodied in a League of Nations.[2] In economic terms, freedom of the seas and non-discriminatory trade arrangements would replace a war-engendering system of national commercial barriers and permit thereby the natural processes of an inherently peaceful international capitalism to bring about universal progress and prosperity.[3] In other words, the backbone of the Wilsonian postwar ideology was the political economy of liberal-capitalist internationalism. The President interpreted America's national interest as being one with the maintenance of international liberal stability.

Earlier we have seen that the Wilsonian tendency to oppose European imperialism with a progressive ideology of liberal globalism was evident in both the prewar and the war periods. The pre-1917 mediation efforts of the President and Colonel House were based in large part on the notion that the progressive liberal-exceptionalism of a missionary America could show an atavistic Europe the way to move beyond militarism to a rational com-mercial and political world system of liberal order. After April 1917, however, the reformist zeal of Wilsonian liberal messianism was directed not, as formerly, against a diffuse "European" im-perialism but almost solely against Germany, whose autocratic militarism was judged in Washington to be extraordinary in its imperialistic atavism even by European standards.[4] Yet, despite the Administration's wartime definition of German militarism as the central imperialistic challenge to world order, some of the pre-1917 Wilsonian tendency to see imperialism as a general Euro-pean rather than a purely German phenomenon persisted in the President's disapproval of the secret treaties and more extremist Allied economic and political plans for the postwar period.[5]

It did, of course, remain largely true during the war that, in the interests of maintaining a unified war effort, Wilson and House sought to postpone, until a future peace conference, any overt clash with the Allies over the Entente's more extreme war aims.[6] By September 1918, however, shortly before the collapse of Ger-many, the President and House decided that the time was right for a major address by Wilson designed, in part, to bring the Al-lies into line behind the Wilsonian program for a liberal postwar settlement.[7] On his way to deliver the September 27, 1918, ad-dress, Wilson confided to Tumulty his fears concerning postwar Allied imperialism:

They (Meaning the Allies) will not like this speech, for there are many things in it which will displease the Imperialists of Great Brit-ain, France, and Italy. The world must be convinced that we are playing no favourites and that America has her own plan for a world settlement, a plan which does not contain the germs of another war. What I greatly fear, now that the end seems inevitable, is that we shall go back to the old days of alliances and competing armaments and land grabbing. We must see to it, therefore, that there is not an-other Alsace-Lorraine, and that when peace finally comes, it shall be a permanent and a lasting peace. We must now serve notice on every-body that our aims and purposes are not selfish. In order to do this and to make the right impressions we must be brutally frank with friends and foes alike.[8]

Clearly, with Germany's defeat near, the President was preparing to meet, at least to a greater extent than before, the challenge to his conception of postwar world stability posed by militant Allied nationalism.

During the Armistice negotiations with Germany in October and November of 1918, Wilson often spoke with dismay regard-ing both the intolerant hatred of Germans and the desire for a vengeful peace exhibited by the Entente leaders and by many anti-Wilsonian Republicans in America.[9] In public statements made directly after the Armistice, the President emphasized in various ways the theme that there ought not to be an imperialistic vic-tor's peace which would breed "a constantly recurring sense of in-justice." [10] Then too, Wilson's instructions to Colonel House, in regard to the freedom of the seas and other issues to be discussed at the inter-Allied meetings in Paris of October–November 1918, revealed a firm presidential desire to have the recalcitrant Allies accept the Wilsonian vision of an open international commercial system stabilized politically and legally by a League of Nations.[11] The President returned to these concerns on board the *George Washington*, en route to the Paris Peace Conference, when he criticized Entente plans to exact an exorbitant reparations bill from Germany, attacked what he saw as England's tendency to-ward naval aggrandizement, and affirmed again that "it must be a peace of justice to the defeated nations or it will be fatal to all the nations in the end." [12]

At the center, then, of Wilson's conception of his postwar role was the idea of an American mission to complete the work of lib-erating the Old World from the atavistic restraints of pre-liberal militarism begun in the successful crusade against German autoc-racy. America's liberal-exceptionalist duty was to inspire a con-tinued progressive reform of the old international political-economy and in the process to create "a peace secure against the violence of irresponsible monarchs and ambitious military coteries and made ready for a new order, for new foundations of justice and fair dealing." [13] As for Germany, a dominant concern of Wilson's wartime addresses had been to assure German liberals that there would be a place for the commerce of a democratized Germany in the President's projected liberal-international system.[14] In a private conversation on November 8, 1918, concerning America's role in the readjustment of the postwar world, Wilson expressed clearly his reintegrationist orientation toward Germany by saying that he felt the Germans "had shaken off the imperialistic rule and the military aristocracy and that being an industrious people, and naturally orderly, they might, if properly treated, ultimately be a bulwark for peace in Europe." [15] In 1918–19, then, with Germany defeated and in the process of internal liberalization, it would seem that a crucial Wilsonian task at Paris would be to check Allied imperialism and construct a new world order of liberal-capitalist stability into which a reformed Germany could be reintegrated.

At this point, however, it is crucial to grasp that the Wilsonian reintegrationist approach toward Germany was also strongly reinforced by the Administration's desire to check the expansion of Bolshevism in the immediate postwar period. First of all, in general terms Wilsonians saw their opposition to Allied imperialism at Paris as serving the correlative function of supplying the broad masses with a reformist anti-imperialist alternative to revolutionary-socialism. Secondly, and more specifically related to the question of German reintegration, it is a fact that the President and his advisers were greatly concerned in 1918–19 not only that the German Revolution might move too far to the Left, but also that Allied opposition to a moderate reintegrationist settlement would inhibit Wilsonian efforts to steady German moderates and would lead to a destruction of Germany's new democratic structure by Bolshevism.

In the broadest terms it is clear that there was an inherent conflict between Wilsonian and Bolshevik goals in the immediate aftermath of World War I.[16] The Wilsonian attempt to stabilize the international-capitalist system challenged the assumptions of revolutionary-socialists whose hopes for a postwar series of revolutions were based in part on the conviction that world capitalism could not reform its war-producing contradictions from within. It cannot be overemphasized that if Wilsonian ideology was anti-imperialist it was in no way sympathetic to revolutionary-socialism. Indeed, the President conceived his form of moderate opposition to the Right as a barrier to more radical anti-imperialist tendencies. Wilson refused to join Lenin in ascribing the cause of imperialism and war to the institution of the liberal-capitalist nation-state itself. Instead, in almost classical liberal fashion, the President preferred to see such pre-liberal phenomena indigenous to traditional European politics as militarism, autocracy, and great power rivalries over the control of weaker states as constituting the real basis for international instability.[17] In this context, it is easy to see how Wilsonians were able to rank Imperial Germany, a country in which pre-liberal feudal and military institutions were especially strong, as exceptional in its imperialism when judged by the non-feudal values of America's liberal anti-imperialism. During the war Wilson often sought to make it clear that American opposition to Imperial Germany was directed not against legitimate German economic expansion but rather against what Wilson saw as the atavistic efforts of Germany's autocratic ruling groups to combine military with commercial expansion.[18] For the President, in short, operating with the perspective of American liberal-exceptionalism, the answers to the Old World's atavistic imperialism were progressive forms of democratic-capitalist nationalism and internationalism as opposed to any form of revolutionary-socialism which rejected liberal as well as feudal values.

During the war years, as we have seen earlier, the President and Colonel House sought to control and to co-opt the forces of international radicalism by offering a Wilsonian ideology of war-liberalism as a substitute for revolutionary-socialist values. Indeed, until the end of the war it remained one of Wilson's dominant concerns to bind the Allied Left securely to the Entente cause by convincing them that a victory for Allied arms was also a triumph for anti-imperialist values in general.[19] Moreover, the problem of containing Entente radicalism was one of the factors which helped to give a more positive tone to the President's response to the German armistice appeals of October 1918. On October 16, 1918, Wilson told the British diplomatic agent Wiseman that while he, Wilson, did not trust the present German Government, he could not shut the door to peace negotiations since "the spirit of the Bolsheviki is lurking everywhere, and there is no more fertile soil than war-weariness."[20] With the defeat of Germany accomplished, however, it became as necessary to prevent radicalism from upsetting an orderly liberal settlement as it had been to contain the challenge of the Left to liberal war.

Even apart from the issue of whether the majority of the Allied people were in fact not conservatively and nationalistically oriented in the 1918–19 period, there can be no doubt that the President, rightly or wrongly, saw it as one of his most urgent postwar tasks to win the loyalty of the broad masses for moderate liberal-reformism as opposed to Bolshevism. Wilson was convinced that liberal anti-imperialism had to satisfy popular demands for a change in the traditional organization of international politics or revolutions would result. On the eve of his departure for Europe in December 1918 Wilson reflected pessimistically on his inability to change the world overnight and expressed concern that the disappointed common people might turn on him as a false messiah.[21] A few days later, at sea aboard the George Washington, the President spoke of the necessity to build a new world order, among other reasons because the "poison of Bolshevism" was accepted readily by the world as a "protest against the way in which the world has worked."[22] Shortly after

his arrival in Europe, the President received a cable from Tumulty which succinctly conveyed the essence of the Wilsonian fusion of liberal anti-imperialism and liberal anti-Bolshevism:

Clemenceau's speech demonstrated necessity for and wisdom of your
trip, and has set stage for final issue between balance of power and
League of Nations. If America fails now, socialism rules the world
and if international fairplay under democracy cannot curb nationalistic ambitions, there is nothing left but socialism upon which Russia
and Germany have already embarked. You can do nothing more ser-
viceable than without seeming to disagree with Clemenceau, drive
home in your speeches differences between two ideals, one, the balance of power means continuance of war; other, concert of nations
means universal peace. One has meant great standing armies with
larger armaments and burdensome taxation, consequent unrest and
bolshevism. If the statesmanship at Versailles cannot settle these
things in the spirit of justice, bolshevism will settle them in a spirit of
injustice. The world is ready for the issue.[23]

At Paris the President would reveal his complete agreement with
Tumulty's analysis by expressing the view that Bolshevism was
likely to advance in a world which rejected his program of
moderate-liberal reforms.[24] Finally, it should be noted that in
two of the speeches given during his brief return to the United
States from Paris in the late winter of 1919 Wilson also developed the concept of an American-inspired liberal peace as a barrier to the possible appeal of revolutionary-socialism among the
restive European masses.[25]

    In late 1918 and early 1919, however, the Wilson Administra-
tion's concern regarding European Bolshevism was focused most
specifically on events in Germany. The President's aim of moderate political democratization in Germany had remained constant to the end of the war. Wilson's notes in response to the
German armistice requests of October 1918 indicated his determination to negotiate peace only with a liberalized Germany in
which the military autocrats were subject to popular control.[26]
Yet these Presidential Notes, by focusing attention on the Kaiser

as the main barrier to a compromise peace, helped to set in motion a revolutionary process in Germany which came close to destroying the hopes of centrist and democratic-socialist German elements for a carefully controlled "revolution from above" in the national interests of the German state.[27] By mid-November 1918, the threat of a victory by the revolutionary-socialist minority in Germany was such that moderate German socialists and traditional military groups had become loosely allied against the far Left.[28] At the same time, in Russia, Bolshevik leaders entertained great hopes for the radical prospects of the long-awaited German Revolution.[29]

In the face of these developments, Washington decision-makers found themselves confronted with a Germany in which the Wilsonian encouragement of moderate democratization had inadvertently helped to create a disturbingly revolutionary politics. By late November 1918, American diplomats were urging in their cables to Washington that the United States use economic and political pressure in Germany to defeat revolutionary-socialism and to ensure orderly democratic processes.[30] These concerns were not lost on Secretary Lansing who, despite his desire to see democracy dominant in Germany, became increasingly worried, in the autumn of 1918, lest the developing revolutionary process in Germany end in Bolshevism.[31] On October 28, 1918, Lansing wrote an agonized letter to Elihu Root, in which, after some speculation as to the desirable form and extent of Germany's necessary democratization, the Secretary moved on to the heart of the problem that faced Wilsonian statesmanship in postwar Germany:

On the other hand how far should we go in breaking down the present political organization of the Central Empires or by military operations render them utterly impotent? This latter question is even more difficult because of the situation which confronts us. There are two great evils at work in the world today, Absolutism, the power of which is waning, and Bolshevism, the power of which is increasing. We have seen the hideous consequences of Bolshevik rule in Russia, and we know that the doctrine is spreading westward. The possibility of a proletariat despotism over Central Europe is terrible to contemplate. Democracy *without* education and Autocracy *with* education are the great enemies we have to face today. But I believe the former is the greater evil since it is destructive of law and order. How can we best utilize the hostility of these two principles, which are at opposite poles of political thought, so that both will be weakened? How much encouragement should we give to radicalism in Germany in the effort to crush out Prussianism? We cannot dismiss these questions with an assertion of disbelief that Bolshevism cannot become a factor among an enlightened people, because the doctrine of the "social revolution" is gaining adherents in every land. This we know. The situation must be met. What is the best way? How does it effect our policy toward Germany? [32]

We shall see shortly that Lansing answered his last question with a firm commitment to the reintegrationist orientation toward Germany at Paris.

For his part, Wilson was no less concerned than Lansing about the radical potential latent in the politics of the German Revolution. At the Cabinet meeting of October 8, 1918, Wilson expressed his conviction that he could not negotiate with an autocratic Germany, but he also conveyed his anxiety that "unless some sort of Gov. offers medium of communication, we might witness bolshevikism worse than in Russia." [33] A week later, the President told William Wiseman that while he [Wilson] did not trust the present German Government nor wish to negotiate with them, "we should consider too the condition of Germany. If we humiliate the German people and drive them too far, we shall destroy all form of government, and Bolshevism will take its place." [34] During the course of a Cabinet meeting on October 23, 1918, the President reflected in a similar vein on the course of events in Germany and, according to Interior Secretary Lane, the President said "he was afraid of Bolshevism in Europe, and the Kaiser was needed to keep it down—to keep some order. He really seemed alarmed that the time would come soon when there would be no possibility of saving Germany from the Germans." [35] Finally, on

[handwritten annotation: Wilson is struggling against two destructive political ideologies: imperialism which is on the decline, and bolshevism/communism which is on the rise]

November 5, 1918, Wilson returned to the theme of a Bolshevik conspiracy in Europe and its threat to Germany.[36] It should come as no surprise then, that by the end of November 1918 the Administration was actively seeking methods by which to aid moderate anti-Bolshevik German elements.[37]

We have already seen that in broad terms Wilsonians were convinced that Allied imperialism, if unchecked, could inspire a generalized Bolshevik response in Europe. It remains here to make the point, more specifically in relation to the German rein-tegration issue, that members of the Administration were also concerned lest an excessively punitive Allied orientation toward postwar Germany would help to foster German Bolshevism. During October and November 1918 Secretary Lansing's letters and memoranda revealed his fear of an irrational anti-German passion on the part of the American public, coupled with an awareness that "Bolshevism is raising its abominable head, and a Germany crushed might become a prey to that hideous movement."[38] Lansing became increasingly convinced that in a Europe threatened by social revolution, any purely one-dimensional policy of bitter anti-Germanism that refused to distinguish between the Kaiser's and Ebert's Germany would be disastrous for social order. "We must look to the future," wrote Lansing in November, "even though we forget the immediate demands of justice. Reprisals and reparations are all very well, but will they preserve society from anarchy and give to the world an enduring peace."[39] For Lansing, then, America's postwar anti-imperialist struggle against Allied extremism was inextricably fused with the Wilsonian anti-Bolshevik effort.

Just prior to the Armistice, Assistant Secretary of State Breckinridge Long was also critical of extreme Allied plans for a defeated Germany on the grounds that "Bolshevism there rampant will mean the same thing at a later date in France, Italy and England, even in America, and the peace, order and safety of the civilized world will be endangered. Germany can not safely be annihilated."[40] Moreover, it is highly significant that while representing Wilson at the Armistice negotiations in Paris Colonel House saw fit to point out to the French "the danger of bringing about a state of Bolshevism in Germany if the terms of the armistice were made too stiff." [41] General Tasker Bliss, also present at these negotiations, shared House's concern that Allied intransigence might foster Bolshevism in a crushed Germany.[42] For his part, Wilson also realized that a relationship existed between the spirit of anti-German vengefulness and the Bolshevik danger in Germany. On October 16, 1918, the President told William Wiseman that a policy which sought the humiliation of Germany would destroy all German governmental forms and leave a vacuum for Bolshevism to fill.[43] It is clear then, that at least one of the dominant tendencies of Wilsonian policy at Paris would move in the direction of reintegrating Germany into a new liberal world order in a effort to check both Allied imperialism and German Bolshevism.

Within the Wilsonian delegation to the Paris Peace Conference the reintegrationist position toward Germany was most consistently upheld by Henry White, General Tasker H. Bliss, and Secretary of State Lansing. It should be noted that these three men were partly isolated from the President and the actual decision-making process at Paris.[44] It is therefore possible to argue that both natural resentment at being excluded from power and general freedom from involvement in concrete situations demanding compromise with the Allies tended to produce in these three men an abnormally critical orientation toward the Paris scene. Yet whatever weight one chooses to assign to such personal factors, the crucial point to be stressed for the purposes of an analysis here is that these three commissioners consistently expressed their alienation at Paris in reintegrationist terms which fused opposition to Allied extremism with a pervasive concern lest Germany be overcome by Bolshevism. Moreover, as will soon be evident, their concerns were not ignored at Paris by such American decision-makers as Hoover, Baruch, House, and Wilson.

The retired diplomat Henry White was the only Republican chosen by Wilson to join the Peace Commission, and even

White in no sense reflected the strong pro-Allied position which was dominant in the Republican party in the winter of 1918–19. Indeed, Wilson and House appointed White to the Commission in full knowledge that he was not strongly pro-Allied, that he had personal connections in Germany, and that he favored a moderate settlement of reconciliation.[45] This background lends added interest and significance to the extensive correspondence which White carried on with Senator Henry Cabot Lodge from Paris. One gets a sense in reading this correspondence that the two men, while retaining personal respect for one another, were talking past each other politically. Lodge was an outspoken protagonist for the French position of an extremely punitive peace. White, by contrast, was almost pro-German in his attitudes, and his letters to Lodge reflected many of the assumptions of the reintegrationist view. White responded to Lodge's bitter pro-French and anti-German statements with discussions which criticized what White saw as unreasonable French militarism and which also warned of the threat of Bolshevism in Germany unless the Peace Conference sought to support German moderate elements with a speedy peace of reconciliation.[46]

As a firm exponent of the values of liberal-internationalism, General Tasker Bliss was as different politically from General Pershing as was Henry White from Senator Lodge.[47] Bliss was convinced that only general disarmament and a moderate peace could prevent a catastrophic second world war, and he feared that the defeat of German militarism was being followed in Europe by the growth of an equally dangerous Allied militarism.[48] Moreover, Bliss at Paris became increasingly concerned that Bolshevism might be stimulated by continued militarism and by Allied action in Germany that had created mass despair.[49] Bliss favored policies which would be fair to Germany and help to "build up there a strong democratic government which will be the natural barrier between Western Europe and Russian Bolshevism." [50] For Bliss, then, the reintegration of German into a new liberal world order would check both war and revolution.

We have already seen that Secretary Lansing became disturbed in the fall of 1918 lest the destruction of German autocracy, which he had sought since 1915, lead to the victory of revolutionary-socialism in Germany. In consequence, even before arriving at Paris Lansing had begun to retreat from his wartime "hard-line" orientation toward Germany and to adopt a more conciliatory reintegrationist viewpoint critical of Allied extremism. At Paris, the Secretary continued to be both obsessed by a fear of expanding Bolshevism and strongly opposed to most Allied, and especially French, policy goals in relation to Germany.[51] Speaking in Paris on March 11, 1919, at a dinner given by the French Club of the Foreign Press for the American Commissioners, Lansing tried to make explicit his conception of the way a defeated Germany ought to be treated in the new postwar world:

And now that the mighty conflict is ended and the great war engine of Prussia is crushed we have new problems to solve, new dangers to overcome. East of the Rhine there are famine and idleness, want and misery. Political chaos and outlawry have supplanted the highly organized government of imperial Germany. Social order is breaking down under the bitterness of defeat and the hopelessness of the future. Like the anarchy which for a year has made an inferno of Russia, the fires of terrorism are ablaze in the states of Germany. Through the ruins of this once great empire the flames are sweeping westward. It is no time to allow sentiments of vengeance and of hatred to stand in the way of checking the advance of this conflagration, which will soon be at the German borders threatening other lands. We must change the conditions on which social unrest feeds and strive to restore Germany to a normal though it be a weakened social order. Two words tell the story—Food and Peace. To make Germany capable of resisting anarchism and the hideous despotism of the Red Terror, Germany must be allowed to purchase food; and to earn that food industrial conditions must be restored by a treaty of peace. It is not out of pity for the German people that this must be done and done without delay, but because we, the victors in this war, will be the chief sufferers if it is not done.[52]

A little more than a quarter of a century later, at the end of another European war, Secretary of State George Marshall would echo views similar to Lansing's in outlining a vision for German reintegration into a postwar Europe which the Truman Administration, like its Wilsonian predecessor, saw as threatened by communism.

Having briefly traced the ideological roots and development of the Wilsonian reintegrationist orientation toward Germany, we must now consider more specifically those aspects of Wilsonian policy at Paris which most reflected this approach. For purposes of this analysis we may roughly distinguish two broad policy areas in which the Administration's linked opposition to Allied extremism and to Bolshevism was either dominant or strongly operative. The first of these concerns the interrelated problems of relief, reparations, and general American economic policy at Paris. The second centers around the Administration's position on the political and territorial issues involving German unity and Germany's borders.

In the late fall and early winter of 1918–19 there was a complete consensus among Wilsonians on the necessity to get immediate food relief into Germany in order to aid German moderate political elements against revolutionary-socialism.[53] Relief Director Herbert Hoover, one of the most effective defenders of the reintegrationist orientation at Paris, was from the end of the war a leading advocate of this humanitarian—and politically motivated —policy of combating German Bolshevism with food.[54] Henry White reflected this pervasive American concern with anti-Bolshevik relief when he cabled to Senator Lodge seeking support in early January, 1919, for Wilson's requested congressional appropriation of $100 million for European relief:

Feel I should no longer delay laying before you condition which has been gradually forcing itself upon our Delegation and which now dominates entire European situation above all else; namely; steady westward advance of Bolshevism. It now completely controls Russia and Poland and is spreading through Germany. Only effective barrier now apparently possible against it is food relief, as Bolshevism thrives only on starvation and disorder.[55]

The crucial problem, however, was that the French, who were relying on the maintenance of the wartime blockade to control
Germany and who also feared loss of reparations payments if
Germany were allowed to buy its own food, resisted American
and British efforts to arrange for German food relief.[56] This
French resistance to the prompt extension of food relief to Germany, in the face of the threat of German revolutionary socialism, naturally upset Hoover, Wilson, and others in the Administration.[57] Colonel House expressed the frustration of many Wilsonians in a letter to Norman Hapgood:

I cannot make anyone realize some situations as I see them. For instance, Bolshevism is steadily creeping westward. Intervention would
only aggravate it. We have had too much of that already. Not only
would it aggravate it, but it is so interlocked with other questions that
it would be impossible to realize even if it were advisable and just.
There is not a western country that could safely send troops into Russia without creating labor troubles at home. It seems to me therefore
that a barrier should be raised by helping the Central Powers to bring
about stable, democratic governments of the right sort. To do this it
is necessary to send food there and lift the blockade and other restrictions. When this is proposed, one is constantly met by objections of
the most puerile sort. The governing classes are the last to see the
hand-writing on the wall. They do not seem to understand that while
today quiet and comparative contentment reigns, tomorrow, through
mob psychology, the whole situation may change.[58]

House, as usual, was assuming here the stance of the sophisticated
progressive who seeks to convince existing elites that it is in their
enlightened self-interest to head off revolution with timely reform. More broadly, however, it could be said that the French, by
their actions on the blockade issue, provided real confirmation for
the reintegrationist conviction that at Paris the American liberal
struggles against Allied extremism and Bolshevism were, in fact,
one struggle.

The issues surrounding the relief of Germany were, however,
merely one section of a much larger cluster of problems concern-

ing the economics of the peace settlement. Perhaps the central economic problem at Paris was the question of German reparations, an issue on which Wilsonians found themselves almost constantly at odds with the French, and often with the British as well. The heart of the American position, developed by such financial advisers as Norman Davis, Bernard Baruch, Thomas Lamont, and John Foster Dulles, was the desire to give Germany both a reasonable fixed sum and a definite time limit to count on in the management of repayments.[59] Wilsonians were basically concerned at Paris that, unless the reparations settlement were made in a reasonable enough manner to leave Germany the possibility of economic recovery and to give the international banking community confidence in German bonds, the result would be continued German and European economic dislocation, heightened international tension, and radical social unrest.[60] It was perhaps the banker and Presidential adviser Norman Davis who, in a memorandum for the President dealing with the German reply to the Allied conditions of peace, most clearly stated this Wilsonian position:

Unless Germany is permitted to retain a requisite working capital and is given the necessary freedom of action for re-establishing her industrial life, it will be utterly impossible for her to pay anything at all, and she might get in the same position that Austria is in today; namely, that credits will have to be given to her for the purchase of food with which to keep her people alive, instead of collecting from her, as will be possible if a constructive policy is pursued. If Germany is not at work and consequently is in a chaotic situation and unprosperous, it is impossible for the rest of Europe to get to work and to be prosperous. It is most essential for the future stability of Europe that confidence and credit be restored at the earliest possible moment, and these can never be restored as long as any large nation in Europe is struggling under a financial burden which the investors of the world think she cannot carry. There is nothing, in our opinion, which could be done which would go further toward re-establishing confidence, credit, and the normal economic and industrial life, than to make an agreement with Germany which the business people of the world think is just and can be carried out, so that the bonds so issued by

Germany can act as a basis of credit. After all, the crux of the whole matter is really not so much what Germany will be able to pay, as what the business men, bankers, and investors of the world think she will be able to pay, and they are most likely to think she will be able to pay any reasonable amount which Germany herself admits she can pay. Six to twelve months delay in getting the masses of Europe at work will cost more, from an economic and financial standpoint, than the extra amount which might be gotten out of Germany by following the present indefinite, so called elastic plan, even assuming that such a plan could be eventually worked out. And if the conditions in Germany and the rest of Europe should become worse from a social, economic, and financial standpoint, which in our opinion is very probable if steps are not taken as above indicated, then the loss will simply be irreparable and far in excess of any amount that anyone has hoped could be gotten out of Germany. The solution of the problem of our friends in Europe is bound up with a practical treatment of the reparation problem in respect to Germany.[61]

In high level negotiations at Paris, Wilson himself often expressed the view that only through relief, blockade relaxation, and a rational reparations program could Germany conquer economic chaos and incipient Bolshevism and gain socio-political stability.[62] In May 1919 the President revealed his concern for German stability in a discussion of the financial and economic terms of the treaty:

President Wilson said that the letter which had just been considered gave a conclusive reply to the German letter but provided no ray of hope. It merely said that the Treaty was right and nothing more. He had understood that the experts who had discussed with the German Financial Experts at Villette found Herr Melchior a very sensible man. Melchior was now one of the German Delegates, and he was a representative of the kind of people in Germany who wanted to get their industries going again, and he wanted to avoid the chaos and the confiscations of property and looting which had occurred elsewhere. These people wanted to get their country started again, and they would listen to what our experts had to say. The United States Experts had, all along, said that the present scheme of reparation would not yield much. This was Mr. Norman Davis' view, and Mr. Keynes, the British expert, shared it. He himself wanted the Allies to get reparation. He feared they would get very little. If it could be shown to Melchior that the Reparation Commission was allowed to consider the condition of Germany and to adjust the arrangements accordingly from time to time, it might enable him to persuade the German people.[63]

Clearly, reintegrationist considerations concerning Germany's social stability and her postwar role in the political economy of an orderly non-Bolshevik Europe were central to the Wilsonian approach to the reparations issue.

Some historians, however, have seen fit to place a good deal of the blame on Wilson personally for the failure of the Paris Peace Conference to construct a more rational economic settlement. They argue that it was unreasonable for the President to have expected the Allies to be sensible on the reparations issue while America remained aloof from all British efforts at inter-Allied economic integration, opposed any plan by which Allied debts to America could be either lessened or absorbed into the reparations settlement, and favored the primary use of private, especially American, investment as the means of world economic recovery.[64] In short, Wilson and his financial advisers are accused of having injured the prospects for European economic unity and recovery by the practice of economic nationalism and the overzealous defense of free enterprise.

It is certainly true that, despite the hopes of Colonel House, neither of Wilson's Secretaries of the Treasury was prepared to offer a scaling down of Allied war debts to America.[65] It is also true, that in early February 1919 Wilson, Baruch, and Davis all expressed concern over what they saw as efforts being made by the Allies to have the United States assume a larger share of war indebtedness through the creation of economic plans involving America in the unsound financial structure of Europe.[66] Yet America's very real economic nationalism at Paris cannot be completely understood without some discussion of its relationship both to the specific issue of German reintegration and to the more inclusive Wilsonian goal of constructing, under American leadership, a peaceful and open order of world liberal-capitalism free from military and economic alliances and from socialist revolution.

As has been noted earlier, Wilson approached the Peace Conference with a deep mistrust of Allied economic goals.[67] Clearly, any successful effort on the part of the Allies to maintain an exclusionist unity in the economic area would have been fatal to Wilsonian hopes for German reintegration into a new liberal-capitalist international system. In this connection it is significant that in late 1918 Hoover and House were agreed that American control of relief operations would be superior to inter-Allied control, in that what Wilsonians saw as American "disinterestedness" could thereby be in a position to head off any possible Allied use of the relief program for political purposes.[68] In short, the President and his advisers entered the Conference with the sense that inter-Allied economic co-operation was to be avoided, not simply in the interests of America's independent economic strength, although this was an important consideration, but also in the interests of the larger Wilsonian goal of constructing a new liberal world order which was to include Germany.

Events at Paris served to confirm many of the Administration's worst fears as to the nature of Allied economic policy. We have already discussed the largely unsuccessful efforts of Wilsonians to bring the French, and often the British as well, to a realization of the necessity for rational relief, blockade, and reparations policies if Germany were to play a role in European economic recovery and if social revolution were to be avoided. Indeed, these concerns were to reach a climax in May 1919, when Wilson, Hoover, Vance McCormick, and others showed strong sentiment against seeking to coerce Germany to sign the Treaty through any reimposition of a strict blockade.[69] The Paris experience, in sum, reinforced the Wilsonian sense that American economic freedom from Allied political manipulation was essential to the rational reconstruction of a peaceful and orderly world.

It is in this general context that the Wilsonian rejection in late

April 1919 of the Keynes Financial Plan advanced by the British
is best understood. The Keynes Plan would have brought the Allies and America together in one co-operative economic scheme
seeking general European recovery by merging both inter-Allied
debts and German reparations into one rational program.[70]
Members of the Administration were quick to notice on the negative side, however, that the Keynes Plan envisioned the United
States as the basic underwriter for all German bonds to be issued,
and left America, in effect, both the prime creditor of Germany
and the central financial support for the entire European economic structure.[71] Moreover, of equal importance was the fact
that Lloyd George had advocated Keynes's financial plan without
the Keynes corollary of reasonable reparations.[72] The Keynes
Plan, in short, would have absorbed American financial power
into an Allied-sponsored economic program which the President
and his advisers saw not only as detrimental to America's national
economic interests, but also as an expression of a more general irrational Allied approach to the issues of reparation and German
economic reintegration at Paris.[73] Wilson stated both these concerns plainly in his letter to Lloyd George of May 5, 1919, rejecting the Keynes Plan:

America has, in my judgement, always been ready and will always
stand ready to do her full share financially to assist the general situation. But America has grave difficulties of her own. She has been
obliged within two years to raise by means of war loans and taxes the
sum of forty billion dollars. This has been a very heavy burden, even
for our well-to-do commonwealth, especially in view of the fact of the
short period during which such sums of money had to be raised; and
our Treasury informs me that our investing public have reached, and
perhaps passed, the point of complete saturation in respect of investments. Such is our situation. You have suggested that we all address
ourselves to the problem of helping to put Germany on her feet, but
how can your experts or ours be expected to work out a *new* plan to
furnish working capital to Germany when we deliberately start out by
taking away all Germany's *present* capital? How can anyone expect
America to turn over to Germany in any considerable measure new

working capital to take the place of that which the European nations have determined to take from her? [74]

In a similar vein, Herbert Hoover had taken the occasion of a meeting of the Supreme Economic Council on April 23, 1919, to criticize the French both for their failure to understand that only a productive Germany led by its middle classes could pay reparations and resist Bolshevism and for France's efforts to seek an answer to economic difficulties by increasing the credit burden on the United States.[75] Basically, then, Wilsonians were insisting that the essence of any rational economic settlement was not unlimited American credits but rather the reintegration of a prosperous Germany into a productive liberal-capitalist Europe.

By way of a rough summary at this point, the economic policies of the leading powers at Paris can be briefly sketched as follows. The French were primarily concerned with extorting the largest possible reparations from Germany, and they saw inter-Allied economic co-operation at Paris as a means of extending Entente unity into an economic war with Germany.[76] British policy was more ambiguous. On the one hand, Keynes and Lloyd George shared many Wilsonian concerns as to enabling Germany to resist Bolshevism and to play a productive role in a general program of European recovery. Indeed, we have already seen that the British tended to support the United States on the issues of blockade and relief, and also that Keynes advanced in late April the most significant of a series of British efforts to create programs of international co-operation for economic and financial stability. The central problem was, however, that Lloyd George, probably because of pressure from the Right in England, rejected the Keynes orientation on reparations in favor of the position advanced by his more hard-line experts and the French.[77]

Basic American economic policy at Paris was oriented toward seeking an end to inter-Allied political interference in Europe's economic life and toward creating, as far as possible, a system of international free trade. Wilsonians tended to assume that the healing effects of the myriad activities of private capitalists, acting freely in an international commercial arena liberated from Allied political controls, would create economic recovery and social stability.[78] A natural corollary to this Wilsonian emphasis on general free trade was the desire to allow Germany access to the markets of the world. On April 25, 1919, the President spoke of Germany's commercial plight to the Council of Four:

President Wilson said. . . . The Treaty would hit them very hard since it would deprive them of their Mercantile Marine; would affect their international machinery for commerce; would deprive them of their property in other countries; would open their country by compulsion to enterprising citizens of other countries without enabling their enterprising citizens to try and recover their position in foreign countries. He did not think that the fact had been sufficiently faced that Germany could not pay in gold unless she had a balance of trade in her favour. This meant that Germany must establish a greater foreign commerce than she had had before the war if she was to be able to pay. Before the war the balance of trade in Germany's favour had never equalled the amounts which she would now have to pay. If too great a handicap was imposed on Germany's resources we should not be able to get what Germany owed for reparation. Moreover, if the business world realized that this was the case the securities on which the payment of reparation would depend would have no value. If this reasoning was sound it provided a formidable argument. He only looked towards reaching a peace and in doing so putting Germany in the position to build up a commerce which would enable her to pay what she ought to pay in order to make good the robbery and destruction she had perpetrated.[79]

Thus, if Wilsonian policy was in one sense exclusive in its rejection of inter-Allied economic co-operation in the immediate post-war period, it was in another sense inclusive in its ultimate vision of a universal liberal-capitalist harmony which would include Germany.

America's insistence at Paris was not on pure Manchesterian free trade but rather on the creation of a modified free trade system which would outlaw discriminatory trade barriers and exclusive economic blocs and which would in effect establish the principles of the Open Door and the "most-favored-nation arrangement" on a worldwide basis.[80] Such a world commercial system would also be made to order for what Wilsonians had always seen as America's need to expand her exports in order to maintain domestic prosperity.[81] It is worth noting that one of Herbert Hoover's concerns in establishing American control over relief operations in postwar Europe was to make certain that America's glutted domestic farm markets would be cleared at advantageous prices.[82]

Yet, as was normal in Wilsonian thought, the needs of America's expanding capitalism were joined ideologically with a more universal vision of American service to suffering humanity and to world stability. Wilsonian ideology permitted one to believe sincerely that there was no contradiction between the particular pursuit of American national interest and the more universal Wilsonian goals of alleviating world deprivation and defending international liberal order against challenges from the Right and the Left. In Wilson's own terms, the relief question was bound up with "The high mission of the American people to find a remedy against starvation and absolute anarchy." [83] A telegram to Washington from the Commission to Negotiate Peace concerning relief appropriations perfectly conveys the Wilsonian fusion of idealism and self-interest:

It would be well to impress upon Congress that there is in the United States at present a considerable stock of surplus food especially wheat and pork which was accumulated principally for supplying the Allies and which would have been required by them had the war continued but which must now be disposed of in order to relieve storage and financial facilities in the United States because the Allies are now able to purchase and transport food at lower prices from their own possessions. While it is most important for us to dispose of this surplus in order to avoid difficulties in the United States, it is most fortunate that we have this surplus which is necessary to save human lives and stem the tide of Bolshevism in Europe.[84]

Moreover, Hoover and the President's other economic advisers at Paris almost always related their conceptions of a commercially expansionist America's need for economic independence from Allied price and credit control plans with the larger problem of using American private credits and investments judiciously to foster the recovery of a peaceful and prosperous international-capitalist system. Such a system was to include Germany and was to be both receptive to the products of American agriculture and industry and resistant to the interrelated dangers of irrational nationalism and socialist revolution.[85]

It was perhaps Wilson himself who, in a cabled message to the Congress in May, 1919, best expressed this faith that American and world economic welfare were inextricably bound together;

Peculiar and very stimulating conditions await our commerce and industrial enterprise in the immediate future. Unusual opportunities will presently present themselves to our merchants and producers in foreign markets, and large fields for profitable investment will be opened to our free capital. But it is not only of that that I am thinking. Many great industries prostrated by the war wait to be rehabilitated, in many parts of the world where what will be lacking is not brains or willing hands or organizing capacity or experienced skill, but machinery and raw materials and capital. I believe that our business men, our merchants, our manufacturers and our capitalists will have the vision to see that prosperity in one part of the world ministers to prosperity everywhere: that there is in a very true sense a solidarity of interest throughout the world of enterprise, and that our dealings with the countries that have need of our products and our money will teach them to deem us more than ever friends whose necessities we seek in the right way to serve. . . . America has a great and honorable service to perform in bringing the commercial and industrial undertakings of the world back to their old scope and swing again, and putting a solid structure of credit under them.[86]

For Wilson then, liberal-nationalism and liberal-internationalism were ideologically joined so inseparably as to make certain that America best served world capitalism by developing her own commercial potential. In Wilsonian terms, the needs of international-capitalism were always defined so as to be compatible with America's economic self-interest.

In the realm of ideology, therefore, it was possible for Wilsonians to reconcile the apparent contradiction between, on the one hand, their commitment to assist in the reconstruction of a viable European economic order into which Germany could be reintegrated, and, on the other hand, their refusal to entertain Allied plans for a co-operative economic settlement to include both inter-Allied debts and German reparations. The contradiction was resolvable because Wilsonians believed that, above all else, the moral and material power of America's liberal-exceptionalism had to be preserved from European control and remain the prime agent of the world's movement from traditional imperialism to liberal rationality, without socialist revolution. On a different plane of analysis, the real exclusiveness of America's economic policy at Paris was perceived by Wilsonians as necessary to the ultimate attainment of a higher and more universal form of liberal-capitalist harmony into which the Allies and the Germans could both be led by America's commercial and political leadership. Wilsonian ideology permitted the Administration honestly to see its pursuit of American economic self-interest, in the matter of the Allied debts, as compatible with America's mission to lead the world toward liberal-international harmony.

The general policy area of relief, reparations, and credits has been discussed at some length because it was in this area of policy formation at Paris that the Wilsonian reintegrationist approach to Germany was most operative. It is possible, however, to see somewhat similar American tendencies of opposition to Allied extremism partially at work in a second and more purely political area of policy at the Peace Conference. This can be seen in the Franco-American conflicts at Paris concerning the political questions relating to the maintenance of German unity and the determination of Germany's borders.

France emerged from the World War with her male population decimated, with some of her most productive regions in ruins, and clearly in a position of growing inferiority to a more populous Germany in both industrial and military potential. It is not surprising, then, that the French statesmen at Paris sought to annex the Saar Basin and to detach the entire left bank of the Rhine permanently from German sovereignty in the form of a Rhenish Republic under French protection.[87] Indeed, even Clemenceau, devoted to the maintenance of French security within the traditional context of international power politics, occasionally found himself under attack from Marshall Foch and others on the powerful French Right for alleged softness on the issues of territory and security in the Rhineland.[88]

Wilsonians were concerned with moderating these extreme French demands in the interests both of a fair, lasting peace and of Germany's liberal political order and unity. It could be argued that the President's most difficult task at Paris was to get the French to accept compromise arrangements in the Saar and the Rhineland—to provide for French reparations and security while trying not to sow dragon's teeth by alienating either area irreparably from German sovereignty.[89] The evidence suggests that, if the French were inclined to tighten excessively the Armistice military controls on Germany and to support Rhenish and Bavarian separatism in an effort to dismember postwar Germany, the Wilson Administration, opposed French extremism in all these matters and sought to buttress a unified and liberalized Germany, possessed of sufficient military capability to defend the German state from internal or external Bolshevik pressures, and integrated into a League of Nations structure of mutual security and disarmament.[90]

In the negotiations concerning the Rhineland, and to a much lesser degree in discussions on the Saar, Wilson received the support of the British against the French.[91] These differences were not lost on such ardent supporters of German reintegration as Lansing, Bliss, and White, who often singled out Great Britain for praise for British stands at Paris on non-economic issues.[92]

Within the British delegation itself, in addition to Keynes, the re-integrationist orientation had another strong champion in the influential South African statesman J. C. Smuts, who favored a moderate settlement with Germany which would both ensure future peace and make Germany a strong bulwark against communism in the East.[93] More significantly, however, Lloyd George's Fontainebleau Memorandum of March 25, 1919, reveals that he also was well aware of the threats posed in the present by Bolshevism and in the future by a revived German nationalism to any peace treaty which was unduly harsh on Germany and which thereby disappointed mankind's hopes for a reformed international order.[94] Clemenceau responded to the Fontainebleau Memorandum with a clear statement of the French anti-reintegrationist view that by strongly supporting Eastern European nationalism as an anti-German and an anti-Bolshevik bulwark it would be possible for the Entente to fashion a lasting peace based on Allied military control of both Germany and Bolshevism.[95] In broad terms, it could be said that the problem of Germany's borders at the Paris Peace Conference contained in embryonic form many of the issues that would evolve into the full-grown appeasement debates of the 1930's, in which fear of communism and fear of Germany would be dialectically intertwined.

The moderate-socialists and liberal-centrists who emerged, with the aid of the military, as Germany's postwar leaders sought in their own way to appeal to liberal and anti-Bolshevik reintegrationist sentiments among the Allies. At the Armistice negotiations in November 1918, for example, Erzberger argued successfully for the right of Germany to delay the immediate evacuation of her troops from eastern territories threatened by Bolshevism. He also attempted, with less success, to win further concessions for Germany by emphasizing the immediate danger of German revolutionary-socialism.[96] Before and during the Peace Conference itself, the German Government developed two interrelated arguments in an effort to win concessions from the Allies. On the one hand, the German leaders expressed a willingness, if fairly treated, to eschew militarism and bring a reformed Germany into Wilson's new liberal world of legal and commercial order guaranteed by a League of Nations.[97] At the same time, moderate-socialist, liberal, and nationalist Germans sought in 1919 to convince the Allies that the existing German Government, if supported by relief and generally conciliatory peace terms, could provide a firm defense against German Bolshevism and serve as a potential ally against Bolshevik pressures in Eastern Europe.[98] In short, the postwar German Government, much to the displeasure of Germany's revolutionary-socialists, who rejected both Clemenceau and Wilson in favor of Lenin, decided to further the interests of German liberal-nationalism at Paris in an alliance with Wilsonian and British reintegrationist tendencies against both Allied extremism and Bolshevism. Yet this alliance proved to be a shaky one at best, and we must now turn to a consideration of some of the strains and tensions present in the attempt to create an anti-Bolshevik and anti-imperialist community of interest among Wilsonian-British reintegrationists and German moderate-nationalists at the Paris Peace Conference.

V

Peace and Revolution, II: The Wilson Administration, The League of Nations, and the Problem of German Control.

So far our discussion of the Paris Peace Conference has been focused almost entirely on the ideology and politics of the Wilsonian reintegrationist approach to Germany. Historical forces are, however, rarely without their internal contradictions, and if we are really to understand Wilsonian policy at Paris in all its true complexity, we must now complicate the picture by discussing the tension in Wilsonian theory and practice between the desire to reintegrate Germany and the desire to punish and control Germany. Yet even this is not all. We must also come to understand the relationship of this reintegrationist-punitive dialectic, played out in Wilsonian ideology and policy, to the larger Wilsonian program of constructing, under American guidance, a postwar liberal-international order safe from traditional imperialism and socialist revolution.

The final terms of the Versailles Treaty were a bitter disappointment to the moderate-socialist and liberal-nationalist German leaders who had hoped to be able to protect Germany's national interest through a centrist alliance with Wilson against the extremes represented by Clemenceau and Lenin.[1] In this connection, there is no doubt that the Treaty was of enormous assistance to the German Right, in that the Treaty seemed to discredit Wilsonian promises of a liberal peace as hypocritical, and to deny, in effect, that it was possible for Germany to defend its national interests in a context of loyalty to liberal-internationalist values.[2] Then too, Germany's radical-socialists, rightly fearful that the Treaty would cause a new wave of German chauvinism and drive the Government further to the Right, criticized all expressions of traditional nationalism by the Government and called for reliance on European revolutionary developments to overturn the Versailles Treaty.[3] In brief, then, it could be argued that in one sense the Versailles Treaty represented Wilson's failure to reintegrate Germany into a new European order in a manner satisfactory to those postwar German leaders who most completely adhered to Wilsonian values. Actually, the Treaty had an effect which was the obverse of reintegration, in that it further discredited the German liberal-nationalist center in the eyes of its domestic opponents on the Right and the Left.

The problem was that Germany's leaders had partly misjudged Wilsonian intentions toward the defeated Germany. It was true that Wilsonians were interested in protecting postwar Germany against Bolshevism and in moderating extreme Allied political and economic demands on Germany in the interests of social stability and a more lasting peace. Yet it was also true that at Paris the President and his advisers were not so much seeking real solidarity with the newly democratized Germany as they were seeking a stable and docile German democratic Government that would willingly accept a moderated, but nonetheless still harsh, dictated settlement. For, just as during the war Wilson was unwilling to make the types of concessions to German expansionism in Eastern Europe demanded by liberal-nationalist Germans in search of a compromise anti-Bolshevik peace with the Allies, so too the President was unprepared in the immediate postwar period to support entirely the conception of a just peace held by German democratic-nationalism. In short, the central contradiction of Wilsonian policy at Paris was reflected in the tension between the President's desire to reintegrate a liberal Germany into a peaceful and non-revolutionary world order and his almost equally strong punitive determination to avoid any appeasement of Germany. Let us turn now, therefore, to a consideration of some of the ideological and structural sources of the Wilsonian punitive orientation toward Germany.[4]

1. WILSONIAN PUNISHMENT AND CONTROL OF GERMANY

One source of the contradiction noted above lay in Wilson's ambivalent attitude toward the German Revolution of 1918–19. On the one hand, the President, as we have seen, was concerned lest the Revolution go too far to the Left and was, therefore, insistent that Germany be allowed the necessary food, economic relief, and military force to defend her fragile liberal political and economic institutions against revolutionary-socialism. In effect, then, Wilsonians supported the decision of Germany's moderate-socialists, backed by the army and the majority of the German people, to limit the Revolution to the area of formal constitutional democracy while leaving largely untouched the underlying social supports of German traditionalism in the form of conservative civil servants, army officers, Junker landowners, jurists, and large industrialists.[5] Yet, having done all he could to prevent the radical revolutionists from dismantling the German social order root and branch, Wilson could not escape the paradoxical but related problem of the threat to German liberal stability posed by the still powerful German Right. How could Wilson be sure that the mild German Revolution he supported had really destroyed the roots of German militarism?

The evidence suggests that, beginning with his firm demands for German democratization in the pre-Armistice exchange of notes with the Government of Prince Max, the President remained concerned with the threat to Germany's new liberal order from the traditionally militaristic Right throughout the Peace Conference period. On several occasions Wilson revealed a belief that Germany ought not to be admitted to the League of Nations until she had passed through a probationary period, testing the staying power of her new liberal institutions and the sincerity of her complete disavowal of militarism.[6] Thus, just as in the President's pre-1917 mediation efforts and in his wartime attempts to appeal to German liberalism, so too, at Paris, a central problem for Wilsonian ideology and policy remained the inherent difficulty of reintegrating a Germany, perceived as extraordinary in its traditional militarism, into a projected liberal-capitalist international community. While it was natural for the Administration to support German liberalism against socialist revolution, could Wilsonians then trust the ability or the will of German liberalism to control the German Right?

In sum, Wilson feared the potential influence of the German Right in the postwar period, but he could not seek a destruction of the German Right by the German Left because, among other reasons, of his concern lest Bolshevism result and Germany be irrevocably lost to world liberal order. Inevitably, then, the President came to accept, with some efforts to moderate its severity, the basic Allied notion of the necessity of establishing postwar military and political control of the German state, a notion which became central both to the nature of the Armistice agreements and to the makeup of the very organizational structure of the Paris Peace Conference itself.[7] The records of one negotiating session at Paris in February 1919 report Wilson as affirming that "he felt that until we knew what the German Government was going to be, and how the German people were going to behave, the world had a moral right to disarm Germany, and to subject her to a generation of thoughtfulness."[8]

For dominant French opinion the German Revolution created no real ideological dilemmas since the leading French publicists and decision-makers were convinced that the socio-political structure of Germany had been unchanged by the revolution and that, in any event, a unified and democratic Germany could be as great a threat to France as a more traditional Germany.[9] In essence, the French, along with many of Wilson's Republican opponents at home, developed a critique of the German Revolution which, in many of its particulars, was paradoxically close to that of the German revolutionary-socialists themselves. Yet, while the German revolutionists hoped to destroy the German Right from within, Lodge and Clemenceau hoped to contain both Germany and revolution with military force. Wilson, torn between his reintegrationist and punitive orientations toward Germany, ultimately opted for a moderate system of military controls on a probationary German state. The irony was that, by partially accepting the basic assumption underlying the Paris Peace Conference, the assumption that a liberalized Germany was still a suspect nation to be controlled and dictated to rather than negotiated with as an equal, Wilsonians inadvertently played their own role in the creation of a self-fulfilling prophecy about the character of the postwar German state.

There is also much evidence to suggest that, whatever his attitude toward German reintegration and the German Revolution, the President approached the Peace Conference with an extremely moralistic attitude of judicious, but nonetheless punitive, righteousness toward Germany. Wilson's desire for a "temper of high-minded justice" in the treatment of postwar Germany definitely ruled out Allied extremism but was not incompatible with a more punitive desire to make the German settlement an example of the harsh wages of international sin.[10] Wilson felt it was possible to combine justice, rationality, and harshness in the creation of a German settlement. Thus, while it is important to emphasize Wilson's reintegrationist-oriented desire for a rational reparations settlement, it is equally important to stress that the issue between the President and the Allies on reparations was in reality a struggle over the method of collection from Germany and not a disagreement over the underlying assumption, accepted by both Wilsonians and the Allies, that a guilty Germany ought to be forced to pay large reparations. On one occasion, Wilson made quite explicit this fusion of rationality and harsh justice:

He [Wilson] only looked towards reaching a peace and in doing so putting Germany in the position to build up a commerce which would enable her to pay what she ought to pay in order to make good

the robbery and destruction she had perpetrated. But if the robber
was to be in such a position that he could not pay the penalties
would be inoperative. The penalties ought to be operative and real.
We ought to see that Germany could put herself in a position where
she could be punished.[11]

It could be said that the President's reintegrationist approach toward Germany, modified by his punitive orientation, represented
not so much a desire to accept the postwar liberalized German
state on terms of equality and solidarity, as it represented an effort
to curb Allied extremism just enough to permit Germany to be
punished and controlled in a manner that would neither encourage
Bolshevism nor prevent a lasting peace. In his Fontainebleau Memorandum, Lloyd George, well aware of the essential reintegrationist
concerns over war and revolution, joined Wilson in the comfort-
ing assumption that the peace terms "may be severe, they may be
stern and even ruthless, but at the same time they can be so just
that the country on which they are imposed will feel in its heart
that it has no right to complain." [12]

The President's response on May 16, 1919, to a critical letter
from General J. C. Smuts on the final peace terms reveals that,
whatever its contradiction to his reintegrationist approach, Wilson retained throughout the Peace Conference a moralistic desire
to make Germany an example to mankind of the severe results of
international criminality:

No apology was needed for your earnest letter of the fourteenth. The
treaty is undoubtedly very severe indeed. I have of course had an
opportunity to go over each part of it as it was adopted and I must
say that though it is in many respects harsh I do not think that it is
on the whole unjust in the circumstances, much as I should have
liked to have certain features altered. I am in entire agreement with
you that real consideration should be given to the objections that are
being raised against it by the Germans, and I think I find a growing
inclination to treat their representations fairly. As it happens, they
have so far addressed their criticisms only to points which are substantially sound. I feel the terrible responsibility of this whole busi-

ness, but invariably my thought goes back to the very great offense against civilization which the German state committed and the necessity for making it evidence once and for all that such things can lead only to the most severe punishment. I am sure you know the spirit in which I say these things and that I need not assure you that I am just as anxious to be just to the Germans as to be just to anyone else.[13]

While Wilson was not unwilling to reconsider the terms of the Treaty in the light of Germany's counter proposals, he was somewhat less receptive to such a reconsideration than either General Smuts or the ardent reintegrationists in the American delegation. Indeed, in May 1919, such committed reintegrationists as Lansing, Hoover, Bliss, and White were convinced that the terms of the Treaty ought to be revised in Germany's favor and were, therefore, happy when Lloyd George was moved by some of his advisers and his own doubts to call for last-minute revision of some of the harsher terms of the settlement.[14]

On June 3, 1919, a full meeting of the American Peace Commission was held to consider Lloyd George's proposals. At this meeting, Lansing, Bliss, White, Norman Davis, and Hoover all argued from a reintegrationist orientation in an effort to win as many concessions for the Germans as possible.[15] Wilson found himself in agreement with the ardent reintegrationists on some issues, especially in matters concerning the reparations settlement and the plans for a continued military occupation of Germany, but the President's remarks to Lansing at one critical juncture of the meeting reveal that Wilson never lost his sense of punitive righteousness when dealing with policy matters relating to Germany:

Mr. Lansing was asking me if I did not think that it would be a good idea to ask each of our groups to prepare a memorandum of what might be conceded, and while I do not want to be illiberal in the matter, I should hesitate to say "yes" to that question. The question that lies in my mind is: "Where have they made good in their points?" "Where have they shown that the arrangements of the treaty are essentially unjust?" Not "Where have they shown merely that they are hard?," for they are hard—but the Germans earned that.

And I think it is profitable that a nation should learn once and for all what an unjust war means in itself. I have no desire to soften the treaty, but I have a very sincere desire to alter those portions of it that are shown to be unjust, or which are shown to be contrary to the principles which we ourselves have laid down.[16]

Clearly, whatever his desire to reintegrate Germany into a postwar liberal world order safe from war and/or revolution, the President was less prepared than his most ardently reintegrationist advisers to make concessions to the new Germany in the process.

Finally, it should be noted that, on issues related to Germany's eastern frontiers with Poland and Czechoslovakia, the President was influenced both by his own pro-Slavic biases and by the strategically oriented advice of some anti-German experts serving on the staff of the American Inquiry at Paris. As a result, Wilson accepted territorial arrangements in the East which, if far too moderate by French, Polish, and Czechoslovakian standards, were definitely harsh from the standpoint of the German people assigned, for economic or strategic reasons, to the new Slavic states.[17] Moreover, it is clear that, on Polish frontier issues in particular, Wilson, while in no sense acquiescing in all Polish demands, often stood somewhat closer to the Poles than did Lloyd George, whose Fontainebleau Memorandum had emphasized the dangers from Bolshevism and German nationalism latent in Poland's claims. [18] The crucial point is not that Wilson was oblivious either to the dangers of postwar Polish militarism or to the reintegrationist insights of the Fontainebleau Memorandum, but rather that the President was not prepared to follow reintegrationist logic if it should lead, by way of appeasing German nationalism in the East, to any compromising of his vision of justice to long-oppressed Slavic peoples.

2. WILSONIAN LIBERALISM, THE LEAGUE OF NATIONS, AND THE GERMAN PROBLEM

Up to this point in our discussion, we have chosen, for analytic purposes, to treat separately the Wilsonian reintegrationist and

punitive approaches toward Germany at Paris. By way of conclusion, however, it is important to attempt to speak of Wilsonian
policy at the Paris Peace Conference in more comprehensive
terms capable of subsuming the reintegrationist-punitive dialectic
into a larger analytic synthesis. Ultimately we shall see that, for
Wilson himself, the League of Nations served the function of re-
solving whatever contradictions were inherent in his efforts to
create a European settlement which would control and punish
Germany and which would, at the same time, also insure against
war or revolution.

On the eve of the Peace Conference, there were some serious
misconceptions in Europe and America as to the probable nature
of Wilson's role in postwar world politics. Perhaps most indica-
tive of this situation is the fact that in late 1918 and early 1919
some European political elements expected the President to play
an openly radical, if non-Bolshevik, role in European politics.
Hopes for some form of open radical solidarity with Wilson
against the Entente Establishment were shared by the majority of
Europe's social democrats who often found themselves torn between liberal and revolutionary anti-imperialism.[19] Moreover, the
Allied governments and the Republican opposition in the United
States were concerned in late 1918 that the presence of the President in Europe, which would make direct contact between Wilson and the people probable, might lead to just such an overt Wil-
sonian-radical union against an extremist peace.[20] Yet such radical hopes and conservative fears proved largely groundless, because they were based on an underestimation of the extent to
which Wilsonians, for all their missionary American opposition to
Old World imperialism, still remained fundamentally committed
to the non-revolutionary politics of centrist liberalism, to the accepted practices of international relations, and to inter-Allied
unity against a defeated Germany. Let us turn then, to a more
detailed analysis of the reasons behind Wilson's failure to satisfy
his would-be allies among the non-Bolshevik European Left.

Part of the problem was that Wilson's supporters on the postwar Left seriously underestimated the extent to which the President and his advisers conceived of the Peace Conference in somewhat conventional terms, as a gathering of victorious Allies meeting to impose just but severe terms on a defeated criminal enemy. Social democratic hopes notwithstanding, Wilson was extremely reluctant at Paris ever to risk either inter-Allied unity or Entente political and military control of Germany in the process of attempting to check Allied extremism. [21] Many European and American non-revolutionary radicals who hoped that Wilson would use the Peace Conference as a forum from which to launch an anti-imperialist assault on the Allies, failed to comprehend that much of the President's crusading liberalism remained, even in the postwar period, directed primarily at German imperialism in particular rather than at European imperialism in general. Indeed, it is possible, after understanding Wilson's ambivalent attitude toward the German Revolution, to describe the President's reintegrationist critique of Allied extremism operationally as an effort to moderate an essentially punitive peace. In sum, then, the non-Bolshevik radical vision of postwar democratic-socialist solidarity between Wilson, the German revolutionaries, and the Allied Left against both Allied and German imperialism was checked in part by the fact that Wilson ultimately chose moderated Allied military and political power, and not some form of social-demoratic solidarity, as his prime response to the threat of German imperialism.[22]

Yet it must also be clear from what has just been said that, in the maintenance of his reluctance to play a more openly radical role at Paris in opposition to Allied extremism, Wilson's own commitment to the reformist politics of ordered liberalism was as important an element as was his punitive orientation toward Germany. It should be noted that Wilson had, as an historian, looked favorably on Edmund Burke's opposition to the French Revolution, and that the President had interpreted Burke's position as one based on progressive liberal pragmatism and oriented toward "a sober, provident, and ordered progress in affairs." [23]

Probably it was in an address delivered before the International Law Society at Paris in the spring of 1919 that the President best expressed both his deeply felt opposition to any form of socio-political radicalism and his sense of the tension implicit in the role of the moderate reformer who seeks to contain utopian impulses within the framework of international liberal legality:

May I say that one of the things that has disturbed me in recent months is the unqualified hope that men have entertained everywhere of immediate emancipation from the things that have hampered and oppressed them. You cannot in human experience rush into the light. You have to go through the twilight into the broadening day before the noon comes and the full sun is on the landscape; and we must see to it that those who hope are not disappointed, by showing them the processes by which that hope must be realized—processes of law, processes of slow disentanglement from the many things that have bound us in the past. You cannot throw off the habits of society immediately any more than you can throw off the habits of the individual immediately. They must be slowly got rid of, or, rather, they must be slowly altered. They must be slowly adapted, they must be slowly shapen to the new ends for which we would use them. This is the process of law, if law is intelligently conceived.[24]

The past must be overcome, but by an evolutionary rather than a revolutionary process. In the postwar period, then, Wilson did not hesitate to support the moderate politics of the anti-imperialism of liberal order against both the passions of Jacobin-like Bolsheviks and the class-oriented politics of Europe's social democrats.

There is no doubt that Wilson was anxious to avoid playing an inflammatory role in the tense class politics of postwar Europe. Especially significant here is the evidence that at Paris Wilson put his confidence in the strongly anti-socialist A.F. of L. leader Samuel Gompers as against the democratic-socialists of Europe who sought a basis of more radical solidarity with Wilsonians.[25] Indeed, Wilson had been informed before Gompers left America that the French and British governments desired Gompers in Eu-

rope during the Peace Conference to act as a "steadying influence" on restive labor and socialist elements in the Allied countries.[26] Nor was Lansing any more anxious than the President to
exacerbate European class tensions on behalf of Wilsonian liberal
goals. Of specific interest in this connection is Lansing's concern
in November 1918 over the fact that the French Socialists were
constantly espousing Wilson's policies. This concern reflected not
only Lansing's desire clearly to separate Wilsonianism from all
forms of socialist anti-imperialism, but also the Secretary's fear
that the growth of radicalism was leading to the supplanting of
the nation-state by the class as the basic unit in the political
structure of the world.[27] Writing to Wilson in the fall of 1918 to
oppose William Bullitt's suggestion that the United States urge
Allied leaders to isolate Bolshevik tendencies through a policy of
co-operation with the moderate Left, Lansing argued that:

While there is a certain force in the reasoning as to the peril from extreme radicalism under the leadership of such men as Liebknecht and
the Independent Socialists, who affiliate with the Bolsheviks, the danger of compromise with any form of radicalism and the unwisdom of
giving special recognition to a particular class of society as if it possessed exceptional rights impress me as strong reasons for rejecting
such a proposal. Kerensky's experience in compromise and the results
which have followed the exaltation of class at the expense of the rest
of society, (whether the class be aristocratic, land owning or labor)
are not encouraging to adopting the course suggested.[28]

While there is no reply from Wilson to Lansing's letter on
record, other evidence shows that the President shared the Secretary's reluctance to give any special recognition to socialist or
working class politics in the postwar period.[29]

As for Colonel House, it is true both that he did not share
Lansing's negative attitude toward the non-Bolshevik Left and
that during the war the Colonel once even fantasized on his own
possible role at a future peace conference as a socialist suddenly
rallying the world's peoples against the secret machinations of
Old World diplomats.[30] Yet, in practice at Paris, House proved

as reluctant as Lansing to counsel the President to run the risk of a direct appeal to Europe's moderate radicals over the heads of established governments. Essentially, House favored a policy of behind-the-scenes contacts between the Administration and the non-Bolshevik Left in the hopes of harnessing moderately radical elements to the Wilsonian cause on the carefully controlled terms of the anti-imperialism of liberal order.[31] Whatever their desires to oppose Allied imperialism at Paris, Wilsonians were not prepared to abandon the politics of liberal legitimacy and international decorum for any type of class-oriented radical anti-imperialism.

It is true, of course, that Wilson was very much in favor of including a provision in the League of Nations Covenant that would seek to raise the general standards of labor's working conditions on a worldwide basis.[32] Yet it should be noted that the President did not conceive of such a labor "Magna Carta" in the League Covenant in anything approaching class-conscious or radical terms. Rather, Wilson appears to have hoped that the provision would help to curb worldwide labor unrest by reproducing, on a global scale, the same type of non-radical and progressive labor-management co-operation which the Administration saw as the answer to America's own industrial unrest.[33] In an address delivered at Tacoma, Washington, on September 13, 1919, the President articulated this vision of a progressive liberal society in which the differences between labor and management were resolved in a larger harmony based on the public interest:

I call you to witness, my fellow citizens, that our present civilization is not satisfactory. It is an industrial civilization, and at the heart of it is an antagonism between those who labor with their hands and those who direct labor. You cannot compose those differences in the midst of war, and you cannot advance civilization unless you have a peace of which you make the peaceful and healing use of bringing these elements of civilization together into a common partnership, in which every man will have the same interest in the work of his community that those have who direct the work of the community. We have got to have leisure and freedom of mind to settle these things. This was a war against autocracy; and if you have disorder, if you have disquieted populations, if you have insurgent elements in your population, you are going to have autocracy, because the strongest is going to seize the power, as it has seized it in Russia. I want to declare that I am an enemy of the rulership of any minority, however constituted. Minorities have often been right and majorities wrong, but minorities cease to be right when they use the wrong means to make their opinions prevail. We must have peaceful means; we must have discussion. . . .[34]

Clearly, then, Wilson's basic tendency was to avoid class-oriented radicalism, and to search instead for ways to unite workers and capitalists in a liberal and co-operative framework of classless majoritarian consensus.

An analysis of the President's speeches delivered in Europe reveals both that Wilson remained loyal to his liberal progressive ideology of class harmony, and that he avoided direct appeals, on anything approaching class lines, to workers and socialists on behalf of his international program. The President often spoke directly to public audiences in Europe, during late 1918 and early 1919, but he invariably spoke in such a manner as to blur the more radical potentialities latent in his very presence. Wilson's references were usually to such diffuse entities as "world opinion," "humanity," "people," "great moral tide," "the conscience of the world," "voice of humanity," "mankind," "liberal men everywhere," and "the heart of the world," accompanied by no real attempt to root the support for his postwar program more concretely in the democratic-socialist movement of Europe.[35] Moreover, the central message conveyed by many of Wilson's European speeches—to the effect that the Allied statesmen were prepared to follow the lead of their liberal peoples and to construct a forward-looking peace along popular lines—was calculated more to assuage than to exacerbate whatever radical potential for class conflict may have been latent in the contact between Wilsonian anti-imperialism and the more radicalized social groups of postwar Europe.[36] As we shall now see, the League of Nations concept also expressed the general tendency of Wilsonian reform-

ist ideology to remain fixed between the orthodox positions of
classless liberal-nationalism and classless liberal-internationalism,
while eschewing any affirmative approach toward national or
international class conflict. In other words, the League gave Wilson a way to buttress further his confidence in the inseparable
connection between a classless American liberal-nationalism and
an international liberal order safe from socialist revolution.

Since he was unwilling to risk either the control of Germany or
world liberal order by openly moving toward solidarity with the
non-Bolshevik Left in opposition to German and/or Allied imperialism at Paris, Wilson was forced to devise another policy for
the defense of his international goals. The President needed a
moderately reformist program which would oppose both traditional imperialism and revolutionary-socialism, while remaining
well grounded in the twin legitimacies of a liberal-capitalist nation-
state system and of Allied-American dominance over Germany.
Somehow a program would have to be devised which, while permitting Germany to be punished and controlled, would nonetheless retain enough reintegrationist features to assure the gradual reabsorption of Germany into a viable non-Bolshevik world of
liberal order. Moreover, such a program would also have to be
able to legitimize ideologically the co-opting of American power
into the maintenance of a basically anti-German peace settlement, by providing a liberal vision going beyond mere punitive
righteousness. Such a program would have to hold out the promise that America's complete involvement in world politics represented not a destruction of America's liberal-exceptionalism, but
rather the possibility of restructuring world politics, under the in-
spiration of America's liberal idealism, into a new international
order safe from imperialist war and from socialist revolution.
Ultimately such a program was available to Wilsonians in the
form of the League of Nations. It will be important, therefore, to
turn now to an analysis of the Wilsonian conception of the
League of Nations, in order to understand how, for the President,

the League seemed to resolve all the contradictions latent in his policies at the Paris Peace Conference.

The League of Nations issue is perhaps best viewed as an institutional and ideological microcosm containing all the tensions present in the postwar Wilsonian approach to the German question. On one level of analysis, therefore, it could be argued that, along with whatever more purely reintegrationist tendencies it certainly contained, Wilson's attitude toward the League also included his related but somewhat contradictory desire to punish and to control the defeated Germans. In his major address of September 27, 1918, Wilson made it clear that, for him, one of the essential functions of a projected League of Nations would be to enforce just peace terms on a probationary Germany:

If it be in deed and in truth the common object of the Governments associated against Germany and of the nations whom they govern, as I believe it to be, to achieve by the coming settlements a secure and lasting peace, it will be necessary that all who sit down at the peace table shall come ready and willing to pay the price, the only price, that will procure it; and ready and willing, also, to create in some virile fashion the only instrumentality by which it can be made certain that the agreements of the peace will be honored and fulfilled. That price is impartial justice in every item of the settlement, no matter whose interest is crossed; and not only impartial justice, but also the satisfaction of the several peoples whose fortunes are dealt with. That indispensable instrumentality is a League of Nations formed under covenants that will be efficacious. Without such an instrumentality, by which the peace of the world can be guaranteed, peace will rest in part upon the word of outlaws and only upon that word. For Germany will have to redeem her character, not by what happens at the peace table, but by what follows.[37]

In this connection, it is important to note that Wilson often made clear his belief that Germany ought to be excluded from the League of Nations, for a probationary period, while the Allied democracies made certain that Germany's autocratic political structure and imperialistic foreign policy had both been sufficiently liberalized.[38] Moreover, it is also significant that on many occasions during 1919, the President spoke of the League's important role in guarding Poland and the other newly liberated states of Eastern Europe against any future economic or political aggression from Germany.[39] Then, too, reflecting the interrelatedness of punitive and reintegrationist tendencies among Wilsonians at Paris, it is worth noting that, while Colonel House and General Bliss were more prepared than Wilson to admit Germany to the League immediately, both House and Bliss also saw the League, in part, as a device for controlling Germany.[40]

Wilson and House also argued on occasion that the League of Nations could serve specifically as a defense for France against the threat of another German attack.[41] Indeed, without some emphasis on the League as an anti-German bulwark, it is doubtful that Wilsonians would have been as successful as they were in moderating some of France's most extreme postwar designs on Germany. In a letter responding to Elihu Root's measured opposition to possible American over-involvement in European politics, David Hunter Miller, the Wilsonian expert on international law at Paris, succinctly conveyed his awareness of the real necessity of assuring France of America's commitment to the League of Nations, as an instrument of security against German aggression, in order to win French approval of more moderate peace terms:

The question discussed is not only one of the highest political importance but of immediate importance. France does not think that our interest in a future attack of Germany on France is secondary but primary, and feels that that possibility should be the first concern of the world in general and of America in particular, while admitting that no such attack for the next few years is possible. Whether this feeling on the part of France is right or wrong is not the question, for it exists in a degree which it is almost impossible to overstate, and any attempt to limit our responsibility in the matter would defeat the whole Covenant, for France would prefer then to make a different kind of peace with Germany and not to have a League. Certainly without the League we could hardly refuse her the right to make a peace with Germany which would let her feel secure, but such a peace would then be made as would be contrary to everything we have stood for.[42]

David Hunter Miller's analysis of the anti-German security aspects implicit in the League as it emerged at Paris points up for us anew one of the central paradoxes of Wilsonian policy at the Peace Conference. In its efforts to check Allied extremism and to provide for the reintegration of a liberalized Germany into a new non-revolutionary world order, the Wilson Administration was partly inhibited by the fact that the President, and many of his advisers, retained a punitive and a suspicious orientation toward the postwar German polity. Yet, even when they did disagree on German questions with the British and French, Wilsonians were also inhibited from more direct conflict with the Allies by the fear that an overt U.S.-Entente break might somehow give encouragement to manifest and latent revolutionary-socialist tendencies in postwar Europe. It followed, therefore, that to whatever extent the President and his advisers did choose to oppose Allied, and especially French, extremism at Paris, the Americans were not prepared to rely on the tactic of radical mass mobilization against imperialism. Instead, Wilsonians sought to moderate Allied policies behind the scenes by the implicit and explicit use of America's one viable weapon: namely the threat of the possible withdrawal of the economic, political, and military power of the United States from the immense task of guaranteeing the final European settlement. It must be noted, however, that, paradoxically, the employment of such tactics meant that every concession on the German question which the Administration won in negotiation with the Entente only served to bind American power more securely to the task of guaranteeing the peace settlement. The willingness of Wilson and House, despite the reintegrationist objections of Lansing, White, and Bliss, to join Great Britain and France in a special anti-German security treaty in return for French concessions to moderation in Rhineland negotiations was the classic case in point. In sum, then, part of the American conception of the League of Nations involved anti-German security considerations.

For their own part, unlike Wilson and his advisers, the postwar leaders of France saw the League only as a *de facto* military alliance to protect France from Germany.[43] The French would accept moderation of their demands in the Rhineland only after the United States and Great Britain agreed to sign a special security treaty guaranteeing France against unprovoked German aggression.[44] Thus, so deeply interrelated at Paris were the Wilsonian reintergrationist and punitive orientations toward Germany that, whatever the inherent tension between them, both these approaches often coexisted in the Wilsonian response to such issues as the reparations tangle and the question of the League and French security.

In any event, there is no doubt that on one level Wilsonians were definitely prepared to conceive of the League partly as an instrument for enforcing the final peace terms on Germany, notwithstanding whatever inherent contradiction such a view might involve for the Administration's equally strong desire to reintegrate a democratized Germany into a non-revolutionary liberal-capitalist world order. In this sense, the Wilsonian orientation toward the League tended to merge well with the world views of such leading British statesmen as Lloyd George, who envisioned the absorption of American power permanently into the maintenance of a peace settlement in Europe which would fuse punitive and reintegrationist features in an uneasy balance.[45] It is also interesting to observe that, during 1919, many security-conscious elements of the French Center and Right moved from opposition to later support of the President, as it became clear that he meant to pledge American power to the protection of France and to the maintenance of the severe peace settlement through the League of Nations and the related security treaty.[46]

Yet if, during 1919, the French and British leaders moved to support Wilson and the League, it is true that, conversely, Europe's democratic-socialists and Left-liberals tended to move from

initial support of the President to an increased rejection of Wilsonian policies. Desperate in their search of a way to end imperialism without socialist revolution, many democratic-socialists
hoped that Wilson would create a League which, rather than
being made up exclusively of the representatives of various foreign
offices, would instead reflect the diversity of class and party interests in each member country, and would, thereby, provide a world
forum capable both of being strongly influenced by socialist values and of transcending the nation-state system of world politics.[47] However, having underestimated Wilson's loyalty to liberal-nationalist legitimacy, his distaste for any form of socialist
politics, and his desire to control Germany by reliance on Allied
armed power rather than through more radical means, the democratic socialists were necessarily disillusioned by the actual League
of Nations, which emerged as a union of governments implicitly
pledged, in part, to enforce an anti-German peace.[48] Radicals
could see clearly that, far from ending such contradictions in
world politics as the German question by any sort of revolutionary transformation, the League created by the statesmen at
Paris was itself partially based on those very contradictions.

Within the Wilsonian delegation itself, at Paris, a critical approach toward the postwar Allied-American political agreements
also developed among such ardent reintegrationists as Lansing,
Bliss, White, and Hoover. Convinced of the necessity strongly to
oppose the Allies in the interests of a moderate settlement which
would strengthen Germany as a bastion of liberal political and
economic stability, these committed reintegrationists were often
fearful that, in secret negotiations, House and Wilson would allow American power to be absorbed fully by the Allies into the
maintenance of a severely anti-German peace capable of produc-
ing war or social revolution.[49] Lansing, for one, even went so far
as to be deeply critical of the League of Nations, which he saw as
basically an alliance of the victorious powers formed primarily to
enforce harsh peace terms on Germany.[50] Lansing had envisioned
instead a League with no real powers of enforcement which, by

immediately including a liberalized Germany and by bringing all nations to pledge allegiance to the principles of liberal-internationalism on an equalitarian basis, could not have implicitly become a postwar extension of the Entente alliance.[51] In part, then, Lansing, Hoover, and Bliss became somewhat "isolationist" in their reactions to events at Paris, in that they sought to keep America free from entangling economic and political ties to the Allies. Yet, their "isolationism" was always ambivalent at best, since these ardent reintegrationists also hoped, in their own way, to make possible, under the guidance of a liberal-exceptionalist America uncontaminated by power politics, the creation of a more inclusive international system of political and economic liberalism, safe from either traditional imperialism or Bolshevism.

It is true that at Paris neither Wilson nor House was indifferent either to general reintegrationist criticism of Allied policy or to the desire of the most committed American reintegrationists to defend America's political and economic freedom against possible Allied absorption. At the same time, and to a greater extent than Lansing, Bliss or White, both Wilson and House were also prepared to view the League as a device making possible the involvement of American power in the tasks of controlling Germany and of enforcing the peace settlement. Indeed, Wilson's defense of the League Covenant in America during the summer and early fall of 1919 was partly based on the argument that the League was needed to maintain American-Allied unity in the face of a Germany which had suffered severe but just punishment.[52] This apparent contradiction could be wholly resolved in the realm of ideology, if not so completely in the area of practice, since both House and the President also saw the League of Nations as having strong counterbalancing reintegrationist potentialities.

Along with their more static vision of the League as a defender of the Versailles settlement, both the President and Colonel House also saw the League as a potentially flexible instrument through which the imperfect decisions made at Paris could be readjusted in the future.[53] Unwilling completely to share the view of such reintegrationist critics as Lansing, Wilson and House preferred to view the League more broadly and hopefully as a living liberal institution capable of constant adaptation and growth. "A living thing is born," said Wilson of the League at one point, "and we must see to it that the clothes we put on it do not hamper it—a vehicle of power, but a vehicle in which power may be varied at the discretion of those who exercise it and in accordance with the changing circumstances of the times." [54] Similarly, the President hoped that America's postwar participation in the work of the Reparations Commission would make possible a rational readjustment of the problematic reparations settlement which Wilsonians had been forced to accept at Paris. For Wilson, then, the League was the means of extending to the world scene an American vision of pragmatic and progressive change within the confines of a liberal order.

In this general context it is of interest to note that even such ardent reintegrationists and critics of the Paris settlement as Hoover, Lansing, Bliss, and White were in no sense immune to the notion that the League might prove to be useful in an imperfect world, by assuring some degree of continued international cooperation in the interests of world stability.[55] Lansing's memoirs make clear that, for him, his eventual support of the cause of treaty ratification represented no change of heart from his critical stance at Paris, but rather a sense that American ratification of the Treaty and the League Covenant was necessary to the prevention of social chaos:

My own position was paradoxical. I was opposed to the Treaty, but signed it and favored its ratification. The explanation is this: Convinced after conversations with the President in July and August, 1919, that he would not consent to any effective reservations, the politic course seemed to be to endeavor to secure ratification without reservations. It appeared to be the only possible way of obtaining that for which all the world longed and which in the months succeeding the signature appeared absolutely essential to prevent the widespread disaster resulting from political and economic chaos which seemed to threaten many nations if not civilization itself. Even if the Treaty was bad in certain provisions, so long as the President remained inflexible and insistent, its ratification without change seemed a duty to humanity.[56]

It is quite probable that, considering his general world view, Lansing had Bolshevism in mind when he referred to a "widespread disaster resulting from political and economic chaos which seemed to threaten many nations if not civilization itself." Ironically, Colonel House, a man whose constant efforts to compromise with the Allies had drawn Lansing's wrath at Paris, had been himself moved to compromise in the interests of a speedy peace partly because of a fear that Bolshevism was growing in the atmosphere of postwar uncertainty.[57] In any event, it could be said that, in the aftermath of the Paris Peace Conference, the differences between Wilson and such reintegrationist critics within the Administration as Hoover and Lansing tended to be submerged in a unified Wilsonian effort to attain both Treaty ratification and the maintenance of world liberal-capitalist stability in the face of intransigent criticism of the Versailles Peace from the Left and the Right in the United States.

In the realm of ideology, Wilson's reintegrationist conception of the League was more powerful than his somewhat contradictory vision of the League as a means for controlling Germany and enforcing the peace settlement. After all, the President did feel that Germany would be admitted to the League after having proved her liberal sincerity, and that Germany's eventual admittance could help to ease certain problems latent in the terms of the Treaty.[58] On September 13, 1919, Wilson clearly affirmed his idea of the future reintegration, after a period of probation, of a truly liberalized Germany:

I read you these figures in order to emphasize and set in a higher light, if I may, the substitute which is offered to us, the substitute for war, the substitute for turmoil, the substitute for sorrow and despair. That substitute is offered in the Covenant of the League of Nations.

America alone cannot underwrite civilization. All the great free peoples of the world must underwrite it, and only the free peoples of the world can join the League of Nations. The membership is open only to self-governing nations. Germany is for the present excluded, because she must prove that she has changed the processes of her constitution and the purposes of her policy; but when she has proved these things she can become one of the partners in guaranteeing that civilization shall not suffer again the intolerable thing she attempted.[59]

Thus, Wilson's conception of the League as an inter-Allied instrument to control a justly punished Germany was ultimately transcended by the President's related but broader vision of the League of Nations as an inclusive concert of liberal powers into which a reformed Germany could eventually be reintegrated.

As early as spring 1918 the President had urged that the League ought not to be "an alliance or a group formed to maintain any sort of balance of power, but must be an association which any nation is at liberty to join which is willing to cooperate in its objects and qualify in respect of its guarantees." [60] Similarly, at Paris, Wilson affirmed that "there must now be, not a balance of power, not one powerful group of nations set off against another, but a single overwhelming, powerful group of nations who shall be the trustee of the peace of the world." [61] Of course, it is clear that, for a time, the powerful trustees would be the victorious Allied powers, but it is significant, as Colonel House made plain, that one of the reasons for America's rejection of the French plan for an official League army was the Wilsonian concern lest the French succeed in turning the League completely into an anti-German instrument.[62] In sum, then, the basic Wilsonian reintegrationist conception of the League, as an inclusive community of liberal states mutually pledged to defend international law and one another's territorial integrity, had the potential of ideologically transcending the actual anti-German context from within which the League emerged at Paris.[63]

At one point, while in England late in 1918, the President spoke of the League in terms which contained many of the ambiguities already discussed:

I wish that it were possible for us to do something like some of my very stern ancestors did, for among my ancestors are those very determined persons who were known as the Convenanters. I wish we could, not only for Great Britain and the United States, but for France and Italy and the world, enter into a great league and covenant, declaring ourselves, first of all, friends of mankind and uniting ourselves together for the maintenance and the triumph of right.[64]

On the one hand, both the direct mention of the Allied powers as forming the moral core of the League, and the reference to stern covenanted unity in "the maintenance and the triumph of right," could imply the creation of a League simply to defend a righteously punitive settlement against Germany. On the other hand, however, such phrases as "and the world" and "friends of mankind" obviously suggest the more inclusive and reintegrationist possibilities of Wilsonian liberal-internationalism.

There can be no doubt that the President saw the League of Nations, in part, as a postwar inter-Allied police force growing naturally out of the progressive nucleus of the Allied-American liberal alliance which had defeated the special reactionary challenge to world liberalism posed by German autocratic imperialism.[65] Yet, beyond the necessary defeat of atavistic German imperialism, there also existed the larger Wilsonian hope to so reorganize world politics as to prevent any other nation from repeating Germany's imperialistic actions in the future. In his defense of the Versailles settlement, the President was concerned not only with reforming and controlling Imperial Germany; he also sought to liberalize the entire imperialistic system of European politics within which an autocratic Germany had simply played the most militant and aggressive single role.[66] The President often combined an argument to the effect that the League was the necessary culmination to the triumph of world liberalism over German imperialism with a broader argument that the League was also the means by which world liberalism would finally reform the Old World's traditional balance-of-power system.

The point is that, speaking theoretically, Germany's eventual

reintegration was latent in the Wilsonian critique of the traditional imperialistic system. Had Wilson joined the French in
merely seeking to punish and to control German imperialism
alone, the League of Nations would have been only a postwar extension of the Entente alliance. To be sure, the League was, in
part, just such a peacetime extension of the anti-German wartime
alliance, yet the Wilsonian critique of European imperialism also
contained an implicit condemnation both of any continued Allied
reliance on the old diplomacy of the balance of power and of any
Allied failure to live up to liberal values in the future. For the
President, then, the League Covenant projected the vision of a
liberal world order, transcending the historical and traditional restraints of power politics, into which a liberalized Germany could
eventually be reintegrated as a full partner.

Wilson conceived the essence of the League as an orderly social
contract among the nations. The international social contract represented by the Covenant of the League was to rescue the world
from an insecure "Hobbesian" state of nature in which nations
could find temporary security only through armaments and the
balance of power. The President saw the League Covenant as establishing a new co-operative international society, governed by
liberal norms, whose nation-state members would be pledged to
substitute public discussion and peaceful arbitration under world
law for the reactionary diplomatic practices of secret diplomacy or
armed conflict.[67] Indeed, Wilson always put far more emphasis
on the universal moral force of world liberal opinion, focused in
an association of self-governing states, than he did on the armed
power of the League members.[68]

In Wilson's new "Lockeanized" international environment, in
which formerly hostile nations had been theoretically transformed
into equal law-abiding liberal world citizens, all countries, weak
and strong alike, were to eschew power politics and were also to
covenant together, under Article X of the League of Nations
Covenant, to defend each other's legal rights and territorial integrity.[69] On one occasion, the President pithily expressed his or-

derly liberal desire to transform a world political system in which, historically, might had made right, by remarking that he hoped "to make a society instead of a set of barbarians out of the governments of the world." [70] The League Covenant, then, ultimately represented for Wilson the fulfillment of America's historic mission to lead the Old World away from the traditional war-producing diplomacy of the balance of power to an harmonious American-inspired liberal world order of international responsibility under law. In the eyes of the President the League Covenant was the embodiment of American and world liberalism's final triumph over the imperialistic and atavistic restraints of the pre-liberal historical past. [71]

There can be little doubt that, without his faith that the League offered a new liberal beginning in world politics, in which the concept of a universal concert of powers replaced the old notion of a balance of power, the President would not have been willing to involve the United States so permanently in European affairs. [72] Given Wilson's missionary conception of the universality of America's liberal-nationalism, the League legitimized for him the involvement of American power in world politics by permitting him the assumption that, far from being absorbed as another competing element into the traditional global political reality, American strength was enabled, by the League, to enter world politics at the very moment that world politics was transcended by liberal-internationalism. For Wilson America's involvement in world affairs was inseparably joined with America's effort to lead a liberal anti-imperialist transformation of global reality through the League of Nations. In a theoretical sense, then, the League may be seen as Wilson's answer to reintegrationist critics, such as Hoover and Lansing, who feared lest Allied absorption of America's political and economic power might end hopes for the establishment of an American-inspired world of liberal-capitalist harmony.

For Wilson, the ultimate mission of a liberal exceptionalist America was to lead the rest of the world, without socialist revo-

lution, to a universal liberal triumph over all elements of pre-
bourgeois reaction and atavistic imperialism. The war years had
seen a strengthening of the President's faith that, under his
leadership, the United States was fulfilling this historic destiny by
uniting America, the Allies, and common peoples of all countries
in a liberal people's war on behalf of freedom and the creation of
a new anti-imperialist world order.[73] In the postwar period as
well, Wilson was more than ever certain that it was the duty of
the American state to continue to act selflessly as the leader of
world liberalism in the effort to create a new international system
free of power politics and Europe's traditional balance of power.[74]
In this connection, it is not surprising that the President saw
the American-inspired League of Nations as a logical extension, to
the entire world, of America's effort, under the Monroe Doctrine,
to keep European reaction out of the Western Hemisphere.[75] In
essence, therefore, Wilson saw a powerful postwar America as the
leader of the liberal opinion of the world, as the selfless and
trusted arbiter of international problems, and as the disinterested
defender of a new world order against both traditional imperialism and revolutionary socialism.[76] For the President, America's
political, economic, and military self-interest was inseparably
joined to America's missionary idealism, in the Wilsonian struggle
for international liberal stability.

In the final analysis the League of Nations proved to be the
central element in the Wilsonian vision of an Americanized postwar world order in which the contradictions of international politics would be resolved in a new liberal harmony. While it is true
that the League provided a means to enforce a severe peace on
Germany, it is also true that, for Wilson, the League held out the
promise of the eventual reintegration of a reformed Germany into
an American-inspired liberal-capitalist world order safe from war
and/or socialist revolution. Moreover, by maintaining the basic
legitimacy of the nation-state system, the League was a logical
expression of Wilson's effort, based on his ideology of American
liberal-exceptionalism, to combine the leadership of world liberal

anti-imperialism with his somewhat contradictory position as the leader of the militarily powerful American nation-state. Finally, by permitting Wilson to link ideologically American nationalism with liberal-internationalism, the League was the culmination of the President's vision of an orderly American-inspired reform of the traditional world political-economy. Such Wilsonian international reform, by using the League to establish a universal liberal-capitalist stability without class conflict, would ultimately defeat both atavistic imperialism and revolutionary socialism, the two mutually reinforcing barriers to the final realization of America's true national interest and pre-eminence in a liberal world order.

VI

Peace and Revolution, III: Wilsonian Policy
toward Eastern Europe and Russia at the
Paris Peace Conference

Under Wilson the American nation-state began in earnest to play
its ambiguous modern role, both as a great power among other
great powers in a traditional system of power rivalries and as a historical agency for the transformation of the world political system
along the lines of liberal-internationalist ideology. Wilson's ambivalent efforts to reintegrate a reformed Germany into a new liberal world order beyond class conflict and imperialist rivalry
should be recalled in this general connection. The present chapter
is concerned with the Administration's efforts to establish a postwar liberal order in Eastern Europe and in Russia. It will become
clear that the Wilsonian vision of a peaceful liberal-capitalist triumph over pre-liberal reaction, a triumph which was to make revolutionary-socialism unnecessary, was as central to the Administration's approach to the postwar politics of Eastern Europe and
Russia as the same missionary vision had been to the determination of America's orientation to the German question at Paris.
In the unsettled areas of Eastern Europe and Russia the postwar
Wilsonian centrists opposed the contradictory yet mutually reinforcing extremist challenges of imperialism on the Right and of
revolutionary-socialism on the Left, in the interests of establishing, under the League of Nations, an American-inspired international order of rational commercial and political stability in
which the moral and the material expansion of American liberal-
capitalism could take place freely in a world at peace.

1. NATIONALISM AND COMMUNISM IN POSTWAR EASTERN EUROPE

In the vast area of Eastern and Southern Europe lying between Germany and Russia and stretching from the Baltic states on the north to Yugoslavia on the south, the Wilson Administration faced severe postwar challenges to the President's vision of liberal-international harmony.[1] On the one hand, the collapse of the Austro-Hungarian Empire led, in the immediate postwar period, to the development of bitter nationalist rivalries among the militant successor states. On the other hand, internal and external Bolshevik pressures created the reality of a revolutionary-socialist challenge to Administration hopes for postwar Eastern Europe. Somehow, Wilsonians would have both to moderate tendencies toward militant nationalism on the Right and to check the threat of Bolshevism on the Left, if a viable centrist political-economy of liberal-nationalism and internationalism were to be constructed in Eastern Europe by the Paris Peace Conference.

The Wilson Administration had a real interest in the success of national self-determination in postwar Eastern Europe. Despite their reintegrationist approach toward Germany, it is clear that Wilsonians shared, to a limited extent, the French concept of a band of pro-Allied Eastern European states, to be anchored by a strong Poland, and to be constructed as a barrier of nationalism to both German aggression from the west and Bolshevik expansion from the east.[2] Indeed, Wilson and House remained especially sympathetic throughout the Peace Conference to the difficulties of the new Poland menaced on the one side by Germany and on the other by Bolshevism.[3] Then too, it could be argued that the United States was the principal supporter, at the Peace Conference, of the new Yugoslavian state against the threat of Italian imperialism in the Adriatic area.[4] Nonetheless, regardless of the general Wilsonian commitment to Eastern European nationalism, there developed among many Americans at Paris a good deal of criticism of the militant and expansionist chauvinism exhibited by Poland and the other Eastern states allied with France during the immediate postwar period.[5]

Within the American delegation at Paris, the strongest critics of the French-inspired militant nationalism that characterized the postwar behavior of Poland and the other pro-Allied states in the East were the ardent reintegrationists Lansing, White, and Bliss.[6] Moreover, whatever his basic commitment to the defense of legitimate Polish national aspirations, Wilson also joined the other Peace Commissioners in their strong concern over the evidence of French-inspired Polish imperialism revealed in the report brought back from Eastern Europe in April 1919 by General Francis Kernan, the chief American representative on the Inter-Allied Commission to Poland.[7]

In early June 1919 General Bliss wrote to Wilson in terms highly critical of the tendency of the new Eastern European states to war among themselves and to neglect the more basic task of containing the expansion of Russian Bolshevism:

Permit me to suggest that if the Allied and Associated Powers were to take this attitude and to actually carry it into effect, not only in the case of Hungary—Roumania—Czecho-Slovakia, but also with respect to other areas where senseless and unjustified war is being carried on, it would, in the opinion of many of us, go a long way toward correcting the situation. If definite boundaries could be drawn in all cases where it has not yet been done; if all parties concerned could be informed that under no circumstances whatever would the Great Powers recognize any other boundaries and that every man lost and dollar expended in trying to amplify boundaries would be a sheer waste; and finally, if they were informed that all assistance of any kind whatsoever would be immediately withdrawn unless these new States stopped fighting amongst themselves and devoted their attention solely to resisting aggression of the Russian Bolsheviks,—if that attitude were taken and faithfully lived up to by the Powers, I think we might bring about a state of reasonable peace in Europe. As it stands now the United States is giving millions of dollars worth of food supplies to these nations which take the money thus saved and expend it on unjustified military operations.[8]

In his reply, Wilson thanked Bliss for his letter and added, "I think that my colleagues are coming more and more to the view that we must put the utmost pressure upon the Middle European States, and I need not tell you with what sympathy of judgement I have read your suggestion." [9] Clearly, Wilsonians would have to control the danger of imperialism latent in the realization of self-determination by nations in Eastern Europe, if that area were to be secured from war and revolution for the values of orderly liberal-nationalism and internationalism.

One possible answer to the destabilizing threat of excessive nationalism in postwar Eastern Europe lay in the creation of new forms of political authority and economic unity among the successor states to replace the direction once provided for much of the area by the Dual Monarchy. In late 1918, in a pamphlet on the League of Nations, which made an extremely favorable impression on Wilson, General Smuts argued that the League had a crucial role to play as the successor to the Austro-Hungarian Empire in accomplishing what Smuts saw as the interrelated tasks of containing Bolshevism and controlling the potentialities for great power imperialism and/or chaotic chauvinistic rivalry latent in the effort to create new states in Eastern Europe:

The peoples left behind by the decomposition of Russia, Austria and Turkey are mostly untrained politically; many of them are either incapable of or deficient in power of self-government: they are mostly destitute and will require much nursing towards economic and political independence. If there is going to be a scramble among the victors for this loot, the future of Europe must indeed be despaired of. The application of the spoils system at this most solemn juncture in the history of the world, a repartition of Europe at a moment when Europe is bleeding at every pore as a result of partitions less than half a century old, would indeed be incorrigible madness on the part of rulers, and enough to drive the torn and broken peoples of the world to that despair of the state which is the motive power behind Russian Bolshevism. Surely the only statesmanlike course is to make the League of Nations the reversionary in the broadest sense of these Empires. . . . A gigantic task will thereby be imposed on the League as the successor of the Empires. The animosities and rivalries among the independent Balkan States in the past, which kept the pot boiling and occasionally boiling over, will serve to remind us that there is the risk of a similar state of affairs arising on a much larger scale in the new Europe, covered as it will be with small independent States. In the past the Empires kept the peace among their rival nationalities: the League will have to keep the peace among the new states formed from those nationalities.[10]

Smuts, like such other ardent advocates of German reintegration as Bliss and Lansing, tended to combine a strong faith in the anti-Bolshevik stabilizing potential of postwar Germany with a deep concern over the destabilizing potential of Eastern European nationalism.

For their part, some Wilsonian Central European experts had also given a good deal of thought to the desirability of some type of economic or political federalism for the Danubian region, since, until the late spring of 1918, it had been the Administration's policy rather than to seek the dismemberment of the Austro-Hungarian Empire to, try instead to influence the Dual Monarchy to move both toward a more liberal internal policy of national federalism and toward a separate peace with the Entente.[11] Indeed, Charles Seymour, the Chief of the Austro-Hungarian Division of the American Peace Commission, makes clear that it was America's unrealized desire at Paris to encourage, through the League, any stabilizing tendencies toward economic or political federalism which should appear among the newly independent nationalities.[12] Moreover, it should come as no surprise that the threat of Bolshevism in Eastern Europe made it even more urgent, from the Administration's point of view, to use the League and American influence to control irrational nationalism among the successor states in the interests of postwar commercial and political order.

In late 1918 and early 1919, there was general concern among members of the Wilson Administration lest revolutionary socialism make successful inroads into Eastern Europe. In late Decem-

ber 1918, Allen Dulles, then an American diplomat in Switzerland, sent word to Washington of the pressing danger to Poland
and Lithuania posed by the advance of the Russian Bolsheviks toward the west.[13] However, whatever their very real concern over
the westward military movement of the Russian Bolsheviks, Wilsonians were even more worried, on the eve of the Paris Peace
Conference, over the possibility that the sudden collapse of traditional authority in the Austro-Hungarian Empire might open the
door to the internal development of revolutionary-socialism in
some of the successor states. As in the case of postwar Germany,
the President and his advisers feared that orderly liberal-nationalist elements in the successor states might be unable to control the
revolutionary process.

On November 2, 1918, Secretary of War Newton D. Baker
wrote to Wilson urging him to make clear to the newly independent nations being formed from the wreckage of the Dual Monarchy that America did not favor violent revolution and that the
United States wanted the new states to "observe orderly processes
in these revolutionary days and refrain from acts of violence." [14]
Ten days later, Wilson was warned by Thomas Nelson Page, the
American Ambassador in Italy, that "It is reported here, not publicly, but by those who are usually well informed, that Bolshevikism is getting under way already along the other side of the
Adriatic and that in Austria the Red Guards are already at
work." [15] At the State Department, in early November 1918, Assistant Secretary Breckinridge Long speculated in his Diary on
ways to check Bolshevism in the new nations "about to be born
of the Austro-Hungarian parent." [16] Finally, Secretary Lansing
was convinced in late 1918 that the prevailing political and economic upheaval in Central Europe could well lead to a revolutionary-socialist solution, and he hoped that the free nations
would aid the states newly liberated from autocratic oppression
and now threatened, in Lansing's view, with a "class despotism"
of the Left rather than the Right.[17]

For his part, Wilson expressed many of these concerns in the conclusion to his Armistice Address of November 11, 1918, in which he tried to convince the peoples of the newly liberated states to reject any form of revolutionary violence:

For with the fall of the ancient governments which rested like an incubus upon the peoples of the Central Empires has come political change not merely, but revolution; and revolution which seems as yet to assume no final and ordered form but to run from one fluid change to another, until thoughtful men are forced to ask themselves, With what Governments, and of what sort, are we about to deal in the making of the covenants of peace? . . . Excesses accomplish nothing. Unhappy Russia has furnished abundant recent proof of that. Disorder immediately defeats itself. If excesses should occur, if disorder should for a time raise its head, a sober second thought will follow and a day of constructive action, if we help and do not hinder. The present and all that it holds belongs to the nations and the peoples who preserve their self-control and the orderly processes of their governments. . . . The peoples who have but just come out from under the yoke of arbitrary government and who are now coming at last into their freedom will never find the treasures of liberty they are in search of if they look for them by the light of the torch. They will find that every pathway that is stained with the blood of their own brothers leads to the wilderness, not to the seat of their hope. They are now face to face with their initial test. We must hold the light steady until they find themselves. And in the meantime, if it be possible, we must establish a peace that will justly define their place among the nations, remove all fear of their neighbors and of their former masters, and enable them to live in security and contentment when they have set their own affairs in order.[18]

In Wilson's view, the new nations were to be rescued from their arbitrary and autocratic pasts by stable liberalism and not by revolutionary-socialism. In short, the President's Armistice Address called upon the new states of Eastern Europe to choose the road of orderly liberal-nationalism over the Russian path of violent socialist revolution, and also asked the new nations to follow the lead of the Allied powers in the creation of a peaceful liberal-international order secure against all forms of armed aggression.

Of course, the question of the best way to check the postwar

Bolshevik threat to Eastern Europe also concerned the other main Allied powers. In general terms it could be said that, while the French hoped to control both Germany and Bolshevism through a militant policy of armed assistance to Poland, Czecho-slovakia, and Roumania, the British, being more oriented toward German reintegration into a viable postwar system of European state relations, tended to be suspicious of French-inspired Polish militarism and to opt for efforts, in line with the views of General Smuts quoted above, to stabilize Eastern Europe and contain Bolshevism through the League of Nations.[19] For its part, the Wilson Administration, although concerned with the defense of Eastern European liberal-nationalism from direct German or Bol-shevik attack, tended to share British fears that the French might foster destabilizing chauvinistic tendencies in Poland and the rest of Eastern Europe by supporting a one-dimensional policy of mil-itary reaction to the Bolshevik danger.

Early in January 1919, at a meeting of the Council of Ten, Wilson responded to Marshal Foch's proposal that the Polish Army in France and Italy be hurried home to defend Poland against both German and Bolshevik pressures by suggesting that:

It might be unwise to discuss a proposal of this sort on its individual merits, since it formed part of the much larger question of checking the advance of Bolshevism to the Westward. There was room for great doubt as to whether this advance could be checked by arms at all. Hence he felt doubtful whether it would be wise to take the kind of action proposed by Marshal Foch until we had agreed on a general policy as to how to meet the social danger of Bolshevism.[20]

While the President did eventually come to favor the dispatch of the Polish troops in question, for purely defensive purposes, he never lost his awareness that a reliance on arms alone was not necessarily the most effective way to meet what he and his advis-ers saw as the social danger of Bolshevism. In this sense, Generals Bliss and Kernan were definitely expressing Wilson's own orienta-tion in their warnings that the French, by encouraging the destabilizing militarism of Poland and other new nations, were only aggravating the problem of Bolshevism in Eastern Europe. Bliss and Kernan, aware that arms could not entirely stop a revolutionary ideology, favored seeking ways to check the spread of revolutionary-socialism, without direct Allied or American military involvement, by using the tools of progressive liberal socio-economic reconstruction to remove the social, economic, and political roots of Bolshevism.[21]

In any event, the evidence suggests that the major emphasis in the Wilsonian policy used against Bolshevism in postwar Eastern Europe was not on American support for the French concept of militant anti-communist nationalism. Instead, the Administration largely sought to rely on the skillful utilization of food relief programs by Herbert Hoover to check whatever revolutionary socialist tendencies emerged among the new nations.[22] In the last analysis, this Hoover-directed program of anti-Bolshevik food relief, with its emphasis on the breaking down of nationalistic barriers to trade and economic recovery, was a classic expression of the more general proto-Marshall Plan tendency of Wilson and his advisers to use America's expansionist economic power in the postwar period to establish international liberal-capitalist stability in the face of threats to world order from irrational nationalism on the Right and from revolutionary-socialism on the Left.[23]

Many of the themes which have so far been developed in this chapter, concerning Wilsonian attitudes toward nationalism and the threat of revolution in postwar Eastern Europe, are perhaps best summarized through a consideration of the Wilson Administration's relations with Bela Kun's short-lived Soviet Hungarian Republic during the spring and summer of 1919. In the process of such a consideration, one finds that the Wilsonian opposition to Bolshevism in Hungary was mixed with a strong liberal desire to prevent the struggle against Bela Kun's Bolshevism from abetting either the French-inspired imperialism of Roumania or the hopes of some autocratic Hungarian elements for a return to power under an anti-Bolshevik banner.

The Hungarian Bolshevik Revolution of March 1919 was naturally of great concern to many Wilsonians at Paris, who feared that radical-socialist revolution might spread from Bela Kun's Budapest to engulf the rest of Eastern Europe and Germany.[24] In response to the threat of communist expansion, Wilson and Hoover agreed during April on a program of manipulating food and relief supplies in such a manner as to isolate and contain the Hungarian Revolution.[25] Indeed, the evidence suggests that at first the President was concerned with containing, but not with destroying, the Soviet Hungarian Republic. Wilson, Bliss, and Hoover tended to put their emphasis, in the spring of 1919, on preventing the expansion of Bolshevism from Hungary through a containment program which combined diplomatic pressures on Bela Kun, applied for the Allies by General Smuts, with the normal American stress on relief, economic recovery, and just territorial settlements.[26] Hoover and Wilson were especially interested in adopting a liberal-reintegrationist approach, in regard to Austrian relief and the diplomatic treatment of the defeated Austrians in general, in an effort to prevent the possible spread of Bolshevism from Budapest to Vienna.[27]

Moreover, whatever their distaste for Bela Kun's Hungarian Bolshevism and their desire to protect Hungary's neighbors against its spread, few Wilsonians were prepared, during the first months of the Kun regime, to accept the French-supported policy which called for a Roumanian military crusade against the Hungarian communists. Wilson, Bliss, and Lansing were all convinced that Roumanian imperialism, supported by France, had played a role in causing the Bolshevik Revolution in Hungary, and also that the threat of Roumanian aggression kept many purely patriotic Hungarians loyal to Bela Kun on grounds of nationalism alone.[28] It could be argued that in some ways the Wilsonian orientation toward the defeated Hungarians ran parallel to the Administration's more reintegrationist approach toward postwar Germany, which sought, by controlling Allied extremism, to check the danger of German Bolshevism.[29] In this general connection, Wilson's remarks at a meeting of the Council of Four in early June 1919 revealed both the President's specific suspicion of Roumanian imperialism in Hungary and his general philosophy as to the most efficacious means of countering the radical extremism of the Left. Bratiano, the Roumanian spokesman, had just charged the Germans with a wartime plot to unite Hungarian and Russian Bolshevism across Roumania:

President Wilson said that he had no doubt intrigues of this kind had been started by Germany. Unquestionably Germany had tried to make the situation in Eastern Europe impossible for the Allies. It was, however, one thing to stir up trouble by means of propaganda and another to do it by aggression. The Allies must see that they do not contribute to it by giving anyone just ground to dread them. As an example, he mentioned that in the United States there was an organization known as the Industrial Workers of the World which was largely an anarchistic organisation of labourers but one that was opposed to agreements with anyone. When opportunity offered they took action by means of sabotage. The policy of the United States Government had been to check this by ensuring, as far as possible, that no grievances should exist among the army of working people. He would not say that there were no grievances but where these grievances had been removed the activities of the Industrial Workers of the World had been checked. The right thing, therefore, must be done. Whatever the reasons might be, it was certain that under the terms of the armistice the Roumanian troops had no right on the Theiss. So long as they remained there they were helping to create Bolshevism in Hungary even more than propaganda would. This situation was one of provocation to Hungary. He was surprised at what had been told him as to the Roumanian and Czecho-Slovak Delegations knowing nothing of the proposed boundaries for them. . . . The first question was to settle boundaries and have some understanding in regard to them which could be observed. When the boundaries were settled, he thought the Bolshevist support would be weakened.[30]

In short, Wilson sought to project onto the world scene his conception of America's internal success in containing revolutionary radicalism through the processes of orderly liberal reform. In this sense, the preferred Wilsonian remedy for Bolshevism in Eastern

Europe was not militarism but the establishment of a just liberal-international order.

By July 1919, however, the continued militancy of the Bela Kun regime had led American policy-makers to move from an ambivalent containment policy of uneasy coexistence with Hungarian communism to a search for ways to end completely the Bolshevik rule in Budapest. On July 5, 1919, Hoover told a meeting of the Heads of Delegations of the Five Powers of the threat posed by the military and ideological power of Hungarian Bolshevism to the political and economic stability of Central and South-Eastern Europe:

Mr. Hoover said that the problem was that of the economic rehabilitation of Central Europe. As matters stood, there was no hope of removing and distributing the Hungarian harvest unless the Danube and the railways across Hungary were re-opened for traffic. The question, therefore, was not merely an internal Hungarian question. It was one of external economic relations. The action of the Hungarians had tied up the Danube and with it a large proportion of the river craft used on it. . . . In order, therefore to set the economic life of Central Europe going again, it was necessary to have control of these essential means of transport. The third aspect of the question was largely political. Bolshevik ideas were impregnating the working classes throughout the area. Unless some means could be devised of abating the infection, the economic regeneration of Central and South-Eastern Europe would be difficult. Bela Kun's government was spending a great deal of money on sending Bolshevik missionaries to industrial centres outside Hungary. This re-acted on production. Moreover, the military power of the Hungarian Government was growing. A kind of nationalist passion was thereby put at the service of the revolutionary theories advocated by the Government. It was not likely that Bela Kun would abstain from spreading his theories outside the borders of Hungary by the help of this military force. The next probable victim after Czecho-Slovakia was Austria. . . . Bela Kun's party until the last three weeks had not represented methods of violence. Latterly, however, executions had increased, which indicated that opposition was growing in the country and that the methods of red terror were being resorted to. Previously, it might have been possible to treat the Hungarian revolutionary party with indulgence. Now that it showed a tendency to overflow its frontiers, it must be considered as an economic danger to the rest of Europe.[31]

On July 9, Lansing indicated his willingness to see a military destruction of the Kun regime in order to protect Allied prestige and to prevent the spread of Bolshevism.[32] On July 17, even General Bliss, despite his continuing opposition to the annexationist designs of Hungary's neighbors, indicated that he was not opposed to the "general purpose" of destroying Hungarian communism by force of arms.[33] By the end of July, American and Allied policy-makers seemed to have settled on a plan, put forward by Hoover, which sought to use a strict military and economic blockade of Hungary as a lever to bring about an overthrow of Bela Kun from within, in the interests of a social democratic regime. Hoover and the Allies hoped to avoid the necessity for a full-scale military advance on Hungary by the French and the neighboring states, lest the Hungarian people be rallied to their Bolshevik leaders.[34]

Nonetheless, despite American and Allied hopes in Paris for an orderly internal overthrow of the Hungarian communist regime, Roumanian troops successfully entered Budapest in early August 1919, carrying the banner of anti-Bolshevism. The Wilsonian response to this Roumanian advance was necessarily ambivalent. While the final destruction of Hungarian Bolshevism was welcome to Washington, Wilsonians were concerned that the Roumanians would both satisfy their annexationist designs at Hungary's expense and destroy any possibility of Hungarian democracy by establishing an autocratic regime in Budapest.[35] Having hoped that the Kun regime would be followed by an orderly and progressive social-democratic government in Hungary, Wilsonians were naturally upset over the Roumanian efforts to establish a purely rightist regime in Hungary under the Hapsburg Archduke Joseph.

Hoover had written to Wilson as early as March 28, 1919, only one week after Bela Kun's seizure of power, to warn against the

danger that counterrevolutionary military intervention in European revolutions could lead to the re-establishment of reactionary
classes in power.[36] It is not surprising then, to find that Hoover
was especially concerned over the possibility of a Hapsburg restoration in Budapest, and to find that Hoover also feared that any
movement back to the Right, after the overthrow of Hungarian
Bolshevism, would help to confirm the Leninist view of the Allies
as reactionaries and thereby aid the Bolsheviks elsewhere in Eastern Europe and in Russia.[37] Frank L. Polk, speaking for the
United States at a meeting of the Heads of Delegations on August 7, 1919, made it clear that he shared Hoover's viewpoint on
Hungarian political developments:

> Mr. Polk said that in the opinion of the American Delegation, inter-
> ference in the domestic affairs of Hungary would do more to en-
> courage Bolshevism than any event in the last six months. Lenin
> would point to the example of what had taken place on the downfall
> of the Soviet Government in Hungary, in order to scare Russia and
> preserve his own regime. The setting up of a reactionary Government
> in Hungary in place of a moderate Socialist Government was a very
> threatening feature in the situation.[38]

As always, Wilsonian ideologists sought a centrist position of progressive liberalism between pre-bourgeois imperialist autocracy on
the Right and revolutionary-socialism on the Left. Yet, as was
clear in Hungary and elsewhere in postwar Europe, a Wilsonian
policy which totally rejected socialist revolution in favor of an
orderly reform of the international *status quo* also ran the risk of
preserving and inadvertently aiding political elements of the traditional Right whose anti-Bolshevism was in no sense mixed with
liberal reformism.

In sum, then, the Wilson Administration's policy in response
to the Bolshevik Revolution in Hungary may be seen as containing all the elements of the general Wilsonian policy toward the
problems of nationalism and revolution in postwar Eastern Europe. Broadly speaking, the President's policy sought to contain

both autocratic imperialism and Bolshevism in the hopes of establishing, under American and League guidance, a stable liberal order among the new nations. Moreover, as we shall now see, also related in both method and intent to America's orientation toward Hungarian communism, were the Administration's less successful postwar efforts to return Russia to the lost liberalism of the March Revolution.

2. THE WILSONIAN RESPONSE TO BOLSHEVISM IN POSTWAR RUSSIA

The central aims of the Wilson Administration's postwar Russian policy were to end Bolshevik rule and to recreate a unified liberal-nationalist Russia. Wilsonians remained firmly opposed, during and after the Paris Peace Conference, to any recognition or acceptance of Bolshevik control over all or part of Russia. Yet the Administration's committed anti-Bolshevism did not prevent tensions from developing, at Paris and elsewhere, between Washington and the other anti-Bolshevik forces active in the immediate postwar period. In this connection, it is clear that White Russian and Allied anti-communists were often angered by the Wilsonian liberal scrupulousness which inhibited Washington from giving wholehearted support either to extensive armed intervention in Russia or to Russian anti-Bolshevik elements of a more reactionary type. Then too, Japanese military leaders occasionally followed policies in Siberia which, despite their strongly anti-Bolshevik character, hindered the realization of the Wilsonian goal of helping to establish, with Japanese co-operation, a non-communist and democratic Siberia as a possible stepping stone to the successful fostering of liberal nationalism throughout Russia. In essence, Wilsonian policy at Paris and in postwar Russia sought to oppose Bolshevism on the Left and Allied-sponsored reaction on the Right, in the interests of aiding the recovery of a true "Russia," which, for Wilsonians, was always seen as the unified liberal-nationalist Russia of the March Revolution.

Up to and immediately following the defeat of Germany, the Wilson Administration pursued an implicitly anti-Bolshevik policy both in the northern Russian area around Murmansk and Archangel and in the Siberian region to the east. In both these zones of American intervention, the President and his advisers hoped to buttress indigenous anti-German and anti-Bolshevik forces of liberal order through programs of political and economic assistance. After a brief analysis of the nature of Wilsonian anti-communism in both of these Russian areas, during late 1918 and early 1919, we shall be in a position to understand more completely the ideological dynamics of the Administration's approach to Russian Bolshevism at the Paris Peace Conference.

During the summer and fall of 1918, American policy in the northern zone of Allied intervention in Russia was largely determined by Ambassador David R. Francis, a man who despised Bolshevism and believed that it was the duty of America and the Allies to assist anti-German and anti-Bolshevik Russian elements, in the northern region and elsewhere, in their efforts to re-establish liberal-nationalist order in Russia.[39] With the approval of Lansing and Wilson, Francis sought to use American political power in the Archangel-Murmansk area, during late 1918, to support a liberal civilian regime against the local threats of Bolshevism on the Left and of British-supported Russian military reaction on the Right. After Francis's departure from the northern region, Consul Dewitt C. Poole vigorously supported the continued use of British and American troops to protect those anti-Bolshevik Russians who had rallied to the Allies against both Germany and Bolshevism, and had formed a liberal regime in the Murmansk-Archangel area.[40] Poole did not convince Wilson, however, since the President, for all his willingness indirectly to support non-Bolshevik Russian elements in the north and elsewhere, was not prepared to combat the Bolsheviks directly with American troops. Thus, Wilson and Bliss rejected projected British military programs in the north and withdrew all American troops from the northern zone by June 1919.[41] In Siberia, how-

ever, Washington found a more fertile field in 1919 for the application of the Wilsonian tactics of indirect anti-Bolshevism.
During late 1918 and early 1919, the Wilson Administration
sought to co-operate with Japan in an inter-Allied effort to buttress democratic and anti-Bolshevik political elements in Siberia.
It is true, of course, that the Wilson Administration caused some
concern among its Allies and White Russian elements because of
America's unwillingness in the fall of 1918 to advocate the retention of Czech troops on the Volga front, to support the concept
of an inter-Allied political directorate for Siberia, or officially to
recognize an anti-Bolshevik Russian government in Siberia.[42] Yet
it is also true that, in the fall of 1918, Secretary Lansing was at
great pains to assure the Allies and the anti-Bolshevik Russians
that American political neutrality in Siberia was a neutrality in
regards only to the conflicts among anti-communist Siberians for
political power, and that Washington's neutral stance in these
matters in no sense represented any lessening of the over-all
American commitment against a Bolshevik solution in the Russian East.[43] In this connection, Lansing cabled some significant
general instructions to Ernest L. Harris, the strongly anti-Bolshevik American Consul General at Irkutsk, on October 23, 1918:

The Government of the United States . . . desires you personally, if
practicable, and certainly through your subordinates and without
committing this Government, to keep in touch with the leaders of all
movements and report regularly the progress of their endeavors, the
development of the various efforts to establish law and order which
are being made, and the strength and character of support from the
Russian population which they attract. . . . For your guidance, the
Government of the United States is not prepared to recognize any
new government in Russia; but this must not be construed as a lack
of sympathy with the efforts of the Russian people to erect a government which is able to protect individual rights and to perform its international obligations. The Government of the United States has
stated that it desires where practicable to steady any efforts at self-
government or self-defense in which the Russians themselves may be
willing to accept assistance and you may authorize consular represen-

tatives wherever opportunity offers to give aid and advice to local governments in their efforts to improve local conditions. This, of course, applies only to local and municipal authorities and not to any others.[44]

Clearly, in Lansing's view, the Bolsheviks in no sense represented "a government which is able to protect individual rights and to perform its international obligations." [45]

In general terms, Washington hoped, in late 1918 and early 1919, to use judiciously its political, military, and economic power in a broadly conceived foreign aid program designed to support indigenous Siberian liberal-democratic elements in their spontaneous efforts to bring stability to a Siberia rescued from Bolshevik or German control by the Czech troops.[46] Of course, Japanese imperialism represented a major threat to the realization of this Wilsonian anti-communist program in Siberia. Indeed, during the months immediately following the Wilson Administration's decision to intervene in Siberia, tensions did exist between Washington and Tokyo as a result both of the independent aggressiveness of the Japanese military in Siberia and of the Japanese tendency to take sides in the conflicts among anti-Bolshevik Siberian elements.[47] Yet, the Administration's basic response to Japanese pressures remained an effort to orient toward more moderate elements in Tokyo in the interests of co-opting Japanese power into an American-inspired program to buttress a non-Bolshevik Siberian order. In this connection, the President and Lansing were especially pleased in January 1919 by the seeming success of Ambassador Roland S. Morris's long efforts to win Japanese approval of a plan calling for inter-Allied control and operation of the Siberian and Chinese Eastern Railroads in the interests of the development of non-Bolshevik commercial and political order in eastern Russia.[48] In other words, Washington hoped that Japan's absorption into a co-operative international plan of railroad management, under the American engineer John F. Stevens, would serve both the interrelated Wilsonian purposes of aiding "Russia" (that is, a liberal non-Bolshevik Russia) and of controlling the threat of Japanese imperialism to the Open Door and to the international stability of the Far East in general.

On January 31, 1919, Lansing sent a long cable from Paris to the Acting Secretary of State, Frank L. Polk, in which Lansing said that he and the President wanted Polk to go before a closed session of a Congressional Committee and defend the Administration's Siberian policy, then under fire from some Senate liberals:

. . . You will then develop the strategic importance both from the point of view of Russia and of the United States of the Trans-Siberian Railway as being a principal means of access to and from the Russian people and as affording an opportunity for economic aid to Siberia where the people are relatively friendly and resistant to Bolshevik influence and where there are large bodies of Czech-Slovaks who rely upon our support as well as large numbers of enemy prisoners of war whose activities must be watched and in all cases (if necessary) controlled. The potential value of this railroad as a means for developing American commerce particularly from the west coast of the United States to Russia might be mentioned. You may then narrate in considerable detail the difficulties which we have had with Japan with reference to this railway and in particular the action of Japan in practically seizing the Chinese Eastern Railway, thereby in effect controlling all intercourse to and from Russia via the Pacific. You might mention the number of troops sent by Japan for the purpose and point out that such number was far in excess of that contemplated by the arrangement under which troops of the Associated Governments were landed in Siberia. The nature of the activities of Japan including disposition of their troops and Japanese commercial activities should then be referred to (followed by) a statement of the efforts of the Government of the United States to restore the railroad to a condition where it would not be exclusively dominated by any one power. . . . The conversations of the President and Secretary of State with the Japanese Ambassador, the negotiations of Ambassador Morris under instructions from the Department and the economic pressure applied by the War Trade Board may be referred to. You should then describe the successful conclusion of these efforts of the United States as evidenced by the arrangements for administration of the railway by Stevens as a Russian employee and the withdrawal of substantial numbers of Japanese troops. We feel that these proceedings and their conclusion can properly be described as a very important and constructive achievement which may be of inestimable value to the people of Russia and to the United States as well as the world in general, provided they are followed through, thereby giving practical effect to the principle of the open door.[49]

In essence, the Administration hoped to persuade Japan to join in a co-operative anti-Bolshevik effort to assist in the establishment of a commercially and politically stable Siberia, open to the moral and economic expansion of American liberalism and safe from either Bolshevism or Japanese imperialism. Moreover, in this succinct summary, Lansing managed, in classic Wilsonian fashion, to fuse ideologically America's commercial and political self-interest with the broader idealistic goal of constructing a liberal-internationalist order opposed both to revolutionary-socialism and to traditional imperialism.

The essential point to be made in regard to American policies and long-range goals in Siberia, during late 1918 and early 1919, is that Wilsonian decision-makers had evidenced a commitment against Bolshevism and in favor of supporting some form of indigenous Russian democratic order. The Administration was clearly searching in postwar Siberian politics for some social-democratic and/or liberal middle ground between Bolshevism and reaction. In this connection, Lansing wrote to Wilson, shortly before the opening of the Paris Peace Conference, to argue that, in regard to the problem of Russia:

I believe a third point should be insisted upon, namely, that in distinguishing between representatives of order and any others, we do not at all oppose socialistic movements or governments as such but only where they are definitely undemocratic and unrepresentative of the majority will. Finally, it seems to me vital that we should not only offer but carry out immediate economic assistance wherever we can come in contact with elements desiring to maintain democratic principles. In other words, while we must set our faces sternly against anarchy and the class tyranny and terror of Bolshevism, we must at the same time cut to the root of the sore and relieve the misery and exhaustion which form such a fertile soil for its rapid growth.[50]

On a broad level, there is an obvious interrelationship between these liberal anti-communist views of Lansing in regard to Russia, and the Secretary's efforts at Paris, discussed in the previous chapter, to check German Bolshevism by advocacy of a proto-Marshall Plan reintegrationist orientation toward Germany.

More specifically, however, Lansing also made clear, in the same letter quoted above, that at Paris the United States ought, in his view, to look beyond the temporary partition of Russia to the interests of Russian liberal-nationalism as a whole:

First of all, I would suggest we inform the French, British, Italians and Japanese that we will use our best efforts to see to it that Russia's interests are safeguarded and that we propose to urge that Russian questions be considered as parts of a whole and not as separate problems resulting from what may prove, for the most part, temporary disintegration. . . . Russia played a part as a great nation in staving off the early victory of Germany and to that extent her people have earned a right to assistance and counsel in their present attempts to establish control over their own affairs. The second point I would suggest, would be a statement that only delegates from a Constituent Assembly or from some general government of Russia based on democratic principles will be admitted as signatories to the peace treaty; that in the interim approved representatives from existing elements of order in Russia will be welcomed to appear before the conference and will be heard on all questions relating to their affairs and where Russian interests may be concerned.[51]

Evidently, on the eve of the Paris Peace Conference, Lansing saw beyond the protection of such "existing elements of order" as those in Siberia and the northern region, to an eventual triumph of liberal democracy throughout Russia. In this hope for the reconstitution of Russian liberal-nationalism Lansing was also joined in late 1918 by members of the staff of the Inquiry, who were preparing American position papers on Russia for use at the coming Peace Conference.[52] With this background in mind, we can move on now to an analysis of the President's approach to the problem of Russian Bolshevism at the Paris Peace Conference.

It is possible, on one level of analysis, to see Wilson's Russian policy at Paris during early 1919 as an effort to move America and the Allies away from a program of armed intervention in Russia and toward some sort of a negotiated settlement with the Bolsheviks. Yet, it should also be noted that Wilson did not intend such negotiations with the Bolsheviks to result in either the recognition of the Bolshevik regime or the betrayal of White Russian trust in the United States and its Allies. Rather, the President seems to have hoped to bring about a reconciliation of all Russian political factions in a new liberal-nationalist synthesis into which the Bolsheviks would be absorbed. Moreover, despite his very real opposition to any large-scale policy of Allied armed intervention in Russia, Wilson did continue his own Administration's political and economic support of Siberian liberal anti-Bolshevism throughout the first months of 1919.

In the opening weeks of the Paris Peace Conference, the President, who had always been ambivalent about the purely military aspects of the Administration's Russian intervention, made clear his opposition to any efforts to expand or continue a policy of armed Allied intervention.[53] Wilson argued that a program emphasizing military support for isolated and possibly reactionary pockets of anti-Bolshevik resistance could only postpone their inevitable destruction, and could neither win the enthusiasm of Allied troops nor guarantee a "common effort to establish order throughout Russia." [54] Then too, the President became increasingly convinced that foreign military intervention in Russia tended actually to serve "the cause of Bolshevism," in that the Bolsheviks were enabled to win popular support by picturing the Allies as reactionary imperialists anxious to bring the old regime back to Russia.[55] In taking this general position on Russian affairs at Paris, Wilson was strongly supported by General Bliss, who was similarly opposed to any primary reliance on the use of military force against revolutionary-socialism in either Eastern Europe or Russia.[56]

Somehow the President had to find a liberal Russian policy

which would contain and ultimately dissolve Bolshevism, avoid the reactionary excesses of purely military anti-communism, and preserve the democratic achievements of the March Revolution. Indeed, the Wilsonian approach to Russian affairs, at the Paris Peace Conference and after, is really comprehensible only if one grasps at the outset the deep inner ambivalence of the President's anti-Bolshevik orientation. This ambivalence reflected the tension between, on the one hand, the desire to end the single-party rule of the Bolsheviks and to return Russia to the liberal order of the March Revolution, and, on the other, Wilson's fear that Allied or American intervention in Russia might encourage military reaction and thereby inadvertently assist the very Bolshevism against which it was directed. An awareness both of Wilson's ambivalence concerning intervention in Russia and of the President's implicit faith in the eventual triumph of liberal values in Russia is necessary to resolve the apparent paradox of the often ambiguous interaction in Wilson's postwar Russian policy between a tendency to attempt to aid Russian liberal anti-Bolshevism directly, and a seemingly contradictory tendency to advocate the termination of American and Allied involvement in Russia's internal affairs.[57]

During the early weeks at Paris, despite Wilson's opposition to increased Allied military intervention in Russia, the Administration remained, nonetheless, implicitly involved in a general inter-Allied effort to prevent the expansion of Russian Bolshevism beyond the base it had already secured in European Russia.[58] Indeed, it should be noted that in the period immediately following the Armistice the Allies agreed to leave some German forces in the Baltic States to act as a temporary barrier against the advancing Bolsheviks.[59] The efforts of America in Siberia may also be seen as having formed a component of this containment orientation. Yet we have noted as well that the President had serious reservations as to the ability of a purely military containment policy either to check Bolshevism or to bring permanent liberal stability to Russia. It is not surprising, then, that in early 1919 at

Paris Wilson began to consider the possibility of reaching a liberal-nationalist settlement in Russia through negotiations leading to the possible inclusion of the Bolsheviks in a final reconciliation of all the competing Russian political factions and governments.

At the beginning of January 1919, Wilson authorized a mission by William H. Buckler to Stockholm, where Buckler was to meet with the Bolshevik representative Maxim Litvinov. Apparently Buckler was to attempt to discover the exact nature of the foreign and domestic goals of the Bolshevik regime.[60] He reported a generally "conciliatory attitude" on the part of the Bolsheviks, reflected by Litvinov's general willingness to negotiate an armistice with the Allies, to be based on Soviet promises of greater moderation in their domestic and foreign policies. It should be noted, however, that all of Litvinov's offers concerning political amnesty, economic concessions, and a curbing of Bolshevik revolutionary propaganda abroad were based on one crucial implicit assumption: the assumption that the Allies were prepared to recognize the existing Bolshevik regime.[61] This assumption represented a misreading of Wilson's intentions.[62]

It is probable that Litvinov's generally moderate tone was an important factor in leading the President, in January 1919, to support the plan proposed by Lloyd George to bring representatives of all the competing Russian political factions, including the Bolsheviks, together on Prinkipo Island in the Sea of Mamara for a truce conference designed to seek ways to end the Russian Civil War.[63] Yet, while it is clear that Wilson's support for the idea of a Prinkipo Conference reflected his general desire to find an early and peaceful solution to the Russian problem through negotiations with the Bolsheviks, the evidence also suggests that the President intended such a possible conference to lead toward a liberal-nationalist Russian settlement, rather than toward any Allied acceptance or recognition of the existing Bolshevik regime in European Russia.

At a meeting of the Council of Ten on January 16, 1919, Wilson defended Lloyd George after the British leader had presented his argument in favor of a policy of seeking to arrange an all-Russian political conference, a program opposed to the two other possible alternative Allied Russian policies consisting either of attacking or of simply containing Lenin's regime. In the first part of his statement, the President spoke of the over-all necessity to meet the worldwide revolutionary-socialist problem by liberal-reformist measures, designed to unite capital and labor in the task of curing genuine popular grievances.[64] The President then went on to apply his liberal anti-Bolshevik approach to the specific problem of postwar Russia:

President Wilson stated that he would not be surprised to find that the reason why British and United States troops would not be ready to enter Russia to fight the Bolsheviki was explained by the fact that the troops were not at all sure that if they put down Bolshevism they would not bring about a re-establishment of the ancient order. . . . President Wilson believed that those present would be playing against the principle of free spirit of the world if they did not give Russia a chance to find herself along the lines of utter freedom. He concurred with Mr. Lloyd George's view and supported his recommendations. . . . There was one point which he thought particularly worthy of notice, and that was the report that the strength of the Bolshevik leaders lay in the argument that if they were not supported by the people of Russia, there would be foreign intervention, and the Bolsheviki were the only thing that stood between the Russians and foreign military control. It might well be that if the Bolsheviki were assured that they were safe from foreign aggression, they might lose support of their own movement. President Wilson further stated that he understood that the danger of destruction of all hope in the Baltic provinces was immediate, and that it should be made very clear if the British proposal were adopted, that the Bolsheviki would have to withdraw entirely from Lithuania and Poland. If they would agree to this to refrain from reprisals and outrages, he, for his part, would be prepared to receive representatives from as many groups and centers of action, as chose to come, and endeavor to assist them to reach a solution of their problem. He thought that the British proposal contained the only suggestions that led anywhere. It might lead nowhere. But this could at least be found out.[65]

First of all, it is important to note that Wilson's argument for an all-Russian conference approach was presented in the context of the over-all need to contain the expansion of Russian Bolshevism. Beyond mere containment, however, the President's statement also revealed his hope that Lloyd George's concept of bringing all Russian factions, including the Bolsheviks, together for truce negotiations, would weaken the Bolshevik regime itself, by denying to Lenin the popular role of revolutionary-nationalist which the Bolshevik leader had been able to assume in the face of foreign intervention. Finally, his statement also makes clear that Wilson implicitly assumed that the Bolshevik movement would be undercut if the Allies could encourage a situation of peace and orderly political freedom in Russia.

A few days later, while defending the Prinkipo idea against the criticisms of some of the more traditional Allied statesmen, Wilson was even more explicit in regard to his liberal anti-Bolshevik desire to use the Prinkipo Conference as a means to weaken Bolshevism in Russia by removing fear of Allied sponsored reaction as a lever which Lenin could continue to use to win Russian popular support:

President Wilson ventured to think that what was back of Baron Sonnino's suggestion was an antipathy to the Bolsheviki, and a natural repulsion against their acts. He would observe, however, that by opposing the Bolsheviki by armies, the cause of the Bolsheviki was being served by the Allies. They were being given a case. They could say to their followers that the imperialistic and capitalistic governments were desirous of destroying Russia. They would represent the Allies as the advocates and supporters of reaction. If the Allies could make it appear that this was not true, most of the moral influence of the Bolsheviki would break down, as their case would be gone. They could no longer allege that it was the purpose of the Allies and the United States to enslave the Russian people and to take charge of their affairs. It was therefore desirable that the Allies show that they are ready to hear the representatives of any organized group in Russia, provided they are willing and ready to come to one place, to put all their cards on the table, and see if they could not come to an understanding. He ventured to think that such a line of action, if adopted, would bring about more reaction against the cause of the Bolsheviki than anything else the Allies could do.[66]

In large terms, the President's conception of the Prinkipo Conference may be seen as a specific example of Wilson's more general tendency to search always in international politics for an American-inspired liberal alternative to both reaction on the Right and revolutionary-socialism on the Left.

The proclamation which the Allies issued on January 22, 1919, inviting all Russian political factions to a conference on Prinkipo Island, was based on a draft written by Wilson.[67] The final text read, in part, as follows:

The single object the representatives of the associated Powers have had in mind in their discussions of the course they should pursue with regard to Russia has been to help the Russian people, not to hinder them, or to interfere in any manner with their right to settle their own affairs in their own way. They regard the Russian people as their friends not their enemies, and are willing to help them in any way they are willing to be helped. It is clear to them that the troubles and distresses of the Russian people will steadily increase, hunger and privation of every kind become more and more acute . . . unless order is restored, and normal conditions of labour, trade and transportation once more created, and they are seeking some way in which to assist the Russian people to establish order. They recognize the absolute right of the Russian people to direct their own affairs without dictation or direction of any kind from outside. They do not wish to exploit or make use of Russia in any way. They recognize the revolution without reservation, and will in no way, and in no circumstances, aid or give countenance to any attempt at counter-revolution. It is not their wish or purpose to favour or assist any one of those organized groups now contending for the leadership and guidance of Russia as against the others. Their sole and sincere purpose is to do what they can to bring Russia peace and an opportunity to find her way out of her present troubles.[68]

When Wilson affirmed Allied recognition of "the revolution without reservation," and when he denied any Allied desire to abet a "counterrevolution," what did he mean? All the evidence concerning the theory and practice of Wilsonian diplomacy in Russia suggests that the President narrowly defined counterrevolution to mean the restoration of pre-1917 military reaction, a possible development opposed by the Administration, and that Wilson did not define the replacement of Lenin's Bolshevik rule by Russian liberal-nationalism, a possible development favored by the Administration, as counterrevolutionary. Since Wilson assumed that the Russian people were inherently liberal, it is perhaps not unfair to suggest that when he used the phrase "Russian Revolution," the President implicitly meant the liberal democracy of the March Revolution, and not the radical revolutionary-socialism of the anti-liberal November Revolution. Moreover, Wilson's references, in the proclamation quoted above, to "the Russian people," to "all sections of the Russian people," and to the general Allied desire to bring normal order back to Russia through a reconciliation of all the Russian political factions, clearly all conveyed an implicit rejection of any continued one-party dominance by the Bolsheviks.[69] In broad terms, it could be said that Wilson's Prinkipo Proclamation was analogous to his Fourteen Points Address of the previous year, in which the President had, in effect, also called upon the Bolsheviks and their supporters to trust the Allies and to enter into a new pluralistic Russian liberal-nationalist coalition.

Wilsonians were prepared to view the Bolsheviks either as a criminal force to be excluded from the political process, or as one Russian political faction among many to be absorbed into a pluralistic and competitive liberal order. Wilsonians were not, however, prepared to accept a situation in which the Bolsheviks would abolish liberalism and maintain single-party rule. In this connection, it is probable that any Bolshevik efforts to win recognition for their regime at Prinkipo would have encountered the firm opposition at Paris of such members of the Administration as Lansing, Hoover, and the experts on the staff of the Russian Section of the American Peace Commission, all of whom were strongly anti-Bolshevik and anxious to see Russia united under a liberal-democratic regime.[70] Significantly, on February 8, 1919, Lansing cabled D. C. Poole, the strongly anti-Bolshevik American Consul in Archangel, to reassure him that it was not the intention of the American Government in arranging the Prinkipo Conference "to barter in matters of principle with the Bolshevik Government." [71] Moreover, even the suggestion of any form of reconciliation with the Bolsheviks was anathema to the anti-Bolshevik Russian groups and officials who retained close contact with American diplomatic personnel in Siberia, Washington, and Paris. Indeed, despite all American efforts to convince them that the Prinkipo plan was not intended to be pro-Bolshevik, the White Russians, with French support, ultimately rejected the whole notion of the conference out of a fear that Prinkipo might appear to give added dignity and recognition to the Bolsheviks.[72]

For their part, the Bolsheviks appeared to assume that the Prinkipo proposal represented an Allied effort to bargain with the existing Soviet regime for a military truce and a political *modus vivendi*.[73] Assuming that the Allies meant to leave Bolshevik power essentially intact, the Soviet leaders offered the Entente wide-ranging concessions of a political and economic nature, while still continuing, for bargaining purposes, to emphasize the growing military success of the Red Army.[74] In the context of our analysis here, it is not crucial to decide whether or not the proposed Bolshevik concessions regarding a military truce, a political amnesty, and a curbing of Soviet revolutionary propaganda abroad were completely sincere. The central point to note is the fact that the Bolsheviks mistakenly assumed that the Prinkipo proposal had reflected a general Allied willingness to extend *de facto* recognition to the Soviet regime in return for economic concessions and promises of future Bolshevik political moderation.[75]

It is true that a policy of postwar reconciliation with the existing Soviet regime was strongly advocated by such American Left-liberals as Raymond Robins, Lincoln Colcord, and Lincoln Steffens. These and other American Left-liberals, positioned around *The Nation* and *The New Republic,* believed that the best way to end what they saw as the radical excesses of revolutionary-socialism in Russia was for the Allies to seek a sympathetic understanding with the more moderate and orderly Bolshevik leaders through a policy of recognition and aid.[76] Within the American Peace Commission at Paris, the essentials of the Left-liberal position on Russia were supported by two young diplomats, William H. Buckler and William C. Bullitt.[77] Significantly, Buckler had recommended the acceptance of the moderate Soviet peace proposals offered to him by Litvinov in Stockholm, arguing that the Allies would thereby be "obviating conquest and policing and reviving normal conditions as a disinfectant against Bolshevism." [78] For Buckler and Bullitt, extremist Bolshevism was to be checked by accepting more moderate Bolshevism.

Buckler, Bullitt, and other American Left-liberals saw a moderated and liberalized Soviet regime as a vehicle through which the positive reformist qualities of the Russian Revolution could be preserved. It does not seem, however, that the President really shared this viewpoint. It is true that in early 1919 Wilson was willing to seek an end to Russian revolutionary extremism through negotiation rather than through the use of armed force. Yet the evidence suggests that Wilson was not prepared to extend *de facto* recognition to even a more moderate Soviet regime in European Russia as the final product of the Russian Revolution. Instead, the President appears to have envisioned the proposed Prinkipo Conference as an opportunity to find a liberal and pluralistic Russian settlement acceptable to all Russian political factions. The fact that Wilson's goal was a political impossibility should not obscure the fact that, unlike the Left-liberals, Wilson did not see Prinkipo as the occasion merely for a Soviet-Allied *rapprochement.* Ultimately, this subtle but real difference which existed between the President and the Left-liberals, concerning the essential purpose of postwar negotiations with the Bolsheviks, was perhaps most fully revealed in the issues raised by the Bullitt mission to Russia.

By February 15, 1919, Wilson had left Paris for a brief return to the United States, and the Prinkipo proposal had been effectively aborted by White Russian opposition. At some point within the next few days, William C. Bullitt received instructions from Lansing and House to proceed to Russia and to interview the Soviet authorities.[79] In his Diary entry for February 16, 1919, Lansing, who felt only contempt for the Bolsheviks, referred half-humorously to a conversation "with House about sending Bullitt to Russia to cure him of Bolshevism." [80] Moreover, while terming Bullitt's mission "entirely unofficial and for information purposes solely," Lansing also agreed with Acting Secretary of State Frank L. Polk that care had to be taken lest Bullitt's activities redound to the propaganda advantage of the Bolsheviks.[81] At no point did Lansing indicate any awareness that Bullitt might be taking British or American peace terms to the Soviet leaders.

For his part, however, Bullitt was convinced that he had been officially sanctioned to make peace between the Allies and the Soviet regime. Apparently, in the days immediately following Wilson's departure on February 15, 1919, Bullitt succeeded in obtaining both from Philip Kerr, Lloyd George's Secretary, and from Colonel House, supposedly authoritative British and American peace proposals to take to the Bolsheviks.[82] The substance of these Kerr-House terms suited the Left-liberal Bullitt perfectly, since these terms (which essentially called for a stationary armistice in the civil war, a withdrawal of foreign troops from Russia, an establishment of trade relations between the Soviets and the Allies, and a pledge of political moderation in their foreign and domestic policies by the Soviet authorities in European Russia) were closely parallel to the peace proposals which had already been put forward by the Bolsheviks themselves during early 1919, and were terms which implicitly conveyed an Allied willingness to extend *de facto* recognition to a moderate Soviet regime in European Russia.[83] In Bullitt's own words, "the plan was to make a proposal to the Soviet Government which would certainly be accepted." [84]

In this connection, it seems evident that Bullitt and House were prepared to ignore White Russian opposition to any armistice in the civil war which extended *de facto* recognition to Bolshevik control over European Russia. Indeed, since it had been the anti-Bolshevik Russians and not the Bolsheviks who had rejected the original Prinkipo proposal, it made little sense to send Bullitt to Moscow with another Prinkipo type of proposal unless the White Russians were to be shunted aside in the process of an Allied-Soviet *rapprochement* aimed at getting the Bolsheviks to accept socialism in part of one country. Such an Allied-Soviet *rapprochement* at the expense of anti-Bolshevik hopes in European Russia seems to have been the implicit intention of Bullitt and House, but not, as we shall shortly see, of Wilson. Then too, it is highly probable that like the Soviets, but unlike the President, Bullitt and House had interpreted the first Prinkipo proposal as an indication of American readiness to recognize the Soviet regime. In any case, it is little wonder that the Bolshevik leaders, who, with the exception of Trotsky, were anxious to gain the breathing space which would result from an armistice with the Allies, leaving the Soviets in control of most of European Russia, were quick to accept the Kerr-House proposals proffered by Bullitt, with only minor changes.[85]

Several points must be suggested at this juncture, however, in order to correct Bullitt's partly self-created image of America's Russian policy. First, as has been mentioned above, the strongly anti-Bolshevik Lansing was probably unaware of the existence of the extremely liberal House-Kerr peace terms which Bullitt planned to submit to the Bolsheviks. Indeed, when Bullitt cabled the Soviet peace terms to Paris on March 16, 1919, House, who had in effect already approved the terms before Bullitt's departure, spoke in favor of the Bolshevik proposals. Lansing, however, joined Henry White and David H. Miller in opposition.[86] Secondly, Wilson, who had been on his way back to America from Paris when the Bullitt mission took its final form, had absolutely no knowledge of the Kerr peace proposals taken by Bullitt to

Russia.[87] Then too, since the "American" peace proposals which originated with Colonel House were elicited from House verbally by Bullitt, and since there is no available record showing that House informed Wilson of the details of this conversation with Bullitt, it seems fair to assume that the President was also in the dark concerning House's half of the House-Kerr terms.[88] Moreover, while it is true that Wilson had told the Council of Ten on February 14, 1919, the day before his departure from Paris, of his willingness "that informal American representatives should meet representatives of the Bolsheviks," it is also true that the President made plain on the same day that he sought clear information for a Russian settlement, but "not a rapprochement with the Bolsheviks." [89] Taken all in all, the evidence suggests that House and Bullitt were probably alone among the American Peace Commissioners in seeking to co-operate with the British in finding a *rapprochement* with the Soviets during February–March, 1919, on the basis of a *de facto* recognition of Lenin's regime in European Russia.[90]

This general interpretation is borne out by the events which followed upon Bullitt's return to Paris from Russia in late March 1919. Bullitt burst back onto the Paris scene, full of Left-liberal enthusiasm for what he saw as a successful and increasingly moderate Soviet regime, and convinced that the Allies should immediately accept the liberal Soviet peace terms which he conveyed from Lenin.[91] Indeed, since Lenin's terms were substantially the same as the House-Kerr proposals which Bullitt had taken to Russia, Bullitt was confident that the Allies would quickly accept them. Yet, had Bullitt stopped to reflect more dispassionately on the real nature of his mission, it might have given him pause in his enthusiasm to realize that all he had really done was to take back to the Soviets, in the form of the House-Kerr proposals, the same armistice terms which the Bolsheviks themselves had already offered to the Allies without success earlier in 1919, and then to return to Paris with a fresh Soviet ratification of their old peace terms.

In any event, Bullitt came back to Paris during the last week in March 1919, almost directly following Bela Kun's Bolshevik Revolution in Hungary, to discover that Allied decision-makers did not share his enthusiasm for the latest version of the postwar Soviet peace offers. Official French opinion was outraged by the Bullitt proposals.[92] Lloyd George, when confronted by a sharp attack from the British Right, quickly moved away from his earlier support for Bullitt's orientation toward the Bolsheviks.[93] Then too, among the personnel of the State Department and the American Peace Commission, Bullitt's Left-liberal views on Bolshevism and the Soviet armistice terms found an ambiguous reception in which some grudging support was mixed with a general skepticism.[94] Indeed, in late March 1919, only Colonel House showed any strong desire to accept Bullitt's vision of an official truce with the *de facto* Soviet Government.[95] In his Diary for March 26, 1919, House recorded some of the arguments he had used to influence Orlando:

If we did not make terms with them, [i.e., the Soviet regime] it was certain that as soon as we made peace with Germany, Russia and Germany would link up together, thereby realizing my prophecy that, sooner or later, everything east of the Rhine would be arrayed against the Western Powers. If we did come to terms, the general Russian dislike for Germany would give the Entente a dominating influence in Russia. It seemed to me footless to say we preferred some other plan. As far as I could see, there was no other. It was either to reckon with the De facto Government, or remain in a state of war, or semi-war. We cannot intervene, everyone admits that, because we cannot get troops to go into Russia and fight. I suggested that we proceed to draw up a treaty with Russia, practically upon our own terms, provided they were just, and send this treaty to Moscow for their signatures, promising to sign it ourselves in the event it was agreed upon there. I did not think we should make another Prinkipo proposal or try to have a meeting in some neutral country.[96]

Both this statement and House's approach to the Bullitt mission make clear that the Colonel hoped to extend *de facto* recognition to the Soviet regime in the context of an over-all effort to absorb the Soviets into an orderly Allied-dominated European settlement. House's rejection of another Prinkipo conference further suggests that his aim was to make peace in Russia, without consulting the anti-Bolshevik Russians, by means of a direct *rapprochement* with the Bolsheviks. In this regard, House's sophisticated diplomacy may be contrasted with the less realistic, but more ideologically principled, efforts of Wilson to create a Russian settlement at Prinkipo by bringing all the competing Russian political factions, including both the Bolsheviks and their opponents, together for rational truce discussions.

Yet, as House came to realize the prevailing Wilsonian hostility toward any official *rapprochement* with the Bolshevik regime, he slowly shifted his support from Bullitt's proposal to a new plan designed to pacify Russia with food relief.[97] This Russian food relief program (the Hoover-Nansen Plan) was developed in the American Peace Commission during the weeks immediately following Bullitt's return to Paris, and it represented an uneasy compromise between the Bullitt-House approach to Russia and the more firmly anti-Bolshevik position of such other Wilsonians as D. H. Miller and Herbert Hoover.[98] Apparently, as the plan developed, food relief was to be used as a lever to bring about both a truce in the Russian Civil War and an Allied presence on Russia's rails, without the *de facto* recognition of the Soviet regime which had been implicit in Bullitt's proposals.[99] In regard to the whole issue of the tendency of most Americans at Paris to oppose Bullitt's proposals, and to support instead a food relief program which did not involve any real legitimization of Bolshevik rule, the following letter from Joseph Grew, Secretary-General of the American Peace Commission, to William Phillips, in the State Department, is of special interest:

As regards the Russian matter, I had the Bullitt reports prepared to cable to the Department but the Secretary stopped them and they were only sent considerably later. The Commission and the personnel thereof has been considerably torn with dissension on this subject. I am personally in entire accord with the food proposition: Bolshevism thrives on hunger and armed opposition; if you fight it with arms it will grow; if you fight it with food it will die a natural death.[100]

In a broad sense, America's projected food relief program in Russia may be seen as another specific example of the more general proto-Marshall Plan effort of Wilsonians to check the expansion of revolutionary-socialism in postwar Europe with food and economic aid instead of arms.

It is difficult to find evidence defining the exact role played by the President in the formation of America's Russian policy during late March and early April of 1919. It does seem clear, however, that Wilson was not favorably impressed by the Bolshevik peace proposals which Bullitt had brought back from Russia.[101] At first glance this may appear puzzling, since Lenin's proposals included the offer of a new Prinkipo conference. The crucial point, however, is that Lenin was offering to attend a new Prinkipo conference only on the basis of a prearranged agenda which implicitly conferred *de facto* Allied recognition upon the control which the Soviet regime exercised over most of European Russia.[102] It goes without saying, of course, that such a proposal was unacceptable to almost all anti-Bolshevik Russians.[103] Moreover, the Bolshevik terms could hardly have been fully acceptable to Wilson, since, as we have seen, the President had apparently conceived of the Prinkipo conference as a possible forum for the rational discussion of differences by all the competing Russian political factions in the interests of creating a liberal and pluralistic settlement for Russia. In short, the Bullitt mission was probably doomed to fail from its inception, because both Bullitt and House had structured the mission around the mistaken assumption that Wilson's intention was to use a Prinkipo conference as a way to recognize a moderate Bolshevik regime in European Russia. Bullitt and House wrongly assumed that Wilson was as indifferent to the hopes of anti-Soviet Russians for a reunified non-Bolshevik Russia as they were themselves.

In retrospect, it is apparent that House was in favor of a policy which would have sought to contain Russian Bolshevism by extending *de facto* recognition to the authority of the Soviet regime over much of European Russia, in return for Bolshevik promises not to advance on Siberia, Poland, and the Baltic States.[104] In other words, House hoped to pacify Russia by a program of partition, a position he formulated as early as the fall of 1918:

I am not in agreement with the President as to leaving Russia intact. She is too big and too homogeneous for the safety of the world. I would like to see Siberia a separate republic, and European Russia divided into three parts. The British Empire does not present the same menace to the world as would the Russian Empire under a monarchy.[105]

At Paris, House, retaining a willingness to see Russia partitioned, moved toward the view that Russian Bolshevism could best be tamed and contained by changing the Bolshevik regime itself from an ideologically and militarily expansionist center of revolutionary-socialism into a moderate-socialist regime in European Russia, content with socialism in a part of one country, and prepared to be co-opted into an orderly community of nation states ruled by the norms laid down at Paris. Yet, while some British policy-makers may have been in favor of plans to partition postwar Russia, House could not win support for a partition of Russia in a Wilson Administration which would, throughout 1919 and 1920, remain essentially loyal to the President's vision of a Russia ultimately reunified under the control of its liberal-nationalists.[106] It is true, of course, that Lansing and Wilson were both concerned with the containment of postwar Bolshevik expansion within Russia. It must be stressed, however, that, unlike House, Lansing and Wilson did not seek to freeze this containment process into a partition of Russia based on the *de facto* recognition of Soviet control in European Russia.[107] It is probable that Wilson preferred Hoover's plan for Russian food relief over Bullitt's proposals, because the food relief program seemed to promise an humanitarian way to bring both peace and aid to Russia, and to contain Bolshevism, without extending any official recognition to the Soviet regime in European Russia.[108] It cannot be overemphasized that, regardless of his willingness to negotiate with the Bolsheviks in the immediate postwar period, the President was never prepared to renounce completely his hopes for a democratic Russia, reunited under progressive bourgeois nationalism, into whose liberal and pluralistic politics Bolshevism could successfully be integrated.

At the innermost heart of Wilson's Russian policy there lay the implicit desire to find a way, preferably through peaceful negotiations, to help Russia regain the lost liberal-nationalist order of the March Revolution. The realization of such a liberal anti-Bolshevik desire was often threatened, however, both by advocates of armed foreign intervention, such as Winston Churchill and Marshall Foch, and by advocates of an immediate *rapprochement* with the existing Bolshevik regime in European Russia, such as William Bullitt and Colonel House. Nonetheless, during the first months of 1919, the President attempted to maintain his centrist vision of an eventual liberal-nationalist Russian settlement against such threats from the Right and the Left at the Paris Peace Conference. The following chapter will conclude the analysis of postwar Wilsonian Russian policy by considering the attitude of the Wilson Administration, during the remainder of 1919, toward the possibility of aiding Russian liberal-nationalism through assistance to the anti-Bolshevik regime of Admiral Kolchak in Siberia.

VII

Peace and Revolution, IV: The Wilsonian
Search for Postwar Liberal Order in
Siberia and the Underdeveloped World

Throughout 1919, the Wilson Administration sought to co-
operate with the Japanese in the creation of a viable program of
economic and logistical aid designed to support and to liberalize
the anti-Bolshevik regime of Admiral Kolchak in Siberia. In one
sense, this Siberian aid program may be seen as a last Wilsonian
effort to keep alive the possibility of Russia's return to liberal-
nationalism. In even broader terms, however, it is also possible to
see America's attempted collaboration with Japan in an implicitly
anti-Soviet Siberian policy as having been related to the over-all
postwar Wilsonian endeavor to sublimate Japan's imperialist energies by absorbing the Japanese into an American-inspired order
of liberal-capitalist harmony among the great powers interested in
Asian commercial developments. Moreover, just as Wilsonians
sought to co-opt Japan into a new Far Eastern order, free from
traditional imperialism and violent revolution, and open to the
moral and material expansion of American liberalism, so too, in a
related fashion, the President's colonial mandate program evolved
at Paris into a non-revolutionary and reforming effort to absorb
all the other imperial powers into an American-inspired system
for more peaceful and progressive colonial development under the
League of Nations. Ultimately, for Wilsonians, traditional imperialism was to be curbed, and the rights of backward peoples were
to be protected, by means of the slow processes of liberal world
reform in a universal League of Nations, and not by means either
of socialist or of nationalist revolution.

1. THE WILSON ADMINISTRATION AND THE KOLCHAK REGIME IN
SIBERIA

It could be argued that, during the first half of 1919, the Wilson
Administration was highly ambivalent in its orientation toward
the anti-Bolshevik military regime of Admiral Kolchak in Siberia.
While it is true that Wilsonian liberal scrupulousness often angered Kolchak and his supporters, it is also true that the over-all
intent of America's actions in Siberia during 1919 was to give material and moral support to Kolchak's anti-communist program.
Indeed, when confronted by what appeared to be a choice between Kolchak and Lenin, it is clear that almost all Wilsonians,
whatever their liberal doubts, opted for a hopefully liberalized
version of White Russian rule.

The attitude of General William S. Graves, commander of
America's forces in Siberia, did much to exacerbate whatever tensions were latent in the postwar relationship between Washington and the Kolchak regime in Omsk. Graves possessed a liberal
distrust of all types of military reaction in Russia, and he was especially angered by what he saw as a general effort on the part of
the Kolchak regime to repress democratic and Left-of-Center Siberian political elements. Alienated by all forms of White Russian authoritarianism in Siberia, and suspicious of the Kolchak
regime's tendency to label all its opponents as "Bolsheviks,"
Graves was reluctant to use American troops to suppress anti-
Kolchak activity.[1] Needless to say, General Graves's declared policy of strict neutrality in Siberian internal politics, and his refusal
to commit his American forces to overtly anti-Bolshevik operations, earned for Graves both the animosity of the Kolchak authorities at Omsk and that of Kolchak's supporters among the
Allied representatives in Siberia.[2]

Yet, within the Wilson Administration, General Graves's approach to Siberian politics was more than counterbalanced by the
influence of the State Department, where firm anti-Bolshevism

and sympathy for Kolchak were the prevailing sentiments on all levels.[3] Moreover, the American Consul General at Omsk, Ernest L. Harris, was an especially committed anti-communist, whose own strong support for the Kolchak government was based on a conviction that the long-term interests of Russian liberal-nationalism could best be served through a temporary military regime dedicated to maintaining order and to preventing "untrustworthy" Left-of-Center civilian politicians from permitting Siberia to drift back into Bolshevism.[4] Not surprisingly then, there developed a good deal of tension, in the postwar period, between General Graves and the State Department as a result of Graves's unwillingness or inability to pursue the sorts of subtle anti-Bolshevik policies through which the State Department hoped to support a non-communist liberal order in Siberia.[5]

Ultimately, however, the President compromised the differences between General Graves and the State Department, and, during the first half of 1919, the Wilson Administration pursued an implicitly pro-Kolchak policy in Siberia which completely satisfied neither the zealous anti-Bolsheviks in the State Department nor the more politically neutral General Graves. In essence, this American policy sought to assist Kolchak, not by giving him direct military support against the Soviets at the front, but rather by aiding the White Siberians, behind the lines, both through extending economic aid to Siberia and through guarding and maintaining the Trans-Siberian and Chinese Eastern Railroads upon which the Kolchak regime was completely dependent for all its supplies.[6] General Graves, for his part, was angered by the fact that the American troops guarding Siberia's rails were actually assisting the White Russians, who controlled all the traffic and the towns on the Trans-Siberian.[7] Moreover, pro-Kolchak Wilsonians also continued their often unsuccessful postwar efforts to absorb Japan into a carefully limited co-operative international plan for the policing of Siberia's railroad lines, in the hope that such co-operation with moderate Japanese statesmen would enable Washington to check the persistent tendency of the Japanese military to intervene directly in Siberian politics and to ally with disruptive anti-Bolshevik and anti-Kolchak Cossack elements under Semenov and Kalmikov.[8] Thus, while it is true that the Administration neither officially recognized the Kolchak regime nor sent American troops into combat alongside the White Siberians, it is also true that the Administration's continuing efforts to co-opt Japan into an orderly program of economic and transportation assistance behind White Siberian lines were meant implicitly to buttress Kolchak's anti-Bolshevik government.

During May 1919 the apparently triumphant westward advance of Kolchak's forces brought the problems of postwar Siberian politics before the Paris Peace Conference itself, and provided the occasion for Wilson to reveal clearly his basic desire for a non-Bolshevik liberal democratic settlement in Russia. With Kolchak's troops in the midst of a seemingly successful spring offensive against the Soviets, the President, and such liberal anti-Bolsheviks as Alexander Kerensky, all expressed concern that the supposedly imminent defeat of the Bolsheviks by the White Russian armies might lead to a reinstitution of landed aristocracy and military reaction in Russia instead of to a re-establishment of the liberal democratic order of the March Revolution.[9] In this connection, the instructions given by President Wilson in mid-May 1919 to Roland S. Morris, the American Ambassador in Japan, conveyed the essence of the President's ambivalent liberal response to Kolchak's authoritarian anti-communism:

The President has cabled me to instruct you to proceed to Vladivostok and after learning all you care to know from Graves to proceed westward, if you can with safety, to the headquarters of the Kolchak Government for the following purposes: To obtain from that Government, official and definite assurances as to the objects that they have in view with regard to the future Governmental regime in Russia and the methods by which they mean to set a new regime up, asking particular assurances with regard to the reform in land tenure, and the extension and security of the suffrage, and the choice and projected action of a constituent assembly, and also learn as definitely as possible the influences that Kolchak is under. The President states his ob-

ject is to satisfy himself as to whether the Kolchak Government de-
serves the recognition, or at least the countenance, if not the support,
of our Government. . . . President directs me to request that you
particularly inquire as to the kind of men and influences surrounding
Kolchak and ask whether in your opinion Kolchak is strong enough
and liberal enough to control them in the right direction.[10]

In Council of Four meetings at Paris, Wilson successfully insisted
that Allied pressure be brought to bear on Kolchak to gain his
public acceptance of liberal-democratic goals for Russia. Indeed,
in June 1919, the President joined the Allies in what amounted to
a pledge of continued material assistance to Kolchak's regime, but
only after the White Russian Admiral had officially promised
that, after the military defeat of the Soviets, his government
would use the electoral process to create a self-governing liberal-
nationalist Russia.[11] In the final analysis, however, it would be
fair to say that, since military reverses quickly denied Kolchak any
opportunity he might have had actually to lead the Russian state,
Wilson's insistence upon Kolchak's liberal pledges remains historically significant primarily as evidence of the President's continuing desire to help recreate a liberal Russia safe both from Bolshevism on the Left and from reaction on the Right.

In any event, Wilson apparently considered that his public
avowal of support for Kolchak in June 1919 had obligated the
United States neither to the formal recognition of the Omsk regime nor to the commitment of American troops to service on
the main Siberian fighting front. In actual practice, the President
and his advisers moved, during the late spring and early summer
of 1919, simply to make more explicit and financially secure the
implicitly anti-Bolshevik American program of economic and railroad assistance to the White Siberians, which the Administration
had been developing in Siberia since autumn 1918.[12] It was further understood in Washington and Paris that Ambassador R. S.
Morris would proceed on his summer mission to Omsk in order
to investigate the political potential of the Kolchak regime.[13]

Perhaps the clearest general expression of the methods and

aims of Wilsonian policy in Siberia during the summer of 1919 was provided by a letter on the Siberian Intervention sent by the President to the Senate on July 22, 1919.[14] Wilson began by stating succinctly his conception of the original purposes behind America's intervention in Siberia:

This measure was taken in conjunction with Japan and in concert of purpose with the other Allied powers, first of all to save the Czecho-Slovak armies, which were threatened with destruction by hostile armies apparently organized by and often largely composed of enemy prisoners of war. The second purpose in view was to steady any efforts of the Russians at self-defense, or the establishment of law and order in which they might be willing to accept assistance.[15]

Moving beyond the anti-Bolshevik implications of such a liberal phrase as "the establishment of law and order," the President described in some detail the manner in which the United States and Japan had come to co-operate in a joint postwar program of military and technical assistance to the railroads of a non-Bolshevik Siberia.[16] Then, following his discussion of the Inter-Allied Railroad plan, Wilson continued with a more general analysis of the role of the American military and civilian personnel in Siberia:

The instructions to Gen. Graves direct him not to interfere in Russian affairs, but to support Mr. Stevens wherever necessary. The Siberian Railway is not only the main artery for transportation in Siberia, but is the only open access to European Russia to-day. The population of Siberia, whose resources have been almost exhausted by the long years of war and the chaotic conditions which have existed there, can be protected from a further period of chaos and anarchy only by the restoration and maintenance of traffic on the Siberian Railway.[17]

After thus linking American railway assistance to the preservation of Siberian social stability, the President concluded his letter to the Senate with an extended description of America's policy in Siberia during the summer of 1919:

Partisan bands under leaders having no settled connection with any organized government, and bands under leaders whose allegiance to any settled authority is apparently temporary and transitory, are constantly menacing the operation of the railway and the safety of its permanent structures. The situation of the people of Siberia meantime is that they have no shoes or warm clothing; they are pleading for agricultural machinery and for many of the simpler articles of commerce upon which their own domestic economy depends and which are necessary to fruitful and productive industry among them. . . . The population of western Siberia and the forces of Admiral Kolchak are entirely dependent upon these railways. The Russian authorities in this country have succeeded in shipping large quantities of Russian supplies to Siberia, and the Secretary of War is now contracting with the great cooperative societies which operate throughout European and Asiatic Russia to ship further supplies to meet the needs of the civilian population. The Kolchak Government is also endeavoring to arrange for the purchase of medical and other Red Cross supplies from the War Department, and the American Red Cross is itself attempting the forms of relief for which it is organized. All elements of the population in Siberia look to the United States for assistance. This assistance can not be given to the population of Siberia, and ultimately to Russia, if the purpose entertained for two years to restore railway traffic is abandoned. The presence of American troops is a vital element in this effort. The services of Mr. Stevens depend upon it. . . . From these observations it will be seen that the purpose of the continuance of American troops in Siberia is that we, with the concurrence of the great Allied powers, may keep open a necessary artery of trade and extend to the vast population of Siberia the economic aid essential to it in peace time, but indispensable under the conditions which have followed the prolonged and exhausting participation by Russia in the war against the Central Powers.[18]

A careful reading of this statement makes absolutely clear that, whatever he meant by non-interference in Russian affairs, the President, in mid-1919, was in fact quite prepared to endorse publicly a program of railroad aid and economic assistance for the areas behind the lines of the Kolchak regime in Siberia. Moreover, this implicitly anti-Bolshevik foreign aid program was also to be partially policed by American troops acting as railroad guards against all forms of anti-Kolchak guerrilla activities by partisan bands. Thus, almost a year after the Wilsonian decision to intervene in Siberia, the anti-communist motive, which had been implicit in America's Siberian policy from the outset, became more-

explicit in the form of a limited Wilsonian commitment to the
egime of Admiral Kolchak.

As matters turned out, however, the White Siberians proved
ultimately incapable of using limited Allied aid either to destroy
the Soviet regime in European Russia or to prevent Bolshevism
from returning to Siberia itself. In postwar Siberia, as in all
White Russian dominated areas, the inability of the anti-Bolshevik military and civilian elements to co-operate on a basis of
mutual trust and respect led ultimately to a Bolshevik victory.[19]
By late summer and autumn 1919, the Kolchak regime, having
alienated much of the Siberian population and many of its Czech
allies by following policies of repression and conscription, found
itself both forced to retreat before the advancing Bolshevik armies
in western Siberia and harassed by pro-Soviet partisan peasant
bands in its rear areas.[20]

During his mission to the Kolchak headquarters at Omsk, in
July and August 1919, Ambassador Roland S. Morris reported to
Washington on conditions of imminent military defeat and popular discontent, conditions Morris tended to blame largely on the
reactionary and corrupt military clique which surrounded an honest but naïve Admiral Kolchak. Believing that it was finally a
question of Kolchak or Bolshevism in Siberia, Ambassador Morris, despite his generally pessimistic appraisal of the political potential of the Omsk regime, tried his best to work out plans for
an improved and extended program of American aid to the
White Siberians. Moreover, with the support of Lansing and
Wilson, Morris sought to urge the Kolchak authorities both to
improve their organizational techniques and to adopt a generally
more liberal and democratic approach toward the civilian population of Siberia in order to win them over to the anti-Bolshevik
cause. Needless to say, Morris's liberal anti-Bolshevik advice was
not well received by the more reactionary and anti-American
members of Kolchak's entourage, who resented what they saw as
Washington's "neutrality" in Siberia and wanted to move toward
an open military alliance with Japan. Nevertheless, Kolchak him-

self appeared quite prepared to work with Morris for liberal and organizational reforms in his regime in the hope of winning a marked increase in the American aid he was already receiving.[21]

With obvious reluctance, however, Lansing was forced, on August 25, 1919, to cable Morris with the news that political considerations in Congress made "unfortunately impracticable" the acceptance by the Administration of Morris's full recommendations for the recognition of Kolchak and for a greatly expanded American program of military and economic assistance to the White Siberians. Lansing wanted Kolchak to be reassured, however, both that American assistance would be continued in its previous form and that Kolchak's anti-Soviet efforts had the moral support of Washington.[22] Indeed, there is no doubt that, during the fall and early winter of 1919, the Administration did its best to maintain and to improve its limited program of moral and material aid to Kolchak. In essence, Wilsonians sought, in late 1919, to resolve persistent differences with the Japanese military in Siberia, so that Washington could co-operate with Japan more effectively in continuing inter-Allied anti-Bolshevik efforts to buttress the threatened Kolchak regime with limited technical, economic, and military assistance.[23] On September 20, 1919, the President himself took time out from his western speaking tour in defense of the League of Nations in order to "fully approve" the State Department's plans "with regard to furnishing such supplies as are available to the forces under Kolchak."[24] Moreover, despite a brief delay caused by General Graves, a large shipment of rifles from the United States did reach Kolchak in the fall of 1919.[25] Finally, by way of marked contrast to such continued American efforts to supply the White Russian controlled areas of Siberia, it should be noted that, during the summer of 1919, the United States gave unofficial moral support to the maintenance of an Allied commercial blockade against Soviet Russia.[26]

The autumn months of 1919 were a time of great trial for Secretary of State Lansing, as he watched disaster steadily overtake the Kolchak regime in spite of America's continued limited efforts

to buttress a non-Bolshevik Siberia. As much as he despised Bolshevism and hoped for Kolchak's success, Lansing remained,
nonetheless, too well aware of the basic political and military
weakness of the often reactionary and politically inept White Siberians to advise full American recognition of Kolchak.[27] Yet, in
late October 1919, the apparent military success of the White
Russian forces under General Yudenitch in the vicinity of Petrograd encouraged Lansing to the extent that the Secretary excitedly
cabled to the American railroad expert in Siberia, John F. Stevens, to urge Stevens to continue his pro-Kolchak railroad program in the hopes that the military tide had suddenly turned decisively against Russian Bolshevism:

As you may be aware already, the anti-Bolshevik forces in European
Russia, have recently had decisive military successes. It is now more
probable than at any time in the past that the Bolshevik Government
will fall. On this account it is more important than ever that Kolchak
be supported. Everything possible is being done to this end in Washington. A withdrawal of the Allied railway inspectors will bring about
a most difficult situation for Admiral Kolchak at the very moment
when everything else is more favorable to the success of his movement
than at any time in the past. It is unfortunate that Allied troops are
not available to replace the Czechs West of Lake Baikal. I understand thoroughly that under the conditions which existed a short time
ago the absence of Allied troops would have necessitated unquestionably the departure of the Allied inspectors. The reports received during the last two days reveal, however, so radical an improvement in
the general situation in Siberia that I feel justified in asking you that
the inspectors be retained under Russian guard at least until the culmination of the critical events now taking place in European Russia.
It would seem the more practicable to do this as the anti-Bolshevik
successes in the West will certainly have a deterrent effect on Bolshevik agitators in Siberia.[28]

Lansing's optimism quickly proved mistaken, however. As matters
turned out, Yudenitch did not take Petrograd, and, with conditions continuing to worsen for Kolchak in Siberia, the Administration decided in late December of 1919 to withdraw American

troops from Siberia rather than to engage in direct combat with the steadily advancing Bolshevik forces.[29]

In early 1920, after Kolchak's eventual defeat and assassination, Lansing tried to defend the Administration's Siberian policy, in a letter to the strongly anti-Bolshevik Russian expert, George Kennan, by claiming that "we simply did the best we could in an impossible situation, which resulted from Kolchak's inability to create an efficient Russian army to replace the Czecho-Slovaks." [30] The long Wilsonian Siberian aid effort, designed around the use of limited American technical, economic, and military assistance to buttress a pro-Allied and non-Bolshevik liberal Siberia—on the foundations provided by the original defeat of Siberian Bolshevism by the Czecho-Slovak troops in summer 1918—had ended in failure, because of the political and military incapacity of the White Siberians.

It is true, of course, that President Wilson was never fully reconciled to the presence of Allied or American troops in Russia. At one point in early May 1919, the President, upset over news he had just received concerning dangerous tensions in Siberia between the forces of Kolchak and the American troops under General Graves, blurted out that "he [Wilson] had always been of [the] opinion that the proper policy of the Allied and Associated Powers was to clear out of Russia and leave it to the Russians to fight it out among themselves." [31] Then, too, it should be noted that, during 1919, the President moved steadily to remove American troops from the northern region in Russia, despite the risk involved in such a removal to the anti-Bolshevik regime which had been established under Allied protection in the Murmansk-Archangel zone of intervention.[32] Moreover, in late June 1919, when Herbert Hoover suggested that the United States ought to participate in a broad inter-Allied economic program designed to buttress a non-Bolshevik socio-political reconstruction of Russia, Wilson demurred on the ground that "it was impossible for an Inter-Allied body to give such aid without getting mixed up in politics to some extent." [33] The President went on to add that in his view "the Russian people must solve their own problems without outside interference and that Europe had made a great mistake when they attempted to interfere in the French Revolution. He said it seems hard on the present Russian generation, but in the long run it means less distress for Russia." [34]

There can be no doubt then, both that Wilson opposed extensive political and military intervention in the Russian Civil War and that the President wanted to see the Russians settle their own affairs. Yet, the evidence also suggests that Wilson was in no sense indifferent to the outcome of such an internal Russian struggle. Indeed, as has been amply illustrated by the example of the Administration's Siberian policy, Wilson was perfectly prepared to extend assistance to those portions of Russia where indigenous anti-communist forces appeared to be potentially capable of establishing the basis for a non-Bolshevik liberal order. It is also important to note that, throughout 1919, the President remained anxious to extend American economic and political support to indigenous forces resisting Bolshevism in the Petrograd and Baltic States areas of Russia.[35] Moreover, Wilson's statement of July 27, 1919, expressing moral, but not official, support for a policy of economic sanctions against the Bolshevik areas of Russia, spoke volumes as to the President's real sympathies in the Russian Civil War:

The President is convinced that if proper representations are made to the neutral countries during the war they can be induced to prohibit traffic in arms and munitions with the portions of Russia controlled by the Bolsheviks. The avowed hostility of the Bolsheviks to all Governments and the announced programme of international revolution make them as great a menace to the national safety of neutral countries as to Allied countries. For any Government to permit them to increase their power through commercial intercourse with its nationals would be to encourage a movement which is frankly directed against all Governments and would certainly invite the condemnation of all peoples desirous of restoring peace and social order. The President cannot believe that any Government whose people might be in a position to carry on commerce with the Russian ports referred to would be so indifferent to the opinion of the civilized world as to permit it.[36]

It is clear that, whatever his very real ambivalence concerning intervention in Russian affairs, President Wilson was in fact quite prepared occasionally to use limited American moral and material power to help contain the internal expansion of Russian Bolshevism. In the last analysis, the apparent contradictions in Wilson's approach to postwar Russia were perhaps resolved for the President, on an ideological plane, by his implicit conviction that limited material aid to the one "true Russia"—that is, to the anti-Bolshevik liberal Russia of the March Revolution—did not really constitute interference in Russia's internal affairs.

Of course, it is true both that Wilson indicated, at Paris, a desire to negotiate with the Bolsheviks, and that, on occasion, he even appeared somewhat receptive to a generally Left-liberal approach to the Russian question.[37] Yet an analysis of the Prinkipo conference issue and of the Bullitt mission revealed that in practice Wilson did not really share the Left-liberal desire to extend *de facto* recognition to the Soviet regime in the hopes that the Bolsheviks would liberalize themselves in response to Allied conciliation. Unlike the Left-liberals, Wilson was never really prepared to accept the existing revolutionary authoritarianism of the Soviet system as being a truly representative expression of Russia. In practice, the President's hand was extended to the Bolsheviks only on condition that they give up their forceful efforts to bring revolutionary-socialism to Russia by means of their own single party rule. It was perhaps on his western tour, in the fall of 1919, that Wilson most clearly expressed the reasons behind his orthodox liberal opposition to Bolshevism in Russia:

My fellow citizens, it does not make any difference what kind of a minority governs you if it is a minority, and the thing we must see to is that no minority anywhere masters the majority. That is at the heart, my fellow citizens, of the tragical things that are happening in that great country which we long to help and can find no way that is effective to help. I mean the great realm of Russia. The men who are now measurably in control of the affairs of Russia represent nobody but themselves. They have again and again been challenged to call a constitutional convention. They have again and again been challenged to prove that they had some kind of a mandate, even from a single class of their fellow citizens, and they dare not attempt it. They have no mandate from anybody. There are only thirty-four of them, I am told, and there were more than thirty-four men who used to control the destinies of Europe from Wilhelmstrasse. There is a closer monopoly of power in Petrograd and Moscow than there ever was in Berlin, and the thing that is intolerable is, not that the Russian people are having their way, but that another group of men more cruel than the Czar himself is controlling the destinies of that great people.[38]

Clearly, in the President's non-revolutionary ideological universe of middle class liberal majoritarianism, the concept of the forceful maintenance of minority rule by a revolutionary-socialist vanguard was anathema. As a pragmatic and reformist-minded neo-Lockean liberal, Wilson never could sympathize with the revolutionary passion of the Jacobin-Bolshevik minority which seeks to transform society totally by force.

Like Wilson, Secretary Lansing was prepared to accept the Bolsheviks only when, in effect, they ceased to be Bolsheviks and became social democrats who accepted a socio-political order of liberal pluralism. On November 24, 1919, Lansing succinctly expressed his orthodox liberal criteria for judging Soviet political behavior in a cable to John W. Davis, the American Ambassador to England:

It would seem most unfortunate if the Government of Great Britain should give to the Bolsheviki at this critical juncture the moral support they would derive from negotiations of a general nature with Great Britain or an expectation of recognition. It would not alter the situation if the Bolsheviki were actually making overtures to other socialist parties, as any movement toward really democratic reformation would be halted rather than encouraged by developments which might give the Bolsheviki ground for hoping that they could still maintain themselves without fundamental concessions to other political elements in Russia.[39]

In his own fashion, Lansing was answering here such Left-liberals as William C. Bullitt, who, from the perspective of orthodox

Wilsonianism, were too prepared to accept prematurely a moderated Soviet regime as the genuinely liberal article.

On December 4, 1919, Lansing, apparently still hopeful at that point about the Siberian railroad plan, sent Wilson a memorandum in which the Secretary argued that the long-term prospects for an eventual triumph of Russian liberalism were good, so long as the United States continued to oppose Russian Bolshevism with programs of economic and technical assistance.[40] Early in this memorandum, Lansing presented a brief but complete historical description of the character and purposes of the Wilson Administration's postwar defense of Russian liberal nationalism:

It is clear that the early settlement of the difficulties by which Russia is now distracted is of vital concern to the United States. Russia is among the largest factors in the complicated system of production and distribution by which the world is clothed and fed. It is not to be expected that economic balance can be regained and living costs brought once more to moderate levels while its vast area . . . is rendered sterile by civil distraction. It is not less vitally important to the United States that there should be established in Russia with the least possible delay a government expressive of the will of the people and capable of performing its international obligations, and that Russian resources should be no longer at the disposal of adventurous revolutionaries, seeking to subvert democratic governments everywhere, or within reach of a possibly renascent imperialism which might conspire once more to establish itself in forcible control of the world's affairs. These conditions led the government during the past year to adopt every measure with respect to Russia which gave promise of hastening the end of civil war, the establishment of orderly constitutional government, and the relief of the material distress of the people. The experience of these efforts proved that it was impossible to attain the ends desired by dealing with the so-called Bolshevik group which controls the central position of European Russia and part of Western Siberia. On the other hand, written assurance was obtained, through Admiral Kolchak and his associates, that the coordinated anti-Bolshevik movements would direct their efforts, if they succeeded in driving the Bolsheviki from Moscow and Petrograd, to the democratic rehabilitation of the Russian state. They expressly repudiated all attempts to revive the former land system or to impose again upon the

Russian people the regime of caste and privilege which the revolution destroyed. . . . Pursuant to the policy laid down in the note of May 26th, this Government has cooperated with Admiral Kolchak and his associates, as far as has been possible under existing legislation, in order that they might establish themselves as the Government of all Russia and convene, upon the establishment of public order, a constituent assembly capable of expressing the will of the Russian people with respect to their future political institutions.[41]

In essence, during 1919, Wilsonian policy-makers had sought, with the limited means at their disposal, to assist in the recreation of a liberal-nationalist Russia, loyal to the values of the March Revolution, and safe from the political extremes of Bolshevism and reaction. Moreover, in still broader terms, such a liberal Russia was to have constituted but one important element in the larger postwar Wilsonian grand design, calling for the establishment of an American-inspired peaceful liberal-capitalist order on a worldwide basis.

2. THE WILSONIAN SEARCH FOR LIBERAL ORDER IN POSTWAR ASIA AND AFRICA

The Administration's attempt to co-operate with Japan in an inter-Allied program of support for Siberian anti-Bolshevism may also be seen, in a wider context, as simply one facet of a broader postwar Wilsonian effort to absorb Japan into a co-operative liberal program of American-inspired international-capitalist harmony in Asia. Essentially, the Wilson Administration hoped to bring moderate Japanese statesmen to the realization that Japan's true political and economic interests lay in co-operation with the United States and the Western powers, through the League of Nations and the financial Consortium, in an over-all Far Eastern approach which would guarantee the political and territorial integrity of China, while ensuring, at the same time, peaceful access to economic opportunities in China for all the great powers. Moreover, in a related fashion, in and beyond the Far East, the

Wilsonian-supported League of Nations Mandate program provided a way, without violent revolution, to make more peaceful and progressive the entire process by which the advanced capitalist powers could expand economically into the underdeveloped world.

Ultimately, Wilsonians hoped to construct a non-revolutionary international commercial order, transcending traditional military and political imperialism, in which the human, political, and territorial rights of underdeveloped peoples would be respected, and in which the dangers of conflict among the advanced powers would be overcome by policies of peaceful free trade and great power co-operation in the non-Western areas. Of course, such a League-supported system of global non-discriminatory trade and peaceful international capitalist economic penetration of the world's underdeveloped areas could not help but benefit an American nation-state bursting with expansive commercial energies and well able to utilize effectively an Open Door to the markets and raw materials of Africa and Asia.[42] In other words, the postwar Wilsonian effort to lead an orderly non-revolutionary reform of the traditional imperial colonial system reflected the ideological fusion of American economic self-interest with American liberal-internationalist idealism.

It is certainly true that there were constant tensions during 1919 between Washington and Tokyo concerning Japan's tendency to support disruptive armed Cossack elements in Siberia and to inhibit the realization of an effective pro-Kolchak policy of integrated inter-Allied management on the Siberian railroads.[43] Yet it is also true that the Wilson Administration continued, throughout 1919, to try to attain its two related policy goals in Siberia, consisting of a commercial Open Door on Siberia's railroads and of a liberal non-Bolshevik Siberian social order, by means of efforts to convince moderate Japanese statesmen that Japan's true interest lay both in abandoning all independent Japanese military and political efforts to establish a traditional Japanese sphere of influence in Siberia, and in joining with

America to implement a co-operative Open Door program of implicitly pro-Kolchak political and economic activities in the Russian East.[44] A memorandum written by Lansing on November 30, 1919, revealed Lansing's belief that a basic community of interest existed between Japan and America in regard to the containment of revolutionary-socialism in the Far East:

> I suppose the announcement of our proposed withdrawal, when it is made, will cause the Japanese to grumble a bit, but they will in the end accept the situation with a good grace and adjust their policy to the new conditions. My belief is that they will send reinforcements to Siberia and attempt to strengthen Seminoff's forces. I can not see how the Japanese Government can adopt any other policy in view of the very real peril to Japan if the Bolsheviks should gain a foothold in Manchuria and cooperate with the Korean revolutionists. Certainly in the circumstances we ought not to raise any objection to Japan sending a sufficient force to check the Bolshevik advance for the spread of Bolshevism in the Far East would be a dreadful menace to civilization.[45]

It is important to note that the eventual announcement of America's intention to withdraw its troops and civilian personnel from Siberia in early 1920 was accompanied by assurances to Japan that the United States would not object if the Japanese decided to keep troops in Siberia to continue policing the railroads for the non-Bolshevik Siberians.[46]

In postwar Siberia, Wilsonian policy-makers sought to oppose both Bolshevism and Japanese imperialism through a policy designed to absorb a more moderate Japan into a co-operative American-inspired program of assistance to Russian liberal-nationalism. Similarly, in postwar China the Wilson Administration attempted to co-opt Japan into an inter-Allied Banking Consortium for Chinese commercial development, designed, in part, to protect China's political independence and territorial integrity by offering to the Japanese the possibility of peaceful economic expansion in China, under the legitimizing auspices of international-capitalism, as an alternative to Japan's more traditional policies of military and political imperialism at China's expense. Washington hoped to use the projected inter-Allied Banking Consortium as a lever to pressure Japan into accepting the Wilsonian vision of a unified, liberal, and progressive China, no longer split into separate spheres of influence by traditional imperialism, and completely open, on a non-discriminatory basis, to the goods and investments of America and all the other advanced capitalist powers.[47] In both Siberia and China, then, Japan was somehow to be won away from her policies of militant imperialism, and brought to share, with America, the progressive but non-revolutionary liberal anti-imperialist task of maintaining international-capitalist stability against all forms of disorder.

At the Peace Conference, however, tensions arose between Washington and Tokyo concerning the ultimate disposition of the old German sphere of influence on the Shantung Peninsula in China. A young nationalist Chinese delegation at Paris demanded the unconditional return of Shantung to China, while the Japanese, armed by treaties with both the Allies and the Chinese, insisted that Japan, having captured the Peninsula from the Germans during the war, had a clear legal right to inherit all the privileges which Germany had enjoyed in Shantung.[48] Needless to say, this Sino-Japanese impasse created a difficult dilemma at Paris for a Wilson Administration committed both to maintaining the territorial integrity and commercial openness of China, and to co-opting Japan into a peaceful and stable international-capitalist framework of great power co-operation in the Far East.

In the view of Wilson and his leading advisers on Far Eastern matters—all of whom desired to see a unified, orderly, and politically independent China, liberated from the divisive control of the great powers, and completely open to the expansion of American goods, investments, and liberal values—the Chinese had far more justice on their side than did the Japanese.[49] During April 1919, therefore, when the Shantung issue was considered at Paris, Wilson and Lansing sought, without success, to gain Japanese acceptance of a plan under which Japan would manage Shantung as the designated agent of a five-power trusteeship arrangement un-

der the League of Nations.[50] At the Council of Four meeting of
April 22, 1919, the President made an especially powerful plea to
Japan to accept a trusteeship solution of the Shantung issue, as a
possible first step toward ending the imperialistic great power
practice of carving out separate political and economic spheres of
influence in China:

What he feared was that Japan, by standing merely on her treaty
rights, would create the impression that she was thinking more of her
rights than of her duties to China. The world would never have peace
based on treaty rights only unless there were also recognized to be re-
ciprocal duties between States. . . . The central idea of the League
of Nations was that States must support each other even when their
interests were not involved. When the League of Nations was formed
then there would be established a body of partners covenanted to
stand up for each other's rights. The position in which he would like
to see Japan, already the most advanced nation in the Far East with
the leadership in enterprise and policy, was that of the leader in the
Far East standing out for these new ideas. There could be no finer
nor more politic role for her. That was what he had to say as a friend
of Japan. When he had seen the Japanese Delegates two days ago he
had said that he was not proposing that Kiauchau should be detached
from the treaty engagements but that it should be ceded to the Powers as trustees with the understanding that all they were going to do
was to ask how the treaties were to be carried out and to offer advice
as to how this could best be done by mutual agreement. . . .
What he was after was to attain a more detailed definition as to how
Japan is going to help China as well as to afford an opportunity for
investment in railways etc. He had hoped that by pooling their interest the several nations that had gained a foothold in China (a foothold that was to the detriment of China's position in the world)
might forgo the special position they had acquired and that China
might be put on the same footing as other nations, as sooner or later
she must certainly be. He believed this to be to the interest of everyone concerned. There was a lot of combustible material in China and
if flames were put to it the fire could not be quenched for China had
a population of four hundred million people. It was symptoms of that
which filled him with anxiety.[51]

Essentially, the President was calling upon Japan to accept Wilsonian values and to join with the other powers in a Consortium-

League of Nations system of Far Eastern liberal stability under international law. Moreover, Wilson also hoped that, within such a new liberal Far Eastern order, a non-revolutionary form of progressive Chinese nationalism could be nurtured by Japan and other advanced capitalist nations interested in commercial opportunities in China. In effect, Wilson's Chinese and Siberian policies were linked by the fact that they both reflected an Administration desire to harness Japan's energies to America's liberal-internationalist struggle against war and revolution in Asia.

Ultimately, however, Wilson's efforts to compromise the Shantung issue, by absorbing Japan's special claims into a five-power trusteeship under the League, were frustrated due to the firm insistence of the Japanese on their legal rights in Shantung. Japan was willing to promise to turn all political control in the Peninsula back to the Chinese in the near future, retaining only the economic rights previously held by Germany, but the Japanese were not willing to permit any great power supervision of Sino-Japanese relations, especially in view of the fact that none of the other powers was willing to renounce its special privileges in China.[52] In the face of Japan's intransigence, the best that Wilson could achieve through negotiation at Paris was a face-saving formula which whittled away at Japan's political and military prerogatives in Shantung, and permitted the United States to accept the substance of the Japanese position without either recognizing the imperialistic Sino-Japanese treaties of 1915 and 1918 or appearing to confer on Japan any more rights than Germany had formerly possessed in Shantung.[53]

Repeatedly, during the fall of 1919, on his western speaking tour in defense of the Treaty and the League, Wilson would seek to justify his Shantung settlement as the best that America could have obtained for China, considering the political realities which had existed at Paris:

America, as I have said, was not bound by the agreements of Great Britain and France, on the one hand, and Japan on the other. We were free to insist upon a prospect of a different settlement, and at the instance of the United States Japan has already promised that she will relinquish to China immediately after the ratification of this treaty all the sovereign rights that Germany had in Shantung Province—the only promise of that kind ever made, the only relinquishment of that sort ever achieved—and that she will retain only what foreign corporations have all over China—unfortunately but as a matter of fact—the right to run the railroad and the right to work the mines under the usual conditions of Chinese sovereignty and as economic concessionaires, with no political rights or military power of any kind. It is really an emancipation of China, so far as that Province is concerned, from what is imposed upon her by other nations in other Provinces equally rich and equally important to the independence of China herself. So that inside the League of Nations we now have a foothold by which we can play the friend to China.[54]

Thus, by emphasizing both Japan's promises and the ultimate reforming potential of the League, Wilson sought to present the most optimistic possible view of his compromise at Paris with Allied and Japanese imperialism. During the summer of 1919, however, the essential ambiguity of the Shantung settlement was revealed by a series of disagreements between Washington and Tokyo concerning just what it was Japan had promised in the compromise agreement reached at Paris.[55]

At Paris, the Shantung settlement was denounced as a betrayal of China by the Chinese delegation and by many members of the American Peace Commission.[56] Even Secretary Lansing, who, as we have seen, was generally committed to seeking Japanese-American co-operation in the Far East, felt that Wilson had been wrong to compromise with Japan on the Shantung issue.[57] Indeed, only Colonel House, who was more sympathetic to Japan's expansionist aims and methods in China than was Lansing, entirely approved of Wilson's accommodation with the Japanese over Shantung. In general, House felt that Japanese imperialism in China was no worse than Allied imperialism elsewhere in the world, and the Colonel preferred, therefore, not to isolate Japan but rather to try to hold the Conference together in the hope of future world reform under the League of Nations.[58]

For his part, the President definitely distrusted Japanese intentions in the Far East, but he felt compelled, nonetheless, to yield to Japan's demands in regard to Shantung because he feared that the intransigent Japanese would refuse to join the League of Nations if they were denied any part of their treaty rights on the Chinese Peninsula.[59] On the evening of April 30, 1919, Ray Stannard Baker recorded in his Notebook the substance of a conversation with the President which clearly revealed Wilson's concern lest the Shantung issue destroy his hopes of maintaining world liberal order through an inclusive League of Nations:

I saw the President at 6:30 as usual and he went over the whole ground (of the Japanese settlement) with me at length. He said he had been unable to sleep the night before for thinking of it. Anything he might do was wrong. He said the settlement was the best that could be had out of a dirty past. . . . The only hope was to keep the world together, get the League of Nations with Japan in it and then try to secure justice for the Chinese not only as regarding Japan but England, France, Russia, all of whom had concessions in China. If Japan went home there was the danger of a Japanese-Russian-German alliance, and a return to the old "balance of power" system in the world, on a greater scale than ever before. He knew his decision would be unpopular in America, that the Chinese would be bitterly disappointed, that the Japanese would feel triumphant, that he would be accused of violating his own principles, but, nevertheless, he *must* work for world order and organization, against anarchy and a return to the old militarism.[60]

Wilson obviously felt that the establishment of an inclusive and stable world order, against all forms of international disorder, was more basic than an uncompromising American defense of China against Japanese and Allied imperialism.

In the final analysis, the willingness of Wilson and House to compromise with Japan over Shantung is perhaps best seen, despite Lansing's readiness to risk isolating Japan on this one issue, as a logical and consistent extension of the Administration's overall postwar effort to control Japanese imperialism by absorbing Japan's expansive energies into America's liberal programs for international-capitalist order in the Far East. We have seen that, both in relation to Washington's anti-Bolshevik policy in Siberia and in regard to Wilsonian plans for a great power Banking Consortium in China, the Wilson Administration's emphasis was on co-opting Japan into progressive programs designed to buttress a non-revolutionary and non-military order of commercial freedom and peace in East Asia. By the same token, therefore, Wilson and House naturally felt that it was essential to bring Japan under the control of the League of Nations, lest an isolated and militant Japanese imperialism be encouraged to disrupt irrevocably the projected Wilsonian vision of international legality and harmony for the Far East. Moreover, House and Wilson also hoped that the United States would be able to use the League of Nations to defend the territorial integrity of China, if necessary, and eventually to bring all the great powers, including the Japanese, to accept a new liberal Asian order, in which equal commercial access to a unified, progressive, and orderly China, would replace the traditional imperialistic system of separate spheres of influence in China.[61]

On a still more theoretical level, however, it is possible to see the Administration's attempt to co-opt Japan into a Consortium-League of Nations framework for Far Eastern liberal-capitalist stability as a classic example of the Wilsonian liberal and non-revolutionary form of anti-imperialism. Ideologically unable to move toward a revolutionary socialist position, Wilsonian liberalism could choose one of two alternative ways in which to oppose traditional imperialism. On the one hand, militant imperialism could be opposed by means of using American military power in the context of a conventional war refashioned into a liberal ideological crusade. This, of course, was the orientation adopted by Wilsonians toward German imperialism after the announcement of unlimited submarine warfare in 1917. On the other hand, however, Wilsonians could oppose traditional imperialism by means of efforts to absorb and to sublimate aggressive imperialistic forces. In terms of this sublimating approach, the Wilsonian emphasis would be on offering more legitimate and orderly forms of peaceful international-capitalist activity as a rational alternative to military imperialism. Clearly, such an absorptive orientation was adopted at Paris by the Wilson Administration in its non-revolutionary efforts to bring Allied and Japanese imperialism under the stable reformist control of the League of Nations. Moreover, we shall now see that this Wilsonian propensity to sublimate traditional imperialism by absorbing it into a peaceful League of Nations framework of legitimate international-capitalist expansion was the basis of the Administration's advocacy of the mandate program at the Paris Peace Conference.

At Paris, the Wilson Administration sponsored a mandate program designed in part to show the world that the Peace Conference wished to go beyond the traditional practice of dividing the colonial spoils of war in an imperialistic fashion. Under the provisions of Wilson's mandate plan, portions of the former German and Turkish Empires in Africa, the Far East, and the Near East were to be governed as mandates under international supervision by advanced nations acting as the trustees of the League of Nations. The President hoped that such a mandate program would both end traditional economic and military forms of colonial exploitation and provide for indigenous political self-development toward independence under the disinterested tutelage of advanced countries. Then, too, it was also understood by Wilsonians that an Open Door for the investments and the trade of the United States and all the other advanced capitalist powers was to prevail in the mandated areas.[62]

It was perhaps Colonel House, in a speech delivered in autumn 1920, who best captured the essential elements of the Wilsonian conception of the mandate program:

The question of mandates is one in which the American people should have much concern. It is not alone a new departure in international ethics, but it is one in which we have an economic interest. Until now, backward countries have generally been controlled or exploited by some Power for selfish purposes, and the good which has come from such control or exploitation has been merely incident thereto. These backward communities have been a constant source of friction between the more civilized states, friction which has often resulted in war. Until the Paris Conference there had been no attempt to reach a general understanding or fixed policy between the more powerful nations regarding the control or betterment of such states or territories. The system hitherto practised was admittedly so bad that when the Conference came to the disposition of the late German colonies there was a general agreement that a more enlightened policy should be inaugurated. . . . The fact that hereafter each Power holding such a mandate will be under close observation must have a tendency to promote the best administration possible. The report which must be given each year to the council of the League will in itself stimulate rivalry, and the Power giving the best account of its stewardship will be the one to hold the highest place in the esteem of the world.[63]

House placed prime emphasis in this statement on the duty of the mandatory power, closely scrutinized by world liberal opinion, to assist the political and economic development of the under-developed area put under its care. Clearly, this was far from a static conception of perpetual colonial dominance. Moreover, the Colonel also stressed the contribution of the mandate program to the important task of avoiding the great power rivalries and wars which had traditionally characterized the international politics of the underdeveloped world.[64] Finally, Colonel House was obviously mindful of America's own economic stake in maintaining the commercial Open Door to the raw materials and the markets of all the mandated areas.[65] In sum then, the Wilsonian mandate program was meant to serve the interrelated functions of extending liberal values and institutions to backward peoples, of pacifying the potentially war-producing contradictions latent in the process of international-capitalist expansion into the underdeveloped areas, and of opening hitherto closed portions of Asia and Africa to American trade and investment. As always in Wilsonian ideology, a sense of America's own expansive economic self-interest was combined with a vision of America's broader liberal mission to lead the world toward a stable and progressive system of universal commercial and political harmony.

Wilson had come to Paris hoping to assign the German and Turkish colonies as mandates to the smaller powers. At the Peace Conference, however, the President was confronted with the fact that the Allies had already distributed the colonial spoils in a series of wartime secret treaties. The best that Wilson was able to achieve by bargaining, therefore, was Allied acceptance of a system of graded mandates as the means through which the prearranged distribution of German and Turkish holdings would take place. In other words, the secret treaties were to stand, but the Allies would receive their colonial gains as mandates rather than as outright annexations.[66]

Considering these facts, it is possible to argue, of course, that all the President had really achieved through the adoption of his mandate program at Paris was the legitimization of the reality of Allied imperialism with the covering liberal rhetoric of League trusteeship. Yet, for Wilson, whose basic orientation was reformist rather than revolutionary, the mandate compromise was seen, nonetheless, as a significant breakthrough for the principles of political liberalism and international responsibility in the colonial areas.[67] Indeed, the very pragmatic and gradualistic character of the mandate settlement expressed quite well the progressive but judicious quality of the liberal Wilsonian temperament.

It cannot be overemphasized that on the colonial issue, as on so many other postwar issues, the Wilsonian position was one of careful and orderly liberal reformism, as opposed to a position of radical or revolutionary anti-imperialism. On December 30, 1918, Secretary Lansing wrote a confidential memorandum in which he made perfectly clear his own concern over the revolutionary possibilities latent in the concept of self-determination:

The more I think about the President's declaration as to the right of "self-determination," the more convinced I am of the danger of putting such ideas into the minds of certain races. It is bound to be the basis of impossible demands on the Peace Congress, and create trouble in many lands. What effect will it have on the Irish, the Indians, the Egyptians, and the nationalities among the Boers?

Will it not breed discontent, disorder and rebellion? Will not the Mohammedans of Syria and Palestine and possibly of Morocco and Tripoli rely on it? How can it be harmonized with Zionism, to which the president is practically committed? The phrase is simply loaded with dynamite. It will raise hopes which can never be realized. It will, I fear, cost thousands of lives. In the end it is bound to be discredited, to be called the dream of an idealist who failed to realize the danger until too late to check those who attempted to put the principle into force.[68]

In actual practice, however, if not so explicitly in theory, Wilson proved to be no more anxious than Lansing to support violent nationalist revolutions in the postwar colonial areas. Significantly, when reports of revolutionary nationalist and/or Bolshevik inspired riots in Egypt reached Paris, Wilson, House, and Lansing all favored swift American action to help stabilize the situation by means of officially recognizing the British Protectorate over Egypt.[69] In terms of the Wilsonian anti-imperialism of liberal order, self-determination was to be obtained slowly through legal processes, and not by means of violent nationalist revolution. In other words, unlike Lenin, Wilson was not prepared in the immediate postwar period to challenge the entire imperialist system with a call for the instantaneous and universal establishment of self-determination for all colonial peoples.[70]

This is not meant to imply that Wilson was less than sincerely committed to bringing about the eventual attainment of universal self-determination for all peoples. Indeed, in his speeches defending the Versailles Treaty, the President often argued that the Paris settlement should be seen principally as a liberating people's peace, which had been created by men eschewing traditional annexationist power politics and using liberal procedures to defend the rights of weak nations to freedom and self-determination.[71] In particular, Wilson constantly emphasized that the Treaty gave self-determination to Eastern European peoples liberated from the imperialistic domination of the Central Powers.[72] Moreover, the President would occasionally even go beyond praise simply for

the destruction of German, Austro-Hungarian, and Turkish imperialisms, to argue that Articles X and XI of the League Covenant gave hope of future American moral and political assistance
to weak peoples, oppressed by non-Germanic forms of imperialist
domination, who had not been liberated by the Paris Peace Conference.[73] The point is, however, that, in contrast to Lenin's violent revolutionary orientation, Wilson hoped to universalize self-
determination by means of utilizing world opinion and legal procedures in the ordered quasi-constitutional context of the League
of Nations. Thus, while it is true that the President, at times,
affirmed an abstract belief in the universal right of liberal revolution on the American model, there can be no doubt that the
main tendency of Wilsonian diplomacy, both in theory and in
practice, was in the direction of establishing a stable and liberalized world community in which political and national freedoms
could be obtained and preserved by non-violent constitutional
means under international law.[74] In a world in which revolutionary-socialism existed, Wilsonians could never be entirely sanguine about any form of violent revolutionary activity.

What Wilson sought was not a sudden or immediate end to
the Western colonial structure, but rather a slow reform of the
imperialist system under the progressive guidance of the League
of Nations. The President appeared implicitly to envision an Afro-
Asian world, open to the penetration of America's expansive commerce and liberal values, and free to evolve toward eventual self-
government under the benevolent tutelage of the more advanced
nations. Moreover, while Wilson did oppose all traditional forms
of military, economic, and political exploitation in the colonial
areas, he did also believe that the great powers, including the
United States, had important commercial and governmental services of a progressive nature to perform in the underdeveloped regions of the world.[75] In short, Wilson was opposed more to the
form than to the substance of the existing economic and political
hegemony of the West in the international arena.

In the final analysis, Wilson's reformist anti-imperialism was basically absorptive rather than exclusive in its orientation. While radicals sought a revolutionary break with the past, Wilson wished to reform the past more gradually by transforming it within the liberal institutional framework of the present. As we have seen, in Russian and Eastern European politics, the Bolshevik spirit sought to restructure society rapidly, by means of revolutionary-socialist power, whereas the President favored, in both Russia and Eastern Europe, a more gradualistic political solution of pluralistic liberalism which would include the past in the very act of transforming it. Similarly, on the world scene, Wilson was prepared to accept far more pluralism than was Lenin. In this sense, the President avoided Lenin's total assault on imperialism, and sought instead to make the existing imperialist system more rational, progressive, and peaceful, through the liberal instrumentality of the League of Nations.

Ultimately, then, the League of Nations was seen by Wilson as creating an orderly legal structure within which the existing elements of world politics could be reformed. For the President, the quest for a new liberal world order was not a revolutionary vision encompassing the immediate transformation of all international political situations which did not measure up to American liberal norms. Rather, Wilson essentially envisioned a liberal-international system to be the existing world socio-political status quo placed under a framework of law and hopefully made more predictable, humane, and peaceful. Basic to the realization of the Wilsonian vision of world order was the willingness of the advanced powers to follow American leadership and to agree to conduct their international relations and commercial-political expansion into the underdeveloped areas in a peaceful global atmosphere of capitalist harmony and rationality.

Wilson apparently had little doubt that the League could liberalize previously imperialistic elements in world politics by means of co-optation. The Administration's efforts to absorb an expansionist Japan into the legitimate controls of a Consortium-League system of international-capitalist stability in the Far East was a manifestation of this belief. In a similar fashion, the President also hoped to co-opt the British Navy into his projected postwar liberal world order. Wilson conceived of a possible progressive role, as a defender of world order, for a British Navy made responsible to the control of world liberal opinion through the League of Nations.[76] The League was to become the Wilsonian instrument for the movement of mankind, without violent revolution if possible, from the war-producing pre-liberal past of imperialist rivalry, to an American-inspired pluralistic future of liberal-capitalist harmony based on international law. Moreover, within such a stable open world of commercial and political order, safe from the interrelated threats of traditional imperialism and revolutionary-socialism, the missionary Wilsonian vision could finally be realized completely in the moral and economic pre-eminence of the liberal-exceptionalist American nation-state.

EPILOGUE

During the summer and autumn of 1919, the Wilsonian peace was subjected to harsh criticism by American liberals and socialists on the Left and by the Lodge Republicans on the Right. The President's critics on the Left argued that the severe terms of the Treaty had laid the foundations for another world war, and as radicals they objected, therefore, to the involvement of American power, through the League of Nations, in what they saw essentially as an imperialistic and anti-revolutionary postwar extension of the Entente alliance. The President's critics on the Right approved of the Treaty's severity, but, seeking to maintain America's freedom of decision in foreign affairs inviolate, the Lodge Republicans opposed the League of Nations as a device for absorbing American power far too directly into the defense of the pro-Allied European settlement.

Thus, starting from entirely different premises, Wilson's critics on the Left and on the Right arrived at a similar condemnation of the League as a means for involving a pure America in the power politics of the Old World. In other words, despite their completely different attitudes toward the peace treaty with Germany, the President's radical and Republican critics both tended to denounce the League of Nations as an institution likely to absorb America into the wars of Europe and to make the United States, in effect, an instrument of the Allied powers. This isolationist fusion of radical and conservative anti-Wilsonianism was perhaps best exemplified in the complex ideology of Senator William E. Borah, who joined Lodge in defending America's complete independence of action in foreign relations, and also joined the *New Republic* in attacking the League as a conservative alliance designed to check revolution and to guarantee Allied imperialism around the world.

The President thus faced considerable criticism, both from radicals and conservatives, directed at the Allies, the Versailles Treaty, and the League of Nations. Somehow Wilson had to convince the American people that the Allies were progressive and not imperialistic, and that the League was a device built to prevent wars and not to create them. Moreover, since, in their different ways, the President's critics on the Left and the Right both argued for the maintenance of America's isolation from European politics, Wilson had to establish that the Treaty and the League together represented an Americanization or a liberalization of world politics, rather than an absorption of a liberal-exceptionalist America into the complexities of the Old World's imperialistic diplomacy. Ultimately, the President would argue that only America's involvement in the League of Nations could make it possible to secure the continued triumph of liberalism over Germany's autocratic imperialism, to create an inclusive liberalized international order of peace and legality transcending the traditional European balance of power system, and, finally, to defend the stability of such a projected liberal world order against the threat of revolutionary-socialism. In this broad sense, then, the ideological structure of Wilson's final speeches embodied a last passionate restatement of the President's vision of a new American-inspired liberal world order, safe both from traditional imperialism and from revolutionary-socialism, in which the moral and economic expansion of American liberalism could take place freely in an ordered open atmosphere of global harmony and legality.

At the heart of Wilson's defense of the Versailles Treaty and the League of Nations Covenant lay his idea that the results of the Paris Peace Conference represented the fulfillment of America's liberal-exceptionalist mission to liberate oppressed peoples and to reform the traditional war-producing diplomacy of the European balance of power. In the President's view, it was fitting for an American nation-state, whose own national tradition was based on an original triumph of progressive liberal values over European reaction, to be the disinterested and trusted leader of mankind at the moment of liberal-internationalism's final victory over the atavistic restraints of traditional reaction.[1] For Wilson, the United States had a moral duty to participate in the American-inspired League of Nations, not only to ensure fully the triumph of world democracy and Slavic self-determination over German imperialism, but, more broadly, to support a new "Lockeanized" world order, under international law, within which American liberal values would remain victorious over Europe's traditional balance of power diplomacy.[2] For all these reasons, the President sought to commit America to give its liberal leadership to the League of Nations, thereby ensuring that the triumph of world liberalism over German and/or European imperialism would remain a permanent triumph.

Yet, while the main emphasis in Wilson's defense of the Versailles Treaty and the League Covenant was on America's responsibility to fulfill its liberal anti-imperialist mission through leadership in the League, the President did not ignore the related function of the progressive League program in containing revolutionary-socialist pressures. Time and again during our analysis of the theory and practice of Wilsonian diplomacy, we have had occasion to remark upon the manner in which the Administration's liberal anti-imperialism also served a related anti-Bolshevik function. Indeed, it is clear that the essential Wilsonian endeavor to reform international politics from within in a non-revolutionary manner was implicitly anti-Leninist in its values and assumptions. It is not surprising, then, that on several occasions, during his final speaking tour in early autumn 1919, Wilson chose to defend the Treaty and the League as liberal barriers to possible revolutionary-socialist tendencies among the world's restless masses. In his speeches the President often argued that America had a duty to support a progressive liberalization of the old imperialistic world power structure, partly to show restive peoples everywhere that the evils of international politics could be reformed without socialist revolution.[3]

At Bismarck, North Dakota, on September 10, 1919, Wilson made quite explicit his sense of the relationship between America's missionary anti-imperialism and America's liberal anti-Bolshevism:

It is a noble prospect. It is a noble opportunity. My pulses quicken at the thought of it. I am glad to have lived in a day when America can redeem her pledges to the world, when America can prove that her leadership is the leadership that leads out of these age-long miseries into which the world will not sink back, but which, without our assistance, it may struggle out of only through a long period of bloody revolution. The peoples of Europe are in a revolutionary frame of mind. They do not believe in the things that have been practiced upon them in the past, and they mean to have new things practiced. In the meantime they are, some of them, like pitiful Russia, in danger of doing a most extraordinary thing, substituting one kind of autocracy for another. Russia repudiated the Czar, who was cruel at times, and set up her present masters, who are cruel all the time and pity nobody, who seize everybody's property and feed only the soldiers that are fighting for them; and now, according to the papers, they are likely to brand every one of those soldiers so that he may not easily, at any rate, escape their clutches and desert. Branding their servants and making slaves of a great and loveable people! There is no people in the world fuller of the naive sentiments of good will and of fellowship than the people of Russia, and they are in the grip of a cruel autocracy that dares not, though challenged by every friendly Government in Europe, assemble a constituency; they dare not appeal to the people. They know that their mastery would end the minute the people took charge of their own affairs. Do not let us expose any of the rest of the world to the necessity of going through any such terrible experience as that, my fellow countrymen. We are at present helpless to assist Russia, because there are no responsible channels through which we can assist her. Our heart goes out to her, but the world is disordered, and while it is disordered—we debate! [4]

Obviously, the Wilsonian liberal struggle against imperialism and war was ideologically fused with the Wilsonian liberal struggle against Leninist revolutionary-socialism.

Finally, however, it must be re-emphasized that Wilson's anti-imperialist and anti-Bolshevik sense of America's liberal-exceptionalist missionary idealism was perfectly compatible with his sense of America's national self-interest. It is clear, for instance, that the President saw America's future commercial expansion as assured, providing that the United States chose to maintain its moral and financial world leadership by doing its part, through the League of Nations, to support an economically stable and non-revolutionary liberal-international order.[5] On September 5, 1919, speaking in St. Louis, Wilson succinctly conveyed his sense of the inseparable relationship between, on the one hand, America's economic and political national interests and, on the other, America's missionary liberal duty to the rest of mankind:

I have sometimes heard gentlemen discussing the questions that are now before us with a distinction drawn between nationalism and internationalism in these matters. It is very difficult for me to follow their distinction. The greatest nationalist is the man who wants his nation to be the greatest nation, and the greatest nation is the nation which penetrates to the heart of its duty and mission among the nations of the world. With every flash of insight into the great politics of mankind, the nation that has that vision is elevated to a place of influence and power which it cannot get by arms, which it cannot get by commercial rivalry, which it can get by no other way than by that spiritual leadership which comes from a profound understanding of the problems of humanity.[6]

In sum, then, the President envisioned America as the moral and the commercial leader of a new liberalized international order, safe both from traditional imperialism and from revolutionary-socialism, in which world trade and world politics would henceforth be conducted on America's liberal terms.

It is important to note that there was something in the President's defense of the Treaty and the League for practically every shade in the spectrum of postwar American public opinion. The more conservative pro-League elements, centered on William Howard Taft and *The New York Times,* could take heart from the more explicitly pro-Allied, anti-German, and anti-Bolshevik portions of Wilson's speeches. For their part, more business-oriented and liberal-internationalist elements, centered on men such as Herbert Hoover and Thomas Lamont, could support Wilson's fusion of America's expansive economic interests with the larger task of reintegrating Germany into an anti-Bolshevik European liberal-capitalist order. Finally, moderate-liberals, led by journals such as *The Public* and the *Springfield Republican,* could respond to Wilson's claims that while the Covenant might not have brought immediate utopia, it had nevertheless succeeded in establishing the machinery for American leadership in the future maintenance of international justice and peace. Indeed, many pro-League liberals insisted that it was necessary to abandon danger-ous utopian visions and to seek instead to reform the world from within an ordered system of controls which discouraged both im-perialist aggression and socialist revolution.

Wilsonian ideology was unable, however, to co-opt all Amer-ican elements into the liberal-internationalist consensus. Many Republican critics, gathering around Henry Cabot Lodge, ap-proved the basically punitive nature of the Versailles Treaty, but they objected to Wilson's having allowed the Allies, through the Covenant, to absorb American power into what appeared to the Lodge group to be a permanent European alliance system. The Lodge Republicans had desired a harsh anti-German peace cou-pled with a strong militant posture against Bolshevism, but they had expected that the European Allies and the new Eastern European states would supply the necessary military and political power. After unleashing the Entente on Germany and Bolshe-vism, the United States, in the opinion of the Lodge group, should have remained only loosely associated with its wartime al-lies, while retaining both its Western Hemisphere sphere of in-fluence and its ultimate freedom of decision in foreign relations inviolate. By the latter half of 1919, therefore, the Lodge Republicans had shifted from an earlier anti-Wilson and pro-Allied position to what was, in effect, an anti-Wilson and anti-Allied position.

At the same time, many on the American Left were unwilling to give up utopian dreams and join in a pragmatic defense of the League of Nations. Their disillusionment with Wilson was all the greater since, in the spring and early summer of 1918, many American Left-liberals and socialists, who had begun by opposing Wilson's liberal war, had come to give *de facto* support to the struggle against Imperial Germany both as a quasi-revolutionary war and as a means of saving the Bolshevik Revolution from German imperialism. Such men (of whom even Eugene Debs was, for a time, one), hoped ultimately for some sort of fusion between Wilsonian and Leninist values which would legitimize their growing implicit support for the war against German imperialism.

Needless to say, however, all those Americans who hoped for any sort of Wilson-Lenin co-operation, either largely on Wilson's terms or on Lenin's were greatly disappointed by the Versailles Treaty. Left-liberals, gathering around the *Nation* and the *New Republic*, were angry that Wilson had made so many concessions to the French and that he had failed to unite with European democratic-socialists to build a new radical liberal world order which would fully embrace both a reformed Germany and a domesticated Lenin. American socialists, for their part, were opposed to the League of Nations in particular and to Wilsonian diplomacy in general, as barriers to revolution. Finally, in Washington, the anti-League Left received the strong support of such radical liberal senators as Borah, Johnson, La Follette, and Norris. The liberal isolationism of these men was born both of disillusioned hopes for a Wilsonian Americanization of world politics and of opposition to what they conceived to be the involvement of America through the League in a reactionary and anti-revolutionary alliance.

It is well known that, through a combination of personal and political factors, Wilsonians were defeated in the Senate on the issue of the League of Nations. Moreover, ensuing Republican Administrations, while in no sense pursuing a strictly "isolationist" foreign policy, did, nonetheless, refuse to play exactly the type of role in international politics that Woodrow Wilson had envisioned for the United States. Yet looking back, what seems clear is that Wilsonianism, even while losing the battle over the League of Nations, eventually triumphed in the more long-term struggle over the ultimate definition of the nature of twentieth-century American foreign policy. Wilson established the main drift toward an American liberal globalism, hostile both to traditional imperialism and to revolutionary-socialism. Many who had been associated with Wilson, or who accepted the essentials of his world view, such as Herbert Hoover, Cordell Hull, Franklin Roosevelt, and John Foster Dulles, would continue in later periods to identify America's expansive national interest with the maintenance of a rational and peaceful international liberal order. Ultimately, in the post-World War II period, Wilsonian values would have their complete triumph in the bi-partisan Cold War consensus.

Abbreviations Used in the Notes for
Woodrow Wilson and World Politics

D.S.N.A.	Records of the Department of State, National Archives.
DLC	The Library of Congress.
Intimate Papers	Charles Seymour, (ed.), *The Intimate Papers of Colonel House* (4 vols., Boston, 1926–1928).
FR	United States Department of State, *Papers Relating to the Foreign Relations of the United States.*
FR, PPC, 1919	United States Department of State, *Papers Relating to the Foreign Relations of the United States, Paris Peace Conference* (13 vols., Washington, 1942–1947).
Life and Letters	Ray Stannard Baker, *Woodrow Wilson, Life and Letters* (8 vols., Garden City, N.Y., 1927–1939).
PPWW	Ray Stannard Baker and William E. Dodd, eds., *The Public Papers of Woodrow Wilson* (6 vols., New York, 1925–1927).
WW&WS	Ray Stannard Baker, *Woodrow Wilson and World Settlement* (3 vols., Garden City, N.Y., 1922–1923).

NOTES

CHAPTER I: WAR AND REVOLUTION, I

1 Ray Stannard and William E. Dodd (eds.), *The Public Papers of Woodrow Wilson* (6 vols., New York, 1925–27), II, p. 375 (hereafter cited as *PPWW*); see also *PPWW*, II, pp. 332, 359, 408; for Wilson's views on the international significance of American

economic growth at the turn of the century and on the Spanish American War, see Woodrow Wilson, *A History of the American People* (5 vols., New York and London, 1902), V, pp. 264-7, 296; William Diamond, *The Economic Thought of Woodrow Wilson* (Baltimore, 1943), pp. 131-55, and William A. Williams, *The Tragedy of American Diplomacy* (New York, 1962), pp. 61-83, are both excellent over-all analyses of Wilson's export orientation.

2 John Wells Davidson (ed.), *A Cross Roads of Freedom, The 1912 Campaign Speeches of Woodrow Wilson* (New Haven, 1956), p. 114; *PPWW*, II, p. 408.

3 Davidson, *Cross Roads of Freedom*, pp. 33, 47, 115, 487-8; *PPWW*, II, pp. 332, 358, 374-5.

4 Davidson, *Cross Roads of Freedom*, pp. 33, 47, 119, 487; *PPWW*, II, pp. 333, 359.

5 Davidson, *Cross Roads of Freedom*, p. 119, see also p. 209; and *PPWW*, II, pp. 232-3, 363-5; for a consideration of the legislation of Wilson's first term in the context of the export issue, see Martin J. Sklar, "Woodrow Wilson and the Political Economy of Modern United States Liberalism," *Studies on the Left*, I, 3 (1960), pp. 17-47.

6 McAdoo to R. L. Henry, Feb. 16, 1915, McAdoo to George W. Norris, June 29, 1915, William G. McAdoo MSS, Library of Congress

7 McAdoo to F. M. Murphy, Nov. 8, 1915, McAdoo MSS; William G. McAdoo, "Address Before the Chicago Commercial Club," Jan. 9, 1915, *Congressional Record*, 63d Cong. 2d sess., pp. 1535-6; William G. McAdoo, *Crowded Years, The Reminiscences of William G. McAdoo* (Boston, 1931), pp. 294-302.

8 McAdoo to P. H. W. Ross, June 26, 1916, McAdoo MSS; McAdoo, *Crowded Years*, p. 198

9 McAdoo to George W. Norris, Aug. 27, 1915, McAdoo MSS; see also McAdoo to Claude Kitchin, Aug. 24, 1915, McAdoo, Speech at Fargo, N.D., Oct. 29, 1915, p. 11, McAdoo MSS; for McAdoo's view that Wilsonian banking, tariff, and shipping legislation formed an interrelated program to aid experts, see McAdoo to J. W. Ashley, Dec. 12, 1914, McAdoo to Henry Lee Higginson, Dec. 15, 1914, McAdoo MSS.

10 *Congressional Record*, 64th Cong. 1st sess., Appendix, pp. 185-8; Edward N. Hurley, Address before Advertising Association, New York, Dec. 1, 1915, Edward N. Hurley, Address before Boston Commercial Club, Mar. 28, 1916, Woodrow Wilson MSS, Li-

brary of Congress, Files 6 and 2, respectively; *PPWW*, III, pp. 267–79; *PPWW*, IV, pp. 167–8; for a discussion of the business-oriented ideology of the FTC under Wilson, see Gabriel Kolko, *The Triumph of Conservatism* (New York, 1963), pp. 255–78.

11 *Congressional Record*, 64th Cong., 1st sess., Appendix, p. 187.

12 Cited in Sklar, *Wilson and the Political Economy*, p. 31; see also Bryan to Wilson, Oct. 6, 1913, Wilson-Bryan Correspondence, National Archives.

13 Sklar, *Wilson and the Political Economy*, p. 31.

14 *PPWW*, IV, pp. 167–8, 228–44, 257–9, 276–8, 287–8, 309–22; see also Woodrow Wilson, "Address to the National Chamber of Commerce, Feb. 10, 1916," *Nation's Business*, IV (Feb. 10, 1916), pp. 18–20.

15 *PPWW*, III, p. 212; see also *PPWW*, III, pp. 216–17, 241–2; *PPWW*, IV, p. 26.

16 *PPWW*, IV, p. 323; see also *PPWW*, IV, pp. 6–7, 117–18.

17 *PPWW*, IV, p. 301; see also *PPWW*, IV, pp. 243–4.

18 *PPWW*, III, p. 227.

19 *PPWW*, IV, p. 233.

20 Tien-yi Li, *Woodrow Wilson's China Policy, 1913–1917* (New York, 1952), pp. 12–13; Burton F. Beers, *Vain Endeavor, Robert Lansing's Attempt to End the American-Japanese Rivalry* (Durham, N.C., 1962), pp. 16–18; Sklar, *Wilson and the Political Economy*, pp. 44–6.

21 Roy Watson Curry, *Woodrow Wilson and Far Eastern Policy, 1913–1921* (New Haven, 1957), pp. 19–24; Arthur S. Link, *Wilson: The New Freedom* (Princeton, 1956), pp. 283–8; Tien-yi Li, *Wilson's China Policy*, pp. 33–9.

22 Williams, *Tragedy of American Diplomacy*, pp. 74–7; Tien-yi Li, *Wilson's China Policy*, pp. 46–7, 163–5; Beers, *Vain Endeavor*, pp. 72–92; Diamond, *Economic Thought of Woodrow Wilson*, pp. 147–8; Russell H. Fifield, *Woodrow Wilson and the Far East, The Diplomacy of the Shantung Question* (New York, 1952), pp. 90–93.

23 Wilson to McAdoo, Nov. 3, 1914, Aug. 26, Oct. 5, 1915, McAdoo MSS; McAdoo to Senator W. J. Stone, Jan. 15, 1915, and McAdoo, Speech at Chapel Hill, N.C., May 30, 1916, McAdoo MSS; Redfield to Wilson, Sept. 17, Nov. 21, 1914, Wilson MSS, File 2.

24 Josephus Daniels, Address at Banquet of Federation of Trade Press Associations, n.p., Sept. 8, 1915, Josephus Daniels MSS, Library of Congress.

25 Link, *The New Freedom*, pp. 327–46; Arthur S. Link, *Wilson:*

The Struggle for Neutrality, 1914–1915 (Princeton, 1960), pp. 495–550; see also United States Dept. of State, *Papers Relating to the Foreign Relations of the United States, The Lansing Papers, 1914–1920* (2 vols., Washington, D.C., 1939), II, pp. 459–70, for evidence that the expansion of American trade and orderly liberal values into the Caribbean area, by forceful means on occasion, was related in part to the Administration's desire to keep strong European economic and/or political influence out of the strategic Caribbean area.

26 The Private Diary of Colonel House, Nov. 28, 1915, House MSS, Yale University Library (hereafter cited as House MSS Diary).

27 *PPWW,* III, pp. 111–22; *PPWW,* IV, pp. 339–42; Link, *The New Freedom,* pp. 347–415; Link, *The Struggle for Neutrality,* pp. 488–94.

28 *PPWW,* III, pp. 45–6, 339–40, 400–405; *PPWW,* IV, p. 343; Wilson to Walter Hines Page, June 4, 1914, Ray Stannard Baker MSS, The Library of Congress; Wilson to Bryan, Mar. 17, 1915, Wilson-Bryan Correspondence, United States National Archives; Link, *The New Freedom,* pp. 382–9, 410–15; Link, *The Struggle for Neutrality,* pp. 458–84.

29 Wilson to Sir William Tyrrell, Nov. 22, 1913, cited in Ray Stannard Baker, *Woodrow Wilson, Life and Letters* (8 vols., Garden City, N.Y., 1927–1934), IV, p. 292 (hereafter cited as *Life and Letters*); in relation to the question of foreign property in Mexico, see Robert Lansing, Remarks at Luncheon for American-Mexican Joint Commission, New York, Sept. 4, 1916, p. 4, Wilson MSS, File 6, Box 56; on the Wilson-Tyrrell negotiations see Link, *The New Freedom,* pp. 374–7.

30 *PPWW,* III, pp. 64–9, 113; see also *PPWW,* IV, pp. 341–2; *PPWW,* V, pp. 227–8; House MSS Diary, Nov. 25, 1914; George Creel, "The Next Four Years, An Interview with President Wilson," *Everybody's Magazine,* XXXVI (Feb. 1917), p. 132.

31 Charles Seymour (ed.), *The Intimate Papers of Colonel House* (4 vols., Boston, 1926–1928), I, pp. 207–34 (hereafter cited as *Intimate Papers*); Link, *The New Freedom,* pp. 324–7.

32 *Intimate Papers,* I, p. 209.

33 *PPWW,* IV, p. 104; see also *PPWW,* III, pp. 250–51, 406.

34 *PPWW,* IV, p. 59; see also *PPWW,* IV, p. 116.

35 *PPWW,* IV, p. 391; see also *PPWW,* IV, pp. 229, 378–9.

36 *PPWW,* III, p. 303; see also *Life and Letters,* VI, pp. 377–8.

37 *PPWW,* IV, p. 141.

38 E. M. House, *Philip Dru: Administrator* (New York, 1912), p. 273.

39 *Intimate Papers*, I, pp. 238–75; *Life and Letters*, V, pp. 20–50; Burton J. Hendrick, *The Life and Letters of Walter H. Page* (3 vols., Garden City, N.Y., 1924–1926), I, pp. 270–300.

40 House MSS Diary, Apr. 10, 1914.

41 House to Gerard, Aug. 17, 1914, cited in *Intimate Papers*, I, pp. 319–20.

42 House MSS Diary, Mar. 19, Mar. 24, 1915; House to Wilson, Feb. 28, Mar. 19, Mar. 26, Mar. 29 (cable), Apr. 12, 1915, Wilson MSS, File 2: *Intimate Papers*, I, pp. 369, 400–402, 410–11, 430–31.

43 House MSS Diary, Sept. 28, 1915; see also House to Wilson, Nov. 19, 1915, Wilson MSS, File 2.

44 House MSS Diary, June 21, 1914; see also House MSS Diary, July 3, 1914; *Intimate Papers*, I, pp. 264–7, 275; Hendrick, *Life and Letters of Walter H. Page*, I, pp. 270–75.

45 House, *Philip Dru: Administrator*, pp. 273–4.

46 House to Wilson, Apr. 11, 1915, Jan. 15, Feb. 9, 1916, Wilson MSS, File 2; House MSS Diary, Mar. 23, 1915, Feb. 7, 1916; *Intimate Papers*, I, pp. 238–9, 246, 260; *Intimate Papers*, II, p. 291; *Life and Letters*, VI, p. 150, n. 5.

47 Robert Lansing, *War Memoirs of Robert Lansing* (New York, 1935), p. 212; David F. Houston, *Eight Years with Wilson's Cabinet, 1913–1920* (2 vols., Garden City, N.Y., 1926) I, p. 229; *Intimate Papers*, II, p. 412; Tien-yi Li, *Wilson's China Policy*, pp. 11–12.

48 Laurence W. Martin, *Peace Without Victory, Woodrow Wilson and the British Liberals* (New Haven, 1958), pp. 7–13, 55–84; Arno J. Mayer, *Political Origins of the New Diplomacy, 1917–1918* (New Haven, 1959), pp. 25–7, 54–7; E. M. Winslow, *The Pattern of Imperialism* (New York, 1948), p. 102; Henry R. Winkler, *The League of Nations Movement in Great Britain* (New Brunswick, N.J., 1952), pp. 28–49, 200–203.

49 Wilson to House, May 16, 1916, House MSS; House to Grey, May 10, 1916, House to Wilson, May 21, 1916, Wilson MSS, File 2; *Life and Letters*, V, pp. 73–4; *Life and Letters*, VI, pp. 204–5, 216–17.

50 Wilson to House, Dec. 24, 1915, House MSS.

51 *PPWW*, IV, p. 289.

52 U.S. Department of State, *Papers Relating to the Foreign Rela-*

tions of the United States, The Lansing Papers, 1914–1920 (2 vols., Washington, D.C., 1939–1940), I, pp. 19–23 (hereafter all volumes in this *Foreign Relations* series of the State Department will be cited by the abbreviation *FR*, to be followed by the appropriate subtitles); see also Martin, *Peace Without Victory*, p. 127; William A. Williams, "American Intervention in Russia, 1917–1920," *Studies on the Left*, III (Fall 1963), 29.

53 *PPWW*, IV, pp. 75, 186–7, 194–5, 348, 381–2; see also Wilson to House, May 16, 1916, House MSS; House to Wilson, May 21, 1916, Wilson MSS, File 2.

54 *PPWW*, IV, pp. 360–61.

55 John H. Kautsky, "J. A. Schumpeter and Karl Kautsky: Parallel Theories of Imperialism," *Midwest Journal of Political Science*, V (May 1961), 120.

56 J. H. Kautsky, "Schumpeter and Kautsky," pp. 118–19.

57 V. I. Lenin, *Collected Works* (Vols. 4, 13, 18–20, 21; three of these volumes in two books, New York, 1927–1942), XVIII, p. 288 (hereafter cited as Lenin, *Works*).

58 Winslow, *The Pattern of Imperialism*, pp. 156–7; Lenin, *Works*, XIX, p. 164; J. H. Kautsky, "Schumpeter and Kautsky," pp. 121–2; Herbert Marcuse, *Soviet Marxism* (New York, Vintage Russian Library, 1961), pp. 18–19.

59 Lenin, *Works*, XIX, pp. 92–144, 151–4, 156–62.

60 Lenin, *Works*, XVIII, p. 290; Lenin, *Works*, XIX, pp. 147–8, 163–5.

61 Lenin, *Works*, XIX, p. 167.

62 Lenin, *Works*, XVIII, pp. 269–72, 291; Lenin, *Works*, XIX, pp. 186–9; C. Dale Fuller, "Lenin's Attitude Toward an International Organization for the Maintenance of Peace, 1914–1917," *Political Science Quarterly*, LXIV (June 1949), pp. 245–61.

63 Lenin, *Works*, XVIII, pp. 206–8, 247–8, 289, 295–7, 317, 402–3; Lenin, *Works*, XIX, pp. 62, 70–71, 187, 339, 430; Lenin, *Works*, XX, Bk. 1, pp. 111–13, 146–7; Mayer, *Political Origins*, pp. 50–51; Alfred G. Meyer, *Leninism* (Cambridge, Mass., 1957), pp. 242–52.

64 Lenin, *Works*, XVIII, pp. 162–4, 292–5; Lenin, *Works*, XIX, pp. 91, 155, 180–83, 352–61; Mayer, *Political Origins*, pp. 52–3; Winslow, *The Pattern of Imperialism*, pp. 183–5.

65 Lenin, *Works*, XIX, pp. 417–26; Meyer, *Leninism*, p. 150.

66 Lenin, *Works*, XVIII, pp. 149, 180–81, 268, 370; Lenin, *Works*, XIX, pp. 51, 63, 67–9, 73, 219, 258, 314–21, 413, 427–35; Lenin, *Works*, XX, Bk. 1, pp. 138–9, 248–50

67 Lenin, *Works*, XXI, Bk. 1, pp. 95–6, 118–26; Mayer, *Political Origins*, pp. 194–5, 240–41; Merle Fainsod, *International Socialism and the World War* (Cambridge, Mass., 1935), Ch. 8 *passim*.

68 Lenin, *Works*, XVIII, pp. 368–72; Lenin, *Works*, XIX, pp. 53–7, 248–53, 269–76; Leon Trotsky, *The Bolsheviki and World Peace* (New York, 1918), pp. 72–3; Mayer, *Leninism*, pp. 151–52; Mayer, *Political Origins*, pp. 298–300.

69 Lenin, *Works*, XVIII, pp. 235–6, 373; Lenin, *Works*, XIX, pp. 50, 253–6; Lenin, *Works*, XX, Bk. 1, pp. 310–14; Lenin, *Works*, XX, Bk. 2, pp. 26–9, 253–4; Mayer, *Leninism*, pp. 153–5; Richard Pipes, *The Formation of the Soviet Union, Communism and Nationalism 1917–1923* (Cambridge, Mass., 1954), pp. 44–5.

70 Lenin, *Works*, XVIII, pp. 264–8; Lenin, *Works*, XIX, pp. 42–4, 72; Lenin, *Works*, XX, Bk. 2, pp. 30–31, 43–4; 91–2, 181–3, 224–5.

71 Lenin, *Works*, XVIII, pp. 69, 224, 367; Lenin, *Works*, XIX, pp. 169–74, 277–303; Meyer, *Leninism*, pp. 145–50; Pipes, *The Formation of the Soviet Union*, pp. 35–43, 48–9; E. H. Carr, *The Bolshevik Revolution* (3 vols., London, 1950–1953), III, pp. 229–34; Stanley W. Page, *Lenin and the World Revolution* (New York, 1959), p. 141.

72 Page, *Lenin and the World Revolution*, p. 142; Mayer, *Political Origins*, p. 295; Richard H. Ullman, *Anglo-Soviet Relations, 1917–1921, Intervention and the War* (Princeton, 1961), pp. 28–9; Robert D. Warth, *The Allies and the Russian Revolution, From the Fall of the Monarchy to the Peace of Brest Litovsk* (Durham, 1954), pp. 199–200; Louis Fischer, *The Soviets in World Affairs: A History of Relations between the Soviet Union and the Rest of the World, 1917–1929* (Princeton, Vintage Russian Library, 1960), pp. 12–13.

73 *PPWW*, IV, p. 381; see also *PPWW*, IV, p. 185.

74 *PPWW*, IV pp. 89–90.

75 *PPWW*, IV, pp. 30, 37–8, 109–10.

76 On the economic importance of American-Allied wartime trade to the American economy, see Alice M. Morrissey, *The American Defense of Neutral Rights* (Cambridge, Mass., 1939), pp. 4–24, 90–104, 132–53; Ernest R. May, *The World War and American Isolation* (Cambridge, Mass., 1959), pp. 156–7, 336–46; Daniel M. Smith, *Robert Lansing and American Neutrality* (Berkeley, 1958), pp. 92–5; Edward H. Buehrig, *Woodrow Wilson and the Balance of Power* (Bloomington, 1955), pp. 85–105; see also the speeches by McAdoo on Sept. 28, 1917, and Oct. 4, 1917, in

McAdoo MSS, Box 563, in which McAdoo argued that German submarine warfare had constituted a threat to America's trade and economic health.

77 *PPWW*, IV, p. 61; see also *PPWW*, IV, pp. 75, 122–3, 171.

78 *PPWW*, IV, p. 44; see also *PPWW*, III, pp. 147–8; *PPWW*, IV, pp. 158, 394.

79 *PPWW*, IV, pp. 282, 430–32; *FR, Lansing Papers*, I, pp. 221–2, 555–8; Lansing to Dr. E. M. Gallaudet, June 2, 1915, Lansing MSS, Library of Congress; House to Wilson, July 17, 1915, Wilson MSS, File 2; May, *American Isolation*, pp. 137–9, 325–35; Arthur S. Link, *Wilson the Diplomatist* (Baltimore, 1957), pp. 40–43.

80 May, *American Isolation*, pp. 110–52; Smith, *Robert Lansing*, pp. 49–61; Buehrig, *Balance of Power*, pp. 18–57; Morrissey, *Neutral Rights*, pp. 50–77.

81 *PPWW*, IV, pp. 4, 8, 26, 55–6, 145.

82 *PPWW*, IV, pp. 127–8.

83 *PPWW*, IV, pp. 347–8.

84 Wilson to House, July 14, 1915, House MSS; House MSS Diary, Feb. 1, 1917; Josephus Daniels's Diary, Mar. 19, Mar. 20, 1917, Daniels MSS; *Intimate Papers*, II, pp. 227–8; *Life and Letters*, VI, p. 358; Joseph Tumulty, *Woodrow Wilson as I Know Him* (Garden City, N.Y., 1921), pp. 233–5.

85 House MSS Diary, Nov. 14 and 17, 1916; Wilson to House, Jan. 24, 1917, Ray Stannard Baker MSS, DLC; *Intimate Papers*, II, p. 390; Arthur S. Link, *Woodrow Wilson and the Progressive Era* (New York, 1954), pp. 254–6; Buehrig, *Balance of Power*, p. 253.

86 House to Wilson, Dec. 22, 1915, Dec. 27, 1916, Jan. 15, 1917, Wilson MSS, File 2; House MSS Diary, Dec. 27, 1916, Jan. 15, 1917; House to Wilson, Jan. 18, 1917, House to Lansing, Jan. 26, 1917, House MSS; *Intimate Papers*, I, p. 318.

87 House MSS Diary, Sept. 28, 1914; *Intimate Papers*, I, pp. 328, 388; *Life and Letters*, V, pp. 64–5; Christopher Lasch, *The American Liberals and the Russian Revolution* (New York, 1962), pp. 12–13.

88 Wilson to House, May 16, May 18, July 23, 1916, House MSS; House MSS Diary, Jan. 14, May 13, June 23, Sept. 24, 1916; House to Wilson, Dec. 20, 1916, Wilson MSS, File 2; Martin, *Peace Without Victory*, pp. 111–12.

89 House MSS Diary, Sept. 3, 1916, Jan. 19, 1917; House to Wilson, Dec. 7, 1915, Wilson MSS, File 2; *Life and Letters*, VI, pp. 208–

9; *Intimate Papers*, I, pp. 284–5; *PPWW*, IV, p. 410; Martin, *Peace Without Victory*, pp. 90–91, May, *American Isolation*, pp. 77–8; for a statement of Wilson's distrust of the war aims of all the major belligerents, see also Wilson to Bryan, Apr. 27, 1915, Wilson-Bryan Correspondence, National Archives.

90 House, *Philip Dru: Administrator*, pp. 272–4.

91 House MSS Diary, Feb. 14, 1916; see also *Intimate Papers*, I, pp. 364, 428.

92 House to Wilson, Nov. 10, 1915, Wilson MSS, File 2; *Intimate Papers*, I, pp. 363–5; *Intimate Papers*, II, pp. 54–5, 87–92.

93 *Intimate Papers*, I, pp. 362–4, 372–5, 380–83; May, *American Isolation*, pp. 82–9.

94 House MSS Diary, Nov. 25, 1914, Nov. 9, 1915, Dec. 15, 1915, Jan. 31, 1917; House to Wilson, Feb. 15, 1915, Apr. 11, 1915, Dec. 22, 1915, Feb. 3, 1916, Mar. 22, 1916, Nov. 6, 1916, Nov. 30, 1916, Jan. 20, 1917, Wilson MSS, File 2; *Intimate Papers*, I, pp. 281–2, 298–300.

95 House MSS Diary, Apr. 22, 1915, Jan. 6, 1916, Feb. 11, 1916, Apr. 30, 1916; House to Walter H. Page, Aug. 4, 1915, House to Wilson, Jan. 11, 1916, Wilson MSS, File 2; *Intimate Papers*, I, pp. 469–70.

96 House to Wilson, Feb. 3, 1916, Wilson MSS, File 2.

97 House to Wilson, Sept. 6, 1914, Wilson MSS, File 2.

98 House MSS Diary, Oct. 15, 1915; see also House MSS Diary, Feb. 20, 1915; House to Wilson, Apr. 18, 1915, Wilson MSS, File 2.

99 House MSS Diary, Feb. 7, 10, 11, 14, 1916; *Intimate Papers*, II, pp. 85–6, 90–1; *Life and Letters*, VI, pp. 124–34, 147–54; May, *American Isolation*, pp. 348–59.

100 Lansing, "Confidential Memoranda and Notes, July 11, 1915, Jan. 9, 1916," Lansing MSS; House MSS Diary, Oct. 13, 1915; Smith, *Robert Lansing*, pp. 60–61; Buehrig, *Balance of Power*, pp. 131–7.

101 Lansing, "Confidential Memoranda and Notes, Sept. n.d., Dec. 3, 1916, Jan. 28, 1917," Lansing MSS; Lansing to Wilson, Dec. 10, 1916, Wilson MSS, File 2; Smith, *Robert Lansing*, pp. 132–7, 146–7; Buehrig, *Balance of Power*, pp. 138–41.

102 Lansing, "Confidential Memoranda and Notes, Dec. 3, 1916," Lansing MSS.

103 Lansing, "Confidential Memoranda and Notes, Feb. 4, 1917," Lansing MSS; *FR, Lansing Papers*, I, pp. 591–2; Smith, *Robert Lansing*, pp. 157–8; Buehrig, *Balance of Power*, pp. 142–7.

104 Lansing to Edward N. Smith, Feb. 27, 1917, Lansing MSS.
105 House MSS Diary, Sept. 22, 1915; see also *Intimate Papers*, I, p. 293; *Intimate Papers*, II, pp. 239–40, *Life and Letters*, V, pp. 214, n. 3, 375–6.
106 *Intimate Papers*, II, pp. 231–2; Martin, *Peace Without Victory*, pp. 98–102; May, *American Isolation*, pp. 351, 356.
107 *Intimate Papers*, II, pp. 390–402; May, *American Isolation*, pp. 358–70; Arthur S. Link, *Wilson: Campaigns for Progressivism and Peace, 1916–1917* (Princeton, 1965), pp. 165–289.
108 House to Wilson, Jan. 20, 1917, Wilson MSS, File 2; on House's fear of a Russian separate peace, see also House to Wilson, Jan. 11, Feb. 9, 1916, Wilson MSS, File 2; *Intimate Papers*, II, p. 129; Lasch, *American Liberals*, pp. 20–23.
109 House MSS Diary, Mar. 17, 1917.
110 House to Wilson, Mar. 17, 1917, House MSS.
111 FR, *Lansing Papers*, I, pp. 626–8; see also pp. 628–9; Lansing, "Confidential Memoranda and Notes, Mar. 20, 1917," Lansing MSS; George F. Kennan, *Soviet American Relations, 1917–1920, Russia Leaves the War* (Princeton, 1956), pp. 14–16.
112 Mayer, *Political Origins*, p. 70; Lasch, *American Liberals*, pp. 27–9.
113 Daniels MSS Diary, Mar. 20, 1917.
114 *PPWW*, V, pp. 12–13.
115 Ibid.
116 House MSS Diary, Mar. 17, 1916; House to Wilson, Mar. 15, 1915, Jan. 15, 1916, Jan. 16, 1916, Apr. 7, 1916, June 1, 1916, June 18, 1916, June 25, 1916, Wilson MSS, File 2.
117 House MSS Diary, Apr. 19, 1916; House to Wilson, May 11, 1915, May 14, 1915, Jan. 8, 1916, Apr. 19, 1916, Apr. 22, 1916, Wilson MSS, File 2; *Intimate Papers*, I, pp. 442–3.
118 House MSS Diary, Jan. 14, 1916; House to Wilson, May 1, 1915, Nov. 19, 1915, Jan. 11, 1916, Wilson MSS, File 2.
119 House to Wilson, Aug 3, 1916, Wilson MSS, File 2.
120 House to Wilson, June 10, July 30, 1916, Wilson MSS, File 2; House MSS Diary, May 3, 1916; House to Frank L. Polk, July 28, 1916, Frank L. Polk MSS, Yale University Library.
121 House to Wilson, May 17, 1916, Wilson MSS, File 2.
122 House MSS Diary, Sept, 24, 1916.
123 *PPWW*, IV, p. 413; see also Wilson to House, June 22, 1916, House MSS; Wilson to Thomas Dixon, Jan. 25, 1917, Wilson MSS, File 7; *Life and Letters*, VI, pp. 372, 388–9, 397.

124 For a recent sophisticated statement of the manner in which the work of Link, Buehrig, and E. May has broadened the concept of Wilson's motivations in the 1914–17 period to include a fusion of both national interest and international idealism, see Daniel M. Smith, "National Interest and American Intervention, 1917: An Historiographical Appraisal," *The Journal of American History*, LII (June 1965), 5–24.

125 Lenin, *Works*, XVIII, pp. 61, 145–6, 299–300.

126 Lenin, *Works*, XVIII, pp. 67–9, 118–29, 142–3, 171–5, 187–90, 220–25, 228, 386–7; Lenin, *Works*, XIX, pp. 77–9, 217–26.

127 Lenin, *Works*, XVIII, pp. 62–6, 70–72, 78–82, 84–9, 112–17, 132–4, 157–8, 197–202, 226, 305, 389–90; Lenin, *Works*, XIX, pp. 15–19, 340–51; Meyer, *Leninism*, p. 156.

128 Lenin, *Works*, XVIII, p. 153; Lenin, *Works*, XIX, p. 74; Lenin, *Works*, XXI, Bk. 2, pp. 159–61, 186–7, 205, 244–6.

129 Lenin, *Works*, XVIII, pp. 76–7, 382–3; Lenin, *Works*, XIX, pp. 65, 231–4, 338, 413; Lenin, *Works*, XX, Bk. 1, pp. 111, 262–3; Lenin, *Works*, XX, Bk. 2, pp. 33–4; Lenin, *Works*, XXI, Bk. 1, pp. 188–9.

130 Lenin, *Works*, XVIII, p. 383; Lenin, *Works*, XIX, pp. 43, 210.

131 Lenin, *Works*, XX, Bk. 1, pp. 23–4, 57–9, 61, 71–3, 173–5, 295; Lenin, *Works*, XX, Bk. 2, pp. 208–9.

132 Lenin, *Works*, XX, Bk. 1, pp. 29–31, 33, 41, 60, 131–2, 234–5; Lenin, *Works*, XX, Bk. 2, p. 58.

133 Robert Paul Browder and Alexander F. Kerensky (eds.), *The Russian Provisional Government, 1917, Documents* (3 vols., Stanford, 1961), II, pp. 1118–9 (hereafter cited as *Provisional Government Documents*).

CHAPTER II: WAR AND REVOLUTION, II

1 Memorandum on Conference with Colonel E. M. House, at Magnolia, Mass., July 27, 1917, A. Lawrence Lowell MSS, Harvard University Library.

2 House MSS Diary, Feb. 24, 1918.

3 *Intimate Papers*, III, pp. 128–35, 378; House MSS Diary, May 19, 1917, Apr. 9, 1918; House to W. H. Buckler, June 10, 1917, House to Wilson, June 23, 1918, House MSS.

4 *Intimate Papers*, III, pp. 57–9, 128–30, 132–5, 153–9, 278–80, 326 n. 2, 339, 354–5; *Intimate Papers*, IV, pp. 61–3; House MSS Diary, Mar. 28, Aug. 29, Oct. 24, Dec. 1, 1917, Feb. 7, Aug. 25,

Sept. 24, 1918; House to Buckler, June 10, July 1, Aug. 11, 1917, House to Wilson, Sept. 4, 1917, House MSS; Anne W. Lane and Louise H. Wall (eds.), *The Letters of Franklin K. Lane* (Cambridge, Mass., 1922), pp. 255–6.

5 *PPWW*, V, pp. 11–12, 61–2, 64–5, 94–6, 119, 129–34, 161–2, 199.

6 *PPWW*, V, p. 95.

7 House MSS Diary, Dec. 4, 1917.

8 *Life and Letters*, VII, p. 546.

9 House MSS Diary, Aug. 19, 1917; *Intimate Papers*, III, pp. 133, 282–4, House to Wilson, Nov. 11, 1917, House MSS.

10 *PPWW*, V, pp. 130–31, 258–61; Wilson to Polk, Aug. 1, 1917, Frank L. Polk Papers, Yale University Library; for Wilson's tendency to use loyal elements of the Left, such as the A. F. of L., to control more radical groups, see Lansing to Wilson, Nov. 30, 1917, with attached note by Wilson, Wilson MSS, File 2.

11 Wilson to House, Aug. 22, 1917, House MSS.

12 Mayer, *Political Origins*, pp. 385–92; Austin Van Der Slice, *International Labor, Diplomacy, and Peace, 1914–1919* (Philadelphia, 1941), pp. 218–57.

13 *FR, Lansing Papers*, II, p. 135.

14 *FR, 1918, Russia*, I, pp. 53–5, 75–7, 172–3, 212–14; *FR, 1917, Supplement 2*, I, p. 166; *Congressional Record*, 65th Cong. 2nd sess., Vol. 56, Appendix, pp. 110–12; Mayer, *Political Origins*, pp. 62, 70–79, 82–3, 96–7, 248–51, 262; Leonard Schapiro, *The Origin of the Communist Autocracy* (Cambridge, England, 1955), pp. 23, 92; Warth, *Allies and the Russian Revolution*, pp. 64–5, 89–90, 149.

15 House to Wilson, Apr. 10, 1917, House MSS; House MSS Diary, July 22, Sept. 29, 1917; *Intimate Papers*, III, pp. 140, 153, 157–8, 167, 204; Lasch, *American Liberals*, p. 48; Kennan, *Russia Leaves the War*, pp. 134–9, 243–4.

16 House MSS Diary, Dec. 31, 1917; *FR, 1917, Supplement 2*, I, p. 352; *FR, 1918, Russia*, I, pp. 254–5, 271; *Intimate Papers*, III, pp. 233–4, 278–9, 284–5, 290, 330–31; Lasch, *American Liberals*, p. 79.

17 *Life and Letters*, VII, p. 355.

18 *PPWW*, V, p. 120.

19 Daniels MSS Diary, Nov, 27, 1917.

20 *PPWW*, V, p. 134; see also Charles E. Russell to Wilson, Nov. 7, 1917, George Creel MSS, Library of Congress; Wilson to Russell,

Nov. 10, 1917, Wilson to Creel, Nov. 10, 1917, Wilson MSS, File 6, Box 93; Lincoln Colcord to Wilson, Dec. 3, 1917, Wilson to Colcord, Dec. 6, 1917, Wilson MSS, File 2; Kennan, *Russia Leaves the War*, pp. 144–7.

21 *FR, 1918, Russia*, I, p. 424, see also pp. 422–3.

22 *FR, 1919, Paris Peace Conference*, I, p. 48; see also Lawrence E. Gelfand, *The Inquiry: American Preparations for Peace, 1917–1919* (New Haven, 1963), pp. 135–7.

23 *FR, 1919, Paris Peace Conference*, I, pp. 45–6.

24 *Intimate Papers*, III, pp. 316–49.

25 House MSS Diary, Jan. 2, 1918; *Intimate Papers*, III, pp. 387–9.

26 *Intimate Papers*, III, p. 331; on Point Six of the Fourteen see *PPWW*, V, pp. 159–60.

27 *PPWW*, V, pp. 156–8; see also Kennan, *Russia Leaves the War*, pp. 253–8.

28 N. D. Baker to Chairman of C.P.I., n.d., N. D. Baker MSS, Box 3, DLC.

29 Lasch, *American Liberals*, pp. 70–83.

30 House MSS Diary, Dec. 22, 1917, Jan. 9, 1918.

31 For Lansing's attitudes, see *FR, Lansing Papers*, II, pp. 32–3, 325; *FR, 1918, Supplement* 1, I, pp. 171–2, 189; Polk to Lansing, Aug. 20, 1917, with enclosures, and Lansing to Wilson, Aug. 20, 1917, File 862.20211/521, Records of the Dept. of State, National Archives (hereafter cited as D.S.N.A.); Gompers to Lansing, Oct. 25, 1917, Lansing to Wilson, Nov. 1, 1917, File 861.00/611, D.S.N.A.; on the anti-radical position of the A. F. of L. during the period of its wartime co-operation with the Wilson Administration, see Louis S. Reed, *The Labor Philosophy of Samuel Gompers* (New York, 1930), pp. 152–6; Bernard Mandel, *Samuel Gompers* (Antioch, 1963), pp. 388–417; Samuel Gompers, *Seventy Years of Life and Labor* (2 vols., New York, 1925), II, pp. 377–472; Henry Pelling, *America and the British Left* (London, 1956), pp. 108–29; Marguerite Green, *The National Civic Federation and the American Labor Movement* (Washington, D.C., 1956), pp. 364–92.

32 *FR, Lansing Papers*, II, pp. 89–90, 338, for Lansing's unenthusiastic attitude toward liberal war aims revision, see also pp. 48–9; *FR, 1917, Supplement* 2, pp. 295–6.

33 *PPWW*, V, pp. 65–6, 130; Wilson to Senator J. S. Williams, Feb. 18, 1918, Wilson MSS, File 7, Box 26; *Life and Letters*, VII, pp. 43–5, 65.

34 *PPWW*, V, pp. 49–50.
35 *PPWW*, V, pp. 120–21; Wilson to William Kent, July 17, 1917, Charles L. Swem Collection of Wilsonia, Princeton University Library; see also Wilson to Gompers, Aug. 31, 1917, Wilson MSS, File 7; Wilson to House, Aug. 31, 1918, House MSS; *Life and Letters*, VII, p. 383.
36 Ray Ginger, *The Bending Cross, A Biography of Eugene Victor Debs* (New Brunswick, 1949), chs. 17–18; Irving Howe and Louis Coser, *The American Communist Party* (Boston, 1957), ch. 1; Robert K. Murray, *Red Scare* (Minneapolis, 1955), ch. 2; H. C. Peterson and G. C. Fite, *Opponents of War* (Madison, 1957), chs. 17–23; see also J. Weinstein, "Anti-War Sentiment and the Socialist Party, 1917–1918," *Political Science Quarterly*, LXXIV (June 1959), 215–39, for an excellent treatment of anti-Wilson radicalism during the war years.
37 Robert Lansing, *The War Memoirs of Robert Lansing* (New York, 1935), pp. 337–8 (hereafter cited as *War Memoirs*).
38 Ibid. p. 342.
39 Ibid. pp. 343–5.
40 Ibid. p. 343; see also *FR, Lansing Papers*, II, p. 348.
41 *FR, Lansing Papers*, II, pp. 343–6; Lansing, *War Memoirs*, p. 342; Creel to Wilson, Dec. 27, 1917, Creel MSS; Daniels MSS Diary, Nov. 30, Dec. 18, 1917, Jan. 4, 1918; Kennan, *Russia Leaves the War*, pp. 170–78; on Manchuria, see *FR*, 1918, *Russia*, II, pp. 2–9.
42 Lansing, *War Memoirs*, p. 340, see also p. 341.
43 Ibid. p. 340.
44 *FR, Lansing Papers*, II, pp. 352–3.
45 Ibid. pp. 346–8.
46 Gordon Auchincloss MSS Diary, Jan. 3, 1918, Auchincloss MSS, Yale Univ. Library.
47 *FR*, 1918, *Russia*, I, pp. 270–71, 300–301, 313–15; see also David R. Francis, *Russia From the American Embassy* (New York, 1921), pp. 190–93.
48 Creel to Wilson, Dec. 27, 1917, Creel MSS.
49 Mezes to House, Dec. 26, 1917, Sidney Mezes MSS, Columbia Univ. Library.
50 Gompers to Wilson, Jan. 19, 1918, Wilson MSS, File 6, Box 92.
51 Kennan, *Russia Leaves the War*, pp. 353–63; Ullman, *Anglo-Soviet Relations*, p. 61.
52 Basil Miles Memoranda, Nov. 28, 1917, Jan. 1, 1918, n.d., Jan. 16, 1918, File 861.00/ nos. 753, 935½, 1048½, 2007, respec-

tively, D.S.N.A.; see also the Basil Miles memorandum of Feb., 1918, cited in William Appleman Williams, "American Intervention in Russia, 1917–1920 (Part 2)," *Studies On the Left*, IV (Winter 1964), p. 40.

53 Wilson to Lansing, Jan. 24, 1918, with enclosure from Senator Owen, File 861.00/1048½, D.S.N.A.; see also Wilson to Lansing, Jan. 20, 1918, with enclosure, R. S. Baker MSS, DLC; the enclosure, a cable of Jan. 14, 1918 from Grant Smith, the Chargé in Denmark, to Lansing, may be found in *FR, 1918, Russia*, I, pp. 337–8.

54 Kennan, *Russia Leaves the War*, pp. 249–50; Victor S. Mamatey, *The United States and East Central Europe, 1914–1918* (Princeton, 1957), p. 174; for other evidence of Wilson's awareness of the Bolshevik threat to the international order see Josephus Daniels MSS Diary, December 21, 1917; *Life and Letters*, VII, pp. 447–9.

55 Wilson to Gompers, Jan. 21, 1918, Wilson MSS, File 6; Wilson to C. W. Eliot, Jan. 21, 1918, Wilson to Thomas Lamont, Jan. 31, 1918, Wilson MSS, File 7; Josephus Daniels MSS Diary, Dec. 11, 1917.

56 Wilson to Lansing, Feb. 13, 1918, with Walling Memorandum enclosed, R. S. Baker MSS, DLC; see also Gompers to Wilson, Feb. 9, 1918, with enclosure, Wilson MSS, File 2; *Life and Letters*, VII, p. 542.

57 Ibid.

58 Lansing, *War Memoirs*, p. 340.

59 *FR, Lansing Papers*, II, pp. 352–3.

60 *FR, 1918, Russian*, I, p. 383, and note 1.

61 Breckinridge Long MSS Diary, Feb. 23, 1918, Long MSS, DLC.

62 Kennan, *Russia Leaves the War*, pp. 495–510; Lasch, *American Liberals*, pp. 88–93; Ullman, *Anglo-Soviet Relations*, p. 82.

CHAPTER III: WAR AND REVOLUTION, III

1 On Robins see Kennan, *Russia Leaves the War*, pp. 62–5, 107–30, 239–41, 378–82, 393–4, 420–29, 488–502, 515–16; George F. Kennan, *Soviet-American Relations, 1917–1920, Vol. II, The Decision to Intervene* (Princeton, 1958), pp. 108–35, 166–84, 208–44; William A. Williams, *Russian-American Relations, 1781–1947* (New York, 1952), chap. 5 *passim*.

2 *FR, Lansing Papers*, II, p. 370.

3 *FR, 1918, Russia,* I, 246–7, 264–5, 275, 399–400, 403; Daniels MSS Diary, Nov. 27, 1917; Louis Fischer, *The Life of Lenin* (New York, 1964), pp. 263–4; Kennan, *Russia Leaves the War,* pp. 191–218, 259–64, 510–13; Ullman, *Anglo-Soviet Relations,* p. 66.

4 V. I. Lenin, *Selected Works* (2 vols. Moscow, 1950–51), II, pp. 385–9, 391–3, 424–30, 432–5; Meyer, *Leninism,* pp. 221–6; Carr, *Bolshevik Revolution,* III, pp. 34, 52; Schapiro, *Origin of Communist Autocracy,* p. 99; Isaac Deutscher, *The Prophet Armed, Trotsky: 1879–1921* (London, 1954), pp. 386–7; Robert V. Daniels, *The Conscience of the Revolution* (Cambridge, Mass., 1960), pp. 72, 78; Fischer, *Life of Lenin,* pp. 192–4, 199–200.

5 Lenin, *Selected Works,* II, pp. 388–9; Meyer, *Leninism,* p. 221; Schapiro, *Communist Autocracy,* pp. 94, 98, 105, 118; Kennan, *Russia Leaves the War,* pp. 496–504; Fischer, *Life of Lenin,* p. 179; David Footman, *The Russian Civil War* (New York, 1961), pp. 138–9.

6 Barrington Moore, Jr., *Soviet Politics: The Dilemma of Power* (Cambridge, Mass., 1956), p. 192; John W. Wheeler-Bennett, *The Forgotten Peace* (New York, 1939), pp. 69, 93–5, 115–6; Carr, *Bolshevik Revolution,* III, pp. 15–21; Fischer, *Life of Lenin,* pp. 144–6, 151–3, 157–8, 160–61, 186–7, 190.

7 Daniels, *Conscience of Revolution,* pp. 39–40; Carr, *Bolshevik Revolution,* III, pp. 32–3; Page, *Lenin and World Revolution,* p. 99.

8 Schapiro, *Communist Autocracy,* pp. 106, 109; Meyer, *Leninism,* p. 223; Deutscher, *Prophet Armed,* p. 374; Moore, *Soviet Politics,* pp. 193–4; Carr, *Bolshevik Revolution,* III, p. 51.

9 Wheeler-Bennett, *Forgotten Peace,* pp. 253–4; Deutscher, *Prophet Armed,* pp. 385–6; Carr, *Bolshevik Revolution,* III, pp. 45–6; Warth, *The Allies and the Russian Revolution,* p. 231.

10 Daniels, *Conscience of Revolution,* p. 73; Moore, *Soviet Politics,* p. 193; Page, *Lenin and World Revolution,* p. 99; Meyer, *Leninism,* pp. 222, 231–2.

11 Carr, *Bolshevik Revolution,* III, pp. 24–31, 44–5; Wheeler-Bennett, *Forgotten Peace,* pp. 136–42, 185–6; Deutscher, *Prophet Armed,* pp. 348, 351–2, 357–9, 385–6; Warth, *The Allies and the Russian Revolution,* pp. 216–17, 231.

12 Ullman, *Anglo-Soviet Relations,* pp. 72–3; see also Fischer, *Life of Lenin,* pp. 222–3.

13 Quoted in Carr, *Bolshevik Revolution,* III, p. 46; on Lenin's will-

ingness to deal on a purely expediential basis with the Entente in the event a German advance left him no choice, see Carr, *Bolshevik Revolution*, III, pp. 47, 70; Warth, *The Allies and the Russian Revoltion*, pp. 235–6; Fischer, *Life of Lenin*, pp. 207–9; Moore, *Soviet Politics*, p. 194.

14 On Lenin's early commitment to revolutionary war as a concept, see Lenin, *Works*, XVIII, p. 383; Fischer, *Life of Lenin*, pp. 190–91; Schapiro, *Communist Aristocracy*, p. 91; Meyer, *Leninism*, pp. 219–20; for Lenin's views at the time of Brest-Litovsk on the proper revolutionary manner in which to conduct war if the Germans made defense necessary, see Lenin, *Selected Works*, II, pp. 436–41; Schapiro, *Communist Autocracy*, p. 103; Fischer, *Life of Lenin*, p. 210.

15 Lenin, *Selected Works*, II, p. 396.

16 J. Bunyan and H. H. Fisher (eds.), *The Bolshevik Revolution* (Stanford, 1934), p. 537.

17 *FR, 1918, Russia*, I, pp. 234–5, 268–9; Kennan, *Russia Leaves the War*, pp. 44–5, 172–3; Kennan, *Decision to Intervene*, pp. 166–84.

18 *FR, 1918, Russia*, I, pp. 385, 400, 484, 490, 518; *FR, 1918, Russia*, II, pp. 65, 593, 601–3; Summers to Lansing, Dec. 26, 1917, and Feb. 19, 1918, File 861.00/ nos. 1209 and 1155, respectively, D.S.N.A.

19 *FR, 1918, Russia*, I, pp. 483, 485–8, 519; *FR, 1918, Russia*, II, pp. 123–4; Cumming and Pettitt (eds.), *Russian-American Relations*, p. 162.

20 Warth, *The Allies and the Russian Revolution*, p. 231; Carr, *Bolshevik Revolution*, III, p. 23; Fischer, *Life of Lenin*, p. 155. 159; Schapiro, *Communist Autocracy*, p. 103, n. 44; Deutscher, *Prophet Armed*, p. 356; Adam Ulam, *The Bolsheviks* (New York, 1965), p. 413.

21 Walter H. Page to Wilson, Dec. 3, 1917, Mar. 7, 1918, Wilson MSS, File 2; House to Wilson, Nov. 9, 1917, enclosing W. H. Buckler's notes of talk with Lord Milner on Nov. 2, 1917, Wilson MSS, File 2; Buckler to House, Dec. 10, 13, 1917, Notes of Buckler Interview with Lansdowne, March 5, 1918, all in William Buckler MSS, Yale Univ. Library; see also *Intimate Papers*, III, p. 279, n. 1; Lasch, *American Liberals*, p. 100; Martin, *Peace Without Victory*, pp. 148–9, 169; Mayer, *Political Origins*, pp. 280–85; Carr, *Bolshevik Revolution*, III, p. 23, n. 6; Henry W. Steed, *Through Thirty Years, 1892–1922* (2 vols., London, 1924),

II, pp. 217–19; Alfred M. Gollin, *Proconsul in Politics* (London, 1964), pp. 551–77; Harold I. Nelson, *Land and Power, British and Allied Policy on Germany's Frontiers, 1916–1919* (London, 1963), pp. 19–20.

22 George F. Kennan, *Russia and the West Under Lenin and Stalin* (Boston, 1960), pp. 41–2, 47–8

23 Henry C. Meyer, *Mitteleuropa in German Thought and Action* (The Hague, 1955), pp. 85–102, 136–52, 160–63, 171–2, 195–208, 215–43, 263–4; Klaus Epstein, *Matthias Erzberger and the Dilemma of German Democracy* (Princeton, 1959), pp. 105–12, 115–7, 210–11; Gordon A. Craig, *Politics of the Prussian Army* (New York, 1955), pp. 308, 325, n. 5; Hans Gatzke, *Germany's Drive to the West* (Baltimore, 1950). pp. 20–21, 54–62, 99–105, 132–3, 203–14, 262, 272–3.

24 Gatzke, *Germany's Drive to the West*, pp. 260–61, Meyer, *Mitteleuropa*, pp. 266–77, Epstein, *Erzberger*, pp. 202–4, 232–4, 238–9; Arthur Rosenberg, *Birth of the German Republic* (New York, 1931), pp. 206–7.

25 Epstein, *Erzberger*, pp. 218–21; Mayer, *Political Origins*, pp. 273, 285–6; Deutscher, *Prophet Armed*, pp. 362–3; Craig, *Prussian Army*, pp. 337–40; Mamatey, *U.S. and East Central Europe*, p. 197; *Intimate Papers*, III, p. 353.

26 *FR, 1919, Paris Peace Conference*, I, p. 32.

27 Wilson to House, June 1, 1917, R. S. Baker MSS, DLC; *Life and Letters*, VII, p. 294; House MSS Diary, Oct. 13, 1917; Louis Gerson, *Woodrow Wilson and the Rebirth of Poland* (New Haven, 1953), pp. 70–71.

28 *PPWW*, V, p. 64; see also *PPWW*, V, pp. 49–50, 63, 118–20, 131–2.

29 *PPWW*, V, pp. 177–80, 199–202, 206, 225, 234–5.

30 Wilson to Frank L. Polk, Aug. 10, 1918, Wilson MSS, File 2; see also *Life and Letters*, VIII, pp. 330–31; *PPWW*, V, p. 255.

31 In this connection, see also Lasch, *American Liberals*, pp. 100–102.

32 *PPWW*, V, pp. 120, 201.

33 On the often unfriendly reception accorded to Wilson's war messages by German moderates and pro-war socialists, see John L. Snell, "Benedict XV, Wilson, Michaelis, and German Socialism," *The Catholic Historical Review*, XXXVII (July 1951), pp. 164–76; Snell, "Wilson's Peace Program and German Socialism, January–March 1918," *The Mississippi Valley Historical Review*, XXXVIII (September 1951), pp. 187–214; Snell, "Socialist

Unions and Socialist Patriotism in Germany, 1914–1918," *The American Historical Review*, LIX (October 1953), pp. 66–77.

34 *FR, 1918, Russia,* III, pp. 108–9; see also Breckinridge Long, "Memorandum of a Conversation with the Chinese Minister, March 11, 1918," Long. MSS, Box 179.

35 *FR, 1918, Russia,* I, p. 397.

36 *FR, 1918, Russia,* I, pp. 395–6, 399–400; see also Fischer, *Life of Lenin,* pp. 224–5; Kennan, *Russia Leaves the War,* pp. 510–13.

37 *FR, 1918, Russia,* I, p. 339.

38 One copy of this memorandum was enclosed with a letter from Basil Miles of the State Department to Elihu Root. See Miles to Root, Dec. 8, 1917, with enclosure, Elihu Root MSS, Box 136, DLC. Miles claimed that the memorandum had also been shown to Lansing, McAdoo, and Creel. On Dec. 13, 1917, the memorandum reached the White House, see Memorandum for the President, from the Secretary, W.F.J. of the White House, Dec. 14, 1917, Wilson MSS, File 2.

39 *Russian Embassy Memorandum,* pp. 1–2.

40 Ibid. pp. 1–4.

41 Ibid. pp. 4–5.

42 Ibid. p. 6.

43 *FR, 1918, Russia,* II pp. 57–65, 99, 101–2, 119–21, 127–8, 141, 159, 164–71, 175, 193–4, 198–9, 205–6, 227–9, 232–3, 272.

44 Lansing, "Confidential Memoranda and Notes, March 18, 1918," Lansing MSS; House MSS Diary, Feb. 25, Mar. 3, 1918; Frank L. Polk MSS Diary, Mar. 1, 12, 1918, Polk MSS, Yale Univ. Library; Daniels MSS Diary, Mar. 1, 29, 1918; Wiseman to Drummond, Mar. 14, 1918, William Wiseman MSS, Yale Univ. Library; *Intimate Papers,* III, pp. 390–402; *FR, 1918, Russia,* II, pp. 12, 23, 31, 37, 45–6, 67, 82, 144–5; Betty M. Unterberger, *America's Siberian Expedition* (Durham, 1956), pp. 24–38.

45 *FR, 1918, Russia,* I, pp. 318, 325, 366–9, 389, 517, 528, 535–8, 540, 545–6, 552, 555, 558, 565, 574–5; *FR, 1918, Russia,* II, pp. 33–4, 43, 62–3, 149, 176, 243; Lansing to Wilson, May 21, 1918, with enclosures, Wilson MSS, File 2; Polk MSS Diary, July 17, 1918.

46 *FR, 1918, Russia,* II, pp. 167–8, 181, 190–91, 206, 221–3, 239–240; W. Sharp to Lansing, Apr. 5, 1918, Poole to Lansing, May 16, 1918, Francis to Lansing, May 29, 1918, File 861.00/nos. 1849, 1927, and 2154, respectively, D.S.N.A.; B. Long Memoranda, May 29, June 24, 1918, Long MSS, Box 187; Francis to Lansing, June

22, 1918, T. N. Page to Wilson, June 11, July 9, 1918, P. H. Stovall to Wilson, June 11, 1918, S. R. Bertron to Wilson, June 24, 1918, Vance Thompson to Wilson, with enclosures, June 12, 1918, all in Wilson MSS, File 2.

47 House MSS Diary, June 14, 1918.

48 Bullitt to House, June 21, 1918, William C. Bullitt MSS, Yale Univ. Library; see also Bullitt to House, June 24, 1918, Bullitt MSS.

49 File 861.00/2146½ D.S.N.A.; The memorandum is unsigned, but the State Dept. Purport Book in the Archives lists it as by Lansing, and the point of view and handwritten corrections do seem to be those of Lansing, although Basil Miles, whose views and writing were similar to Lansing's, is also a possible author. See also *FR*, *1918, Russia,* I, p. 571, for evidence of Lansing's awareness of the threat of German-led counterrevolution in Russia.

50 Lansing, *War Memoirs,* p. 344; see also *FR, 1918, Russia,* I, pp. 203, 235, 239–40, 276–7, 288, 295, 314, 320, 333, 370–78, 381–2; later studies have established that there was some German subsidization of the Bolsheviks, along with other radical and/or separatist Russian elements, in the hope of subverting the pro-Allied Provisional Government, see Gerald Freund, *Unholy Alliance* (London, 1957), pp. 1–2; Z. A. B. Zeman (ed.), *Germany and the Revolution in Russia* (London, 1958), pp. 25–71; Stefan T. Possony, *Lenin, the Compulsive Revolutionary* (Chicago, 1964), pp. 165–276.

51 Lansing, *War Memoirs,* p. 341.

52 Francis, *Russia from the American Embassy,* p. 226; also see *FR, 1918, Russia,* II, pp. 73–4; It is clear that Lenin was willing to take German help only to further Bolshevik goals of world socialist revolution, see Kennan, *Russia Leaves the War,* pp. 455–6.

53 *FR, 1918, Russia,* I, p. 384; see also Francis, *Russia from the American Embassy,* p. 185; *FR, 1918, Russia,* I, pp. 297, 320.

54 See "German-Bolshevik Conspiracy," War Information Series, No. 20, Oct. 1918, issued by the CPI, especially Documents 33, 46, 47, in Edgar Sisson, *One Hundred Red Days* (New Haven, 1931), Appendix; on fraudulent character of the Sisson Documents, see Kennan, *Russia Leaves the War,* pp. 441–56; on Germany's anti-Bolshevik policy in Russian areas under German control after Brest-Litovsk, see Footman, *Russian Civil War,* pp. 23–4; Epstein, *Erzberger,* pp. 238–50; on general Allied fear of expanding German influence in wartime Russia, see John M. Thompson, *Russia,*

Bolshevism, and the Versailles Peace (Princeton, 1966), pp. 26–7.

55 FR, 1918, *Russia,* I, pp. 495–6, 504, 510, 519–21, 540–41, 547, 549–51; *FR, 1918, Russia,* II, pp. 89–91, 93, 102–5, 164–8, 181, 190–91, 220–23, 239–41; see also N. D. Baker to Wilson, Apr. 25, 1918, with enclosed memorandum, Wilson MSS, File 2.

56 Kennan, *Decision to Intervene,* p. 129; Unterberger, *America's Siberian Expedition,* pp. 42–5, 52–4; David F. Trask, *The U.S. in the Supreme War Council* (Middletown, Conn., 1961), pp. 107–14.

57 FR, *Lansing Papers,* II, p. 360.

58 Ibid. pp. 361–2; see also Kennan, *Decision to Intervene,* pp. 354–9.

59 Wiseman to Drummond, May 30, 1918, Wiseman MSS; see also Wiseman to Drummond, June 14, 1918, Wiseman MSS, mentioned in the following paragraph.

60 FR, 1918, *Russia,* II, p. 188; see also p. 189.

61 FR, 1918, *Russia,* II, p. 175.

62 Redfield to Wilson, July 9, 1918, Wilson MSS, File 2; Auchincloss MSS Diary, June 13, 1918; B. Long MSS Diary, May 31, 1918; *Intimate Papers,* III, pp. 408–14; Lasch, *American Liberals,* pp. 103–7; Kennan, *Decision to Intervene,* pp. 381–7; Herbert Hoover, *The Ordeal of Woodrow Wilson* (New York, 1958), p. 12, n. 2.

63 Wilson to Lansing, June 19, 1918, File 861.00/2148½, D.S.N.A.; the dispatch concerning the Cooperative Societies to which Wilson refers is Poole to Lansing, June 12, 1918, *FR, 1918, Russia,* II, pp. 205–6; on Wilson's general interest in liberal-nationalist Russian elements, see C. E. Russell to Wilson, June 20, 1918, with enclosures, and Wilson to Russell, July 3, 1918, Wilson MSS, File 6; Sharp to Lansing, July 9, 1918, and Wilson to Polk, July 12, 1918, File 861.00/2324, D.S.N.A.

64 *Life and Letters,* VIII, pp. 271–2.

65 Schapiro, *Communist Autocracy,* pp. 155–8; Kennan, *Decision to Intervene,* pp. 275–95; James W. Morley, *The Japanese Thrust into Siberia* (New York, 1957), pp. 232–42.

66 FR, 1918, *Russia,* II, pp. 206–7

67 Wilson to Lansing, June 17, 1918, File 861.00/2145½, D.S.N.A.

68 FR, 1918, *Russia,* I, pp. 483, 489, 495–6; *FR, 1918, Russia,* II, pp. 57, 64–7, 76, 92–3, 96–7, 103, 116, 129, 173–4; *FR, Lansing Papers,* II, pp. 357–8; Lansing, "Confidential Memoranda and Notes, March 22, 1918," Lansing MSS.

69 *FR, 1918, Russia,* II, p. 181.
70 *FR, 1918 Russia,* II, pp. 178–9, 181–2, 185–9, 193, 195, 197–8, 203–17, 223, 230–31, 235–8, 241–253, 261–2, 264, 283, 293, 309–14.
71 Ibid. p. 215.
72 State Department Memorandum, June 17, 1918, File 861.00/2146½, D.S.N.A., see also note 49 above, for the possibility that this memorandum was written either by Lansing or by Basil Miles.
73 Ibid.
74 On the issue of a possible Bolshevik invitation, see *FR, Lansing Papers,* II, p. 361; *FR, 1918, Russia,* I, pp. 493–4; *FR, 1918, Russia,* II, p. 160; *Intimate Papers,* III,   pp. 402–3; Unterberger, *America's Siberian Expedition,* pp. 42–3, 62; on the State Department's desire to avoid overt support of anti-Bolshevik elements in May, 1918, see *FR, 1918, Russia,* I, pp. 524–5; *FR, 1918, Russia,* II, pp. 138–9, 150, 153–4, 157; *FR, 1918, Russia,* III, pp. 232–3.
75 On the steadfast opposition of Wilsonians to recognition of a Bolshevik regime, see *FR, 1918, Russia,* II, p. 218; Basil Miles, "Memorandum for the Secretary of State, May 21, 1918," enclosed in Miles to B. Long, May 21, 1918, Long MSS; Wilson to Senator James H. Lewis, July 24, 1918, and Wilson to R. B. Harrison, Aug. 14, 1918, Wilson MSS, File 2; Lansing to Wilson, June 21, 1918, and Lansing to Amembassy, Vologda, June 18, 1918, File 861.00/1945 and 2020, D.S.N.A.; see also Fischer, *Life of Lenin,* p. 267; for Wilsonian fears that any dealings with the Bolsheviks might alienate anti-Bolshevik Russians from the Allies and push them toward the Germans, see *FR, 1918, Russia,* I, pp. 526, 536–8; *FR, 1918, Russia,* II, pp. 123–4; *FR, 1918, Russia,* III, pp. 235–6; *FR, Lansing Papers,* II, p. 361.
76 State Department Memorandum, June 17, 1918, File 861.00/2146½, D.S.N.A.
77 Ibid. pp. 12–13; see also Lansing, "Confidential Memoranda and Notes, June 12, 1918," Lansing MSS
78 For anti-German motivations, see Kennan, *Russia and the West,* pp. 91–106; Lasch, *American Liberals,* pp. 108–118; for anti-Bolshevik motivations, see W. A. Williams, "American Intervention in Russia, 1917–1920 (Part 2)," *Studies on the Left.* IV, (Winter 1964), pp. 39–57.
79 Lansing, "Confidential Memoranda and Notes, July 4, 1918," Lansing MSS.
80 *FR, Lansing Papers,* II, p. 395; *FR, 1918, Russia,* II, p. 241; *FR,*

1918, Russia, III, p. 237; Lansing to Wilson, Aug. 18, 1918, File 861.00/2602½, D.S.N.A.

81 Lansing to Wilson, June 23, 1918, File 861.00/2164½, D.S.N.A.

82 *FR, 1918, Russia,* II, pp. 267–8.

83 Freund, *Unholy Alliance,* pp. 17–31; Carr, *Bolshevik Revolution,* III, pp. 83–7; Ullman, *Anglo-Soviet Relations,* pp. 177–186; Jan H. Meijer (ed.), *The Trotsky Papers 1917–1922* (The Hague, 1964), Vol. I, p. 55.

84 Bliss to N. D. Baker, Aug. 22, 1918, Wilson MSS, File 2; also see Bliss to General Peyton C. March, Feb. 20, 1918, Polk MSS, for evidence that Bliss favored a Siberian intervention if it could achieve a "consolidation of sentiment among the anti-Bolshevists" redounding to the "politico-military advantage" of the Allies.

85 *FR, 1918, Russia,* II, p. 288.

86 Cumming and Pettit (eds.), *Russian-American Relations,* pp. 343–4.

87 *FR, 1918, Russia,* II, p. 290.

88 Lansing, "Confidential Memoranda and Notes, July 4, 1918," Lansing MSS.

89 The George Kennan referred to here should not be confused with the contemporary historian and diplomat, George Frost Kennan. For Wilson's reactions to the George Kennan of his period, see Kennan to Lansing, Aug. 18, 1918, enclosed in Lansing to Wilson, Aug. 22, 1918, and Wilson to Lansing, Aug. 24, 1918, Wilson MSS, File 2; for evidence that Wilson saw aid to the Czechs and the civilian program in Siberia as one integrated program, see Wilson to House, July 8, 1918, R. S. Baker MSS, DLC; Reading to British Foreign Office, July 3, 1918, Wiseman MSS.

90 Lansing to Polk, Aug. 3, 1918, Polk MSS.

91 See *FR, 1918, Russia,* II, pp. 362, 364, 366, 372–3, 382–3; Unterberger, *America's Siberian Expedition,* pp. 90–95.

92 Wiseman to Murray, July 12, 1918, Wiseman MSS; see also Wiseman to Drummond, May 30, 1918, Wiseman MSS; *Life and Letters,* VIII, pp. 246–7; *FR, 1918, Russia,* II, pp. 297–8; for Administration opposition to a new Allied eastern front via Siberia see Trask, *U.S. and Supreme War Council,* pp. 121–9.

93 Lansing to Wilson, Sept. 9, 1918, *FR, Lansing Papers,* II, pp. 381–2.

94 *FR, 1918, Russia,* II, pp. 323–4.

95 Ibid. pp. 389, 392–5, 416–17, 425.

96 Ibid. p. 413.

97 *FR, 1918, Russia,* III, pp. 59–64, 74, 77–8, 87–8, 93–4, 147.
98 *FR, 1918, Russia,* I, pp. 680–700.
99 *FR, Lansing Papers,* II, pp. 386–7; see also *FR, 1918, Russia,* II, pp. 387–90.
100 See A. Whitney Griswold, *The Far Eastern Policy of the United States* (New York, 1958), pp. 223–38; Unterberger, *America's Siberian Expedition,* p. 88.
101 See Beers, *Vain Endeavor,* pp. 120–32; Lasch, *American Liberals,* p. 110; J. A. White, *The Siberian Intervention* (Princeton, 1950), p. 353.
102 House MSS Diary, Aug. 22, 1914, Jan. 25, July 24, 1915.
103 House to Wilson, Sept. 6, 1917, Wilson MSS, File 2.
104 Ibid.
105 House to Wilson, Sept. 18, 1917, *Intimate Papers,* III, p. 25.
106 Beers, *Vain Endeavor,* pp. 16–48; Roy Watson Curry, *Woodrow Wilson and Far Eastern Policy, 1913–1921* (New York, 1957), pp. 114–17.
107 Beers, *Vain Endeavor,* pp. 58–79.
108 Curry, *Woodrow Wilson and Far Eastern Policy,* pp. 170–88; Beers, *Vain Endeavor,* pp. 109–119.
109 Lansing to Wilson, June 25, 1917, Wilson MSS, File 2; B. Long MSS Diary, June 24, Nov, 9, 1917; E. T. Williams Memoranda, June 25, 26, 1917, and B. Long Memorandum, Jan. 22, 1918, Long MSS; Curry, *Woodrow Wilson and Far Eastern Policy,* pp. 189–98; Beers, *Vain Endeavor,* pp. 142–6; Russell H. Fifield, *Woodrow Wilson and the Far East* (New York, 1952), pp. 94–7.
110 Roland Morris to Lansing, Mar. 7, 1918, House MSS; Beers, *Vain Endeavor,* pp. 79–83, 102–8.
111 Lansing to Redfield, Jan. 11, 1918, Long MSS.
112 *FR, 1918, Russia,* II, pp. 58, 74–5, 115, 126, 165–6, 181; Roland Morris to Lansing, Feb. 9, 1918, House MSS; B. Long MSS Diary, Feb. 24, 1918; Bliss to March, Feb. 20, 1918, Polk MSS; Sharp to Lansing, Feb. 19, 1918, Wilson MSS, File 2.
113 Unterberger, *America's Siberian Expedition,* pp. 78–86, 89; Morley, *Japanese Thrust,* pp. 270–300.
114 On Lenin's views, see Fischer, *The Life of Lenin,* p. 234; Kennan, *Decision to Intervene,* pp. 131–5; Kennan, *Russia Leaves the War,* pp. 501–9; for Lenin's and Trotsky's efforts to split the U.S. and Japan, see Carr, *Bolshevik Revolution,* III, pp. 87–8; Fischer, *Soviets in World Affairs,* p. 218; Meijer, ed., *Trotsky Papers,* I, pp. 15–17; for American fears that the Bolsheviks and/or the

Germans might succeed in splitting the U.S. and Japan, see *FR*, 1918, *Russia*, I, pp. 502, 504, 510, 529, 538; *FR*, 1918, *Russia*, II, p. 105; Lansing, Memorandum for A. R. Pinci, Dec. 1, 1917, Lansing MSS; Bullard to House, Aug. 12, 1918, Arthur Bullard MSS, Princeton Univ. Library

115 *FR*, 1918, *Russia*, II, p. 67.

116 Lansing, "Confidential Memoranda and Notes, March 22, 1918," Lansing MSS; see also *FR*, 1918, *Russia*, I, p. 523.

117 Lansing to Polk, Aug. 3, 1918, Polk MSS; see also Lansing to Wilson, Aug. 18, 1918, File 861.00/2602½, D.S.N.A.; for evidence that some moderate-imperialist elements in Japan hoped to use the Siberian situation as a means of *rapprochement* with the United States, see Morley, *Japanese Thrust*, pp. 300–311.

118 B. Long MSS Diary, May 23, July 12, 1918; House MSS Diary, July 2, 6, 25, 1918.

119 House to Wilson, July 6, 1918, Wilson MSS, File 2.

120 Sharp to Wilson, Aug. 8, 1918, Wilson MSS, File 2.

CHAPTER IV: PEACE AND REVOLUTION, I

1 *PPWW*, V, pp. 257–8.

2 *PPWW*, V, pp. 342–3, 353, 364, 377, 437, 453.

3 *PPWW*, V, pp. 95, 159, 181–2, 289, 375, 383; see also Diamond, *Economic Thought of Woodrow Wilson*, pp. 162–76.

4 *PPWW*, V, pp. 64–5, 199–201, 233, 236–7, 278, 285.

5 On Wilson's wartime knowledge of the Allied secret treaties, see Seth P. Tillman, *Anglo-American Relations at the Paris Peace Conference of 1919* (Princeton, 1961), pp. 9–11; for Wilson's wartime concern over Allied postwar plans, see Daniels MSS Diary, Oct. 12, 17, 1917; Wilson to Polk, Aug. 1, 1917, Polk MSS; Wilson to House, Jan. 31, 1918, House MSS; *Life and Letters*, VII, pp. 180–81; *Life and Letters*, VIII, pp. 253, 505, 593.

6 Wilson to House, July 21, Sept 2, 1917, R. S. Baker MSS, DLC; Wilson to House, Aug. 22, 1917, House MSS; *Intimate Papers*, III, pp. 37–9, 51, 134–5, 237.

7 *Intimate Papers*, IV, pp. 64–71.

8 Tumulty, *Wilson as I Know Him*, pp. 301–2.

9 Daniels MSS Diary, Oct. 16, 23, Nov. 5, 1918; *Intimate Papers*, IV, p. 83; Lane and Wall (eds.), *Letters of Franklin K. Lane*, pp. 295–6.

10 *PPWW*, V, p. 307; see also pp. 300–303, 322.

11 *Life and Letters*, VIII, pp. 523, 529–39; Harry R. Rudin, *Armistice, 1918* (New Haven, 1944), pp. 268–274; FR, *Paris Peace Conference, 1919*, I, pp. 134–5 (hereafter cited as FR, PPC, 1919, with appropriate volume number).

12 Unpublished MS of a book on Woodrow Wilson by Charles L. Swem, chap. 21, p. 3, see also Ibid., pp. 2–5, in Swem Collection of Wilsonia, Princeton Univ. Library; see also *Intimate Papers*, IV, pp. 280–83.

13 *PPWW*, V, p. 312; see also Ibid. pp. 342–3, 399, 505, 547.

14 Ibid. pp. 11–12, 61–2, 64–5, 94–6, 119, 129–34, 161–2, 199.

15 *Life and Letters*, VIII, pp. 564–5.

16 The two best theoretical treatments of Wilson's relationship to Bolshevism are to be found in Mayer, *Political Origins*, and W. A. Williams, *Tragedy of American Diplomacy*.

17 FR, PPC, 1919, V, p. 87; FR, PPC, 1919, VI, p. 49; *PPWW*, V, pp. 312, 342–3, 399, 505, 541.

18 *PPWW*, V, pp. 117–18, 131–2, 161–2, 360–61.

19 Ibid. pp. 258–61.

20 John L. Snell, "Wilson on Germany and the Fourteen Points," *The Journal of Modern History*, XXVI, 4 (December 1954), 366; see also *Life and Letters*, VIII, p. 482; Daniels MSS Diary, Oct. 22, 1918.

21 Tumulty, *Wilson*, pp. 336–7; see also R. S. Baker, *Woodrow Wilson and World Settlement* (3 vols., Garden City, N.Y., 1922–1923), I, 8 (hereafter cited as WW&WS, with appropriate volume number). See also Bullitt MSS Diary, Dec. 10 or 11, 1918.

22 *Intimate Papers*, IV, p. 282.

23 Tumulty to Wilson, Dec. 31, 1918, Wilson MSS, File 8A.

24 FR, PPC, 1919, III, pp. 583, 766; see also Isaiah Bowman to R. S. Baker, June 24, 1921, R. S. Baker MSS, Princeton, for further evidence that Wilson felt the pressure of the "working world's" hopes for a new diplomacy at Paris.

25 *PPWW*, V, pp. 447–8; Tumulty, *Wilson*, pp. 368–9.

26 *PPWW*, V, pp. 275, 278–9, 284–5; see also *Intimate Papers*, IV, pp. 77–80.

27 Epstein, *Erzberger*, pp. 264–9; Rudin, *Armistice*, pp. 127–65, 193–264, 324–66; Alma Luckau, *The German Delegation at the Paris Peace Conference* (New York, 1941), pp. 3–23.

28 Craig, *Prussian Army*, pp. 345–50; Richard N. Hunt, *German Social Democracy, 1918–1933* (New Haven, 1964), pp. 26–30; on the minority status of revolutionary-socialism in postwar Germany,

see Werner T. Angress, *Stillborn Revolution, The Communist Bid for Power in Germany, 1921–1923* (Princeton, 1963), pp. 17–20; Fischer, *Life of Lenin*, pp. 312–13.

29 Carr, *Bolshevik Revolution*, III, pp. 91–7; Fischer, *Life of Lenin*, pp. 305–14; Moore, *Soviet Politics*, pp. 196–7.

30 *FR, PPC, 1919*, II, pp. 28–30, 94, 96–7.

31 Lansing, "Confidential Memoranda and Notes, Oct. 7, 22, 29, Nov. 3, 8, 1918," Lansing MSS; Lansing to E. N. Smith, Oct. 12, Nov. 14, 1918, Lansing to W. C. Stebbins, Oct. 18, 1918, Lansing to C. E. Hotchkiss, Nov. 13, 1918, Lansing to R. S. Hungerford, Nov. 14, 1918, Lansing MSS; Lansing to Wilson, with enclosure, Nov. 25, 1918, Wilson MSS, File 2; Gelfand, *Inquiry*, pp. 212–13.

32 Lansing to Root, Oct. 28, 1918, Elihu Root MSS, DLC; see also Lansing, "Confidential Memoranda and Notes, Oct. 26, 1918," Lansing MSS.

33 Daniels MSS Diary, Oct. 8, 1918.

34 John L. Snell, "Wilson on Germany and the Fourteen Points," *The Journal of Modern History*, XXVI, 4 (December 1954), 366.

35 Lane and Wall (eds.), *Letters of Franklin K. Lane*, pp. 295–6.

36 *Life and Letters*, VIII, p. 553; see also Lane and Wall, *Letters of Franklin K. Lane*, p. 298; *PPWW*, V, pp. 300–302.

37 *FR, PPC, 1919*, II, pp. 88, 98–105; Lansing to Wilson, Nov. 18, 1918, Wilson MSS, File 2; Wilson to Lansing, Nov. 22, 1918, Swem Collection of Wilsonia; see also Stephen Bonsal, *Unfinished Business* (New York, 1944), pp. 7–8, for House's fear of postwar German Bolshevism.

38 Lansing to E. N. Smith, Oct. 12, 1918, Lansing MSS; see also Lansing, "Confidential Memoranda and Notes, Oct. 26, 1918," Lansing MSS.

39 Lansing to E. N. Smith, Nov. 14, 1918, Lansing MSS.

40 B. Long MSS Diary, Nov. 1, 1918.

41 *Intimate Papers*, IV, pp. 118–19; see also Grew MSS Diary, Oct. 26, 1918, Joseph C. Grew MSS, Houghton Library, Harvard Univ.

42 *Life and Letters*, VIII, p. 578; on the general Wilsonian concern over Bolshevism in the postwar period, see also J. M. Thompson, *Russia, Bolshevism and Versailles*, pp. 10–20.

43 Snell, "Wilson on Germany and the Fourteen Points," *The Journal of Modern History*, XXVI, 4 (December 1954), 366; see also *PPWW*, V, pp. 300–302.

44 Bonsal, *Unfinished Business*, pp. 42–3; Frederick Palmer, *Bliss, Peacemaker, The Life and Letters of General Tasker Howard*

Bliss (New York, 1934), p. 363: on the closeness of Lansing, White, and Bliss, see Lansing to Polk, July 26, 1919, Polk MSS.

45 Allan Nevins, *Henry White, Thirty Years of American Diplomacy* (New York, 1930), pp. 347–9.

46 White to Lodge, Jan. 14, Mar. 1, Apr. 3, 14, 1919, Henry Cabot Lodge MSS, Mass. Hist. Soc.; White to Lodge, Feb. 10, Mar. 7, 19, July 22, 1919, Root MSS; see also White to Root, Mar. 7, 19, 1919, Root MSS; Nevins, *White*, pp. 395–408.

47 On Bliss-Pershing differences, see W. M. Jordan, *Great Britain, France, and the German Problem 1918–1939* (New York, 1943), pp. 22–5; see also Bliss to N. D. Baker, cable, Oct. 24, 1918, Wilson MSS, File 2.

48 Bliss to General Peyton C. March, Dec. 1, 1918, Bliss to N. D. Baker, Oct. 9, 1918, Bliss to Mrs. Bliss, Feb. 26, 1919, Bliss to Wilson, Mar. 14, 1919, Bliss to S. Prosser, Mar. 16, 1919, Tasker H. Bliss MSS, DLC; Bliss MSS Diary, Jan. 8, Feb. 2, 11, 1919; Bliss to N.D. Baker, Oct. 23, 1918, Newton D. Baker MSS, DLC; Palmer, *Bliss*, pp. 340–47; *FR, PPC*, 1919, I, pp. 521–5.

49 Bliss MSS Diary, Jan. 2, 1919; Bliss to Mrs. Bliss, Jan. 14, 1919, Bliss to Col. A. Hopkins, Feb. 12, 1919; Bliss to S. Prosser, Mar. 16, 1919, Bliss MSS; Bliss to N. D. Baker, Jan. 4, 30, 1919, N. D. Baker MSS; Palmer, *Bliss*, pp. 365–6, 379; *FR, PPC*, 1919, I, p. 525.

50 Bliss MSS Diary, Jan. 7, 1919; Bliss to N. D. Baker, Jan. 30, 1919, N. D. Baker MSS; Palmer, *Bliss*, pp. 415–16, 420–21; Bliss: "The Problem of Disarmament," in Edward M. House and Charles Seymour (eds.), *What Really Happened at Paris, The Story of the Peace Conference* (New York, 1921), pp. 384–7; for an excellent study of Bliss's views on the interrelated threats of Allied militarism and Bolshevism at Paris, see David F. Trask, *General Tasker Howard Bliss and the "Sessions of the World,"* 1919 (Philadelphia, 1966), pp. 5–20.

51 Lansing, "Confidential Memoranda and Notes, Jan. 3, 22, Feb. 3, Mar. 7, 20, 28, Apr. 1, 3, 10, May 5, 6, 8, 1919," Lansing MSS; Lansing MSS Diary, Jan. 3, Mar. 21, 23, 1919; Robert Lansing, *The Peace Negotiations, A Personal Narrative* (Boston, 1921), pp. 110–12; *FR, PPC*, 1919, I, pp. 296–7; *FR, PPC*, 1919, II, pp. 547–50, 568–9.

52 Lansing address of Mar. 11, 1919, Bliss MSS, Box 69; see also Lansing to Polk, Mar. 14, 1919, Polk MSS, for Lansing's views on response to this address.

NOTES FOR PAGES 139–141

53 Daniels MSS Diary, Oct. 17, Nov. 10, 1918; Bliss MSS Diary, Dec. 28, 1918; Lansing, "Confidential Memoranda and Notes, Oct. 28, 1918," and Lansing to E. N. Smith, Nov. 14, 1918, Lansing MSS; Wilson to Lansing, Jan. 10, 1919, Swem Collection of Wilsonia; Wilson to House, Dec. 15, 1918, Lansing to Polk, Jan. 27, 1919, Wilson MSS, File 8A; *PPWW*, V, p. 300; *FR, PPC*, 1919, II, pp. 28–30, 275–6; *FR, PPC*, 1919, III, p. 516; *FR, PPC*, 1919, XI, pp. 47, 150–51.

54 Hoover to Wilson, Apr. 3, 1919, Wilson MSS, File 8A; *FR, PPC*, 1919, II, pp. 680–81; *FR, PPC*, 1919, V, p. 151; Suda Lorena Bane and Ralph Haswell Lutz (eds.), *The Blockade of Germany after the Armistice* (Stanford, 1942), pp. 24–5; Herbert Hoover, *An American Epic* (3 vols., Chicago, 1961), III, pp. 85–7, and chaps. 34–6 *passim*.

55 *FR, PPC*, 1919, II, p. 711; see also White to Lodge, Feb. 17, 1919, Root MSS.

56 David Lloyd George, *The Truth About the Peace Treaties* (2 vols., London, 1938), I, pp. 293–7; Tillman, *Anglo-American Relations*, pp. 264–6.

57 Lansing MSS Diary, Mar. 8, 1919; House MSS Diary, Dec. 26, 1918, Mar. 3, 1919; Bliss MSS Diary, Dec. 28, 1918; Bliss to Hoover, Dec. 30, 1918, Bliss MSS; N. Davis to Rathbone, Mar. 8, 1919, Norman H. Davis MSS, DLC; Vance McCormick MSS Diary, Mar. 1, 3, 5, 8, 1919, Yale Univ. Library; Bane and Lutz (eds.), *Blockade of Germany*, pp. 75–7, 384–6; *FR, PPC*, 1919, III, pp. 516, 709, 712; *FR, PPC*, 1919, IV, pp. 279–80; *FR, PPC*, 1919, V, p. 151; Palmer, *Bliss*, pp. 365–6; Nevins, *White*, pp. 372–3, 377–9; Herbert Hoover, *The Ordeal of Woodrow Wilson* (New York, 1958), pp. 157–78; J. M. Thompson, *Russia, Bolshevism, and Versailles*, pp. 222–30.

58 House to N. Hapgood. Jan. 6, 1919, House MSS; see also House MSS Diary, Mar. 3, 1919.

59 House MSS Diary, Feb. 21, 27, Mar. 6, 1919; McCormick MSS Diary, Feb. 15, 23, Mar. 20, 29, Apr. 2, 1919; Philip Mason Burnett, *Reparation at the Paris Peace Conference* (2 vols., New York, 1940), I, pp. 53, 64–5, 73–5; Tillman, *Anglo-American Relations*, pp. 223–59.

60 "Minutes of the Daily Meetings of the Commissioners Plenipotentiary, Jan. 8, 1919," Grew MSS; Bliss MSS Diary, Jan. 10, 1919; Baruch to Wilson, Mar. 29, 1919, Wilson MSS, File 8A; Lansing, "Confidential Memoranda and Notes, Feb. 20, Mar. 13,

June 5, 1919," Lansing MSS; Norman Davis, "Peace Conference
Notes, July 5, 1919," Davis MSS; McCormick MSS Diary, Mar.
24, 1919; White to Lodge, Jan. 14, Apr. 3, 1919, Lodge MSS;
Harold B. Whiteman (ed.), *Letters from the Paris Peace Conference by Charles Seymour* (New Haven, 1965), pp. 45, 132,
171; Margaret L. Coit, *Mr. Baruch* (Boston, 1957), pp. 259–66;
Nevins, *White*, pp. 381–4; Bernard M. Baruch, *The Making of
the Reparation and Economic Sections of the Treaty* (New York,
1920), pp. 2–5, 51–2, 55; Burnett, *Reparation*, I, pp. 56, 79,
96–7, 107–9; Hoover, *Ordeal*, pp. 220–21; *FR, PPC*, 1919, II,
pp. 554, 599.

61 Burnett, *Reparation*, II, pp. 103–4; see also R. S. Baker, *WW&
WS*, II, pp. 400–407; R. S. Baker, *WW&WS*, III, pp. 470–80;
McCormick MSS Diary, June 2, 3, 7, 9, 1919.

62 *FR, PPC*, 1919, III, pp. 708–9, 712, 901; *FR, PPC*, 1919, VI, pp.
155–6, 262–3, 277–9.

63 *FR, PPC*, 1919, V, p. 801.

64 R. S. Baker, *WW&WS*, II, pp. 314–33, 360–67, 374–5, 407;
Diamond, *Economic Thought*, pp. 182–8; Richard Hofstadter,
The American Political Tradition (New York, 1955), pp. 273–6.

65 *Intimate Papers*, IV, pp. 267–9, 381–2; *FR, PPC*, 1919, II, pp.
538–40, 544–6.

66 McCormick MSS Diary, Jan. 21, 1919; N. Davis to Wilson, Feb.
2, 1919, Baruch to Wilson, Feb. 4, 1919, Wilson to Baruch, Feb.
5, 1919, Wilson MSS, File 8A; House to Hapgood, Jan. 6, 1919,
House MSS; Tillman, *Anglo-American Relations*, pp. 267–9.

67 See p. 127, and note 5, p. 285.

68 Auchincloss MSS Diary, Dec. 14, 15, 1918; *Intimate Papers*, IV,
pp. 230–32, 237–9, 254; *Life and Letters*, VIII, p. 510; Hoover,
Ordeal, pp. 91–101; Tillman, *Anglo-American Relations*, pp. 261–
2; Whiteman (ed.), *Seymour Letters*, p. 44; *FR, PPC*, 1919, II,
pp. 636–9, 658–61.

69 McCormick MSS Diary, May 8, 14, 1919; McCormick to Wilson,
May 13, 1919, Wilson MSS, File 8A; Hoover, *Ordeal*, pp. 234–7;
Intimate Papers, IV, p. 467; *FR, PPC*, 1919, V, p. 600; Bane and
Lutz (eds.), *Blockade of Germany*, pp. 463–4.

70 R. S. Baker, *WW&WS*, II, pp. 289–90, 357–60, III, pp. 336–43;
Tillman, *Anglo-American Relations*, p. 269.

71 McCormick MSS Diary, Apr. 24, 25, 26, 1919; Tillman, *Anglo-
American Relations*, p. 270.

72 R. S. Baker, *WW&WS*, II, p. 89.

73 Ibid. pp. 330-35, 374-5; Tillman, *Anglo-American Relations*, pp. 270-75.

74 R. S. Baker, WW&WS, III, p. 346.

75 *FR, PPC*, 1919, X, pp. 210-12.

76 R. S. Baker, WW&WS, II, pp. 293-302, 416, 420-21, 432-3; George Bernard Noble, *Policies and Opinions at Paris, 1919, Wilsonian Diplomacy, the Versailles Peace, and French Public Opinion* (New York, 1935), pp, 186-205.

77 On British economic policy, see R. S. Baker, WW&WS, II, pp. 353-5, 400-403; Tillman, *Anglo-American Relations*, pp. 229-75 *passim*; on Lloyd George, see Thomas Jones, *Lloyd George* (Cambridge, England, 1951), pp. 172-3; *Lord Riddell's Intimate Diary of the Paris Peace Conference and After* (London, 1933), p. 48.

78 House MSS Diary, Apr. 4, 1919; McCormick MSS Diary, June 9, 10, 13, 1919; Bliss to W. M. Shuster, Feb. 4, 1919, Bliss to S. Prosser, Mar. 16, 1919, Bliss MSS; Baruch to Wilson, Dec. 3, 1918, Wilson MSS, File 8A; *PPWW*, V. pp. 355, 375, 382-3, 513; Bane and Lutz (eds.), *Blockade of Germany*, pp. 504-6; Herbert Hoover, "The Economic Administration during the Armistice," in House and Seymour (eds.), *What Really Happened*, pp. 336-47; Hoover, *American Epic*, III, pp. 211-19; R. S. Baker, WW&WS, II, pp. 343, 356-61, 416-20, III, pp. 331-5; Baruch, *Making of Reparation*, pp. 84-5; *Riddell's Diary*, pp. 12-14; Lansing, *Peace Negotiations*, pp. 110-11, 208-10; Diamond, *Economic Thought*, pp. 162-6.

79 *FR, PPC*, 1919, V, pp. 232-3; see also Bliss MSS Diary, Jan. 10, 1919; Baruch to Wilson, Mar. 29, 1919, Wilson MSS, File 8A; Baruch, *Making of Reparation*, p. 80.

80 See p. 126, and note 3, p. 285; see also Wilson to E. N. Hurley, Aug. 29, Sept. 9, 1918, Wilson MSS, File 2; *FR, 1918, Supplement 1*, I, p. 406.

81 *Congressional Record*, 65th Cong. 3rd sess., Vol. 57, p. 338.

82 Hoover to Wilson, Jan. 8, 1919, Wilson MSS, File 8A; McCormick MSS Diary, Jan. 11, 1919; R. S. Baker, WW&WS, II, pp. 323, 335-40; Hoover, *Ordeal*, p. 153.

83 *FR, PPC*, 1919, II, p. 692.

84 *FR, PPC*, 1919, II, p. 706; see also Auchincloss MSS Diary, Jan. 6, 1919.

85 Baruch to Wilson, Mar. 29, 1919, N. Davis to Wilson, with enclosure, May 9, 1919, N. Davis to Wilson, June 7, 1919, Thomas Lamont to Wilson, June 13, 1919, Hoover to Wilson, June 27,

1919, with enclosed memorandum, all in Wilson MSS, File 8A;
FR, PPC, 1919, X, pp. 462-8; Bane and Lutz (eds.), *Blockade
of Germany,* pp. 512-15; Hoover, *American Epic,* III, pp. 220-
26; Coit, *Baruch,* pp. 231-5; R. S. Baker, WW&WS, II, pp. 325-
34, 360-63, III, pp. 347-62, 373-5.

86 *PPWW,* V, pp. 489-90, see also pp. 549-50; *PPWW,* II, pp.
232-3.

87 *Intimate Papers,* IV, pp. 332-4; R. S. Baker, WW&WS, III, pp.
227-37; Louis A. R. Yates, *The United States and French Security, 1917-1921* (New York, 1957), pp. 21-3, 28-9; Nelson,
Land and Power, pp. 111-16, 130-32, 198-9; Noble, *Policies and
Opinions,* pp. 230-53.

88 Andre Tardieu, *The Truth About the Treaty* (Indianapolis, 1921),
pp. 182-95; Yates, *U.S. and French Security,* pp. 64, 101, 105.

89 House MSS Diary, Feb. 9, 11, Mar. 28, 1919; *Intimate Papers,*
IV, pp. 332-6, 345-6, 358, 360, 383-4, 393-7, 403-7; Frank M.
Russell, *The Saar, Battleground and Pawn* (Stanford, 1951), pp.
13-17; Paul Birdsall, *Versailles Twenty Years After* (New York,
1941), pp. 195-235.

90 Wilson to Clemenceau, May 23, 1919, Swem Collection of Wilsonia; Ellis L. Dresel to Wilson, June 5, 1919, Wilson to Dresel,
June 7, 1919, Wilson MSS, File 8A; Lansing MSS Diary, Apr. 29,
1919; *FR, PPC,* 1919, II, pp. 98-107; *FR, PPC,* 1919, III, pp.
712, 1001-2; *FR, PPC,* 1919, IV, pp. 296-8, 356-7, 520; House
and Seymour (eds), *What Really Happened,* pp. 386-7; Trask,
General Bliss, pp. 25-34, 57-8; Hoover, *Ordeal,* pp. 213-15.

91 Tillman, *Anglo-American Relations,* pp. 177-97; Jordan, *German
Problem,* pp. 1-7, 31-3, 173-93; Nelson, *Land and Power,* pp.
133, 198-281.

92 Lansing, "Confidential Memoranda and Notes, Jan. 3, 22, 1919,"
Lansing MSS; Lansing to Polk, Feb. 11, 1919, Polk MSS; N. D.
Baker to Bliss, Dec. 23, 1918, Bliss to N. D. Baker, Jan. 4, 1919,
N.D. Baker MSS; White to Lodge, Jan. 14, 1919, Lodge MSS;
White to Lodge, Feb. 10, 1919, Root MSS.

93 Nelson, *Land and Power,* pp. 70-71; W. K. Hancock, *Smuts, The
Sanguine Years, 1870-1919* (Cambridge, England, 1962), pp.
510-12; W. K. Hancock and Jean Van Der Poel (eds.), *Selections
from the Smuts Papers* (4 vols., Cambridge, England, 1966), IV,
pp. 79, 83-7, 121.

94 R. S. Baker, WW&WS, III, pp. 449-57; Nelson, *Land and
Power,* pp. 223-6.

95 R. S. Baker, *WW&WS*, III, pp. 249–51; see also Noble, *Policies and Opinions*, p. 182, n. 7.
96 Epstein, *Erzberger*, pp. 277–80; Rudin, *Armistice*, pp. 370, 373; J. M. Thompson, *Russia, Bolshevism, and Versailles*, pp. 23–32.
97 *FR, Lansing Papers*, II, p. 173; *FR, PPC*, 1919, III, pp. 417–20; Epstein, *Erzberger*, pp. 250–51; Gordon A. Craig and Felix Gilbert (eds.), *The Diplomats, 1919–1939* (Princeton, 1953), pp. 133–8; Erich Eyck, *A History of the Weimar Republic* (Cambridge, Mass., 1962), pp. 110–13; Luckau, *German Delegation*, pp. 74–7, 84–7.
98 Garrett to Lansing, Feb. 9, 1919, Stovall to Ammission, Mar. 25, 1919, Grant Smith to Ammission, Apr. 22, 1919, A. L. Conger to Bliss, with enclosure, Apr. 30, 1919, all in Wilson MSS, File 8A; *FR, PPC*, 1919, II, pp. 18–19, 34–6, 40, 43–4, 65, 167–8, 640–41; *FR, PPC*, 1919, IV, pp. 40–41; Mayer, *Political Origins*, p. 391; Alfred D. Low, *The Soviet Hungarian Republic and the Paris Peace Conference* (Philadelphia, 1963), p. 44; Carr, *Bolshevik Revolution*, III, pp. 97–103; Epstein, *Erzberger*, p. 296; Joseph A. Berlau, *The German Social Democratic Party* (New York, 1949), p. 226, n. 26, p. 295, n. 27.

CHAPTER V: PEACE AND REVOLUTION, II

1 Epstein, *Erzberger*, pp. 301–23; Luckau, *German Delegation*, pp. 94–5; Berlau, *German Social Democratic Party*, pp. 285–305, 312–14.
2 Eyck, *Weimar Republic*, pp. 100–105, 110–14, 121–2; William S. Halperin, *Germany Tried Democracy, A Political History of the Reich, 1918–1933* (New York, 1946), pp. 147–53; Craig and Gilbert (eds.), *Diplomats*, pp. 145–8.
3 Luckau, *German Delegation*, p. 99; Berlau, *German Social Democratic Party*, pp. 314–15.
4 Nelson's *Land and Power*, while largely ignoring the reintegrationist side of Wilsonian policy at Paris, contains the best single discussion of the punitive Wilson.
5 Hunt, *German Social Democracy*, pp. 26–32; Berlau, *German Social Democratic Party*, pp. 265–84; on Allied anti-revolutionary policy in postwar Germany see Ernst Fraenkel, *Military Occupation and the Rule of Law, Occupation Governments in the Rhineland, 1918–1923* (New York, 1944), pp. 4, 26–34.
6 James T. Shotwell, *At the Paris Peace Conference* (New York, 1937), p. 74; Whiteman (ed.), *Seymour Letters*, p. 22; *FR, PPC,*

1919, V, p. 700; R. S. Baker, WW&WS, III, p. 494; Nelson, *Land and Power*, pp. 34, 39, 374; on Wilson's fears of continued militaristic tendencies in Germany, see *FR, PPC*, 1919, V, pp. 527–8; *FR, PPC*, 1919, VI, pp. 613, 657.

7 Jordan, *German Problem*, pp. 13–30; F. S. Marston, *The Peace Conference of 1919, Organization and Procedure* (London, 1944), pp. 1–43, 54–5.

8 *FR, PPC*, 1919, III, p. 1002; for Administration willingness, as a last resort, to use the American Army to impose the peace settlement on Germany should the Germans reject it, see *FR, PPC*, 1919, III, pp. 972–4; *FR, PPC*, 1919, V, p. 600; *FR, PPC*, 1919, VI, pp. 543–7.

9 *FR, PPC*, 1919, III, pp. 974–7; R. S. Baker, WW&WS, III, pp. 230–32; David Hunter Miller, *The Drafting of the Covenant* (2 vols., New York, 1928), I, pp. 448–9; Noble, *Policies and Opinions*, pp. 154–61.

10 *Life and Letters*, VIII, pp. 441–2; *Intimate Papers*, IV, p. 243, n. 1; *PPWW*, V, pp. 324–5, 521, 590–93, 644; *PPWW*, VI, pp. 34, 104, 266–7, 400; Nelson, *Land and Power*, pp. 48–9.

11 *FR, PPC*, 1919, V, p. 233; see also *PPWW*, V, p. 592; House and Seymour (eds.), *What Really Happened*, pp. 287–8, 296–304; R. S. Baker, WW&WS, III, p. 499.

12 R. S. Baker, WW&WS, III, p. 450.

13 Wilson to Smuts, May 16, 1919, and Wilson to George D. Herron, Apr. 28, 1919, both in Swem Collection of Wilsonia; Charles T. Thompson, *The Peace Conference Day by Day* (New York, 1920), p. 413.

14 "Conversations with General Bliss, May 19, 1919," Bullitt MSS; McCormick MSS Diary, May 22, 23, June 7, 1919; Lansing, "Confidential Memoranda and Notes, May 19, June 5, 1919," Lansing MSS; Lansing MSS Diary, May 21, 1919; R. S. Baker, WW&WS, III, pp. 505–8; George Curry, "Woodrow Wilson, Jan Smuts, and the Versailles Settlement," *The American Historical Review*, LXVI, 4 (July 1961), 983–5; Tillman, *Anglo-American Relations*, pp. 345–52; Nelson, *Land and Power*, pp. 321–40; Palmer, *Bliss*, p. 399; Nevins, *White*, p. 452; Hoover, *Ordeal*, pp. 245–8.

15 R. S. Baker, WW&WS, III, pp. 469–504; see also Hoover, *Ordeal*, pp. 238–45; Trask, *General Bliss*, pp. 58–60.

16 R. S. Baker, WW&WS, III, p. 498.

17 Nelson, *Land and Power*, pp. 38–43, 283–304, 341–58; Charles

Homer Haskins and Robert H. Lord, *Some Problems of the Peace Conference* (Cambridge, Mass., 1920), pp. 169–80, 217–21; R. S. Baker, WW&WS, III, pp. 481–8, 498–9; Nevins, *White*, pp. 422–3; Gelfand, *Inquiry*, pp. 190–208; Shotwell, *Paris Peace Conference*, pp. 305–6; Whiteman (ed.), *Seymour Letters*, pp. 175–6, 193, 266; FR, PPC, 1919, IV, pp. 417–9; FR, PPC, 1919, VI, pp. 147–55, 212, 303–4.

18 Gerson, *Wilson and Poland*, pp. 124–137; Nelson, *Land and Power*, pp. 49–51, 82–5, 96–100, 145–97; Tillman, *Anglo-American Relations*, pp. 203–9; Titus Komarnicki, *Rebirth of the Polish Republic* (London, 1957), pp. 284–90, 317–47; Piotre S. Wandycz, *France and her Eastern Allies, 1919–1925* (Minneapolis, 1962), pp. 16–58.

19 Mayer, *Political Origins*, pp. 391–2; Van der Slice, *Labor, Diplomacy, and Peace*, pp. 237–43, 246–55; Noble, *Policies and Opinions*, pp. 40–44, 73–6.

20 Sharp to Lansing, Nov. 13, 1918, File 763.72119 so/32, D.S.N.A.; David Hunter Miller, *My Diary at the Conference at Paris* (21 vols., Washington, 1928), I, p. 50; Edith Bolling Wilson, *My Memoir* (New York, 1938), pp. 181, 217, 235; Noble, *Policies and Opinions*, pp. 67–71, 76–8; Van der Slice, *Labor, Diplomacy, and Peace*, pp. 296–300; R. S. Baker, WW&WS, I, pp. 89–91, 99–100; Rene Albrecht-Carrie, *Italy at the Paris Peace Conference* (New York, 1938), pp. 82–4; Whiteman (ed.), *Seymour Letters*, p. 34.

21 McCormick MSS Diary, June 13, 1919, R. S. Baker, WW&WS, III, p. 500; FR, PPC, 1919, III, pp. 609–10; PPWW, V, pp. 350–51, 355–6; for Wilson's public praise of the Allied leaders as liberals, see PPWW, V, pp. 300, 326, 337, 342–3, 390–91, 433, 445; House also favored inter-Allied unity at Paris, see House MSS Diary, May 30, June 2, 1919; *Intimate Papers*, IV, pp. 474–5.

22 For social-democratic hopes of an anti-imperialist postwar alliance with Wilson, see Van der Slice, *Labor, Diplomacy, and Peace*, pp. 314–22; Noble, *Policies and Opinions*, pp. 85–7, 91–3, 155, 339–40; Carl F. Brand, "British Labor and President Wilson," *The American Historical Review*, XLII, 2 (January 1937), p. 248.

23 Woodrow Wilson, "Edmund Burke and the French Revolution," in Ray B. Browne (ed.), *The Burke-Paine Controversy, Texts and Criticism* (New York, 1963), pp. 142–3.

24 PPWW, V. pp. 478–9; see also FR, PPC, 1919, III, p. 583.

25 Gompers, *Seventy Years*, II, pp. 476–85; FR, PPC, 1919, I, pp.

539–41; Van der Slice, *Labor, Diplomacy, and Peace*, pp. 299, 312.

26 Lansing to Wilson, Nov. 29, 1918, Wilson MSS, File 2; see also Van der Slice, *Labor, Diplomacy, and Peace*, pp. 299–312; Shotwell, *Paris Peace Conference*, p. 200; Mandel, *Gompers*, pp. 418–21.

27 Sharp to Lansing, Nov. 13, 1918, and Lansing to Tumulty, Nov. 16, 1918, File 763.72119 so/32, D.S.N.A.; Lansing, "Confidential Memoranda and Notes, Jan. 2, 1919," Lansing MSS.

28 Lansing to Wilson, Nov. 9, 1918, enclosing Bullitt Memorandum, Wilson MSS, File 2.

29 Wilson to F. Morrison, Nov. 22, 1918, Wilson MSS, File 7; Miller, *Drafting*, I, p. 233.

30 Christopher Lasch, *The New Radicalism in America, 1889–1963* (New York, 1965), pp. 242–3.

31 *FR, PPC*, 1919, I, p. 160; House to R. S. Baker, Nov. 16, 1918, R. S. Baker MSS, DLC; Memorandum of Nov. 16, 1918, Conversation with Longuet and Cachin, House MSS; House MSS Diary, Nov. 4, 12, Dec. 7, 1918, Jan. 28, Mar. 3, 1919; House also realized the essential weakness of the Allied Left, see *Life and Letters*, VIII, pp. 377–8; House MSS Diary, Dec. 30, 1919.

32 *PPWW*, VI, pp. 33, 271.

33 *PPWW*, V, pp. 600–601; *PPWW*, VI, pp. 60–62, 86–7, 109–11, 280, 394–5, 401–2; Shotwell, *Paris Peace Conference*, p. 200 *et passim*.

34 *PPWW*, VI, pp. 167–8.

35 *PPWW*, V, pp. 326, 328, 330, 333, 348, 354, 396, 377, 380, 395–6, 403, 480–81.

36 *PPWW*, V, pp. 273, 300, 326, 330, 333, 337–8, 342–3, 354, 369, 376, 390–91, 395–9, 403, 433, 480–81, 505–6; see also *PPWW*, V, p. 378 for Wilson's criticism of class conflict in Italy. When, in April 1919, in his one public attack on Allied imperialism at Paris, the President did appeal to the Italian people on the Adriatic issue, he did so by combining respect for legitimate Italian nationalism with a largely abstract appeal for liberal-internationalist values, see *PPWW*, V, pp. 465–8. At this time, the French and Italian Left was critical of Wilson for saying too little, too late on Allied imperialism, see Noble, *Policies and Opinions*, pp. 339–40; Albrecht-Carrie, *Italy*, pp. 144–7.

37 *PPWW*, V, p. 256; see also *PPWW*, V, pp. 336, 506.

38 *PPWW*, V, p. 631; *PPWW*, VI, pp. 10-11, 24, 33, 71, 272-3, 313, 330-31, 356.

39 *PPWW*, V, 302, 438-9, 445-7, 613-15, 624, 644-5; *PPWW*, VI, pp. 22-3, 36, 122-6,140-41, 175, 250-51, 354-5, 389-90; see also Daniels MSS Diary, July 15, 1919.

40 *Intimate Papers*, IV, pp. 22-3, 239-40, 345-6; Palmer, *Bliss*, p. 403.

41 *PPWW*, V, pp. 392-4, 406-7, 555-7; C. T. Thompson, *Peace Conference*, p. 411; House MSS Diary, Jan. 7, Apr. 14, 1919; R. S. Baker, *WW&WS*, III, p. 477.

42 Miller, *Drafting*, I, p. 300; for similar views on the part of Bliss, see Bliss to Wilson, Mar. 14, 1919, Bliss MSS and Bliss to N. D. Baker, Apr. 3, 1919, N. D. Baker MSS.

43 Miller, *Drafting*, I, pp. 243-60; R. S. Baker, *WW&WS*, III, pp. 236-7; *FR, PPC*, 1919, I, p. 335; *FR, PPC*, 1919, III, p. 301; Noble, *Policies and Opinions*, pp. 103-4, 136-47.

44 Nelson, *Land and Power*, pp. 198-248; Yates, *U.S. and French Security*, pp. 45-63.

45 Nelson, *Land and Power*, pp. 51-2, 95-7, 138-9, 212-13, 216-20, 248, 366-8, 375, 379-80; Tillman, *Anglo-American Relations*, pp. 394-9; Winkler, *League Movement*, pp. 241-2.

46 Noble, *Policies and Opinions*, pp. 124-5, 363, 367, 375-6, 388, n. 112, 406-9; Nevins, *White*, p. 477.

47 Brand, *British Labor*, pp. 246-8; Winkler, *League Movement*, pp. 172-4, 187-9, 192-3; Van der Slice, *Labor, Diplomacy, and Peace*, p. 322.

48 Noble, *Policies and Opinions*, p. 411; Brand, *British Labor*, pp. 250-54; Bonsal, *Unfinished Business*, p. 166.

49 Lansing MSS Diary, Apr. 7, 1919; Lansing, "Confidential Memoranda and Notes, Feb. 3, Mar. 7, 16, 20, Apr. 2, 12, 15, 19, May 5, 1919," Lansing MSS; Hoover to Wilson, Apr. 11, 1919, Lansing to Wilson, Apr. 12, 1919, White to Wilson, Apr. 12, 1919, Wilson MSS, File 8A; Bliss to N. D. Baker, Jan. 11, 1919, N. D. Baker MSS; Bliss to Gen. E. Crowder, Mar. 3, 1919, Bliss to Mrs. Bliss, June 19, 1919, Bliss to Gen. B. H. Wells, Mar. 26, 1919, Bliss MSS; Lansing to Polk, Mar. 14, 1919, Polk MSS; *FR, PPC*, 1919, I, pp. 294-7; *FR, PPC*, 1919, II, pp. 547-9; *FR, PPC*, 1919, XI, p. 130; Palmer, *Bliss*, pp. 376, 387, 420-21; Lansing, *Peace Negotiations*, pp. 178-86; Trask, *General Bliss*, pp. 39, 43-7.

50 Lansing, "Confidential Memoranda and Notes, May 6, 1919," Lansing MSS; *FR, PPC*, 1919, II, pp. 568–9; Robert Lansing, *The Big Four and Others of the Peace Conference* (Boston, 1921), pp. 34–5, 50–55, 130–31; Lansing, *Peace Negotiations*, pp. 45, 77–80, 85, 146–8, 272–5; Roland N. Stromberg, *Collective Security and American Foreign Policy From the League of Nations to NATO* (New York, 1963), pp. 30–31.

51 Lansing, "Confidential Memoranda and Notes, Sept. 30, Oct. 27, Nov. 12, 22, 1918," Lansing MSS; Lansing to House, Apr. 8, 1918, Lansing MSS; Lansing to Wilson, with enclosures, Dec. 23, 1918, Jan. 31, 1919, Wilson MSS, File 8A; Lansing, *Peace Negotiations*, pp. 36–41, 43, 50–59, 67–9, 124–35, 164–7; R. S. Baker, WW&WS, III, p. 494.

52 *PPWW*, VI, pp. 181, 212–13, 230–31, 245–7, 294–5, 302, 322–3, 345–6, 356–7, 402, 413–15.

53 Bonsal, *Unfinished Business*, p. 206; *Intimate Papers*, IV, pp. 281, 410, 487–9; *PPWW*, V, pp. 354, 395, 544–5; Wilson to Hoover, Apr. 15, 1919, Wilson MSS, File 8A; R. S. Baker, WW&WS, III, pp. 478–9; "Conversation with Colonel House, May 19, 1919," Bullitt MSS; *FR, PPC*, 1919, II, pp. 620–23.

54 *PPWW*, V, p. 426.

55 Hoover, *Ordeal*, pp. 248–9; *FR, PPC*, 1919, II, pp. 612–14; Nevins, *White*, pp. 474–6; Trask, *General Bliss*, pp. 68–70.

56 Lansing, *Peace Negotiations*, p. 276.

57 House MSS Diary, Mar. 24, 1919; *Intimate Papers*, IV, pp. 389–91, 397–403; Alexander and Juliette George, *Woodrow Wilson and Colonel House, A Personality Study* (New York, 1956), p. 247.

58 R. S. Baker, WW&WS, III, p. 500.

59 *PPWW*, VI, p. 167.

60 Wilson to J. S. Strachey, Apr. 5, 1919, R. S. Baker MSS, DLC

61 *PPWW*, V, p. 343; see also Chapter IV, p. 126, and note 2, p. 285.

62 House MSS Diary, Mar. 16, 1919.

63 In this connection, see Thompson, *Peace Conference*, pp. 410–11.

64 *PPWW*, V, pp. 355–6.

65 *PPWW*, V, pp. 603–4; *PPWW*, VI, pp. 113, 121, 164–6, 205–6, 273, 281, 301, 323–4, 327–30, 340, 366–8.

66 *PPWW*, V, pp. 548, 593–4, 597, 609, 619, 622–3; *PPWW*, VI, pp. 5–6, 45–8, 51–2, 116–18, 203, 218, 277–8, 295, 310, 346, 388–9.

67 *PPWW*, V, pp. 608–13, 626–9, 642–3; *PPWW*, VI, pp. 28–9,

34–7, 53–5, 71–2, 80–82, 95–6, 134–6, 146–7, 168–9, 177–8, 182–4, 190, 255–9, 274–6, 290–91, 299, 306, 325–6, 360–61, 364, 391–2, 402–3.

68 Miller, *Drafting*, I, pp. 164–6; *PPWW*, V, pp. 330–38, 347–8, 363–4, 397, 410, 425–6.

69 FR, PPC, 1919, V, pp. 128–9; *PPWW*, V, pp. 593, 610–11, 621, 623–6, 631–3; *PPWW*, VI, pp. 11, 25, 90–91, 98, 111–12, 122, 129, 150–52, 186, 203–4, 217, 267, 281, 350–53, 380.

70 *PPWW*, VI, p. 55.

71 See *PPWW*, VI, pp. 326–33, for a clear statement of Wilson's vision of the Paris Peace Conference as the culmination of the Enlightenment's long struggle against European traditional reaction.

72 *PPWW*, V, pp. 353, 397, 452–3; House MSS Diary, Mar. 24, 1919.

73 *PPWW*, V, pp. 3–4, 49–53, 56–7, 85, 95, 111, 133–5, 138, 162, 174, 180–81, 184, 224–5, 231–7, 246–8, 254, 258–9, 264.

74 *PPWW*, V, pp. 325, 333, 337, 353, 380, 397–9, 433–40, 447–55, 483, 502–3, 538–9.

75 *Intimate Papers*, IV, pp. 281, 427; Miller, *Drafting*, I, pp. 444–50; Alfred Zimmern, *The League of Nations and the Rule of Law, 1918–1935* (London, 1936), pp. 215–22.

76 Wilson to Senator Key Pittman, Nov. 7, 1918, Wilson MSS, File 2; Bonsal, *Unfinished Business*, p. 48; Thompson, *Peace Conference*, p. 409; Whiteman (ed.), *Seymour Letters*, p. 24; *Intimate Papers*, IV, p. 280; *PPWW*, V, pp. 447–8; Tumulty, *Wilson*, pp. 368–9.

CHAPTER VI: PEACE AND REVOLUTION, III

1 Mamatey, *The United States and East-Central Europe*, pp. 346–79.

2 See Chapter V, p. 161, and notes 17, 18, pp. 294–5; see also Komarnicki, *Polish Republic*, p. 405; Mayer, *Political Origins*, pp. 280–83.

3 FR, PPC, 1919, VI, pp. 206–7; Gerson, *Rebirth of Poland*, pp. 113–18; *Intimate Papers*, IV, pp. 262–4.

4 Ivo J. Lederer, *Yugoslavia at the Paris Conference, A Study in Frontier-making* (New Haven, 1963), pp. 135–219.

5 The French hoped to erect an anti-German and anti-Bolshevik *cordon sanitaire* in Eastern Europe, see Wandycz, *France and her Eastern Allies, passim*.

6 Lansing MSS Diary, Mar. 28, 31, 1919; Lansing, "Confidential Memoranda and Notes, Jan. 22, Mar. 24, 26, Apr. 1, 10, 1919," Lansing MSS; Lansing to Wilson, Apr. 13, 1919, Lansing MSS; Bliss to Mrs. Bliss, Feb. 26, June 19, 1919, Bliss to N. D. Baker, Apr. 19, 1919, Bliss MSS; White to Wilson, Apr. 12, 1919, Wilson MSS, File 8A; White to Lodge, Apr. 14, 1919, Lodge MSS; *FR, PPC*, 1919, XI, pp. 83–4; Palmer, *Bliss*, pp. 367–8, 375–9, 389–90, 398–9; Trask, *General Bliss*, pp. 54–7.

7 Lansing MSS Diary, Apr. 10, 1919; Lansing to Wilson, Apr. 11, 1919, enclosing the Kernan Report, Bliss to Wilson, Apr. 18, 1919, Wilson to Bliss, Apr. 22, 1919, Wilson to Lansing, May 1, 1919, Wilson MSS, File 8A; Nelson, *Land and Power*, pp. 191–2; R. S. Baker, *WW&WS*, III, pp. 218–24.

8 Bliss to Wilson, June 10, 1919, Wilson MSS, File 8A; see also Bliss to N. D. Baker, Apr. 19, 1919, Bliss MSS, and Palmer, *Bliss*, pp. 389–90.

9 Wilson to Bliss, June 16, 1919, Wilson MSS, File 8A.

10 Smuts, *The League of Nations*, a pamphlet in the Lowell MSS; see also Hancock and Poel (eds.), *Smuts Papers*, IV, pp. 11–16; for evidence that Wilson was favorably impressed with Smuts's pamphlet, see Bliss to N. D. Baker, Jan. 4, 21, 1919, N. D. Baker MSS and George Curry, "Woodrow Wilson, Jan Smuts, and the Versailles Settlement," *The American Historical Review*, LXVI, 4 (July 1961), 968–71; Hancock and Poel (eds.), *Smuts Papers*, IV, pp. 45, 49.

11 Mamatey, *U.S. and East-Central Europe*, pp. 56–9, 69–70, 83–4, 102–5, 135, 175–84, 213, 222–6, 233–40, 252–69; Gelfand, *Inquiry*, pp. 199–204.

12 House and Seymour (eds), *What Really Happened*, pp. 89, 107, 110–11; Whiteman (ed.), *Seymour Letters*, pp. 109, 248, 269–70; Theodore P. Greene (ed.), *Wilson at Versailles* (Boston, 1957), p. 45.

13 *FR, PPC*, 1919, II, pp. 481–3, see also pp. 427–9.

14 N. D. Baker to Wilson, Nov. 2, 1918, N. D. Baker MSS.

15 T. N. Page to Wilson, Nov. 12, 1918, Wilson MSS, File 2.

16 B. Long MSS Diary, Nov. 1, 1918.

17 Lansing to Root, Dec. 3, 1918, Lansing MSS; see also Lansing, "Confidential Memoranda and Notes, Oct. 28, Nov. 2, 1918," Lansing MSS; Lansing to Wilson, Nov. 1, 1918, with enclosure, Wilson MSS, File 2.

18 *PPWW*, V, pp. 301–2.

19 Low, *Soviet Hungarian Republic*, pp. 44–6; Komarnicki, *Polish Republic*, pp. 318–25, 417–18; Wandycz, *France and her Eastern Allies*, pp. 22–34, 40–43, 104–15; C. A. Macartney and A. W. Palmer, *Independent Eastern Europe, A History* (London, 1962), pp. 100–101.

20 *FR, PPC*, 1919, III, p. 471, see also pp. 478–9.

21 Bliss MSS Diary, Dec. 29, 1918, Jan. 7, 1919; Bliss to Col. A. Hopkins, Feb. 12, 1919, Bliss to Gen. B. H. Wells, Mar. 26, 1919, Bliss MSS; Bliss to Wilson, Mar. 26, 1919, Wilson MSS, File 8A; Bliss to N. D. Baker, Apr. 3, 1919, N. D. Baker MSS; Palmer, *Bliss*, pp. 389–90; R. S. Baker, *WW&WS*, III, pp. 218–24; Trask, *General Bliss*, pp. 37–8.

22 *PPWW*, V, pp. 300, 367–8; Hoover to Wilson, Jan. 27, Mar. 31, 1919, Wilson MSS, File 8A; Hoover to Bliss, with enclosures, Feb. 19, 1919, Bliss to Hoover, May 22, 1919, Bliss MSS; D.H. Miller, *My Diary*, III, pp. 113–14; Hoover, *American Epic*, III, pp. 120–21; *FR, PPC*, 1919, II, pp. 628–9, 692–3, 695, 698, 704–7.

23 McCormick MSS Diary, Feb. 26, Mar. 15, 1919; Hoover to Wilson, Feb. 12, 1919, Wilson MSS, File 8A; *FR, PPC*, 1919, X, pp. 462–8.

24 R. S. Baker MSS Diary, Mar. 23, 1919, in Notebook 22, R. S. Baker MSS, DLC; Thompson, *Peace Conference*, pp. 261–4; Whiteman (ed.), *Seymour Letters*, pp. 185–9; White to Root, Mar. 28, 1919, Root MSS.

25 Hoover, *Ordeal*, pp. 135–6; Low, *Soviet Hungarian Republic*, p. 49.

26 Lansing to Wilson, Mar. 24, 1919, enclosing memorandum on Hungary by Allen Dulles, Wilson MSS, File 8A; Low, *Soviet Hungarian Republic*, pp. 47, 51–6, 59, 80; Sherman David Spector, *Rumania at the Paris Peace Conference* (New York, 1962), pp. 117, 119; Bonsal, *Unfinished Business*, pp. 139–40; Trask, *General Bliss*, pp. 40–2.

27 Lansing, White, Bliss, and House to Wilson, Apr. 28, 1919, Wilson MSS, File 8A; *FR, PPC*, 1919, V, pp. 291–2; *FR, PPC*, 1919, VII, pp. 173–6.

28 Lansing MSS Diary, Mar. 31, 1919; Bliss to Wilson, Mar. 28, Apr. 11, 1919, Bliss MSS; *FR, PPC*, 1919, V, pp. 706–7; *FR, PPC*, 1919, XI, pp. 134–5; Low, *Soviet Hungarian Republic*, pp. 44–7, 57–60; Spector, *Rumania*, pp. 104–17, 134–54; J. M. Thompson, *Russia, Bolshevism, and Versailles*, pp. 200–206.

29 Wilson did not, however, oppose Roumanian rearmament for defense against Hungary, nor did he oppose all of Roumania's extreme territorial demands, see Low, *Soviet Hungarian Republic*,
pp. 49, 59, 61–2, 80; Spector, *Rumania*, pp. 113, 120–22; in this
sense, the Wilsonian attitude toward Hungary contained the same
inner tension between punitive and reintegrationist tendencies
which characterized the Wilsonian orientation toward postwar
Germany; see Low, *Soviet Hungarian Republic*, pp. 65–6, for an
excellent discussion of the punitive-reintegrationist dilemma faced
by the Allies in regard to a postwar Hungary threatened by Bolshevism.

30 *FR, PPC, 1919*, VI, pp. 284–5; see also Bliss to Wilson, June
10, 1919, and Wilson to Bliss, June 16, 1919, Wilson MSS, File
8A; see also Spector, *Rumania*, p. 154, for Wilson's consideration
of recognizing Kun in mid-June 1919 because of the Hungarian
Bolshevik leader's apparent willingness to obey the Allied Note of
June 13.

31 *FR, PPC, 1919*, VII, pp. 20–21; see also *FR, PPC, 1919*, XI, pp.
259–60; Hoover had expressed similar views to Wilson early in
June, but at that time, Wilson still hoped that Kun would come
to terms with the Allies, see Hoover to Wilson, June 9, 1919,
with enclosures, and Wilson to Hoover, June 10, 1919, Wilson
MSS, File 8A.

32 *FR, PPC, 1919*, VII, p. 60; see also Low, *Soviet Hungarian Republic*, p. 75.

33 *FR, PPC, 1919*, VII, p. 179; Bliss MSS Diary, July 17, 1919;
Spector, *Rumania*, pp. 159–61.

34 *FR, PPC, 1919*, XI, p. 349; *FR, PPC, 1919*, VII, pp. 254–6,
303–8, 317–22, 348–50; Low, *Soviet Hungarian Republic*, pp. 73–
86; Hoover, *Ordeal*, pp. 137–8.

35 Bliss to N. D. Baker, Aug. 7, 1919, N. D. Baker MSS; Wilson to
Lansing, Aug. 8, 1919, R. S. Baker MSS, DLC; White to Lodge,
Aug. 13, 1919, Root MSS; Polk MSS Diary, Aug. 21, Sept. 2,
1919; *FR, PPC, 1919*, VII, pp. 504–9, 528–33, 694–7, 776–8;
Francis Deak, *Hungary at the Paris Peace Conference* (New York,
1942), pp. 143–5; Spector, *Rumania*, pp. 166–174.

36 Hoover to Wilson, Mar. 28, 1919, R. S. Baker MSS, Princeton.

37 *FR, PPC, 1919*, VII, pp. 774–5, see also p. 21.

38 Ibid. p. 605.

39 Francis to Lansing, Jan. 1, 11, 17, 1919, Lansing MSS; *FR, 1918.
Russia*, II, pp. 553–6, 559–60, 563; *FR, 1919, Russia*, pp. 27–30.

40 *FR, 1918, Russia,* II, pp. 509–13, 516–19, 521–50, 557, 567–8, 572–3; *FR, 1919, Russia,* pp. 604–12, 615, 618–21; *Life and Letters,* VIII, pp. 443–4.

41 J. M. Thompson, *Russia, Bolshevism, and Versailles,* pp. 212–20.

42 *FR, 1918, Russia,* II, pp. 362, 366, 382–3, 396–7; Polk MSS Diary, Oct. 11, 1918; Pauline Tompkins, *American-Russian Relations in the Far East* (New York, 1949), pp. 93–4; Unterberger, *America's Siberian Expedition,* pp. 91–5, 98–101.

43 *FR, 1918, Russia,* II, pp. 413, 416, 425; see also B. Long, "Memorandum of a Conversation with the Russian Ambassador, Sept. 28, 1918," File 861.00/2894, D.S.N.A.

44 *FR, 1918, Russia,* II, p. 417; see also *FR, 1919, Russia,* p. 323.

45 See esp. Lansing to R. J. Buck, Nov. 29, 1918, Lansing MSS.

46 *FR, 1918, Russia,* II, p. 366; *FR, 1918, Russia,* III, p. 294; Polk to Wilson, Sept. 9, 1918, Polk MSS; Basil Miles, "Memorandum for Mr. Polk, Oct. 24, 1918," File 861.00/3458, D.S.N.A.; Cyrus McCormick to Wilson, Sept. 13, 1918, Wilson to Cyrus McCormick, Sept. 20, 1918, Wilson MSS, File 2; B. Long MSS Diary, Jan. 28, 1919; Auchincloss MSS Diary, Oct. 3, 1918; Polk to Roland S. Morris, Dec. 5, 6, 1918, and B. Long to R. S. Morris, with enclosure, Feb. 19, 1919, Roland S. Morris, MSS, DLC.

47 Lansing to House, Nov. 9, 1918, House MSS; B. Long MSS Diary, Dec. 16, 1918; *FR, 1918, Russia,* II, pp. 428, 434–5, 462–7; Curry, *Wilson and Far Eastern Policy,* pp. 238–9; Tompkins, *American-Russian Relations,* pp. 95–8, 105–7, 119–24.

48 Basil Miles, "Memorandum for the Secretary of State, Oct. 28, 1918," Wilson MSS, File 2; *FR, 1918, Russia,* II, pp. 434, 436–7, 465–6; *FR, 1918, Russia,* III, pp. 238, 240, 243, 252, 264, 281–5, 288, 290–94, 299–300, 306–7; *FR, 1919, Russia,* pp. 242–53; Beers, *Vain Endeavor,* pp. 130–40; Unterberger, *America's Siberian Expedition,* pp. 104–17.

49 *FR, 1919, Russia,* pp. 246–7.

50 *FR, PPC, 1919,* I, p. 271.

51 Ibid.

52 Gelfand, *Inquiry,* pp. 213–14; see also J. M. Thompson, *Russia, Bolshevism, and Versailles,* pp. 46–50.

53 Lloyd George, *Truth about the Treaties,* I, p. 188; *FR, 1919, Russia,* pp. 71–2; House MSS Diary, Feb. 17, 1919; *Intimate Papers,* IV, p. 348, n. 1.

54 *FR, PPC, 1919,* III, pp. 1402–3.

55 Ibid. p. 648, see also p. 584.

56 Bliss to N. D. Baker, Feb. 14, Apr. 3, Oct. 5, 16, 1919, N. D. Baker MSS; Bliss to A. Hopkins, Feb. 12, 1919, Bliss to Gen. P. C. March, Sept. 3, Oct. 9, 1918, Feb. 19, 1920, Bliss MSS; Bliss MSS Diary, Jan. 7, 1919; Palmer, *Bliss*, p. 369; Trask, *General Bliss*, pp. 34–9.

57 On Wilson's implicit faith that liberalism would eventually triumph over Russia's "temporary" Bolshevik aberration, see the discussion of Wilson's Russian policy in Ray Stannard Baker's unpublished MS on the Russian Problem at the Paris Peace Conference, pp. 20–22, in the R. S. Baker MSS, Princeton; see also *FR, PPC, 1919,* V, p. 498, for Wilson's view that "Bolshevism must collapse" eventually in Russia.

58 See *Intimate Papers,* IV, p. 348, and n. 1, for the Wilsonian fusion of opposition to armed Allied intervention in Russia with the desire to contain the Bolshevik regime in European Russia.

59 *FR, PPC, 1919,* IV, pp. 589–93, 690–93, 762; Palmer, *Bliss,* pp. 415–16; Hoover, *Ordeal,* pp. 126–7.

60 House MSS Diary, Jan. 1, 1919; Wilson to Lansing, Jan. 10, 1919, Wilson MSS, File 8A.

61 *FR, 1919, Russia,* pp. 15–18; *FR, PPC, 1919,* III, pp. 643–6.

62 On Wilson's opposition to recognition of the Soviets at Paris, see also Williams, *American-Russian Relations,* pp. 157–70.

63 Tillman, *Anglo-American Relations,* pp. 136–8; J. M. Thompson, *Russia, Bolshevism, and Versailles,* pp. 89–106.

64 *FR, PPC, 1919,* III, pp. 583–4, 591–2.

65 Ibid. pp. 591–3.

66 Ibid. pp. 663–4, see also pp. 648–9.

67 Ibid. p. 676.

68 Ibid. pp. 676–7.

69 For Wilson's desire to use the projected Prinkipo Conference to reconcile *all* Russian factions, and not simply to seek an Allied-Bolshevik *rapprochement* based on Bolshevik control of European Russia, see *FR, PPC, 1919,* III, pp. 663, 667, 1042–3; *FR, PPC, 1919,* V, p. 736; Tumulty, *Wilson,* p. 374.

70 Memorandum from the Russian Section of the American Peace Commission, Mar. 31, 1919, initialed by Lansing, in Wilson MSS, File 8A; Hoover, *Ordeal,* pp. 117–19; Hoover to House, Apr. 19, 1919, House MSS.

71 Lansing to D.C. Poole, Feb. 8, 1919, Wilson MSS, File 8A; see also *FR, 1919, Russia,* p. 35; Lansing to Polk, Feb. 11, 1919, Polk MSS; Thompson, *Peace Conference,* pp. 92–3.

72 George D. Herron to House, Feb. 13, 1919, House MSS; Mitchell P. Briggs, *George D. Herron and the European Settlement* (Stanford, 1932), pp. 141–7; Kennan, *Russia and the West*, p. 127; Noble, *Policies and Opinions*, pp. 277–86; J. M. Thompson, *Russia, Bolshevism, and Versailles*, pp. 119–27.

73 Fischer, *Life of Lenin*, p. 349; Carr, *Bolshevik Revolution*, III, pp. 110–11; see also Kennan, *Russia and the West*, p. 124, and J. M. Thompson, *Russia, Bolshevism, and Versailles*, pp. 82–92, 113–18, for an analysis of the Soviet "peace offensive" of early 1919, through which the Soviet leaders hoped to end Allied intervention, achieve Allied recognition of the Soviet regime in European Russia, and gain a breathing spell in the Civil War while awaiting possible further revolutionary success in Europe.

74 FR, 1919, *Russia*, pp. 39–42; significantly, on Jan. 24, 1919, Lenin told Trotsky to seize a few more cities to improve the Soviet bargaining position at Prinkipo, see Deutscher, *Prophet Armed*, p. 429.

75 The Bolshevik response, offering imperialistic concession for recognition angered Wilson, see Tumulty, *Wilson*, p. 374.

76 Lasch, *American Liberals*, pp. 135–8, 146–9, 153–7.

77 "Minutes of the Daily Meetings of the Commissioners Plenipotentiary, Jan. 30, 1919," Bliss MSS; Bullitt to Wilson, Apr. 6, 1919, Bullitt MSS.

78 FR, 1919, *Russia*, p. 18.

79 *The Bullitt Mission to Russia, Testimony before the Committee on Foreign Relations, United States Senate, of William C. Bullitt* (New York, 1919), pp. 32–4; Lasch, *American Liberals*, p. 185.

80 Lansing MSS Diary, Feb. 16, 1919.

81 FR, 1919, *Russia*, pp. 74–5.

82 *Bullitt Mission*, pp. 32–8.

83 This judgment is based on a comparison of the House-Kerr terms, as they appear in *Bullitt Mission*, pp. 34–7, with the Soviet terms that had been conveyed to the Allies earlier in the year by Litvinov. For a similar view, see Beatrice Farnsworth, *William C. Bullitt and the Soviet Union* (Bloomington, 1967), pp. 37–8, and p. 192, n. 15.

84 *Bullitt Mission*, p. 34; on House's desire for a *rapprochement* with the Bolshevik regime at this time, see Lloyd George, *Truth about the Treaties*, I, pp. 373–4.

85 The point about Bullitt's implicit ignoring of the White Russians was originally made by Frederick L. Schuman in his *American*

Policy toward Russia since 1917 (New York, 1928), p. 131; also significant is the fact that the anti-Bolshevik George Herron, who had been appointed by Wilson to be one of America's representatives at the projected Prinkipo Conference, saw the Bullitt Mission as a pro-Bolshevik intrigue on Bullitt's part, see Briggs, *Herron and the European Settlement*, pp. 148–9; on the Bolshevik acceptance of Bullitt's terms, as long as Bullitt was willing to add a specific pledge that the Allies would cease to aid anti-Bolshevik movements in Russia, see J. M. Thompson, *Russia, Bolshevism, and Versailles*, pp. 162–72; Fischer, *Life of Lenin*, p. 351; see also Farnsworth, *Bullitt*, pp. 194–5, n. 28, however, for evidence that Trotsky already opposed any movement toward "socialism in one country" and opposed Lenin's decision for an expediential compromise with the Allies through Bullitt. Trotsky felt increased Allied intervention would bring socialist revolution to France and England.

86 Lansing MSS Diary, Mar. 19, 1919; Miller, *My Diary*, I, p. 189.
87 Wilson to Tumulty, July 17, 1919, Wilson MSS, File 2.
88 The House terms had been partly created by Bullitt himself in the process of asking House a series of leading questions, see *Bullitt Mission*, pp. 34–5.
89 FR, PPC, 1919, III, pp. 1042–3.
90 On the ignorance of the majority of the American Peace Commission concerning Bullitt's mission, see Joseph Grew to William Phillips, Mar. 18, 1919, Grew MSS; FR, 1919, *Russia*, p. 97; Trask, *General Bliss*, pp. 39–40.
91 FR, 1919, *Russia*, pp. 81–9; Kennan, *Russia and the West*, p. 131.
92 Noble, *Policies and Opinions*, pp. 288–9.
93 Ibid. pp. 287–8; see also Tillman, *Anglo-American Relations*, pp. 142–4.
94 Lansing MSS Diary, Mar. 26, 1919; McCormick MSS Diary, Apr. 6, 1919; Auchincloss MSS Diary, Mar. 26, Apr. 23, 1919; Polk to Auchincloss, Apr. 5, 1919, Polk MSS; Grew to Phillips, Apr. 13, 1919, Grew MSS; Bullitt claims to have spent a day on his return to Paris winning over Lansing, White, and Bliss to his Russian peace plan, see *Bullitt Mission*, p. 65. It will be recalled, however, that Lansing and White both opposed the Soviet terms cabled by Bullitt to Paris from Moscow on Mar. 19, 1919, see p. 214, and note 86, above. Moreover, if Bullitt did actually change their minds on his return, there is no evidence of it in the actions of the Peace Commissioners, none of whom supported Bullitt openly or took responsibility for publishing his report.

95 House MSS Diary, Mar. 25, 26, 1919; Miller, *My Diary*, I, p. 206;
   J. M. Thompson, *Russia, Bolshevism, and Versailles*, pp. 235–6.
96 House MSS Diary, Mar. 26, 1919; see also Auchincloss MSS
   Diary, Mar. 26, 1919.
97 House MSS Diary, Mar. 27, 1919; see also Kennan, *Russia and
   the West*, pp. 136–40.
98 Bullitt tried to fuse the food relief plan with his own peace plan,
   see *Bullitt Mission*, pp. 74–92; Lasch, *American Liberals*, pp.
   195–6; yet, Bullitt's efforts were counterbalanced by those of Wilsonians such as Hoover and Vance McCormick who were ada-
   mant that the food relief program should not entail a recognition
   of the *de facto* Bolshevik regime, see McCormick MSS Diary,
   Mar. 29, 1919; *FR, 1919, Russia*, pp. 100–102; see also J. M.
   Thompson, *Russia, Bolshevism, and Versailles*, pp. 247–60, and
   Farnsworth, *Bullitt*, pp. 51–4, for discussions of the Hoover-
   Hansen food relief plan in Russia as a somewhat ambiguous
   compromise between Bullitt and his opponents within the Administration on Russian policy.
99 Kennan, *Russia and the West*, pp. 136–42.
100 Grew to Phillips, Apr. 13, 1919, Grew MSS; for similar views
    held by Hoover at this time, see J. M. Thompson, *Russia, Bolshe-
    vism and Versailles*, pp. 257–9.
101 On Mar. 29, 1919, House advocated the publication of Bullitt's
    report, but Wilson refused; see R. S. Baker, MSS Diary, Mar.
    29, 1919, Notebook XXII, in the R. S. Baker MSS, DLC.
102 *Bullitt Mission*, pp. 39–40.
103 In Russia Bullitt consulted only the Left-Mensheviks and Social
    Revolutionaries who were anxious to come to terms with the Bol-
    sheviks; see *Bullitt Mission*, pp. 60–62.
104 See p. 216, and note 96, above. For House on containment, see
    House MSS Diary, Mar. 29, 1919; *Intimate Papers*, IV, p. 348; on
    House's willingness to extend *de facto* recognition to the Bolshevik
    regime in European Russia in return for Bolshevik promises not to
    advance into non-Bolshevik areas of Russia, see *Bullitt Mission*,
    pp. 34–5.
105 House MSS Diary, Sept. 19, 1918.
106 Lansing to Amembassy, Tokyo, Dec. 5, 1919, Roland Morris
    MSS; *FR, 1919, Russia*, pp. 130, 723–4, 727–8; *FR, PPC, 1919*,
    XI, pp. 253–5; Unterberger, *America's Siberian Expedition*, p.
    175; Komarnicki, *Polish Republic*, pp. 412–13; Spector, *Rumania*,
    p. 131; Ronald Radosh, "John Spargo and Wilson's Russian
    Policy, 1920," *The Journal of American History*, LII, 3 (Decem-

ber, 1963), 552–65; Albert N. Tarulis, *American-Baltic Relations, 1918–1922* (Washington, D.C., 1965), pp. 21–40, 161–206.

107 See Lasch, *American Liberals*, p. 177, for a correct judgment to the effect that Wilson did not intend a partition of Russia to result from a Prinkipo Conference,

108 Also see Lasch, *American Liberals*, p. 202, for an interesting warning from Tumulty to Wilson in Apr. 1919, to the effect that American public opinion was opposed to any move toward a *rapprochement* with the Bolshevik regime.

CHAPTER VIII: PEACE AND REVOLUTION, IV

1 N. D. Baker to Wilson, Mar. 3, 1919, with enclosure from Graves, and Polk to Wilson, Mar. 6, 1919, Wilson MSS, File 8A; *FR, 1919, Russia*, pp. 212–13, 465–72, 474–5, 491–2; William S. Graves, *America's Siberian Adventure, 1918–1920* (New York, 1931), pp. 65–6, 74–6, 92–6, 99–110, 116–18, 122, 143–66, 214–16, 222–3.

2 Lansing to Wilson, Mar. 22, 1919, Bliss to Wilson, May 9, 1919, Wilson MSS, File 8A; *FR, 1919, Russia*, pp. 494–6, 499–500, 502–3; Graves, *Siberian Adventure*, pp. 67–9, 71–3, 81–4, 98–9, 111–12, 202–3; J. A. White, *Siberian Intervention*, pp. 262, 271–3; J. M. Thompson, *Russia, Bolshevism, and Versailles*, pp. 283–7.

3 Polk to Auchincloss, Apr. 5, 1919, Polk MSS; Ammission to Polk, Apr. 1, 1919, Polk to Lansing, Apr. 24, 1919, Wilson MSS, File 8A; *FR, 1919, Russia*, pp. 200–201, 322–5, 331–7, 342–4, 347–8; Tompkins, *American-Russian Relations*, pp. 103–7, 110; Unterberger, *America's Siberian Expedition*, pp. 149–54.

4 *FR, 1919, Russia*, pp. 199–201, 373–4, 464–5; *FR, 1918, Russia*, II, pp. 370, 386–7, 420–21, 426–7, 443–6, 451–6, 458–460.

5 Lansing MSS Diary, May 15, 1919; *FR, 1919, Russia*, pp. 493–4; Graves, *Siberian Adventure*, pp. 97–8, 107, 147, 162, 192–7, 216–18, 225, 295; Unterberger, *America's Siberian Expedition*, pp. 124–5.

6 Ammission to Polk, Apr. 2, 1919, Polk to Auchincloss, May 21, 1919, Wilson to Tumulty, May 23, 1919, Wilson MSS, File 8A; *FR, 1919, Russia*, pp. 256, 260–62, 326, 328, 331, 336–7, 480–81; White, *Siberian Intervention*, p. 311; Schuman, *American Policy*, pp. 140–42; Kennan, *Russia and the West*, p. 111; on the assistance of the Siberian rails to the Kolchak regime, see George Stewart, *The White Armies of Russia* (New York, 1933), pp. 264–5.

7 FR, 1919, Russia, pp. 508–9; Graves, Siberian Adventure, pp. 97, 125, 179–190, 205–6, 242–4, 302; White, Siberian Intervention, p. 273.

8 Polk MSS Diary, Apr. 8, 1919; Basil Miles, "Memorandum for Mr. Polk; the Siberian Situation," May 6, 1919, File 861.00/4976, D.S.N.A.; Ammission to Polk, Apr. 11, 1919, Wilson MSS, File 8A; Caldwell to Amembassy, Tokyo, Apr. 2, 1919, Polk to Amembassy, Tokyo, Apr. 17, May 3, 6, 21, 1919, R. S. Morris MSS; FR, 1919, Russia, pp. 552–68; Tompkins, American-Russian Relations, pp. 127–31; Beers, Vain Endeavor, pp. 170–72.

9 Emile Vandervelde to Wilson, May 15, 1919, and Kerensky, et. al. to Wilson, n.d., Wilson MSS, File 8A, Boxes 48 and 70, respectively; FR, 1919, Russia, pp. 337–8; FR, PPC, 1919, V, pp. 529–30, 544, 725, 735–6; J. M. Thompson, Russia, Bolshevism, and Versaill , pp. 289–93.

10 FR, 1919, Russia, p. 349.

11 FR, 1919, PPC, V, pp. 497–8, 544–5, 735–7, 861–2, 901–3; FR, 1919, PPC, VI, pp. 15–23, 73–5, 233, 321–3, 356; Tillman, Anglo-American Relations, pp. 145–7; see also McCormick MSS Diary, Apr. 21, 24, 26, May 2, 14, 24, 1919, for growing pro-Kolchak sentiment in the American Peace Commission during spring 1919.

12 McCormick MSS Diary, June 23, 1919; Polk to Wilson, July 12, 1919, Wilson MSS, File 2; Close to McCormick, June 7, 1919, Phillips to Ammission, June 16, 1919 (2), Polk to Ammission, June 19, 1919, Polk to Lansing, June 20, 1919, Lansing to Wilson, June 20, 1919, Wilson to Lansing, June 24, 1919, Close to McCormick, June 24, 1919, McCormick to Wilson, June 27, 1919, Lansing and McCormick to Polk, June 26, 1919, all in Wilson MSS, File 8A; FR, PPC, 1919, VI, pp. 15–19; FR, 1919, Russia, pp. 383–7, 390.

13 McCormick MSS Diary, June 17, 1919; FR, 1919, Russia, p. 388.

14 FR, 1919, Russia, pp. 391–4.

15 Ibid. p. 391.

16 Ibid. pp. 391–3.

17 Ibid. p. 393.

18 Ibid. pp. 393–4.

19 See Adam Ulam, The Bolsheviks (New York, 1965), pp. 438–9.

20 White, Siberian Intervention, pp. 267–9, 274–85; Stewart, White Armies, pp. 271, 279; Footman, Civil War, pp. 215–21; FR, 1919, Russia, pp. 226–7, 279–281, 311–15, 395, 419.

21 *FR*, 1919, *Russia*, pp. 394–423; Graves, accompanying Morris, was pessimistic in his political and military judgments of Kolchak's regime, see Graves, *Siberian Adventure*, pp. 208–16, 227–40.
22 *FR*, 1919, *Russia*, pp. 421–2, see also p. 660.
23 B. Long, "Memorandum of a Conversation with the Russian Ambassador, Sept. 4, 1919," Long MSS; Lansing to Wilson, Dec. 4, 1919, with enclosed memorandum by Lansing, Wilson MSS, File 2; Lansing to George Kennan, Feb. 2, 1920, George Kennan Papers, DLC; *FR*, 1919, *Russia*, pp. 123, 214–15, 218, 419–20, 432–43, 548–9, 565–603; Unterberger, *America's Siberian Expedition*, pp. 161–76; Tompkins, *American-Russian Relations*, pp. 130–35.
24 *FR*, 1919, *Russia*, pp. 425–6, see also pp. 119–20.
25 *FR*, 1919, *Russia*, pp. 424–5, 443, 519.
26 *FR*, 1919, *Russia*, pp. 154–7, 161–2; *FR*, *PPC*, 1919, VII, pp. 266, 300–301, 644–5; B. Long, MSS Diary, Aug. 2, 1919; at the same time, the U.S. did supply food relief to areas in the rear of the White Russian forces in the Baltic area under General Yudenitch, see *FR*, 1919, *Russia*, pp. 700–710, 726–7.
27 Lansing, "Confidential Memoranda and Notes, Oct. 9, 1919," Lansing MSS.
28 *FR*, 1919, *Russia*, p. 536; see also Polk to Hapgood, Oct. 23, 1919, House MSS; *FR*, 1919, *Russia*, pp. 729–33.
29 B. Long MSS Diary, Dec. 27, 1919; B. Long, "Memoranda of Conversations with the Russian Ambassador, Dec. 2, 9, 1919," Long MSS; Lansing, "Confidential Memoranda and Notes, Nov. 30, 1919," Lansing MSS; Unterberger, *America's Siberian Expedition*, pp. 176–9.
30 Lansing to Kennan, Feb. 2, 1920, Kennan MSS.
31 *FR*, *PPC*, 1919, V, pp. 528–9.
32 *FR*, 1919, *Russia*, pp. 623–60.
33 McCormick MSS Diary, June 23, 1919; *FR*, 1919, *Russia*, pp. 117–19.
34 McCormick MSS Diary, June 23, 1919.
35 Hoover to Wilson, May 9, 1919, Wilson to Hoover, May 21, 1919, Wilson MSS, File 8A; *FR*, *PPC*, 1919, IV, pp. 752–7; *FR*, *PPC*, 1919, V, p. 737; *FR*, 1919, *Russia*, pp. 673, 678, 691–3, 696–8, 726–8, 737, 747; Hoover, *American Epic*, III, pp. 42–51, 167–70; Hoover, *Ordeal*, pp. 127–34.
36 *FR*, *PPC*, 1919, VII, pp. 644–5.

37 See, Hapgood to Wilson, June 15, 1919, Polk MSS, and Wilson to Hapgood, June 20, 1919, Wilson MSS, File 8A. Since both Wilson and the Left-liberals did a good deal of talking about aiding a vague entity known as "Russia," it was possible for them to appear to agree on the Left-liberal solution of recognition of a moderated Bolshevik Russia, while Wilson really meant a unified liberal Russia when he spoke of "Russia."

38 PPWW, VI, p. 6, see also pp. 15, 70, 100–101, 168, 193.

39 FR, 1919, Russia, p. 125, see also pp. 129–30.

40 Lansing to Wilson, Dec. 4, 1919, with enclosed Lansing Memorandum of Dec. 3, 1919, Wilson MSS, File 2.

41 Lansing Memorandum of Dec. 3, 1919, pp. 1–2, enclosed in Lansing to Wilson, Dec. 4, 1919, Wilson MSS, File 2.

42 See Williams, Tragedy, pp. 112–14.

43 B. Long, "memorandum of a Conversation with the Russian Ambassador, Sept. 4, 1919," Long MSS; FR, 1919, Russia, pp. 292–4, 527–8, 565–78; Tompkins, American-Russian Relations, pp. 129–35.

44 McCormick MSS Diary, June 23, 1919; Lansing to Wilson, Dec. 4, 1919, with enclosed Lansing Memorandum, Wilson MSS, File 2; FR, 1919, Russia, pp. 388, 432–4, 548–9, 574–603. Newton D. Baker favored a policy of early withdrawal from Siberia rather than a policy of continued efforts to move Japan toward co-operation with American goals (see Unterberger, America's Siberian Expedition, pp. 167–8), but, despite Baker's views, Lansing's policy of attempted co-operation with Japan against Bolshevism in Siberia seems to have won out clearly during 1919.

45 Lansing, "Confidential Memoranda and Notes, Nov. 30, 1919," also "July 31, 1919," Lansing MSS.

46 FR, 1920, III, pp. 497–8, 501–2; Unterberger, America's Siberian Expedition, pp. 180–81.

47 B. Long MSS Diary, Aug. 12, Oct. 11, 1918, Mar. 19, June 23, July 9, Aug. 11, 26, 30. Sept. 18, 1919; B. Long, "Memorandum re Consultation with Mr. J. P. Morgan and Mr. John Abbot, Sept. 16, 1918," Memorandum re Conversation with Mr. J. G. Kasai, Nov. 1, 1918," B. Long MSS; H. D. Marshall to Long, May 20, 1919, Lamont to Long, Aug. 30, 1919, Long to Lamont, Dec. 20, 1919, B. Long MSS; FR, 1919, I, pp. 470–503; FR, PPC, 1919, II, pp. 491–7, 507–9, 517–18, 520–25; Gelfand, Inquiry, p. 264; Beers, Vain Endeavor, pp. 142–7, 173–5; Frederick V. Field, Amer-

ican Participation in the China Consortiums (Chicago, 1931), pp. 142-7, 154-64.

48 Fifield, *Wilson and the Far East*, pp. 108-20, 143-57, 174-217; Tillman, *Anglo-American Relations*, pp. 333-5.

49 Lansing to Wilson, Oct. 26, 1918, Wilson MSS, File 2; E. T. Williams to the American Commissioners, Jan 16, 1919, Wilson MSS, File 8A; *Black Book 2*: Outline of Tentative Report and Recommendations, Prepared by the Intelligence Section (i.e. The Inquiry), for the President and the Plenipotentiaries, Feb. 13, 1919, pp. 33, 57-9, 62-3, Wilson MSS, File 8A; *FR, PPC*, 1919, II, pp. 491-6, 507-9, 520-25; *FR, PPC*, 1919, V, pp. 110-11; Fifield, *Wilson and the Far East*, pp. 148, 174-9, 190-94, 208-12, 221-2, 230-38.

50 Lansing MSS Diary, Apr. 21, 1919; *FR, PPC*, 1919, IV, pp. 555-70; Fifield, *Wilson and the Far East*, pp. 155-6, 245.

51 *FR, PPC*, 1919, V, pp. 129-30.

52 Thomas A. Bailey, *Wilson and the Peacemakers* (New York, 1947), pp. 279-83.

53 Curry, *Wilson and Far Eastern Policy*, pp. 267-76.

54 *PPWW*, VI, p. 373, see also pp. 41-2, 132-3, 221-5, 242-3, 316-19, 340-42; *PPWW*, V, p. 630.

55 Curry, *Wilson and Far Eastern Policy*, pp. 285-96; Fifield, *Wilson and the Far East*, pp. 350-53.

56 R. S. Baker, *WW&WS*, II, pp. 254-7; Fifield, *Wilson and the Far East*, pp. 257-60, 298-300, 315-22; Trask, *General Bliss*, pp. 50-53.

57 Lansing to Polk, May 1, 1919, Polk MSS; Lansing, "Confidential Memoranda and Notes, Apr. 28, May 1, 1919," Lansing MSS; Beers, *Vain Endeavor*, pp. 149-59; Lansing, *Peace Negotiations*, pp. 242-267.

58 House to Wilson, Apr. 29, 1919, House MSS; *Intimate Papers*, IV, pp. 451-5; Miller, *My Diary*, I, pp. 116, 119; Fifield, *Wilson and the Far East*, pp. 141, 159, 191, 226, 264, 272, 292; Birdsall, *Versailles Twenty Years After*, pp. 109-15.

59 On Wilson's distrust of Japanese intentions in the Far East, see Miller, *My Diary*, I, p. 100; Birdsall, *Versailles Twenty Years After*, pp. 50, 74; on Wilson's fears over Japan and the League, fears perhaps exacerbated by Japan's disappointment over the racial equality clause in the League Covenant, see Fifield, *Wilson and the Far East*, pp. 263, 291-3; R. S. Baker, *WW&WS*, II, pp. 258-9.

60 R.S. Baker, WW&WS, II, p. 266.
61 House to Wilson, Apr. 29, 1919, House MSS; Wilson to Tumulty, Apr. 30, 1919, Wilson MSS, File 8A; McCormick MSS Diary, July 5, 1919; *FR, PPC*, 1919, V, pp. 145-7, 318; *PPWW*, V, pp. 630-31; *PPWW*, VI, pp. 41-2, 133-4, 223-5, 243-4, 316-19.
62 *FR, 1918, Supplement*, 1, p. 407; *FR, PPC*, 1919, III, pp. 740-41, 765-7; *FR, PPC*, 1919, V, pp. 492, 700; *PPWW*, V, pp. 428-9, 543-4, 601-2; Gelfand, *Inquiry*, pp. 172, 230-2; *Intimate Papers*, IV, pp. 284-5; Benjamin Gerig, *The Open Door and the Mandates System* (London, 1930), pp. 86-96; Quincy Wright, *Mandates under the League of Nations* (Chicago, 1930), pp. 24-9; George Louis Beer, *African Questions at the Paris Peace Conference* (New York, 1923), pp. 425-6.
63 House and Seymour (eds.), *What Really Happened*, pp. 440, 443.
64 It will be recalled that on his mediation trips to Europe prior to 1917, House had also supported plans for great power co-operation in the process of expansion into underdeveloped areas. George Louis Beer, chief of the Colonial Division of the American Peace Commission at Paris, also felt that there was a need to depoliticize the trade and investment questions in Africa as part of a general effort to achieve great power co-operation in Africa for peace and the betterment of the indigenous inhabitants, see Beer, *African Questions*, pp. 213-20, 279-86.
65 In this connection it should be noted that the United States was active, during 1919, in defending its rights of access to Middle Eastern oil resources, see Coit, *Baruch*, pp. 233-4; John A. DeNovo, *American Interests and Policies in the Middle East, 1900-1939* (Minneapolis, 1963), pp. 167-74; see also Gerig, *Mandates System*, however, for evidence that the U.S. did not always follow the Open Door in its own possessions of Puerto Rico and the Philippines.
66 Tillman, *Anglo-American Relations*, pp. 85-100; Gelfand, *Inquiry*, p. 172; Birdsall, *Versailles Twenty Years After*, pp. 49-84.
67 *PPWW*, V, pp. 427-8, 601-2; *PPWW*, VI, pp. 190-91, 336, 358.
68 Lansing, "Confidential Memoranda and Notes, Dec. 30, 1918," Lansing MSS; see also Lansing, Ibid. June 6, 1920, Lansing MSS.
69 Gary, Diplomatic Agent in Egypt, to American Embassy in Paris, Mar. 16, 18, 20, 27, Apr. 24, 25, 1919, and Lansing to Wilson, Mar. 21, 1919, Wilson MSS, File 8A; Wilson to Lansing, Apr. 21, 1919, Swem Collection of Wilsonia; Wiseman to House,

Apr. 18, 1919, Wiseman MSS; House MSS Diary, Apr. 18, 1919.

70 Komarnicki, *Polish Republic*, pp. 17–23, 315–16; on Korea, see Fifield, *Wilson and the Far East*, pp. 205–7; on Ireland, see Nicholas Mansergh, *The Irish Question, 1840–1921* (London, 1965), pp. 277–81; see also Warren I. Cohen, "America and the May Fourth Movement, the Response to Chinese Nationalism, 1917–1921," *The Pacific Historical Review*, XXXV, 1 (February 1966), 88–94, for evidence that some nationalistic Chinese students began to turn to Leninism after the Shantung decision at Paris.

71 *PPWW*, V, pp. 594, 599–602; *PPWW*, VI, pp. 31–3, 49–50, 73, 102–3, 105, 123–4, 151–2, 250–52, 268, 278–9, 304, 358, 369, 385, 400–401.

72 *PPWW*, V, pp. 542, 595–6, 605–6; *PPWW*, VI, pp. 251, 269, 279, 331–2, 400–401.

73 On Wilson's belief that Article X of the Covenant could be used to protect all weak peoples against imperialistic infringement upon their territorial integrity, see *PPWW*, V, p. 631; *PPWW*, VI, pp. 25, 98, 129, 152, 304–5, 363, 380, 407; on Wilson's belief that Article XI of the League Covenant could be utilized to bring all remaining cases of imperialistic dominance under the scrutiny of liberal world opinion, see *PPWW*, V, pp. 597, 616–17; *PPWW*, VI, pp. 72–3, 133–4, 161–2, 170, 224–5, 244, 287, 326, 394, 407.

74 For Wilson's care in stressing that Article X of the League Covenant was meant to guarantee nations against external aggression, and not against internal revolution, see *PPWW*, V, p. 632; *PPWW*, VI, pp. 35, 332–3, 360. Yet it must also be made clear that Wilson felt that a world in which war had been controlled would also be an orderly world in which revolutionary-socialism would not prosper.

75 American policy at Paris in relation to the postwar Middle East provides a fine example of this mixture of a Wilsonian opposition to traditional imperialistic practices in backward areas with a Wilsonian conviction that some form of more progressive Western and/or American economic-political influence in the Middle East was desirable, see Harry N. Howard, *The Partition of Turkey, A Diplomatic History, 1913–1923* (Norman, Okla., 1931), pp. 218–42; De Novo, *American Interests*, pp. 110–25, 167–74; Thompson, *Peace Conference*, pp. 406–7.

76 John L. Snell, "Wilson on Germany and the Fourteen Points," *The Journal of Modern History*, XXVI, 4, (December 1954), 368;

despite his commitment to the freedom of the seas, Wilson was willing to allow the League to apply commercial sanctions against an international lawbreaker, see *PPWW*, VI, pp. 185-6, 312-13; for evidence of the Wilson's Administration's efforts at Paris to use the threat of massive American naval building to bring the British to agree to a naval parity with America and to the use of British naval power in a legal League framework, see Miller, *Drafting*, II, pp. 419-22; George T. Davis, *A Navy Second to None, the Development of Modern American Naval Policy* (New York, 1940), pp. 254-68; Harold and Margaret Sprout, *Toward a New Order of Sea Power, American Naval Policy and the World Scene, 1918-1922* (Princeton, 1940), pp. 47-40.

EPILOGUE

1 *PPWW*, V, pp. 538, 597, 616, 645; *PPWW*, VI, pp. 17-18, 30, 42-4, 52, 56-7, 65-6, 75-80, 82-3, 89, 94-5, 101-2, 127, 150, 173-5, 180, 182, 194, 197-8, 213, 249, 260-61, 265, 295-6, 306-9, 323, 327-31, 344, 396.
2 For Wilson's faith that the Treaty and the League were both based on the values of American liberal anti-imperialism, see *PPWW*, V, pp. 540-41, 549-52, 592-3, 604-5; *PPWW*, VI, pp. 1-2, 12-16, 22, 30-3, 44-5, 55, 104-5, 113, 121-2, 139-140, 171, 191-2, 199-200, 214-19, 234, 277, 289-92, 300-301, 306, 374-5, 414.
3 *PPWW*, VI, pp. 14-17, 66-70, 84-6, 90-91, 106-11, 134-7, 142-6, 162-3, 192-3, 196-7, 248-9, 305-6, 311-12, 334-5, 353-4, 384-5.
4 *PPWW*, VI, pp. 100-101.
5 *PPWW*, V, pp. 560-61, 568-9, 574-6, 624-6, 635-8, 640-41; *PPWW*, VI, pp. 20, 26, 55-6, 58-9, 62-4, 75, 92-3, 126-7, 146, 176, 198-9, 219-20, 252-4, 302-3, 321-2, 396-7.
6 *PPWW*, V, p. 621.

BIBLIOGRAPHY

1. PRIMARY SOURCES

MANUSCRIPT COLLECTIONS

The Archives of the Committee on Public Information, National Archives.
The Archives of the Department of State for 1917–19, National Archives.
The Archives of the American Socialist Party, Duke University Library.
Gordon Auchincloss Papers, Yale University Library.
Newton D. Baker Papers, Library of Congress.
Ray Stannard Baker Papers, Library of Congress.
Ray Stannard Baker Papers, Princeton University Library.
Tasker H. Bliss Papers, Library of Congress.
William H. Buckler Papers, Yale University Library.
Arthur Bullard Papers, Princeton University Library.
William C. Bullitt Papers, Yale University Library.
Charles R. Crane Papers, Columbia University Library.
George Creel Papers, Library of Congress.
Josephus Daniels Papers, Library of Congress.
Norman H. Davis Papers, Library of Congress.
Samuel Gompers Papers, Wisconsin State Historical Society.
Joseph C. Grew Papers, Harvard University Library.
Edward M. House Papers, Yale University Library.
George Kennan Papers, Library of Congress.
Robert Lansing Papers, Library of Congress.
Henry Cabot Lodge Papers, Massachusetts Historical Society.
Breckinridge Long Papers, Library of Congress.
A. Lawrence Lowell Papers, Harvard University Library.
William G. McAdoo Papers, Library of Congress.
Vance McCormick Diary, Yale University Library.
Sidney E. Mezes Papers, Columbia University Library
Roland S. Morris Papers, Library of Congress.

Frank L. Polk Papers, Yale University Library.
Raymond Robins Papers, Wisconsin State Historical Society.
Elihu Root Papers, Library of Congress.
John Spargo Papers, University of Vermont Library.
Charles L. Swem Collection of Wilsonia, Princeton University Library.
William Howard Taft Papers, Library of Congress.
Oswald Garrison Villard Papers, Harvard University Library.
Henry White Papers, Library of Congress.
Woodrow Wilson Papers, Library of Congress.
Wilson-Bryan Correspondence, National Archives.
William Wiseman Papers, Yale University Library.

PRINTED AND PUBLISHED GOVERNMENT DOCUMENTS

United States Congress. *Congressional Record,* 52–57 (December 7,
    1914, to February 24, 1919).
United States Congress, 66th Congress, 1st Session. *Senate Docu-
    ment No. 106, Hearings Before the Committee on Foreign Rela-
    tions, United States Senate on the Treaty of Peace with Germany
    Signed at Versailles on June 28, 1919 and Submitted to the Senate
    on July 10, 1919 by the President of the United States.* Washing-
    ton, D.C., 1919.
United States Department of State. *Papers Relating to the Foreign
    Relations of the United States, 1915.* Washington, D.C., 1924.
United States Department of State. *Papers Relating to the Foreign
    Relations of the United States, 1915, Supplement, The World
    War.* Washington, D.C., 1928.
United States Department of State. *Papers Relating to the Foreign
    Relations of the United States, 1916.* Washington, D.C., 1925.
United States Department of State. *Papers Relating to the Foreign
    Relations of the United States, 1916, Supplement, The World
    War.* Washington, D.C., 1929.
United States Department of State. *Papers Relating to the Foreign
    Relations of the United States, 1917.* Washington, D.C., 1926.
United States Department of State. *Papers Relating to the Foreign
    Relations of the United States, 1917, Supplement 1, The World
    War.* Washington, D.C., 1931.
United States Department of State. *Papers Relating to the Foreign
    Relations of the United States, 1917, Supplement 2, The World
    War.* 2 vols. Washington, D.C., 1932.
United States Department of State. *Papers Relating to the Foreign*

Relations of the United States, 1918, Supplement 1, The World War. 2 vols. Washington, D.C., 1933.

United States Department of State. *Papers Relating to the Foreign Relations of the United States, 1918, Supplement 2, The World War.* Washington, D.C., 1933.

United States Department of State. *Papers Relating to the Foreign Relations of the United States, 1918, Russia.* 3 vols. Washington, D.C., 1931.

United States Department of State. *Papers Relating to the Foreign Relations of the United States, 1919, Russia.* Washington, D.C., 1937.

United States Department of State. *Papers Relating to the Foreign Relations of the United States, Paris Peace Conference 1919.* 13 vols. Washington, D.C., 1942–47.

United States Department of State. *Papers Relating to the Foreign Relations of the United States, the Lansing Papers 1914–1920.* 2 vols. Washington, D.C. 1939.

EDITED COLLECTIONS OF DOCUMENTS AND PAPERS

Ray Stannard Baker, *Woodrow Wilson, Life and Letters,* 8 vols. Garden City, N.Y., 1927–39.

Ray Stannard Baker, *Woodrow Wilson and World Settlement,* 3 vols. Garden City, N.Y., 1922–23.

Ray Stannard Baker and William E. Dodd (eds.), *The Public Papers of Woodrow Wilson,* 6 vols. New York, 1925–27.

Suda Lorena Bane and Ralph H. Lutz (eds.), *The Blockade of Germany after the Armistice, 1918–1919.* Stanford, 1942.

George L. Beer, *African Questions at the Paris Peace Conference,* ed. by Louis H. Gray. New York, 1923.

Robert Paul Browder and Alexander F. Kerensky (eds.), *The Russian Provisional Government, 1917, Documents.* 3 vols. Stanford, 1961.

Philip M. Burnett, *Reparation at the Paris Peace Conference, from the Standpoint of the American Delegation.* 2 vols. New York, 1940.

C. K. Cumming and Walter W. Pettit (eds.), *Russian American Relations, March 1917–March 1920: Documents and Papers.* New York, 1920.

John W. Davidson (ed.), *A Cross Roads of Freedom, the 1912 Campaign Speeches of Woodrow Wilson.* New Haven, 1956.

Vladimir I. Lenin, *Collected Works,* 23 vols. New York, 1927–45.

——, *Selected Works,* 2 vols. Moscow, 1950–51.

David Hunter Miller, *The Drafting of the Covenant*, 2 vols. New York, 1928.
——, *My Diary at the Conference at Paris*, 21 vols. privately printed, Washington, D.C., 1928.
Albert Shaw (ed.), *President Wilson's State Papers and Addresses*, 2 vols. New York, 1917–18.
Z. A. B. Zeman (ed.), *Germany and the Revolution in Russia, 1915–1918, Documents from the Archives of the German Foreign Ministry*. London, 1958.

AUTOBIOGRAPHIES, DIARIES, LETTERS, MEMOIRS, AND
OTHER MISCELLANEOUS PRIMARY SOURCES

Bernard M. Baruch, *The Making of the Reparation and Economic Sections of the Treaty*. New York, 1920.
Stephen Bonsal, *Unfinished Business*. Garden City, N. Y., 1944.
The Bullitt Mission to Russia, Testimony before the Committee on Foreign Relations, United States Senate, of William C. Bullitt. New York, 1919.
George Creel, *Rebel At Large, Recollections of Fifty Crowded Years*. New York, 1947.
Josephus Daniels, *The Wilson Era*, 2 vols. Chapel Hill, 1944–46.
David R. Francis, *Russia from the American Embassy, April 1916–November 1918*. New York, 1921.
Samuel Gompers, *Seventy Years of Life and Labor*, 2 vols. New York, 1925.
William S. Graves, *America's Siberian Adventure, 1918–1920*. New York, 1931.
Cary T. Grayson, *Woodrow Wilson: A Personal Memoir*. New York, 1960.
W. K. Hancock and Jean Van Der Poel (eds.), *Selections from the Smuts Papers*, 4 vols. Cambridge, England, 1966.
Charles H. Haskins and Robert H. Lord, *Some Problems of the Peace Conference*. Cambridge, Mass., 1920.
Burton J. Hendrick, *The Life and Letters of Walter Hines Page*, 3 vols. Garden City, N.Y., 1924–26.
Herbert Hoover, *An American Epic*, 3 vols. Chicago, 1961.
——, *The Ordeal of Woodrow Wilson*. New York, 1958.
Edward M. House, *Philip Dru: Administrator*. New York, 1912.
Edward M. House and Charles Seymour (eds.), *What Really Happened at Paris, The Story of the Paris Peace Conference, 1918–1919*. New York, 1921.

David F. Houston, *Eight Years with Wilson's Cabinet, 1913–1920,* 2 vols. Garden City, N.Y., 1926.

Thomas W. Lamont, *Across World Frontiers.* New York, 1951.

Anne W. Lane and Louise H. Wall (eds.), *The Letters of Franklin K. Lane.* Cambridge, Mass., 1922.

Robert Lansing, *The Peace Negotiations, A Personal Narrative.* Boston, 1921.

——, *The Big Four and Others of the Peace Conference.* Boston, 1921

——, *The War Memoirs of Robert Lansing.* New York, 1935.

David Lloyd George, *The Truth About the Peace Treaties,* 2 vols. London, 1938.

William Gibbs McAdoo, *Crowded Years: The Reminiscences of William G. McAdoo.* Boston, 1931.

Jan M. Meijer (ed.), *The Trotsky Papers, 1917–1922.* The Hague, 1964.

Harold Nicolson, *Peacemaking 1919.* Boston, 1933.

Frederick Palmer, *Bliss, Peacemaker, The Life and Letters of Tasker Howard Bliss.* New York, 1934.

Lord Riddell's Intimate Diary of the Paris Peace Conference and After. London, 1933.

Charles Seymour (ed.), *The Intimate Papers of Colonel House,* 4 vols. Boston, 1926–28.

James T. Shotwell, *At the Paris Peace Conference.* New York, 1937.

Edgar Sisson, *One Hundred Red Days, A Personal Chronicle of the Bolshevik Revolution.* New Haven, 1931.

John L. Snell, "Wilson on Germany and the Fourteen Points," *Journal of Modern History,* XXIV (December 1954), 364–369.

Henry W. Steed, *Through Thirty Years, 1892–1922,* 2 vols. London, 1924.

André Tardieu, *The Truth About the Treaty.* Indianapolis, 1921.

Charles T. Thompson, *The Peace Conference Day by Day.* New York, 1920.

Leon Trotsky, *The Bolsheviki and World Peace.* New York, 1918.

Joseph Tumulty, *Woodrow Wilson as I Know Him.* Garden City, N.Y., 1921.

Harold B. Whiteman, Jr. (ed.), *Letters From the Paris Peace Conference by Charles Seymour.* New Haven, 1965.

Arthur Willert, *The Road to Safety: A Study of Anglo-American Relations.* London, 1952.

Woodrow Wilson, *A History of the American People,* 5 vols. New York, 1902.

NEWSPAPERS

New York *American*, 1917–19.
New York *Call*, 1914–19.
New York Evening Post, 1918–19.
New York *Sun*, 1919.
The New York Times, 1915–19.
New York Tribune, 1918–19.
Springfield Republican, 1917–19.

PERIODICALS

American Federationist, 1914–19.
Harveys' Weekly, 1918–19.
The Independent, 1918–19.
La Follette's Magazine, 1918–19.
The Liberator, 1918.
The Masses, 1914–17.
The Nation, 1914–19.
The New Republic, 1914–19.
The North American Review, 1918–19.
The Outlook, 1917–19.
The Public, 1918–19.
The Survey, 1917–19.

2. SECONDARY SOURCES: HISTORIES, TREATISES,
SPECIAL STUDIES, AND BIOGRAPHIES

Réné Albrecht-Carrie, *Italy at the Paris Peace Conference*. New York,
    1938.
Werner T. Angress, *Stillborn Revolution, The Communist Bid for
    Power in Germany, 1921–1923*. Princeton, 1963.
Thomas A. Bailey, *Wilson and the Peacemakers*. New York, 1947.
Burton F. Beers, *Vain Endeavor, Robert Lansing's Attempt to End
    the American-Japanese Rivalry*. Durham, N.C., 1962.
Samuel F. Bemis, "The First World War and the Peace Settlement,"
    in Theodore P. Greene (ed.), *Wilson at Versailles*. Boston, 1957,
    pp. 1–16.
Joseph A. Berlau, *The German Social Democratic Party*. New York,
    1949.
Paul Birdsall, *Versailles Twenty Years After*. New York, 1941.

Franz Borkenau, *World Communism, A History of the Communist International*. Ann Arbor, 1962.

Carl F. Brand, "British Labor and President Wilson," *American Historical Review*, XLII (January 1937), 244–55.

Mitchell P. Briggs, *George D. Herron and the European Settlement*. Stanford, 1932.

George G. Bruntz, *Allied Propaganda and the Collapse of the German Empire in 1918*. Stanford, 1938.

Edward H. Buehrig, *Woodrow Wilson and the Balance of Power*. Bloomington, 1955.

Edward H. Carr, *The Bolshevik Revolution*, 3 vols. London, 1950–53.

William Henry Chamberlin, *The Russian Revolution, 1917–1921*, 2 vols. New York, 1935.

Warren I. Cohen, "America and the May Fourth Movement, the Response to Chinese Nationalism, 1917–1921," *Pacific Historical Review*, XXXV (February 1966), 88–94.

Margaret L. Coit, *Mr. Baruch*. Boston, 1957.

Rudolf Coper, *Failure of a Revolution, Germany, 1918–1919*. Cambridge, England, 1955.

Gordon A. Craig, *The Politics of the Prussian Army, 1640–1945*. New York, 1955.

Gerda R. Crosby, *Disarmament and Peace in British Politics, 1914–1919*. Cambridge, England, 1957.

George W. Curry, "Woodrow Wilson, Jan Smuts, and the Versailles Settlement," *American Historical Review*, LXVI (July 1961), 968–86.

Roy Watson Curry, *Woodrow Wilson and Far Eastern Policy, 1913–1921*. New Haven, 1957.

William Diamond, *The Economic Thought of Woodrow Wilson*. Baltimore, 1943.

Andreas Dorpalen, *Hindenburg and the Weimar Republic*. Princeton, 1964.

Foster Rhea Dulles, *The Road to Teheran*. Princeton, 1944.

Robert V. Daniels, *The Conscience of the Revolution: Communist Opposition in Soviet Russia*. Cambridge, Mass., 1960.

George T. Davis, *A Navy Second to None, the Development of Modern American Naval Policy*. New York, 1940.

Francis Deak, *Hungary at the Paris Peace Conference, the Diplomatic History of the Treaty of Trianon*. New York, 1942.

John A. De Novo, *American Interests and Policies in the Middle East, 1900–1939*. Minneapolis, 1963.

Isaac Deutscher, *The Prophet Armed, Trotsky: 1879–1921*. London, 1954.

Klaus Epstein, *Matthias Erzberger and the Dilemma of German Democracy*. Princeton, 1959

Erich Eyck, *A History of the Weimar Republic*. Cambridge, Mass., 1962.

Merle Fainsod, *International Socialism and the World War*. Cambridge, Mass., 1955.

Beatrice Farnsworth, *William C. Bullitt and the Soviet Union*. Bloomington, 1967.

Frederick V. Field, *American Participation in the China Consortiums*. Chicago, 1931.

Russell H. Fifield, *Woodrow Wilson and the Far East, the Diplomacy of the Shantung Question*. New York, 1952.

Louis Fischer, *The Life of Lenin*. New York, 1964.

——, *The Soviets in World Affairs: A History of Relations between the Soviet Union and the Rest of the World, 1917–1929*. Princeton, 1960.

David Footman, *The Russian Civil War*. New York, 1961.

Charles Forcey, *The Crossroads of Liberalism; Croly, Weyl, Lippmann and the Progressive Era, 1900–1925*. New York, 1961.

Ernst Fraenkel, *Military Occupation and the Rule of Law, Occupation Governments in the Rhineland, 1918–1923*. New York, 1944.

Gerald Freund, *Unholy Alliance, Russian-German Relations from the Treaty of Brest-Litovsk to the Treaty of Berlin*. London, 1957.

Dale C. Fuller, "Lenin's Attitude Toward an International Organization for the Maintenance of Peace, 1914–1917," *Political Science Quarterly*, LXIV (June 1949), 245–61.

Hans Gatzke, *Germany's Drive to the West, A Study of Germany's Western War Aims during the First World War*. Baltimore, 1950.

Peter Gay, *The Dilemma of Democratic Socialism, Edward Bernstein's Challenge to Marx*. New York, 1952.

Lawrence E. Gelfand, *The Inquiry: American Preparations for Peace, 1917–1919*. New Haven, 1963.

Alexander L. George and Juliette George, *Woodrow Wilson and Colonel House, A Personality Study*. New York, 1956.

Benjamin Gerig, *The Open Door and the Mandates System, A Study of Economic Equality before and since the Establishment of the Mandates System*. London, 1930.

Louis L. Gerson, *Woodrow Wilson and the Rebirth of Poland*. New Haven, 1953.

Ray Ginger, *The Bending Cross, A Biography of Eugene Victor Debs.*
New Brunswick, 1949.

Alfred M. Gollin, *Proconsul in Politics, A Study of Lord Milner in
Opposition and in Power, 1905–1925.* London, 1964.

Harold J. Gordon, Jr., *The Reichswehr and the German Republic,
1919–1926.* Princeton, 1957.

Marguerite Green, *The National Civic Federation and the American
Labor Movement.* Washington, D.C., 1956.

A. Whitney Griswold, *The Far Eastern Policy of the United States.*
New York, 1938.

William S. Halperin, *Germany Tried Democracy, A Political History
of the Reich from 1918–1933.* New York, 1946.

W. K. Hancock, *Smuts, The Sanguine Years, 1870–1919.* Cambridge,
England, 1962.

Maurice P. Hankey, *The Supreme Control at the Paris Peace Conference, 1919.* London, 1963.

Louis Hartz, *The Founding of New Societies.* New York, 1964.

——, *The Liberal Tradition in America.* New York, 1955.

Richard Hofstadter, *The American Political Tradition, and the Men
Who Made It.* New York, 1955.

Hajo Holborn, "Diplomats and Diplomacy in the Early Weimar Republic," in Gordon A. Craig and Felix Gilbert (eds.), *The Diplomats, 1919–1939,* pp. 123–171. Princeton, 1953.

Harry N. Howard, *The Partition of Turkey, A Diplomatic History,
1913–1923.* Norman, Okla., 1931.

Irving Howe and Lewis Coser, *The American Communist Party.*
Boston, 1957.

Richard N. Hunt, *German Social Democracy, 1918–1933.* New
Haven, 1964.

Thomas Jones, *Lloyd George.* Cambridge, England, 1951.

W. M. Jordan, *Great Britain, France, and the German Problem,
1918–1939.* New York, 1943.

John H. Kautsky, "J. A. Schumpeter and Karl Kautsky: Parallel Theories of Imperialism," *Midwest Journal of Political Science,* V
(May 1961), 101–128.

George F. Kennan, *Russia and the West Under Lenin and Stalin.*
Boston, 1960.

——, *Soviet-American Relations, 1917–1920, Russia Leaves the War,*
Princeton, 1956.

——, *Soviet-American Relations, 1917–1920, The Decision to Intervene.* Princeton, 1958.

Gabriel Kolko, *The Triumph of Conservatism*. New York, 1963.

Titus Komarnicki, *Rebirth of the Polish Republic, A Study in the Diplomatic History of Europe, 1914–1920*. London, 1957.

Carl Landauer, *European Socialism, A History of Ideas and Movements from the Industrial Revolution to Hitler's Seizure 'of Power*, 2 vols. Berkeley, 1959.

Christopher Lasch, *The American Liberals and the Russian Revolution*. New York, 1962.

——, *The New Radicalism in America, 1889–1963, The Intellectual as a Social Type*. New York, 1965.

Ivo J. Lederer, *Yugoslavia at the Paris Peace Conference, A Study in Frontiermaking*. New Haven, 1963.

Ivo J. Lederer (ed.), *The Versailles Settlement, Was it Foredoomed to Failure?* Boston, 1960.

Richard W. Leopold, *Elihu Root and the Conservative Tradition*. Boston, 1954.

Arthur S. Link, *Wilson the Diplomatist*. Baltimore, 1957.

——, *Wilson: The New Freedom*. Princeton, 1956.

——, *Wilson: The Struggle for Neutrality, 1914–1915*. Princeton, 1960.

——, *Wilson: Confusions and Crises, 1915–1916*. Princeton, 1964.

——, *Wilson: Campaigns for Progressivism and Peace, 1916–1917*. Princeton, 1965.

——, *Woodrow Wilson and the Progressive Era*. New York, 1954.

Alfred D. Low, *The Soviet Hungarian Republic and the Paris Peace Conference*. Philadelphia, 1963.

Alma Luckau, *The German Delegation at the Paris Peace Conference*. New York, 1941.

C. A. Macartney and A. W. Palmer, *Independent Eastern Europe. A History*. London, 1962.

Victor S. Mamatey, *The United States and East Central Europe, 1914–1918*. Princeton, 1957.

Bernard Mandel, *Samuel Gompers*. Antioch, 1963.

Nicholas Mansergh, *The Irish Question, 1840–1921*. London, 1965.

Herbert Marcuse, *Soviet Marxism*. New York, 1961.

F. S. Marston, *The Peace Conference of 1919, Organization and Procedure*. New York, 1944.

Laurence W. Martin, *Peace Without Victory, Woodrow Wilson and the British Liberals*. New Haven, 1958.

Ernest R. May, *The World War and American Isolation*. Cambridge, Mass., 1959.

Arno J. Mayer, *The Political Origins of the New Diplomacy, 1917–1918*. New Haven, 1959.

Alfred G. Meyer, *Leninism*. Cambridge, Mass., 1957.

Henry C. Meyer, *Mitteleuropa in German Thought and Action, 1815–1945*. The Hague, 1955.

James R. Mock and Cedric Larson, *Words that Won the War, The Story of the Committee on Public Information*. Princeton, 1939.

Barrington Moore, Jr., *Soviet Politics: The Dilemma of Power*. Cambridge, Mass., 1956.

William Morley, *The Japanese Thrust into Siberia, 1918*. New York, 1957.

Alice M. Morrissey, *The American Defense of Neutral Rights*. Cambridge, Mass., 1939.

Robert K. Murray, *Red Scare*. Minneapolis, 1955.

Harold I. Nelson, *Land and Power, British and Allied Policy on Germany's Frontiers, 1916–1919*. London, 1963.

Allan Nevins, *Henry White, Thirty Years of American Diplomacy*. New York, 1930.

George B. Noble, *Policies and Opinions at Paris, 1919: Wilsonian Diplomacy, the Versailles Peace, and French Public Opinion*. New York, 1935.

Harley Notter, *The Origins of the Foreign Policy of Woodrow Wilson*. Baltimore, 1937.

Karl Friedrich Nowak, *The Collapse of Central Europe*. London, 1954.

Robert E. Osgood, *Ideals and Self-Interest in America's Foreign Relations*. Chicago, 1953.

Stanley W. Page, *Lenin and the World Revolution*. New York, 1959.

Henry Pelling, *America and the British Left*. London, 1956.

H. C. Peterson and G. C. Fite, *Opponents of War*. Madison, 1957.

Richard Pipes, *The Formation of the Soviet Union, Communism and Nationalism, 1917–1923*. Cambridge, Mass., 1954.

Stefan T. Possony, *Lenin, The Compulsive Revolutionary*. Chicago, 1964.

Ronald Radosh, "John Spargo and Wilson's Russian Policy, 1920," *Journal of American History*, LII (December 1963), 548–65.

Louis S. Reed, *The Labor Philosophy of Samuel Gompers*. New York, 1930.

Arthur Rosenberg, *The Birth of the German Republic*. New York, 1931.

Harry R. Rudin, *Armistice, 1918*. New Haven, 1944.

Frank M. Russell, *The Saar, Battleground and Pawn*. Stanford, 1951.

Leonard Schapiro, *The Origin of the Communist Autocracy, Political Opposition in the Soviet State, First Phase, 1917–1922*. Cambridge, England, 1955.

Frederick L. Schuman, *American Policy Toward Russia Since 1917*. New York, 1928.

Charles Seymour, "The Paris Education of Woodrow Wilson," *The Virginia Quarterly Review*, XXXII (Autumn 1956), 578–93.

——, "Woodrow Wilson and Self-Determination in the Tyrol," *The Virginia Quarterly Review*, XXXVIII (Autumn 1962), 567–87.

Martin J. Sklar, "Woodrow Wilson and the Political Economy of Modern United States Liberalism," *Studies on the Left*, I (1960), 17–47.

Daniel M. Smith, *Robert Lansing and American Neutrality*. Berkeley, 1958.

——, "National Interest and American Intervention, 1917: An Historiographical Appraisal," *Journal of American History*, LII (June 1965), 5–24.

——, *The Great Departure, the United States and World War One, 1914–1920*. New York, 1965.

John L. Snell, "Benedict XV, Wilson, Michaelis, and German Socialism," *Catholic Historical Review*, XXXVIII (July 1951), 164–76.

——, "Socialist Unions and Socialist Patriotism in Germany, 1914–1918," *American Historical Review*, LIX (October 1953), 66–77.

——, "Wilson's Peace Program and German Socialism, January–March 1918," *Mississippi Valley Historical Review*, XXXVIII (September 1951), 187–214.

Sherman D. Spector, *Rumania at the Paris Peace Conference, A Study of the Diplomacy of Ioan I. C. Bratianu*. New York, 1962.

Harold Sprout and Margaret Sprout, *Toward a New Order of Sea Power, American Naval Policy and the World Scene, 1918–1922*. Princeton, 1940.

George Stewart, *The White Armies of Russia*. New York, 1933.

Roland N. Stromberg, *Collective Security and American Foreign Policy, from the League of Nations to NATO*. New York, 1963.

Albert N. Tarulis, *American-Baltic Relations 1918–1922: The Struggle Over Recognition*. Washington, D.C., 1965.

John M. Thompson, *Russia, Bolshevism, and the Versailles Peace*. Princeton, 1966.

Tien-yi Li, *Woodrow Wilson's China Policy, 1913–1917*. New York, 1952.

Seth P. Tillman, *Anglo-American Relations at the Paris Peace Conference of 1919*. Princeton, 1961.

Pauline Tompkins, *American-Russian Relations in the Far East*. New York, 1949.

David F. Trask, *General Tasker Howard Bliss and the "Sessions of the World," 1919*. Philadelphia, 1966.

——, *The United States in the Supreme War Council, American War Aims and Inter-Allied Strategy, 1917–1918*. Middletown, 1961.

Adam B. Ulam, *The Bolsheviks*. New York, 1965.

Richard H. Ullman, *Anglo-Soviet Relations, 1917–1921, Intervention and the War*. Princeton, 1961.

Betty M. Unterberger, *America's Siberian Expedition, 1918–1920, A Study of National Policy*. Durham, 1956.

Austin Van Der Slice, *International Labor, Diplomacy, and Peace, 1914–1919*. Philadelphia, 1941.

Eric Waldman, *The Spartacist Uprising of 1919*. Milwaukee, 1958.

Piotre S. Wandycz, *France and Her Eastern Allies, 1919–1925*. Minneapolis, 1962.

Robert D. Warth, *The Allies and the Russian Revolution, From the Fall of the Monarchy to the Peace of Brest Litovsk*. Durham, 1954.

Richard L. Watson, Jr., "Woodrow Wilson and His Interpreters, 1947–1957," *Mississippi Valley Historical Review*, XLIV (September 1957), 207–36.

James Weinstein, "Anti-War Sentiment and the Socialist Party, 1917–1918," *Political Science Quarterly*, LXXIV (June 1959), 215–39.

John W. Wheeler-Bennett, *The Forgotten Peace, Brest-Litovsk, March 1918*. New York, 1939.

——, *The Nemesis of Power, The German Army in Politics, 1918–1945*. London, 1953.

John A. White, *The Siberian Intervention*. Princeton, 1950.

William Appleman Williams, "American Intervention in Russia, 1917–1920, Part 1," *Studies on the Left*, III (Fall 1963) 24–48.

——, "American Intervention in Russia, 1917–1920, Part 2," *Studies on the Left*, IV (Winter 1964), 39–57.

——, *Russian-American Relations, 1781–1947*. New York, 1952.

——, *The Tragedy of American Diplomacy*. New York, 1962.

William Appleman Williams (ed.), *The Shaping of American Diplomacy*, 2 vols. Chicago, 1964.

Henry R. Winkler, *The League of Nations Movement in Great Britain*. New Brunswick, 1952.

E. M. Winslow, *The Pattern of Imperialism*. New York, 1948.

Quincy Wright, *Mandates under the League of Nations*. Chicago, 1930.

Louis A. R. Yates, *The United States and French Security, 1917–1921*. New York, 1957.

Alfred Zimmerman, *The League of Nations and the Rule of Law, 1918–1935*. London, 1936.

INDEX